T0385747

DUMBARTON OAKS
MEDIEVAL LIBRARY

Jan M. Ziolkowski, General Editor

THE RHETORICAL EXERCISES

OF NIKEPHOROS BASILAKES

DOML 43

The Rhetorical Exercises
of Nikephoros Basilakes

Progymnasmata from
Twelfth-Century Byzantium

Edited and Translated by

JEFFREY BENEKER
and
CRAIG A. GIBSON

DUMBARTON OAKS
MEDIEVAL LIBRARY

HARVARD UNIVERSITY PRESS
CAMBRIDGE, MASSACHUSETTS
LONDON, ENGLAND
2016

Copyright © 2016 by the President and Fellows of Harvard College
ALL RIGHTS RESERVED
Printed in the United States of America

Library of Congress Cataloging-in-Publication Data available from the Library of Congress

ISBN 978-0-674-66024-3 (cloth : alk. paper)

Contents

Introduction

Nikephoros Basilakes (ca. 1115 to after 1182) was a member of an aristocratic family and active among the imperial elite in Constantinople.[1] He probably held the office of imperial notary, and he is identified as *notarios* (νοτάριος) in the title that appears in some of the manuscripts of his rhetorical exercises *(progymnasmata)*. He was an instructor of rhetoric and about 1140 became Teacher of the Apostle (διδάσκαλος τοῦ ἀποστόλου), a patriarchal appointment with responsibility for teaching the letters of the apostles, especially the Pauline epistles. This position was associated with the so-called Patriarchal School that was attached to the church of Hagia Sophia.[2] According to his own testimony, Basilakes was a very successful teacher, whose popularity attracted the envy of the patriarch.[3] Although we do not know the date of Basilakes's *progymnasmata* or their intended audience, we might suppose that their composition was connected with Basilakes's instruction and performance of rhetoric during this period.[4]

In the midst of his career, Basilakes was involved in a theological debate over the nature of the eucharistic sacri-

fice. Some argued that the sacrifice was offered to the Father alone, while others held that it was offered to all three persons of the Trinity, including Christ himself. The latter position was confirmed as orthodoxy at two synods, held in 1156 and 1157.[5] Basilakes, however, was associated with the views of Soterichos Panteugenos, a deacon who served at Hagia Sophia, was later elected patriarch of Antioch, and was the major proponent of what became the heretical position. For his involvement in this debate, Basilakes was condemned and banished to Philippopolis (now Plovdiv in Bulgaria). It is not certain whether he ever returned to Constantinople, but in any case he does not seem to have continued his teaching career after his banishment.

In addition to the *progymnasmata,* which are presented in this volume, Basilakes's corpus contains many other works in a variety of genres.[6] These include monodies (rhetorical laments) for his brother Constantine and for an anonymous friend, panegyrics for the patriarch Nikolaos IV Mouzalon and the emperor John II Komnenos, orations on a variety of subjects, and four letters. In editing a collection of his orations and letters, Basilakes included a prologue in which he describes his own career and comments on his popularity as a teacher associated with the Church in Constantinople.[7]

PROGYMNASMATA AND RHETORICAL EDUCATION

Progymnasmata are literally "exercises" that are "preliminary" to declamation, which is the composition and delivery of ostensibly impromptu speeches in the guise of fictional, mythical, or historical characters who serve as prosecution or defense in fictitious trial scenarios. From the first century

BCE (or perhaps earlier) to the sixth century CE, elite young men with the leisure and the financial support to pursue an advanced education worked through the sequence of *progymnasmata* in order to learn the art of prose composition, and the influence of this widespread educational program is readily seen throughout imperial-era Greek literature, both poetry and prose. This educational program continued through the Byzantine period under the guidance of one influential textbook: a treatise on the *progymnasmata* by Aphthonios (fourth century CE), which improved upon the one incorrectly attributed to Hermogenes (perhaps third century CE) with a clearer exposition and the addition of one or two models to illustrate each type of exercise. Aphthonios's treatise was the focus of extant commentaries by John of Sardis (ninth century) and John Doxapatres (eleventh century); both of those works drew on other commentaries now lost. Aphthonios's model exercises and those of Libanios (fourth century) also inspired the extensive and influential collection by Pseudo-Nikolaos (perhaps fifth century), which was known to Basilakes and other Byzantine writers of *progymnasmata,* such as John Geometres (tenth century). In the sequence advocated by Aphthonios, students learned to compose fourteen exercises: fable (μῦθος), narration (διήγημα), *chreia* (χρεία), maxim (γνώμη), refutation (ἀνασκευή), confirmation (κατασκευή), common topics (κοινοὶ τόποι), encomium (ἐγκώμιον), invective (ψόγος), comparison (σύγκρισις), ethopoeia (ἠθοποιΐα), ecphrasis (ἔκφρασις), thesis (θέσις), and introduction of a law (εἰσφορὰ τοῦ νόμου). The exercises were arranged in generally increasing order of difficulty, and students could later return to earlier exercises to give them a more advanced treatment.

In the hands of master practitioners, such compositions could serve both as model exercises for students and as impressive literary works in their own right.[8]

Basilakes's collection includes highly polished examples of fable, narration, maxim, refutation, confirmation, encomium, and ethopoeia. A brief review of these exercises as they were practiced in late antiquity and the Byzantine period will be helpful here.

A fable is a fictional story illustrating an explicitly stated ethical or moral truth, usually featuring animals but sometimes also humans and gods as the actors and speakers. Basilakes's fables include many animals and three humans, but no gods. The world of his fables is filled with crafty characters eager to mislead the innocent and with pretenders who get their due. Students are advised to be wary of trusting an enemy, to safeguard their liberty and freedom of speech, to avoid pretense, not to attempt to do "impossible" things beyond their nature or station in life, and not to oppose the powerful. Failure to heed these warnings brings a loss of freedom, status, or even death.

A narration is a clear, concise, and realistic retelling of a story from myth or, less frequently, from history. All of Basilakes's examples come from myth except for one quasi-historical story taken from Plutarch's *Moralia*. His examples do not exhibit the virtue of conciseness recommended in the handbooks and found in other collections. The typical themes of sexual desire (Danaë, Narcissus, Pasiphaë, Myrrha) and metamorphosis (Danaë, Platanos, Narcissus, Pasiphaë, Icarus and Daedalus, Myrrha) are found both together and separately, but they are not as heavily emphasized as in other collections. Three examples concern events that

took place before and after the Trojan War (how Achilles and Odysseus entered the war, how Troy fell, how Polydorus died after the war).

A *chreia* exercise is a detailed examination of a *chreia* statement, which is a morally useful anecdote about the words, actions, or combined words and actions attributed to a famous individual (e.g., "Diogenes, upon seeing a child misbehaving, struck his pedagogue, adding, 'Why do you teach such things?'"). A maxim exercise is a detailed examination of a maxim statement, which is similar to the kind of *chreia* statement that consists only of the speaker's words except that it does not name the speaker (e.g., "A man who is a counselor should not sleep all night"). Even so, a maxim exercise may praise the source of the maxim (in this example, Homer). In Basilakes's maxim exercises, the quotations are taken from Gregory of Nazianzus (Maxim 1) and Sophocles (Maxims 2 and 3), but the speakers are not named in the quotations that serve as the titles of the three exercises, and so the manuscripts divide on whether to call them *chreiai* or maxims. We call them all maxims in our edition because the title quotations do not name the author, even though each exercise does include praise of the author.

Refutation dissects brief mythical or (infrequently) historical narratives and argues that they are unclear, implausible, impossible, illogical, inappropriate, or inexpedient, using whichever of these topics in whatever order makes the most sense. Confirmation does the opposite. In this collection, Basilakes both refutes and confirms the story of how Atalanta was raised and how Hippomenes defeated her in a footrace and thereby won her hand in marriage. Basilakes's exercises are much longer than most of their ancient and

Byzantine counterparts, but they use the same topics of argument and the same framing devices (attacking the poets for telling lies in refutation; condemning those who doubt poetry's divine inspiration in confirmation), and likewise respond to the challenges of hypothetical interlocutors. Ancient and Byzantine theorists saw the value in preparing speakers to attack or defend any position, and they believed that confirmation was a more difficult exercise than refutation.

Encomium is a speech in unmitigated praise of a mythical or (less frequently) historical character and can be extended to other topics, including places, seasons, plants, and animals. In this collection, the recipient of praise is the dog. Although some ancient sources acknowledge the dog as a potential theme for encomium, Basilakes's example is the earliest of three extant examples, the other two being from the fifteenth century.[9] Its framing device alludes to the satirist Lucian, and the encomium itself incorporates an elaborate description of a hunt—which is another type of rhetorical exercise called ecphrasis—as well as a speech attributed to a dog. This makes Basilakes's example more ambitious than the typical encomium found in other collections of *progymnasmata*.

Ethopoeiae occupy a prominent place in Basilakes's collection, as well as in Byzantine rhetorical education more generally.[10] An ethopoeia is a speech of a mythological or historical figure responding to a challenging situation that reveals his or her character (ἦθος), emotional state (πάθος), or both. Although three poetic ethopoeiae featuring biblical characters survive from the fourth century,[11] they did not circulate in later Byzantine book culture and, more impor-

tantly, no prose ethopoeiae on themes from the Bible or early Christian history are found before the early twelfth century. The first extant twelfth-century ethopoeiae on biblical themes are from Basilakes's teacher Nikolaos Mouzalon.[12] Basilakes appears to be the most prominent writer of such pieces; his collection features the largest number of examples known from the twelfth through the fourteenth centuries.[13] In an ethopoeia, the speaker typically describes an experience of terror or grief in the present, contrasts it with good times experienced in the past, and ends with a prediction of an even worse future. However, Basilakes's exercises involving New Testament miracles invert this arrangement: the present is wonderful, the past was bad, and the future looks even brighter. (The reaction of Hades to the resurrection of Lazarus is an exception.) Although Basilakes occasionally reworks traditional themes, many of his themes are not found elsewhere, and his use of characters and situations from the Bible and early Christian history in his ethopoeiae is perhaps his most important contribution to the history of the genre.

Exercises Not Found in Basilakes's Collection

No manuscripts of Basilakes have yet revealed examples of the exercises in common topics, invective, comparison, ecphrasis, thesis, or introduction of a law. Some of these apparent omissions are perhaps understandable from a practical pedagogical standpoint. Invective is simply the opposite of encomium and therefore receives less discussion in Aphthonios's manual. And unlike encomium, invective had no formal counterpart in performance to encourage students

to practice it. Comparison uses both encomium and invective in order to compare two individuals; it also receives less attention in Aphthonios. Admittedly, both invective and comparison proved useful to writers in a variety of literary contexts, but encomium was much more prominent both in classroom instruction and in the daily needs of the Byzantine elite, from encomia of emperors to funeral speeches. Moreover, one role of the Master of the Rhetors, a position that Basilakes might have held, was to produce encomiastic speeches for the emperor on major holidays. Thesis (an extended meditation upon a general question dealing with life in human society, such as the ever-popular "whether one should marry") and introduction of a law, the two most advanced exercises, were sometimes not taught in the Byzantine period because of their perceived difficulty.

The omission of three of these exercises may in fact be illusory, since they appear in abbreviated form within the preserved exercises:

Introduction of a law: The exercise in introduction of a law takes the form of a speech either for or against a proposed or existing law. In Maxim 3, which takes as its prompt a quotation from Sophocles advocating immediate execution for "whoever wishes to act outside of the laws," the speaker (who uses the word "law" ten times in this exercise and refers to the quotation from Sophocles as if it were a law) argues that punishment should always immediately follow a crime and that the mere intention to commit a crime should be subject to the same punishment as the crime itself.

Common topics: The exercise in common topics takes the form of a speech delivered by a prosecutor attempting

to stir the anger of the jurors just before they decide a case against a generic malefactor, such as an adulterer, murderer, temple robber, tomb robber, traitor, or tyrant. All these malefactors are denounced in Maxim 3, along with thieves, ambassadors who take bribes, unscrupulous demagogues, and highwaymen.

Ecphrasis: Basilakes's encomium of the dog includes an ecphrasis of a hunt that displays the typical Byzantine fondness for describing a nature scene as a work of art. This ecphrasis conflates text, oral performance, and the visual arts, self-deprecatingly asking listeners to enjoy the description with their eyes and ears as they would enjoy the painting of a mere amateur.

Major Themes of Basilakes's *Progymnasmata*

Basilakes's exercises draw on myth, ancient history, the Bible, and other Christian texts, and they use specific words and phrases from ancient Greek epic, tragedy, historiography, and other genres. His ethopoeiae in particular emphasize novelty, paradox, and inversion (often expressed in heavy-handed antitheses); the interrelationships of art, nature, and love; the conflict between sexual desire and chastity; and theatricality (that is, life as a drama on stage, the speaker as an actor playing a part, and the reader or listener as the audience). In this way they show the influence of the earlier cultural environment that produced their ancient counterparts, the so-called Second Sophistic revival of classical literature and learning (first through third centuries CE), and they reflect the contemporary environment of new erotic novels, poetry on mythological themes, drama, and

satire, which emerged in what has been called the twelfth-century "revival of fiction" in Byzantium.[14] Moreover, Ethopoeia 13, in its depiction of Saint Peter imagining his heavenly reward just before he is to be crucified by Nero, draws on a common scenario from declamation, the war hero (*aristeus*) who has faced down a tyrant and is to be honored with a special prize.

The *progymnasmata* also feature mythological and biblical stories that Basilakes treats more than once, the most obvious example being his handling of the myth of Atalanta as both a refutation and a confirmation. In other cases, however, he revisits stories so as to highlight different perspectives, changes in disposition, and moral dilemmas. He gives a voice to Joseph, for example, both while he is wrongly imprisoned in Egypt and just after his release (Ethopoeiae 1 and 2). King David speaks in three of the Ethopoeiae: once as he is being pursued by Saul (4), again when he has caught Saul unawares (5), and finally when David himself is being pursued by his son Absalom (6). Basilakes seems to have had a special interest in the myths involving Pasiphaë's love for a bull and her husband Minos's angry response. In the Narrations he tells the story from the point of view of Daedalus (11), Pasiphaë (12), and Icarus (13), while in Ethopoeia 20 he recounts the escape of Daedalus and Icarus from the perspective of a sailor who observes them flying above the sea. Furthermore, the underworld appears in the Ethopoeiae in both a pagan and a Christian context, when Ajax responds to the descent of his enemy Odysseus (16) and when Hades himself reacts to the raising of Lazarus (10).

Basilakes's artistic blending of pagan and Christian sources and worldviews may have been influenced not only

by the earlier works of Prokopios of Gaza (sixth century)[15] and Michael Psellos (eleventh century)[16] but also by contemporary methods of instruction in schedography, in which Basilakes was a self-proclaimed innovator,[17] and contemporary novels.[18] Basilakes also displays originality in his reworking of well-known myths and fables, which makes him important for the study of classical reception in the Byzantine Empire.[19] Thus we find in Basilakes's *progymnasmata* a collection of learned, allusive, high-register prose essays, which, while reflective of their ultimate origin in Hellenistic and late-antique pedagogy, also exemplify the resurgence of literary culture in twelfth-century Byzantium.[20]

About This Text and Translation

Our text and translation of the *progymnasmata* are based on the text of Adriana Pignani (1983), with the exception of Ethopoeia 12, which is based on the text of Wolfram Hörandner (1981). We have made numerous changes to the text of Pignani, which are documented in our notes to the text; we have made no substantive changes to the text of Hörandner. We have arranged the exercises by type, retaining Pignani's order and numbering, and have employed English terms for them (for example, fable for *mythos*) except in the case of ethopoeia, since it is best known even in English-language scholarship by its Greek name. In the case of exercises based on biblical themes, we have documented the passages that serve as inspiration as well as all other references to the Septuagint and the New Testament. When Basilakes quotes from the Bible, the Greek text and translation are both italicized, and the biblical reference is indicated in

the Notes to the Translation. Often he has slightly modified the quotation, changing the form of a noun or verb in order to put it in the mouth of a new speaker. In these cases, we have indicated that the quotation has been modified slightly by the addition of "see" in front of the biblical reference (e.g., "see 1 Kings 17:36"), though the reader will have to compare the biblical text with Basilakes to see the change he has made. Biblical references are to *Septuagint with Apocrypha,* ed. L. C. Brenton (Peabody, Mass., 1986); and *The Majority Text Greek New Testament Interlinear,* ed. A. L. Farstad et al. (Nashville, 2007).

For exercises based on mythological themes, we have not attempted to identify Basilakes's sources, an impossible task given the pervasiveness of myth in Greek literature. Instead, we give references to Apollodorus's *Library* and to Ovid's *Metamorphoses* so that the reader may consult well-known, and in most cases more complete, versions of the myths. When a myth is also the subject of an extant tragedy or appears in Homer, we give that reference as well. All references to ancient texts, except as otherwise noted, are to the Loeb Classical Library editions.

In rendering the *progymnasmata* in English, we have attempted to preserve the sense of Basilakes's learned style and vocabulary, while at the same time producing a clear translation. We have taken special care to translate technical terms consistently, but also to take into account the context in which Basilakes uses them. So, for example, παρθένος is translated as "virgin" in some places and as "maiden" in others, depending on Basilakes's emphasis. We have marked instances where Basilakes borrows a phrase from or alludes to a classical text when the phrase or allusion affects the meaning of a passage, but we have not at-

tempted to document all references to classical texts or to provide a full commentary. For the sake of clarity, we have in some places supplied proper names where Basilakes uses a pronoun or omits a name entirely. In applying pronouns to animals, we have preserved the gender from the Greek, rather than using "it" as is common in English.

We profited from consulting Pignani's Italian translation as well as Hock and O'Neil's translations of Maxims 1 and 2 (Pignani 24–25), Papaioannou's translations of Narration 16 (23) and Ethopoeia 22 (51), and Xenophontos's translation of Narration 4 (11). We would like to thank Sarah Bond, John Caldwell, Robert Cargill, Paul Dilley, Malcolm Heath, Anthony Kaldellis, Joshua Langseth, Ephraim Lytle, J. C. McKeown, and Kent Rigsby for offering helpful advice on various aspects of the translation and notes. We would also like to thank Josh Smith for checking the Greek text, and Molly Harris and Staci Duros for carefully proofreading the full manuscript. Support for this project was provided by the University of Wisconsin, Madison Office of the Vice Chancellor for Research and Graduate Education with funding from the Wisconsin Alumni Research Foundation. We are happily indebted to Nathanael Aschenbrenner, a Tyler Fellow at Dumbarton Oaks, whose careful editorial work greatly improved the book. We are especially grateful to Alice-Mary Talbot and Stratis Papaioannou for their expertise, generosity, and extraordinary patience in reviewing three full drafts of our translation, making numerous corrections and improvements, and answering many questions along the way. Any mistakes that remain are our own.

We dedicate this volume to the memory of our fathers: Roger W. Beneker (1934–2013) and Alvin N. Gibson, Jr. (1942–2012).

NOTES

1 For details of Basilakes's life and career, see "Basilakes, Nikephoros" in *ODB;* Robert Browning, "The Patriarchal School in Constantinople in the Twelfth Century," *Byzantion* 32 (1962): 167–202, at 181–84; Hock and O'Neil, *The Chreia and Ancient Rhetoric,* 280–81; and Magdalino, "The *Bagoas* of Nikephoros Basilakes," 49–51.

2 On the organization of the school, see Magdalino, *The Empire of Manuel I Komnenos,* 325–30; "Patriarchal School" in *ODB.*

3 See Magdalino, "The *Bagoas* of Nikephoros Basilakes," 49–50.

4 See Papaioannou, "On the Stage of *Eros,*" 357.

5 On the controversy, see "Panteugenos, Soterichos" in *ODB;* J. M. Hussey, *The Orthodox Church in the Byzantine Empire* (Oxford, 1986), 151–52. On Basilakes's involvement, see Magdalino, "The *Bagoas* of Nikephoros Basilakes," 50–51.

6 For a list of works, see Browning, "The Patriarchal School in Constantinople in the Twelfth Century," 181–82. Basilakes also wrote in his youth four satires that he later destroyed; see Magdalino, *The Empire of Manuel I Komnenos,* 395–96.

7 See Basilakes's preface in Garzya, *Nicephori Basilacae orationes et epistolae,* sect. 3–4, p. 3.

8 On the *progymnasmata,* see Clark, *Rhetoric in Greco-Roman Education,* 177–212; Kennedy, *Greek Rhetoric under Christian Emperors,* 52–73; Webb, "The *Progymnasmata* as Practice"; Penella, "The *Progymnasmata* in Imperial Greek Education." On Byzantine *progymnasmata,* see Herbert Hunger, *Die hochsprachliche profane Literatur der Byzantiner* (Munich, 1978), 1:92–120.

9 See Craig A. Gibson, "In Praise of Dogs: An Encomium Theme from Classical Greece to Renaissance Italy," in *Our Dogs, Our Selves: Dogs in Medieval and Early Modern Europe,* ed. Laura Gelfand (Leiden, forthcoming).

10 Niels Gaul, "Rising Elites and Institutionalization—*Ethos/Mores*—'Debts' and Drafts: Three Concluding Steps towards Comparing Networks of Learning in Byzantium and the 'Latin' West, c. 1000–1200," in

Networks of Learning: Perspectives on Scholars in Byzantine East and Latin West, c. 1000–1200, ed. Sita Steckel, Niels Gaul, and Michael Grünbart (Zurich, 2014), 235–80, at 263–65; with reference to Basilakes's ethopoeiae in particular, Gaul emphasizes the role of *progymnasmata* in the rhetorical and theatrical shaping of the student's character.

11 See André Hurt and Jean Rudhardt, eds. and trans., *Codex des visions: poèmes divers* (Munich, 1999): P. Bodmer 30 (the words of Abraham, Sarah, and Isaac after Abraham was ordered to sacrifice Isaac), P. Bodmer 33 (Cain's words after he murdered Abel), and P. Bodmer 34 (Abel's words after Cain murders him). For discussion, see Laura Miguélez-Cavero, *Poems in Context: Greek Poetry in the Egyptian Thebaid 200–600 AD* (Berlin, 2008), 330–36.

12 See Ilias Nesseris, "Η Παιδεία στην Κωνσταντινούπολη κατά τον 12° αιώνα" (PhD diss., Ioannina, 2014), 1:108, 258.

13 See the partial catalog of Eugenio Amato and Gianluca Ventrella, "L'éthopée dans la pratique scolaire et littéraire: répertoire complet," in *Ethopoiia. La représentation de caractères entre fiction scolaire et réalité vivante à l'époque impériale et tardive,* ed. Eugenio Amato and Jacques Schamp (Salerno, 2005), 213–31; also see Ioannis Vassis, "Τῶν νέων φιλολόγων παλαίσματα. Ἡ συλλογὴ σχεδῶν τοῦ κώδικα Vaticanus Palatinus gr. 92," Ἑλληνικὰ 52 (2002): 37–68, esp. no. 179, an ethopoeia by Basilakes's likely teacher Nikolaos Mouzalon on what Sarah would say to Abraham when he is about to sacrifice Isaac.

14 For the place of Basilakes's ethopoeiae in this revival, see Stratis Papaioannou, *Michael Psellos: Rhetoric and Authorship in Byzantium* (Cambridge, 2013), 247–49; for the term "revival of fiction," see 247. On literary and cultural aspects of Basilakes's *progymnasmata,* see Panagiotis Roilos, *Amphoteroglossia: A Poetics of the Twelfth-Century Medieval Greek Novel* (Washington, D.C., 2005), 32–40; Anthony Kaldellis, *Hellenism in Byzantium: The Transformations of Greek Identity and the Reception of the Classical Tradition* (Cambridge, 2007), 258–61; Papaioannou, "On the Stage of *Eros,*" (esp. on Narration 16 and Ethopoeia 22); on Narration 9, see Papaioannou, "Byzantine Mirrors," 98–99. On "the self-conscious artistry" of twelfth-century authors, see Magdalino, *The Empire of Manuel I Komnenos,* 396–97. On the broader significance of theatricality in twelfth-century Byzantine rhetoric, see Magdalino, *The Empire of Manuel I Komnenos,* 336–43, 352–56.

15 Edmund Fryde, *The Early Palaeologan Renaissance (1261– c. 1360)* (Leiden, 2000), 60.

16 Papaioannou, *Michael Psellos,* 247–49.

17 We are grateful to Stratis Papaioannou for this suggestion. Originating in the late tenth or early eleventh century, schedography "substituted the intensive study of short, dictated, model compositions for the extensive study of entire ancient texts as a means of learning grammar, syntax, etymology and orthography. . . . [I]t offered a short cut to the acquisition of fairly advanced literate skills" (Magdalino, *The Empire of Manuel I Komnenos,* 329). See Stéphanos Efthymiadis, "L'enseignement secondaire à Constantinople pendant les XIe et XIIe siècles: modèle éducatif pour la Terre d'Otrante au XIIIe siècle," *Νέα 'Ρώμη* 2 (2005): 259–75, esp. 266–75; Panagiotis A. Agapitos, "Grammar, Genre, and Patronage in the Twelfth Century: A Scientific Paradigm and Its Implications," *Jahrbuch der Österreichischen Byzantinistik* 64 (2014): 1–22; Robins, *The Byzantine Grammarians,* 125–48. Robins, 135, 146–47, notes the integration of classical and Christian texts in these exercises. On Basilakes and schedography, see Agapitos, pp. 8–10.

18 Roilos, *Amphoteroglossia,* 32–40; Roderick Beaton, *The Medieval Greek Romance,* 2nd ed. (Cambridge, 1996), 25–26, 80–81, 88, 212.

19 See, for example, the study of Papaioannou, "On the Stage of *Eros.*"

20 For a recent overview of the complex relationship between pedagogical methods and literary production in Byzantium, see Antonia Giannouli, "Education and Literary Language in Byzantium," in *The Language of Byzantine Learned Literature,* ed. Martin Hinterberger (Turnhout, 2014), 52–71.

FABLES

Προγυμνάσματα κυροῦ Νικηφόρου τοῦ Βασιλάκου νοταρίου

I

Λέων ποτὲ ταῦρον ὁρᾷ· καὶ τροφῆς μὲν ἐρᾷ, τὰς δὲ τῶν κεράτων δεδίττεται προβολάς. Καὶ τὸ φάρμακον εὑρών, οὐ θεραπεύει τὸ πάθος· νικᾷ μὲν αὐτὸν ὁ λιμὸς καὶ τῷ ταύρῳ κελεύει συμπλέκεσθαι, ἀλλ᾽ ἐκφοβεῖ τῶν κεράτων τὸ μέγεθος. Τέλος πείθεται τῷ λιμῷ καί, φιλίαν πλασάμενος, εἰς ἀπάτην τὸν ταῦρον ὑπέρχεται· ὅπου γὰρ τὸ κακὸν πρόδηλον, καὶ τὸ ἀνδρεῖον πεφόβηται, κἂν ἴδοι τὸ βίᾳ κρατεῖν οὐκ ἀκίνδυνον, τὸ λάθρα σοφίζεται. "Ἔγωγ᾽ οὖν," φησίν, "ἐπαινῶ σου τὸ καρτερόν, ὑπεράγαμαι τὸ κάλλος. Ὁποῖος μὲν εἶ τὴν κεφαλήν! Ὁποῖος δὲ τὴν μορφήν! Ὅσος δὲ τοὺς πόδας! Ὅσος δὲ τὰς ὁπλάς! Ἀλλ᾽ ὅσον ἐπὶ τῆς κεφαλῆς φέρεις τὸ ἄχθος! Περίελε γοῦν οὕτω ματαίαν ἐπιπλοκὴν καί σοι καὶ κόσμος ἔσται τῆς κεφαλῆς καὶ βάρους ἀπαλλαγὴ καὶ πρὸς τὸ κρεῖττον μεταβολή. Τί δὲ καὶ δεῖ σοι κεράτων, εἰρήνης οὔσης πρὸς λέοντα;" Πείθεται τούτοις ὁ ταῦρος καί, τὴν ἐκ τῶν ὅπλων ἰσχὺν ἀποβαλών, τῷ λέοντι λοιπὸν εὐχείρωτος ἦν καὶ δεῖπνον ἀκίνδυνον.

Progymnasmata of Kyr Nikephoros Basilakes, the Notary

I

A lion once saw a bull, and although he desired to eat him, he feared the bull's prominent horns. Even though he had found the remedy, he could not treat the disease: his hunger was getting the best of him and urging him to grapple with the bull, but the massive horns filled him with fear. Finally, he yielded to his hunger and, feigning friendship, approached the bull with deceit in mind. For wherever trouble is clearly evident, even manly courage experiences fear, and if it sees that winning through violence is risky, it stealthily devises treachery instead. "I praise your power," the lion said, "and I greatly admire your beauty. What a head you have! What a physique! How great your legs are! And your hooves! But what a great burden you carry upon your head! Just rid yourself of that useless, tangled mess, and you'll get beauty for your head, relief from the weight, and a change for the better. Why do you even need horns, when you're at peace with the lion?" The bull was convinced by the lion's words, and after he cast off the strength that came from his armament, he was, in the end, easy for the lion to overcome and so became a danger-free dinner.

2   Οὕτω τὸ πείθεσθαι τοῖς ἐχθροῖς μετὰ τῆς ἀπάτης φέρει καὶ κίνδυνον.

2

Ἦν ὅτε καὶ ὁ ἵππος ἀχείρωτος ἦν καί, πρὶν ἢ τοῖς ἀνθρώποις εἰς χεῖρας ἐλθεῖν, κατὰ λειμῶνα ἐκρόαινε καὶ τρυφὴν ἐποιεῖτο τὸ ἐλευθέριον. Καλὸν μὲν ἦν αὐτῷ καὶ τὸ ἄνετον, οὐ σμικρὸν εἰς εὐμοιρίαν καὶ τὸ χαλινοῦ διάγειν ἔξω καὶ μύωπος. Ἀλλ᾽ ἦν ἄρα καὶ τοῦτο τῆς τύχης οὐδὲν ἧττον τὸ φιλοτίμημα· ἄλσος ἀνθηρὸν ἐπὶ πεδιάδος ἐφηπλωμένον καὶ χλόη τις εἴς τε ποδῶν ἀγωνίαν καὶ τάχους φιλοτιμίαν οὐκ ἄχαρις καὶ πρὸς τροφὴν οὐκ ἀνέραστος. Κατέρρει τὸ ἄλσος καὶ πηγή τις, ὡς μὲν ὀφθῆναι καλή, ὡς δὲ ἡδεῖα πιεῖν. Ἡ δὲ καὶ τὸ χλοάζον ἐχορήγει τοῖς ἄνθεσι καὶ τῷ ἵππῳ τὴν κόμην ἐκάθαιρεν. Ἐπὶ τούτοις ὢν τοῖς καλοῖς, ὁ ἵππος ἔχαιρεν· οὐδὲ γὰρ ἐνέδει τῶν, ὁπόσα καὶ τρυφᾶν ἵπποι νομίζονται.

2   Ἀλλ᾽ εἶδε ταῦτα ἔλαφος καὶ τοῖς τοῦ ἵππου καλοῖς ὀφθαλμὸν ἐπέβαλε βάσκανον καὶ ξένοις ἀγαθοῖς ἐφυβρίζειν οὐκ ἐπῃσχύνετο. Τί μὲν τῆς λόχμης τοῖς κέρασιν οὐκ ἀνώρυττε; Τί δὲ τῶν ἀνθέων τοῖς ποσὶν οὐ κατέκλα; Τί δὲ μὴ ξυνεθόλου τῆς πηγῆς, ὡς ἐφ᾽ ὕβρει καὶ φθόνῳ τῶν τοῦ ἵππου καλῶν ἀναιδῶς ἐπιτρέχουσα; Ἐντεῦθεν ἀλγεῖ μὲν ὁ ἵππος καὶ περισκοπεῖται τὴν ἄμυναν, ἀλλ᾽ οὐκ εἶχεν ὅ τι

Thus, trusting your enemy brings, along with the deceit, 2
also danger.

2

Once upon a time even the horse was untamed and, before he came under human control, he used to gambol in the meadows and enjoy the luxury of freedom. He had autonomy, which is a fine thing, and that he also led a life free from the bit and whip was no small part of his happiness. But the blessings of fortune were no less a matter of pride for him: a blooming grove spread wide over a plain, and some green grass that was quite pleasant for running and for a show of speed, and lovely for grazing. A spring, as beautiful to behold as it was sweet to drink, also flowed through the grove. It gave color to the flowers and cleansed the horse's mane. The horse enjoyed living in these fine conditions, for he lacked none of the pleasures in which horses are reckoned to delight.

But a deer saw all these things, cast a malevolent eye 2
upon the horse's blessings, and did not refrain from abusing another's good fortune. What part of the horse's lair did she not dig up with her antlers? What flowers did she not trample under her hooves? What part of the spring did she not muddy, shamelessly running through it with arrogance and envy of the horse's blessings? The horse, in turn, was pained by this and considered how to defend himself, but did not

καὶ χρήσαιτο. Ὡς οὖν ἐπέγνω κρεῖττον τῆς αὐτοῦ σοφίας τὸ κακόν, ὁρᾷ τινα παριόντα τὸ ἄλσος, διηγεῖται τῆς ἐλάφου τὸ βάσκανον καί, ὅπως ἀμυνεῖται, πυνθάνεται. Ὁ δέ—ἄνθρωπος γὰρ ἦν—ἀπάτῃ καὶ δόλῳ τὸν ἵππον μέτεισι καί, τὸν χαλινὸν ἐπιδείξας, "Εἴγε," φησίν, "ὦ ἵππε, τοῦτον μὲν ἐπὶ στόματος, ἐμὲ δ᾽ ἐπὶ νώτου φέρειν ἀνέξῃ μικρόν, ἐγώ σοι δι᾽ ὀλίγου τὴν ἔχθραν ἀμυνοῦμαι." Ἤκουσεν ὁ ἵππος ταῦτα καὶ πείθεται. Καὶ τὸ ἐντεῦθεν ἡ μὲν ἔλαφος ἀπηλαύνετο τοῦ ἄλσους, ὁ δὲ ἵππος ἐπὶ φάτνης εἱστήκει, μετὰ τῆς χλόης καὶ τῆς πηγῆς προσαφαιρεθεὶς καὶ τὸ ἄνετον.

3   Φυλακτέον ἄρα καὶ τὸ ἐλευθέριον καὶ παρρησίαν οὐ προδοτέον φρονήματος, εἴγε μὴ μέλλοι τις δουλεύειν οὐδὲν ἧττον ἤπερ ἵππος χαλιναγωγούμενος.

4   Ὁ μῦθος οὗτος ἐστὶ μὲν Αἰσώπειος, τὴν δὲ μελέτην ἐκ τῶν Ἑρμογένους προγυμνασματικῶν μεθόδων ἠρανίσατο, πλατύτερον ἐξειργασμένος, ὡς ἐκεῖνος μεθοδεύει ἐν τοῖς περὶ μύθου.

3

Ἁλίσκεταί ποτε καὶ λέων ὑπὸ κάλλους καὶ κόρης ἐρᾷ. Καὶ δὴ πρόσεισι τῷ πατρὶ καὶ λόγους πρὸς γάμον συνάπτει. "Θηρῶν μὲν ἄρχω," φησίν, "ἄνδρας δὲ οὐδ᾽ ἂν τὴν ἀρχὴν τρέσαιμι. Ἐγὼ καὶ λαγωὸν ὑπὸ τάχους εἷλον καὶ κύνας

know what to do. Just as he realized that the deer's wickedness was mightier than his cleverness, he saw someone coming through the grove, described to him the deer's malevolence, and asked how he might defend himself. The man — for "someone" was a human — approached the horse with trickery and deceit. He showed him the bit, and said, "If you, O horse, will consent to take this bit in your mouth and carry me on your back for a little while, I will quickly rid you of this hostile attack." The horse listened to this proposal and was persuaded. From that point on the deer was driven from the grove, but the horse too was put in the stable, deprived of his autonomy along with his grassy field and his spring.

And so one must guard his freedom and not abandon the 3 liberty to speak his mind, if he is to avoid being enslaved just as a horse is led by the bit.

This fable is Aesopic, but its execution was borrowed 4 from Hermogenes's treatise on *progymnasmata,* with the rather extensive elaboration as prescribed by Hermogenes in his instructions concerning Fable.

3

A lion once was captivated by beauty and fell in love with a girl. Then he approached the girl's father and discussed marriage. "I am king of the beasts," he said, "and I would not run away from men at all. I have captured hares with my

ἐφόβησα. Ἐγὼ καὶ ταῦρον ἐπέσχον μυκώμενον καὶ ἵππον κατέσχον μικροῦ τοῖς ποσὶν ἱπτάμενον. Ἔχεις ἕδνα τῆς κόρης τὴν ῥώμην, τὸ κάλλος, τὸ τάχος, τὰς ὁσημέραι θήρας. Ταῦτα πλουτήσεις, ταῦτα εὐδαιμονήσεις, εἰ μόνον κηδεστὴς ἐθελήσεις ἀκοῦσαι λέοντος."

2 Ὁ δέ, οἷς μὲν ἐδεδίττετο, τοὺς λόγους προσίεται καὶ τὸν γάμον οὐκ ἀνένευσε μέν, ἀνεβάλλετο δέ, οἷς δ' ἀπηχθάνετο, τοῦ θηρὸς περιελεῖν τὰ ὅπλα σοφίζεται. "Ἀλλ' ἐγὼ μέν," φησὶν ὁ πατήρ, "καὶ τοῦ κάλλους ἄγαμαι καὶ τῆς ῥώμης ἀποθαυμάζω, καὶ ὡς ἕδνα ταῦτα δέχομαι καὶ τὸν νυμφίον εἰς οὐδὲν ὅ τι καὶ μέμφομαι. Ἀλλ' ἡ κόρη παῖς ἐστιν ἁπαλὴ καὶ τὸ ὅλον γυνὴ καὶ πεφόβηται. Ἂν ἴδῃ τὰς τῶν ὀδόντων ἀκμάς, πέφρικεν· ἂν ἴδῃ τοὺς ὄνυχας, οὐκ ἀνέχεται. Ὀξεῖς εἰσι, συνεχεῖς εἰσι· φοβοῦσι καὶ μόνον φαινόμενοι. Ταῦτα καὶ τὸ σὸν χαροπὸν ἀγριαίνουσι, ταῦτα καὶ τὴν κόρην δειλαίνουσι καὶ τὸν γάμον ἀπείργουσιν. Ἂν σὺ τοὺς ὄνυχας ἐξέλῃς, καὶ ἡ κόρη συνεξέλῃ τῆς ψυχῆς τὸ φοβούμενον. Ἂν σὺ τοὺς ὀδόντας ἐκκόψῃς, κἀκείνη συνεκκόψει τὸ δέος. Αὐτός μοι μόνον τὸν θῆρα περίελε καὶ περίσωζε τὸ χαροπὸν ἀκραιφνὲς καὶ τάχα σε καὶ ἡ κόρη οὐκ ἐκφεύξεται."

3 Ταῦτα ὁ μὲν εἰς ἐπιβουλὴν καὶ δόλον ἔλεγεν, ὁ δ' ἀβασανίστως ἐδέχετο, τυφλὸς γὰρ ἅπας ἐρῶν καὶ ἀπροβούλευτος. Ἐντεῦθεν ὁ μὲν τὴν τῆς φύσεως πανοπλίαν ἀποδύεται, ὁ δὲ τῆς κόρης πατὴρ ἐπιπηδᾷ τῷ δῆθεν νυμφίῳ θρασύτερον, καταγελῶν τῆς ἀσθενείας ἅμα καὶ τῆς ἀνοίας, ὃν οὐδὲ προσβλέπειν ἐθάρρει τὸ πρότερον.

swiftness and struck terror into dogs. I have stopped a bellowing bull and caught a horse that all but flew on its legs. You have as wedding gifts for your daughter my strength, my beauty, my swiftness, and game from my daily hunts. You will have an abundance of these things, and you will be prosperous, if only you are willing to hear yourself called the father-in-law of a lion."

Out of fear, the father assented to the lion's proposal, and 2 while he did not refuse the marriage, he put it off; because of his revulsion, he devised a means to deprive the beast of his weapons. "I indeed am amazed at your beauty," the father said, "and I admire your strength. I accept these things as your wedding gifts and find no fault with you as a son-in-law. But my daughter is a tender child, and as a woman is afraid of everything. When she sees the points of your teeth, she's terrified; when she sees your claws, she can't endure it. They're sharp. They're densely packed. They terrorize just by their appearance. They make your fierce glance look angry. These things strike fear into my daughter and stand in the way of the marriage. But if you extract your claws, my daughter will likewise extract the fear from her soul. If you knock out your teeth, she will also knock out her dread. Strip away only the beast and preserve your fierce glance unchanged, and perhaps even my daughter will not flee from you."

The father said these words as a plot and a trick, and the 3 lion accepted them without a second thought, for everyone who is in love is blind and shortsighted. Then the lion stripped himself of his natural weapons, and the girl's father challenged his presumed son-in-law more boldly, mocking his weakness together with his foolishness, although previously he did not even dare to look at the lion.

4   Μὴ πείθου, ὦ παῖ, τοῖς ἐχθροῖς ἑτοιμότερον, μὴ καὶ γένῃ τούτοις εὐάλωτος, οἷς τὸ πρὶν ἐδόκεις ἀνάλωτος.

4

ᾺΟ ἐπείσακτος κόσμος ἐπικίνδυνος τοῖς χρωμένοις ἐστίν.

2   Ἔδοξέ ποτε τῷ λύκῳ τὴν φύσιν τῷ σχήματι μεταλλάξασθαι, ὡς ἂν οὕτως ἀφθονίαν ἕξει τροφῆς καί, δορὰν οἰὸς περιβεβλημένος, μετὰ τῆς ποίμνης ἐνέμετο, τὸν ποιμένα φενακίσας τῷ μηχανήματι. Νυκτὸς δὲ γενομένης, συναπεκλείσθη καὶ ὁ θὴρ παρὰ τοῦ ποιμένος τῇ μάνδρᾳ καὶ φραγμὸς τῇ εἰσόδῳ περιετέθη καὶ ἀτεχνῶς ὁ περίβολος κατησφάλιστο. Ὡς δὲ ὁ ποιμὴν ἡράσθη τροφῆς, μαχαίρᾳ τὸν λύκον ἀπέκτεινεν.

3   Οὕτως ἄρα ὁ τὸν ἐπείσακτον κόσμον ὑποκριθεὶς τῆς ζωῆς πολλάκις ἐστέρηται καὶ τὴν σκηνὴν εὗρε παραιτίαν μεγάλου συμπτώματος.

5

Κολοιός ποτε, θεασάμενος αἰετὸν ἐφ᾽ ὕψους φερόμενον, ἠθέλησε τούτῳ συναμιλληθῆναι περὶ τῆς πτήσεως.

Do not trust your enemies too readily, my child, so that 4
you do not become easy prey for those to whom you once
appeared unassailable.

4

A false disguise is dangerous to those who adopt it.

Once a wolf thought it a good idea to change his natural 2
form, in order thus to have unlimited food. After putting on
the skin of a sheep, he grazed among the flock, deceiving
the shepherd with his trick. When night came, the shepherd locked the beast in the sheepfold with the other animals. The gate was shut, and the enclosure completely se-
cured. And when the shepherd became hungry, he killed the
wolf with a knife.

And so the one who plays a role in a false disguise is often 3
deprived of his life and finds his pretense to be the cause of a
great downfall.

5

Once a jackdaw, after observing an eagle soaring high in
the sky, wished to contend with him in flight. He began to

Καὶ δὴ ἀρξάμενος ἵπτασθαι, τοῦτον μὲν οὐκ ἠδυνήθη κα-
ταλαβεῖν, ἀνέμου δὲ ἐπιπνεύσαντος σφοδροῦ, αἴφνης
ἐναρπαγεὶς ἡμιθανὴς πρὸς γῆν κατεφέρετο.

2   Οὕτως ὁ τῶν ἀδυνάτων κατατολμῶν μέγιστον ἑαυτῷ
κίνδυνον προξενεῖ.

6

Λέων ποτέ, βουληθεὶς πεῖραν λαβεῖν τῶν ἄλλων θηρῶν,
εἴπερ ὡς βασιλεῖ αὐτῷ πρὸς πᾶν ὑπακούουσι, σύνοδον
τούτων συγκροτησάμενος, παρῄνει λέγων αὐτοῖς·
"Ἐπειδήπερ ἤδη γεγήρακα καὶ θηρᾶν οὐκέτι δεδύνημαι,
ὑμεῖς, καθ᾽ ἑκάστην ἐξιόντες πρὸς θήραν, ἐμοὶ τὰ πρὸς
τροφὴν προκομίζετε." Πάντων δὲ τῷ τούτου ὑποκυψάντων
προστάγματι, μόνος ὁ λύκος οὐδ᾽ ὅλως ἐπείθετο, ὕβρεις δὲ
μᾶλλον τούτου κατέχεεν ὡς ἐγκελευομένου παράλογα. Ὁ
δὲ σφοδρῶς θυμωθείς, κἀντεῦθεν σὺν βρυχηθμῷ κινηθείς,
τοῦτον τοῖς ὄνυξι διεσπάραξεν.

2   Οὕτως οἱ τοῖς ὑπερέχουσιν ἀντιπράττοντες μέγιστον
ἑαυτοῖς προξενοῦσι τὸν κίνδυνον.

fly, but was unable to catch up with the eagle, and when a strong wind came up, he was suddenly caught in the blast and plummeted half-dead down to the earth.

Thus, one who attempts impossible deeds brings the ₂ greatest danger upon himself.

6

Once a lion wished to test the other beasts, to see if they would obey him as king in all respects. When he had brought them together in an assembly, he made this proposal to them: "Since I have now grown old and am no longer able to hunt, all of you should go out hunting every day and bring me food for my nourishment." All the animals submitted themselves to his command. Only the wolf refused to obey in any way, and instead he poured out abuses on the lion, on the ground that he was making unreasonable demands. The lion was greatly angered, and so with a roar he set upon the wolf and tore him apart with his claws.

Thus, those who oppose the powerful bring the greatest ₂ danger upon themselves.

7

Ἔδοξέ ποτε τοῖς ὄρνισιν ἄρχεσθαι, ἵν᾽ οὕτως ἀσφαλεστέραν ἕξουσι τὴν ζωὴν καὶ ἀνεπιβούλευτον, καὶ βασιλέα προελέσθαι τὸν τῶν ἄλλων ὀρνίθων τῷ κάλλει διαφέροντα. Ὡς δὲ καὶ ἡ ψῆφος ἐπεκυρώθη καὶ ἀνεζητεῖτο, τίς ἄρα καὶ εἴη ὁ τὸ κράτος τῆς βασιλείας ἀναδησόμενος, ὑποκριθῆναι κάλλος ἀλλότριον τὸ εἰδεχθέστατον ζῷον καὶ ἀκαλλὲς καὶ φαυλότατον, ὁ κολοιός, ἐτεχνάσατο. Καί, συναγαγὼν ὀρνίθων πτερά, οἷς τὸ φαιδρὸν ἐπήνθει καὶ τὸ διαυγὲς ἐναπέστιλβε, περιεβάλλετο ταῦτα. Καὶ περικαλλὴς ἐντεῦθεν ἐδόκει καὶ καταστράπτων τῇ ὡραιότητι. Μέσον δὲ τῶν ὀρνίθων περιϊπτάμενος καὶ ταῖς ποικίλαις χροιαῖς καὶ λαμπραῖς κάλλος ἔχων ἀμήχανον, εἰς θάμβος τοὺς θεωμένους ὄρνιθας παρεκίνησεν, ὅθεν βασιλεὺς ἀνηγόρευται καὶ πάντες τούτῳ κατεδουλώθησαν. Ὡς δὲ περιεργότερον τὰς ὄψεις τούτῳ προσέβαλον καὶ τὸ οἰκεῖον ἕκαστος ἀνεγνώρισε, τὸν κολοιὸν ἀπεγύμνωσαν καί, καταδρύψαντες τοῦτον τοῖς ὄνυξι, διεσπάραξαν καὶ ἐλεεινὸν πτῶμα κεῖσθαι τὸν πρὶν μακάριον παρεσκεύασαν.

2   Τὸν αὐτὸν ἄρα τρόπον καὶ ὅσοι περιάπτοις κόσμοις ὑπεκρίθησαν τὸ ἐξαίρετον ἔχειν καὶ τὸ μακάριον, τῆς σκηνῆς φωραθείσης, μετὰ γέλωτος καὶ τὴν ψυχὴν αὐτὴν προσαπώλεσαν.

7

The birds once decided to rule themselves, so that they could live more securely and free from intrigue, and to select as their king whichever of them was most outstanding in beauty. When the vote to determine who would be awarded control over the kingdom was taken and counted, the ugliest creature, homely and very plain, namely the jackdaw, contrived to assume a beauty not his own. He gathered up bird feathers that shone brightly and gleamed brilliantly, and clothed himself in them. He thus appeared quite handsome and radiant in his beauty. As he flew among the birds and displayed the extraordinary beauty of his colorful and brilliant feathers, he stirred up amazement in the birds that looked upon him, and so he was declared king and all were made subservient to him. But when they looked at him more carefully and each bird recognized something of himself, they stripped the jackdaw bare, slashed him with their talons, and tore him apart. And the bird that had recently been counted as blessed they left lying dead as a pitiful corpse.

And so in the same manner, all who pretend to be exceptional and blessed by putting on a disguise, when the pretense has been discovered, lose their very life in the midst of ridicule. 2

NARRATIONS

I

Τὸ κατὰ τὸν Θάμυριν

Θάμυρις καλὸς μὲν ἦν καὶ τὴν ὄψιν, σοφὸς δὲ καὶ τὰ μουσικά. Κάλλος μὲν οὖν εἶχε καὶ πρὸς λύραν ᾄδειν ἠπίστατο, σωφρονεῖν δὲ ἄρα πρὸς θεοὺς οὐκ ἐγίνωσκεν. Ἀιδούσας βλέπει τὰς Μούσας καὶ τὸ εὔμουσον εἰς ἀσέλγειαν προβάλλεται καὶ ὕβριν Μουσῶν. Προκαλεῖται καὶ πρὸς ἀγῶνα τὰς θεὰς καὶ "Ὦ Μοῦσαι," φησί, "οὐκ ἄρα Διὸς θυγατέρες ὑμεῖς, οὐδὲ τὴν μουσικὴν Ἀπόλλων ὑμᾶς ἐδιδάξατο, ὅτι μηδὲν μελιχρὸν ὑπηχεῖτε τοῖς ᾄσμασιν. Ὡς ἔγωγε θνητὸς μέν εἰμι, νικῶ δὲ καὶ τὰς Μούσας ὑμᾶς καὶ οὔτε μοι Ζεὺς πατήρ, οὐδὲ μουσικῆς Ἀπόλλων διδάσκαλος. Καὶ εἰ βούλεσθε, ἀγωνιζώμεθα· μόνον ἄθλον ἔστω μοι τῆς νίκης τὸ βούλημα· ἔστω καὶ ὑμῖν ἄθλον, ὅ τι καὶ βούλεσθε καί, νικῶσαι, μὴ φείδεσθε τοῦ Θαμύριδος."

2   Ἀλγοῦσιν ἐπὶ τούτοις αἱ Μοῦσαι καὶ τὴν πρόκλησιν δέχονται. Καὶ λοιπὸν περὶ μουσικῆς ἔρις ἦν Μουσῶν καὶ Θαμύριδος. Μεταχειρίζεται τὴν κιθάραν ὁ Θάμυρις καὶ μέλος ᾄδει τερπνὸν μέν, ἀλλ᾽ οἷον ᾄδουσιν ἄνθρωποι. Παύεται τῆς ἀγωνίας καὶ τὴν νικῶσαν ἤδη θαρρεῖ. Καὶ τὸ ἐντεῦθεν ὁ λοιπὸς ἀγὼν ἦν τῶν Μουσῶν· αἱ δὲ ᾄδουσιν,

The Story of Thamyris

Thamyris was handsome in appearance and also skilled in music. And so he possessed beauty and knew how to sing to the lyre, but he did not know how to act with moderation toward the gods. He caught sight of the Muses singing a song, and asserted his musical talent insolently and hubristically against them. He challenged the goddesses to a contest, saying, "Muses, you are not daughters of Zeus, nor did Apollo teach you the musical art, because you do not create sweet sounds with your songs. Although I myself am mortal, I can still defeat you, even though Zeus is not my father and Apollo was not my music teacher. And if you're willing, let's have a contest. Let there be but one prize for me, the acknowledgment of my victory. If you win, you may have whatever prize you wish: there's no need to spare Thamyris."

The Muses were distressed by these words, and they accepted the challenge. And so there was a musical competition between Thamyris and the Muses. Thamyris took up his lyre and sang a pleasant song, but it was one such as humans sing. He concluded his performance, confident that he had already won. And then the rest of the contest belonged to the Muses. They sang not only so as to defeat

οἷον νικῆσαι μὲν Θάμυριν, ἐμφῆναι δέ, ὡς μουσικῆς αὐταῖς Ἀπόλλων διδάσκαλος. Ἐντεῦθεν ἐδυστύχησε Θάμυρις καὶ μουσικῆς ἀποβολὴν καὶ στέρησιν ὄψεως.

2

Τὸ καθ᾽ Ἡρακλέα

Καὶ πρὸς Ὕδραν ἀγωνιούμενος Ἡρακλῆς ὑπ᾽ Εὐρυσθέως ἐστέλλετο. Ὁ δὲ ἅμα τε ἧκεν ἐπὶ τὴν θρεψαμένην τὸ θηρίον τοῦτο πηγὴν καί, τὸ ξίφος ἐπιβαλών, ἔργου εἴχετο. Ἀλλ᾽ ἦν ἀνίκητον τὸ κακὸν καὶ ὁ ἆθλος ἀτέλεστος. Ἡ μὲν τῶν κεφαλῶν ἐξετέμνετο, ἡ δ᾽ ἀνεφύετο· ἡ μὲν ὑπὸ ξίφους ἔπιπτεν, ἡ δ᾽ ὑπὸ τῆς τομῆς ἀνεδίδοτο. Ἔμενε τὸ θηρίον καὶ πρὸ τῆς τομῆς καὶ μετὰ τὴν τομὴν πολυκέφαλον. Μίαν ἀφηρεῖτο κεφαλὴν καὶ πλείους ἐλάμβανε, καὶ μιᾶς κεφαλῆς ἐκτομὴ πολλῶν ἐγίνετο γένεσις. Ὁ μὲν ἐξεθέριζε τὸ φυόμενον, αἱ δ᾽ οὐκ ἔληγον ἐκτεμνόμεναι. Ὅλον κεφαλῶν ἀνεφύετο λήϊον, τοσούτῳ δὲ μᾶλλον εἰς τομὴν ἀπορώτερον, ὅσῳ μᾶλλον ἐτέμνετο.

2   Ἐπὶ τούτοις διαπορεῖται μὲν Ἡρακλῆς, προσκαλεῖται δὲ σύμμαχον ἑαυτῷ μὲν τὸν Ἰόλεων, τῷ δὲ ξίφει τὸ πῦρ. Καὶ ὁ μὲν τὸ ξίφος ἐπέβαλλεν, ὁ δ᾽ ἐπετίθει τὸ πῦρ, οὔτε τὸ ξίφος εἴα μένειν τῶν κεφαλῶν τὸ φαινόμενον, οὔθ᾽ ὁ

Thamyris, but also to demonstrate that Apollo had indeed been their music teacher. And therefore Thamyris suffered a miserable fate: he lost his musical ability and was deprived of his sight.

2

The Story of Heracles

Heracles was sent by Eurystheus to fight the Hydra. He no sooner arrived at the spring that had nourished this beast than he wielded his sword and applied himself to his labor. But the evil beast was indomitable and the fight unending. When one of its heads was cut off, another grew up in its place. When one fell by the sword, another sprang up from the wound. The beast remained many-headed, both before it was cut and after. Deprived of one head, it would grow more, and the cutting off of a single head gave rise to many others. Heracles would cut off whatever grew, but there were always more heads to cut. An entire crop of heads sprang up, and the more they were cut, the more difficult the cutting became.

At this point Heracles was at his wits' end, but then he called on his helper Iolaus, who added fire to the sword. Heracles then attacked with his sword, while Iolaus applied fire: the sword would not allow the head that was present to

2

καυτὴρ ἀναδίδοσθαι τὸ φυόμενον. Καὶ τὸ ἐντεῦθεν ὁ ἆθλος ἠνύετο.

3

Τὸ κατὰ τὸν Φαέθοντα

Φαέθων ὁ τοῦ Ἡλίου παῖς ἅρματος ἐπιβῆναι τοῦ πατρικοῦ πόθον ἔσχε παράλογον, ὅθεν καὶ ἱκετεύει τὸν φύσαντα, παρακαλεῖ, δυσωπεῖ, δάκρυσι τὴν παράκλησιν ἀνακίρνησι, πένθεσι τὴν αἴτησιν μίγνυσιν. Ἐνδίδωσι τῆς ἐνστάσεως ὁ πατήρ, πείθεται τῷ βιάζοντι, τῷ παρακλήτορι τὴν αἴτησιν ἐκπληροῖ. Τί τὸ μετὰ ταῦτα; Ἐπιβαίνει τοῦ δίφρου, τῆς διφρηλασίας ἀπάρχεται, τῆς ἱππηλασίας ἐξέχεται. Μαστίζονται οἱ ἵπποι, κινοῦνται πρὸς δρόμον μυωπιζόμενοι, ἀεροποροῦσιν, αἰθεροδρομοῦσιν, οὐρανοδρομοῦσι κατὰ τὸ σύνηθες.

2 Ὡς δ' οὐκ εἶχεν οὗτος καταστέλλειν τὸ τῶν ἵππων ἀγέρωχον, μήτε μὴν ἀναχαιτίζειν τὸ θράσος αὐτῶν καὶ τὴν ἄτακτον κίνησιν· πρόσγειοι γίνονται, καὶ τὰ πλείω τῆς περιοικίδος πυρπολοῦνται, καταφλογίζονται, κατατεφροῦνται, καταξηραίνονται, καὶ τέλος ἐπὶ τὸν Ἠριδανὸν ποταμὸν τοῦ δίφρου τὸν ἐπιβάτην ἀποτινάσσουσιν. Δέχεται τοῦτον ὁ ποταμός, παρασύρει τοῖς ῥεύμασι, καταβυθίζει τοῖς κύμασιν, ἀποπνίγει τοῖς ὕδασι.

remain, and the application of fire would not allow a new head to grow. And so the labor was accomplished.

3

The Story of Phaëthon

Phaëthon, the Sun's child, had an extraordinary desire to climb aboard his father's chariot, and so he begged, exhorted, and entreated his father, adding tears to his petitions and mixing grief into his pleas. His father conceded to his insistence, yielded to the pressure, and fulfilled the request of the young suppliant. What happened next? Phaëthon climbed aboard the chariot, started off, and drove carefully. The horses were whipped; spurred on they were urged to run; in their usual manner they traversed the air, took to the sky, and ran through the heavens.

But then Phaëthon could not restrain the horses' high 2 spirits, nor could he rein in their boldness and their frenzied motion. They moved close to the earth, and burned most of the surrounding countryside. They caused it to burst into flames; they reduced it to ashes; they scorched it; and finally they shook out the chariot's passenger into the Eridanus River. The river received him, swept him away with its currents, sank him down beneath its waves, and drowned him in its waters.

4

Διήγημα ὃ καὶ Πλούταρχος ἐν Παραλλήλοις διηγεῖται

Ἀλλ᾽ οὐδὲ γυναικὸς ἐπίνοια τοὺς πάλαι διέλαθεν, ἀλλ᾽ οἷς εἶχέ τι σοφὸν καὶ τὸ θῆλυ τοῦ γένους, εἰκότως θαυμάζουσι, τοῦ δὲ λοιποῦ γένους φθόνον οὐ ποιοῦνται τοῦ θαύματος. Ἦν γάρ τίς ποτε βασιλεὺς τὴν κλῆσιν μὲν ἕτερος, τὴν ψυχὴν δὲ Μίδας, καὶ τὴν γνώμην φιλόχρυσος. Πολλῶν μὲν ἦρχε πόλεων, ἀλλ᾽ οὐχὶ καὶ φιλοχρηματίας ἄρχειν ἠπίστατο. Ἀλλὰ τῶν μὲν ἄλλων ἐκράτει τῷ μεγέθει τῆς τύχης, μόνῳ δὲ τῷ πρὸς χρυσὸν ἐδούλευεν ἔρωτι καί, τἄλλα σωφρονῶν, τοῦτο μόνον, ὡς οὐκ ἔδει, νοσῶν ἀπηλέγχετο. Πάντα χρυσὸς ἦν αὐτῷ τὰ ἐνύπνια, χρυσοῦ καὶ νήφων ἤρα, καὶ μὴ νήφων χρυσὸν νυκτὸς ἐφαντάζετο. Ἐντεῦθεν τί μὲν οὐκ ἔδρα τῶν, ὁπόσα τὸ χρῆμα τοῦτο πορίζουσι; Ποῖος δὲ τρόπος εἰς πορισμὸν οὐκ ἐπενοεῖτο τοῦ χρήματος; Φόροι δύσφοροι τοῖς ὑπηκόοις ἐπεφορτίζοντο καὶ τὰ μέν, ὡς εἶχον, ἐπέφερον, τὰ δὲ προσετίθουν, ἐκ γῆς μεταλλεύοντες. Τὰ μὲν τὴν περιουσίαν ἐξήντλουν, τὰ δὲ τὸ σῶμα κατέτρυχον· καὶ μυρίον εἶδος χρηματισμοῦ προσεπινοοῦντες οὐκ ἔληγον, ἀλλ᾽ ἦν ἡ πᾶσα σπουδὴ τοῦ κρατοῦντος ἀποπλῆσαι τὸν ἔρωτα.

2   Ὁ δὲ εἶχεν ἄρα μετὰ τοῦ φιλοχρύσου καὶ τὸ φιλόθηρον. Καί ποτε καὶ πρὸς τὴν ὕλην ἔξεισι, καὶ τοὺς κύνας

4

A Story also told by Plutarch in the *Parallel Lives*

Not even a woman's intellect escaped the notice of men of old, but they rightly admired the fact that even the female sex possessed some amount of wisdom, and their admiration did not incur the envy of the male sex. For there was once a king who was called by a different name, but really was a "Midas" in his heart and a lover of gold in his mind. He ruled over many cities, but he did not know how to govern his greed. Although he mastered everything else by the greatness of his kingly status, he was a slave only to his desire for gold; although restrained with respect to everything else, he was guilty of weakness in this one matter, even though he should not have been. All his dreams were about gold; while awake he loved gold; while asleep at night he fantasized about it. And so, what did he not attempt in order to obtain this gold? What means of getting it did he not contemplate? He overburdened his subjects with onerous taxes; they paid what they had and added the rest by mining it from the earth. They drained their resources, and then they wore out their bodies. They were ceaselessly devising countless forms of moneymaking, as all their efforts were directed toward fulfilling the desire of their ruler.

This man, in addition to his love of gold, also had a love 2 of hunting. And one day he went out to the forest, taking

ἐπισυρόμενος. Ἐνταῦθα ὁ μὲν ἐλάφοις ἐπέτρεχε καὶ λαγω-
οῖς ἐφιππάζετο καὶ τὸ κυνηγετικὸν ἐπεθώϋζεν· ἡ δὲ βασιλὶς ἑτέραν εἶχε σπουδήν, ὅπως ὑφέλη τῆς ἐς τὸ χρη-
ματίζεσθαι πανταχόθεν ὁρμῆς. Καί πως ἐπιόν, οὕτω κατὰ
δαίμονα, εἰς νοῦν λαμβάνει καὶ μάλα σοφόν τι ἐνθύμιον·
ὡς εἰ μηδὲν εἰς τὸ ζῆν ἐκεῖνος γνοίη τὸν φίλον χρυσὸν
συμβαλλόμενον, τοῦ πάθους ἂν πάντως ἀπόσχοιτο.

3   Τὸ δὲ ἦν, ὡς ἕξει μὲν αὐτὸς μετὰ κόρον τῆς θήρας καὶ
τὴν γαστέρα κορέσων, εὑρήσει δὲ τὸ δεῖπνον ἅπαν χρυσὸν
καί, μικρόν τι λιμώξας, ἐντεῦθεν τὸ τοῦ χρυσοῦ περιττὸν
καταγνώσεται. Ἐδόκει δὴ ταῦτα καὶ τὸ δοκοῦν αὐτίκα
ἐπράττετο. Χρυσὸς μὲν ἦν μυρίος τοῖς χρυσοχόοις, ἐπὶ
μέρος ἀναμετρούμενος, χεῖρες δὲ πολλαὶ διετεχνῶντο τὸ
καινὸν ἐκεῖνο καὶ χρυσοῦν ἄριστον. Ἦν ἐκεῖσε καὶ χρυ-
σήλατος τράπεζα καὶ κρατῆρες καὶ οἰνοχόαι καὶ τὰ πάντα
χρύσεα. Καὶ ἦν ὁρᾶν ὅλον τὸ δεῖπνον χρυσὸν ἐπὶ χρυσῷ
κείμενον· χρυσὸς μὲν ἦν ἡ τράπεζα, χρυσῷ δὲ καὶ τὰ κανᾶ
διεσκεύαστο. Ἐπὶ δὲ χρυσοῖς τούτοις χρυσᾶ καὶ τὰ ὄψα
ἐτίθεντο· πέρδικες ἐκ χρυσοῦ, τοὺς ἀπὸ τῆς ὕλης μιμούμε-
νοι, λαγωοί, ὄρνεις καὶ πάντα ὡς ἀπὸ χρυσοῦ διελάμπετο.
Εἶχέ τι καὶ τοῖς ἐκ πυρὸς ὀπτωμένοις παρόμοιον, οἷς τὸ
τοῦ χρυσοῦ ἄνθος εἰς τὸ πυρωπότερον δίκην ἀνθράκων
ἐπέχρωζεν.

4   Ἐπεὶ δὲ καιρὸς ἦν, ὡς εἰς ἄριστον ἧκεν ὁ βασιλεύς, πολλοὺς τοὺς ἐκ τῆς θήρας ἀποστάζων ἱδρῶτας, καὶ δὴ
παρῆσαν οἱ θεράποντες, χρυσῆν κομίζοντες τράπεζαν, καὶ
ὁπόσα ὡς ἐπὶ τῆς τοιαύτης τραπέζης ἤμελλον κείσεσθαι.
Ὁ δὲ τῶν μὲν ὑπερεώρα, ἕτερα δὲ τὰ πρὸς τροφὴν ἐζητεῖτο.

his dogs along. There he chased deer, pursued hares on horseback, and urged on the hunt. Meanwhile, the queen had a different objective, to secretly take away his impulse to derive income from any and all sources. And somehow, by a god's inspiration, she conceived a very clever idea: if he could realize that his beloved gold contributed nothing to his ability to live, he would free himself completely from his passion.

This was her idea, that after getting his fill of hunting, he 3 would proceed to fill his stomach as well. Then he would find that his entire dinner was made of gold, and when he was about to starve, he would begin to despise his excess of gold. This was her plan, and she implemented it immediately. There was limitless gold for the goldsmiths, measured out into allotments, and many hands crafted that unique, golden meal. A table of worked gold was there, and mixing bowls and wine pitchers, everything made of gold. You could see the whole golden dinner in a golden setting. The table was gold, and the baskets had been prepared in gold too. Upon this gold was placed the golden food: partridges made of gold (in imitation of those from the forest), hares, birds, and everything shining from the gold. There was also something resembling food roasting in the fire, to which the brightness of the gold gave a very reddish-bronze color, like burning embers.

When the time came, the king arrived for his dinner, 4 dripping great drops of sweat from his hunting. His servants were also present, carrying in the golden table and everything that was to be set forth on it. The king regarded all this scornfully, and looked for something else that was

Τί οὖν ἦν; Ἡ βασιλὶς ἅμα καὶ ξύνοικος, "Ἔσθιε," φησίν, "ἀπὸ χρυσοῦ, βασιλεῦ, ἐπειδή σοι καὶ χρυσὸς τὸ φιλούμενον, χρυσὸς ἅπαν ἐστί σοι τὸ σπουδαζόμενον. Ἀπὸ χρυσοῦ τοιγαροῦν καὶ κορέννυσο, ἵνα σοι καὶ ὑπὸ γαστέρα χρυσὸς θησαυρίζοιτο καί σοι καὶ τὸ σῶμα εἴη ὅλον ἐπίχρυσον. Εἰ δ' οὐδὲν ὁ χρυσὸς εἰς τὸ σῶμά σου χρήσιμος, ἀλλὰ θᾶττον ἀπὸ μόνου χρυσοῦ τις λιμώξεται, ἐς τί ἄρα σοι τὸ πολὺ τῆς σπουδῆς καταβάλλεται;" Ἤκουσε ταῦτα ὁ βασιλεὺς καί, τὸ τῆς γυναικὸς σοφὸν μετὰ τοῦ δικαίου προσαιδεσθείς, ἀνῆκε ταῖς πόλεσι μὲν τὸ πολὺ τοῦ φόρου, ἑαυτῷ δὲ τὸ ἐσάγαν χρυσομανές.

5

Τὸ κατὰ τὴν Δανάην

Οὐδὲν ἄρα πατρὸς προμηθέστερον, ἀλλ' οὐδ' εἰς ἐπιβουλὴν σοφώτερον Ἔρωτος. Ἤθελε Δανάην τὴν παῖδα παρθενεύειν Ἀκρίσιος καί, μέγαν οὕτω λειμῶνα κάλλους ὁρῶν, ἐδεδίει τοὺς λάθρα τὸ τῆς παρθενίας ἄνθος ἀποσυλήσοντας. Καὶ δὴ πρὸς φυλακὴν ἐπινοεῖται θριγγίον ἄλλο καινότερον, θάλαμον χάλκεον, ἀτειρές τι χρῆμα, τεῖχος ἀνάλωτον, ἀνδράσιν ἄβατον, ἀνεπιβούλευτον Ἔρωτι. Ἀλλ' ὁρᾷ καὶ κρυπτομένην τὴν κόρην ὁ πάντα ἐφορῶν

edible, but what was there? His queen and wife said, "Dine on gold, my king, since gold is the most beloved thing for you, gold the object of all your attention. Sate yourself with gold, therefore, so your stomach may become a treasure house for gold and your whole body gold-plated. If gold, however, is of no use to your body, but instead you will starve very quickly when there's only gold, why are you focusing your attention on it?" The king heard her words, and, rightly respecting his wife's wisdom, remitted most of the taxes from the cities and renounced his excessive mania for gold.

5

The Story of Danaë

No one exercises more forethought than a father, but no one is more clever at scheming than Love. Acrisius wanted to keep his daughter Danaë a virgin, and observing the great meadow of her beauty, he feared the men who would secretly steal away the blossom of her virginity. And so to keep her under guard he contrived a unique and quite original sort of enclosure: a bronze chamber, an indestructible thing, an impregnable wall, which men could not pass through and Love could not undermine. But then all-seeing Zeus spied

Ζεὺς καὶ δεινὸν ἡγεῖται τοσοῦτον κάλλος ἐγκατορω-
ρυγμένον τῷ χαλκῷ λανθάνειν, ὡς θησαυρὸν ὑπὸ γῆν, ὡς
ἐν νυκτὶ σελήνην, ὡς ἐν κάλυκι ῥόδον, ὡς ἐν κόχλῳ
πορφύραν, ὡς ἐν ὀστρέῳ μάργαρον.

2   Δίεισιν ἐπὶ τούτοις τὸν θάλαμον καὶ περισκοπεῖται τὸν
ὄροφον καί, χαλκὸν ἔχων πολέμιον, εἰς χρυσὸν μετασχη-
ματίζεται, ἵν' εἴη καὶ χαλκοῦ κρείττων χρυσὸς καὶ θεὸς
ἀνθρώπου σοφώτερος, καὶ χρυσῇ τὸ κάλλος παρθένῳ
χρυσὸς ἐραστὴς γένοιτο. Ἐγκολπίζεται τὸν θεὸν ὡς χρυσὸν ἡ παρθένος ἐξ ὀρόφου ῥυέντα. Καὶ τὸ ἐντεῦθεν δρέπε-
ται μὲν τῆς ὥρας εἰς κόρον ὁ Ζεὺς καὶ Δανάη δὲ δῶρον
τοῦ χρυσοῦ καὶ τοῦ γάμου Περσέα κομίζεται.

6

Τὸ κατὰ τὴν Πλάτανον

Πλάτανος καλὴ μὲν ἦν ὡς κόρη, μεγάλη δὲ ὡς Ἀλωέως
θυγάτηρ καὶ τὸ μέγεθος τῶν ἀδελφῶν οὐκ ἐλείπετο. Ἐπεὶ
δ' ἐκείνους, κεραυνῷ βαλών, ὁ Ζεὺς ἔπαυσε, κατὰ τῶν
θεῶν μαινομένους, οὐ φέρει τὴν συμφορὰν ἡ κόρη καὶ τὴν
φύσιν εἰς φυτὸν ἠλλάξατο. Ἀλλ' ἔτι καὶ τὸ κάλλος περι-
σώζει καὶ τὸ μέγεθος οὐκ ἀφήρηται. Τοῦτο τὸ φυτὸν καὶ
Ξέρξης ποτὲ τῆς εὐφυΐας ἠγάσθη καὶ τὸ θαῦμα ἐκεῖνος
ἐδήλου, χρυσῆν φιλοτεχνήσας πλάτανον.

the girl even though she was hidden away, and he thought it terrible that such great beauty should go unnoticed, buried deeply in the bronze chamber, like a treasure underground, like the moon at night, like a rose in bud, like purple in a murex shell, like a pearl in an oyster.

He went all around the chamber, therefore, and carefully 2 examined the roof. Considering the bronze to be his adversary, he changed his own form into gold, so that as gold he might be stronger than bronze and as a god wiser than a human, and he might become a golden lover to the girl who was golden in her beauty. The virgin girl embraced the god-turned-gold who had flowed down from the ceiling. And so Zeus plucked the girl's beauty to his satisfaction, and Danaë received Perseus as a gift from the gold and the union.

6

The Story of Platanos

As a girl, Platanos was beautiful. As the daughter of Aloeus, she was tall and not inferior to her brothers in stature. When Zeus stopped her brothers from raging against the gods by striking them with his lightning bolt, the girl could not endure the calamity and so changed her natural form into a tree. But still she preserves her beauty and has not been robbed of her stature. Even Xerxes once marveled at the fineness of the tree's form and revealed his amazement by fashioning a plane tree out of gold.

7

Τὸ κατὰ τοὺς Ἀλωάδας

Ὧτον καὶ Ἐφιάλτην Ἀλωεὺς παῖδας ηὐτύχησε, τὴν ἰσχὺν ὑπερφυεῖς, τὴν ἡλικίαν ὑπερνεφεῖς. Ἀλλ᾽ ἐκεῖνοι καὶ μείζω τῆς φύσεως φρονεῖν οὐκ ᾐσχύνοντο· μικρὸν ἡγοῦντο κρατεῖν ἀνθρώπων καὶ τηλικούτων σωμάτων ἀνάξιον· ἐπὶ τοὺς θεοὺς τὴν τόλμαν μετάγουσιν, ἐπὶ τὸν οὐρανὸν ἀποχρῶνται τῇ ῥώμῃ καὶ τῷ μεγέθει. Ἤδη κινοῦσι τὰ ἀκίνητα· ὅλα ὄρη ὄρεσιν ἐπεγείρουσι καὶ τὴν εἰς θεοὺς πολιορκίαν ἐπισκευάζονται.

2   Ἀλλὰ κινεῖ τοὺς πρηστῆρας ὁ Ζεὺς καὶ θνητὴν λαχόντες φύσιν μηκέτι κατεπαίρεσθαι τῶν θεῶν ἐπαιδεύοντο. Ζηλοῖ τὸν ἀδελφὸν Δία καὶ Πλούτων καὶ γενομένους ἐν Ἅιδου κολάζει, μεγάλους γύπας μεγάλοις σώμασιν ἐπιστήσας, οἳ καὶ τὰ τούτων σπλάγχνα πλέον τοῖς ῥάμφεσιν ὑπορύττουσιν, ἥπερ ἐκεῖνοι πάλαι τὴν Ὄσσαν. Τοσοῦτον Ἀλωάδαι σωμάτων ἀλόγου μεγέθους ἀπώναντο, ὅσον ἐπὶ γῆς μὲν πολλὴ γενέσθαι σποδός, ὑπὸ γῆν δὲ μεγάλη τράπεζα κεῖσθαι τοῖς τοῦ Πλούτωνος δεινοῖς δαιτυμόσιν.

7

The Story of the Sons of Aloeus

Aloeus was blessed with two sons, Otus and Ephialtes, who were both extraordinary in strength and over-the-clouds in height. But they did not refrain from being more arrogant than their nature. They believed that prevailing over humans was trivial and unworthy of such strong bodies, and so they redirected their boldness toward the gods and wielded their size and strength against heaven. Then they moved the immovable, setting entire mountains upon mountains, and they prepared a siege against the gods.

But Zeus unleashed his lightning bolts, and since the 2 young men were mere mortals by nature, they learned the hard way to disparage the gods no longer. Pluto emulated his brother, Zeus, and punished the young men again when they arrived in Hades, setting giant vultures upon their giant bodies. These birds dug deeper into their entrails with their beaks than the brothers had long ago dug into Mount Ossa. Such was the reward of the sons of Aloeus for the incomparable size of their bodies, that upon the earth they became a great pile of ashes, while below the earth they were set as a magnificent table for Pluto's terrifying dinner guests.

8

Τὸ κατὰ τὸν Ἀχιλλέα

Ἀπόλεμον ἐποίει Πηλέα τὸ γῆρας καὶ τὸν Ἀχιλλέα
νεότης ἀνθώπλιζε καὶ ἡ Ἑλλάς, ἀφέντες τὸν πατέρα, ἐπὶ
συμμαχίαν ἐκάλουν τὸν παῖδα. Ἀλλ' ἡ μήτηρ ἐδεδίει τὸ
Ἴλιον καὶ τὸ μήτηρ εἶναι τοῖς Ἀπόλλωνος βέλεσιν ἀπο-
βαλεῖν ἐμαντεύετο. Οὐκοῦν ἐπινοεῖταί τι σοφώτερον καὶ
τοὺς Ἕλληνας παρακρούεται· ἁρπάζει τῆς Φθίας τὸν
παῖδα, ἐξάγει τοῦ Πηλίου καὶ πρὸς τὸν Λυκομήδους παρθενῶνα μετάγει. Ξυνήρατο τῇ θεῷ τοῦ σοφίσματος καὶ τὸ
τῆς μορφῆς τοῦ παιδὸς ἐπαφρόδιτον, ὅλους ἀπαστράπτον
ἔρωτας καὶ καλαῖς κόραις ἁμιλλᾶσθαι δυνάμενον μεταλ-
λάττει, καὶ τὸ τῆς στολῆς ἀνδρεῖον καὶ ὅσον τοῦ κάλλους
ἀρρενωπότερον εἰς ὥραν ἁπαλὴν μεθηρμόσατο. Οὕτω τὸν
μέγαν ἥρωα τοῦτον καὶ βραχὺς περικρύπτει θάλαμος καί,
ὃν ἐσύστερον ὅλον πεδίον οὐκ ἐχώρει τὸ μέγα τῆς
Εὐρώπης καὶ Ἀσίας μεταίχμιον, ὁ τοῦ Λυκομήδους τηνικαῦτα παρθενὼν ὑποδέχεται.

2   Ἀλλ' Ὀδυσσεύς, καὶ πρὶν ἥκειν εἰς Τροίαν, τοῖς Ἕλλησι
τὸ σοφὸν ἐπεδείξατο καί, δόλιος ὤν, τῆς θεοῦ τὸν δόλον
οὐκ ἠγνόησεν. Ὅπλα καὶ κερκίδας λαβών, περί που τὸν
παρθενῶνα τίθησιν, ἑκατέρῳ γένει δέλεαρ ἐπιτεχνώμενος
οὐκ ἀλλότριον, ἵνα καὶ ταῖς κερκίσι τὰς κόρας ὑπάγοιτο
καὶ τοῖς ὅπλοις τὸν ἄνδρα θηρεύσαιτο.

8

The Story of Achilles

Old age rendered Peleus unfit for war, but youth armed Achilles in his place, and Greece, after discharging the father, summoned the son into an alliance. But his mother feared Ilium and foresaw that she would lose her status as a mother because of the arrows of Apollo. She therefore devised something quite clever and deceived the Greeks. She seized her son from Phthia, dragged him from Mount Pelion, and brought him to the women's apartment in the home of Lycomedes. The king connived in the goddess's trick and altered the appearance of the boy, who became charming, an absolutely radiant object of desire, and able to compete with the finest girls. He also changed the boy's manly clothing and the more masculine aspects of his beauty into a delicate, feminine loveliness. Thus a small chamber entirely concealed this great hero, and the one whom later the whole plain, that great space between Europe and Asia, would not be able to hold, was welcomed then into the women's apartment at Lycomedes's home.

But Odysseus, even before he arrived at Troy, demon- 2 strated his cleverness to the Greeks: since he was tricky himself, the goddess's trickery did not fool him. Taking armor and weaver's shuttles, he placed them casually near the women's apartment, contriving an enticement that was particular to each sex, so that he might attract the girls with the shuttles and lure the man with the armor.

3 Ὁρᾷ τὴν Ὀδυσσέως μηχανὴν Ἀχιλλεύς, οὐ μὲν ὅ τι καὶ βούλεται ξυνορᾷ· ἅμα ἐπὶ τὴν πανοπλίαν ἀνέβλεψε καὶ τὴν ἐκεῖθεν ἐξαλλομένην ἀστραπὴν καὶ ὅλος ὑπεκκάεται τῷ πυρὶ τοῦ θυμοῦ, ἀναμιμνήσκεται τοῦ Πηλίου, τοῦ παρθενῶνος ἐπιλανθάνεται, εἰς νοῦν λαμβάνει τὴν φύσιν, ἀναλαμβάνει τὸ ἀνδρεῖον, αἰσχύνεται τὴν παρθενικὴν στολήν, ἀποτίθεται τὸ δρᾶμα καὶ τὴν σκηνήν. Καὶ τὸ τῆς παρθένου προσωπεῖον ἀποδυσάμενος, ἁρπάζει τὰ ὅπλα καὶ γίνεται θήραμα καλὸν Ὀδυσσεῖ καὶ τὴν ἐπὶ τὸ Ἴλιον στέλλεται, μέγας μὲν τοῖς Ἕλλησι ξύμμαχος, δεινὸς δὲ τοῖς πολεμίοις ἀντίμαχος. Οὕτω τὸν Πηλέως γυναικείαν φύσιν πλαττόμενον ἀπήλεγξεν Ὀδυσσεύς, ὡς ἐκεῖνον Παλαμήδης πρότερον μανίαν σχηματιζόμενον, καὶ τότε πρῶτον Ἕλληνες τῆς Ὀδυσσέως σοφίας ἀπώναντο, οὐχ ἧττον δὲ ἢ ὅτε τὸ παλλάδιον ἐκ μέσης Τροίας ἀφείλετο.

9

Τὸ κατὰ τὸν Νάρκισσον

Νάρκισσος, ὁ νῦν διαπρέπων ἐν ἄνθεσιν, ἐν μειρακίοις πάλαι διέλαμπεν. Εὐανθὴς ἦν τὸν τοῦ προσώπου λειμῶνα, καλὸς τὴν μορφήν, ἄμαχος τὴν θέαν, τὸ κάλλος ἀνίκητος. Ἐφείλκετο μὲν τοὺς τῶν ἄλλων ὀφθαλμούς, ἀλλ᾽ εἶχεν αὐτὸς ἕτερον ἔρωτα, κύνας ἐπισύρεσθαι καὶ πρὸς θήρας ἱππάζεσθαι.

Achilles saw Odysseus's trick, but he did not comprehend 3 his intention. As soon as he glimpsed the armor, which gleamed like lightning, he was completely enflamed with a fiery spirit. He remembered Mount Pelion and forgot the women's apartment; he recalled his own nature and reasserted his manliness; he was ashamed of his girlish clothing, and so he put aside the acting and the stage. Once he had stripped off his maidenly mask, he seized the armor, became a fine quarry for Odysseus, and was sent on his way to Ilium, a great ally for the Greeks and a terrible opponent to his enemies. Thus Odysseus exposed the son of Peleus's artificial femininity, just as Palamedes had earlier exposed Odysseus's pretended madness, and on this occasion the Greeks first made use of Odysseus's cleverness, no less than when he stole the Palladium from the very heart of Troy.

9

The Story of Narcissus

Narcissus, who is now distinguished among flowers, was resplendent long ago among young men. He was blooming in the meadow of his countenance, handsome in form, unconquerable in appearance, unbeatable in beauty. He attracted the eyes of everyone else, but he himself had a different passion, to track with dogs and hunt on horseback.

2   Καί ποτε, πολλοὺς τοὺς ἐκ τῆς θήρας ἀποστάζων
ἰδρῶτας, περιΐσταταί τινα πηγήν, διαφανῆ μὲν ἰδεῖν, ποτι-
μωτάτην δὲ πιεῖν. Ἡ δὲ τὴν μὲν τῆς δίψης φλόγα μαραίνει
τῷ μειρακίῳ, ἕτερον δὲ πῦρ ἀνάπτει τὸν ἔρωτα. Καὶ
διψῶντα μὲν ὕδατος παύει, κάλλους δὲ διψῆν αὖθις βιάζε-
ται· γίνεται τῆς ὥρας κάτοπτρον, ὡς ἐν πίνακι τῷ ῥεύματι
γράφει τὸν Νάρκισσον καὶ τοῖς αὐτὸς αὐτοῦ κάλλεσι
βάλλεται Νάρκισσος καί, ὃ πολλοὺς πρότερον ἔδρασε,
τοῦτο τηνικαῦτα παθών, αὐτὸς ἔλαθε· Νάρκισσος ἐκ πηγῆς τὸ κάλλος ἀνέβλυζε καὶ Νάρκισσος διψῶν οὐκ ἐπίμ-
πλατο· Νάρκισσος ὑπερίστατο τῶν ναμάτων καὶ Νάρκισσος ἕτερος ὑπὸ τὴν πηγὴν διεφαίνετο· ἐμειδία Νάρκισσος
ἄνωθεν καὶ κάτωθεν αὖθις ἀντεμειδία τὸ κάλλος. Ταῦτα
ἦν ἀμφοῖν πάντα ὡς ἐν κατόπτρῳ διαφανεῖ τῇ πηγῇ.

3   Ἀλλ᾽ εἶχέ τι καὶ θαύματος, οἷς διήλλαττε τὸ φαινόμενον·
ὀφθαλμοὶ πρὸς τὴν ὄψιν ἐπεπήγεσαν καὶ τὸ κάλλος
ἐναπέσταζε τῇ πηγῇ· ἡ τῶν ὑδάτων φύσις θᾶττον ἀπέρρει
καὶ τὸ ῥεῦσαν ἐκ τῶν ὀφθαλμῶν ἐν οὐκ εἰδόσι μένειν
ἐπεπήγει τοῖς ὕδασιν. Ἐντεῦθεν ὁ ἔρως θερμότερον ἐπέ-
ζεσε τῷ Ναρκίσσῳ. Ὁ δέ, μὴ φέρων τὸ πῦρ, ἐπαφῆκεν ἑαυτὸν τοῖς ῥεύμασιν, ὡς ἂν καὶ τὸν δοκοῦντα περιπτύξαιτο
Νάρκισσον καὶ τὴν ἔρωτος πυρκαϊὰν ἀποσβέσειεν. Ἀλλ᾽ ἡ
τῶν ὑδάτων φύσις αὐτῷ κάλλει τὸν ἔρωτα ξυναπέσβεσε,
τῷ ζῶντι Ναρκίσσῳ καὶ τὸν δοκοῦντα ξυναποκρύψασα.
Οὐ μιμεῖται τὴν πηγὴν ἡ γῆ, ἀλλ᾽ οἰκτείρει τὴν συμφορὰν
καὶ σοφίζεται τὴν μνήμην τοῦ πάθους καὶ τοῦ καλοῦ μει-
ρακίου καλὸν ἄνθος ἀντιχαρίζεται Ναρκίσσῳ καὶ Ἔρωτι.

Once, dripping wet with sweat from hunting, he stopped 2
alongside a spring that was transparent to the eye and most
sweet to drink. It quenched the flame of the young man's
thirst, but it ignited another sort of fire—erotic desire. It
stopped him from thirsting for water but in turn aroused a
forceful thirst for beauty. It became a mirror for his loveliness, reflecting Narcissus with its current as though in a
painting. Narcissus himself was struck by his own beauty
and did not realize that he was experiencing what he had
done to many others in the past. Narcissus gushed forth
his beauty from the spring, and Narcissus, although thirsty,
could not satisfy his thirst; Narcissus stood over the water
and another Narcissus appeared down in the spring; Narcissus smiled down from above and in return his beauty smiled
back up at him from below. All these actions of both Narcis-
suses appeared in the clear spring as if in a mirror.

But there was also something strange in how the phe- 3
nomenon changed. His eyes were fixed on the sight and his
beauty was dripping into the spring. The water began to
flow more swiftly, and the flow from his eyes became fixed
in the waters that could not remain still. And so Narcissus's
desire boiled up more hotly. And he, no longer able to endure the fire, threw himself into the water, so as to embrace
the imaginary Narcissus and extinguish the flame of his desire. But the nature of the water extinguished his desire together with the beauty, and it hid away the imaginary Narcissus together with the living one. The earth did not imitate
the spring, but it felt pity for the accident and so devised a
remembrance of the passion, returning as a favor to Narcissus and to Love the beautiful bloom of the beautiful young

Οὕτω καὶ μετὰ τελευτὴν περίεστι Νάρκισσος καὶ αὖθις οὐδὲν ἧττον ἢ πρότερον εἰς κάλλος ἀνθεῖ.

10

Τὸ κατὰ τὸν Πολύδωρον

Δέος εἶχέ ποτε καὶ τὴν Τροίαν πεσεῖν καὶ Πρίαμος τὴν ἅλωσιν ἐμαντεύετο· καί, τὴν συμφορὰν ἐπιγνούς, προνοεῖται τοῦ γένους, προμηθεῖται τῆς πόλεως, σωτηρίαν παιδὸς καὶ χρυσοῦ φυλακὴν καὶ φιλίαν Θρᾳκὸς πρὸς τὴν τύχην ὥσπερ ἀντισοφίζεται. Ὁρᾷ τὸν τῶν παίδων χορὸν καὶ τῶν μὲν τὴν ἀκμὴν τοῖς Ἕλλησιν ἀνθιστᾷ καὶ πρὸς τὴν παροῦσαν τύχην μερίζεται. Πολύδωρον δὲ τῆς ἡλικίας ἀπόμαχον ἀποσπᾷ μὲν τοῦ πολέμου, ἐγχειρίζει δὲ Πολυμήστορι καὶ πρὸς τὴν ἐπιοῦσαν τύχην παῖδα καὶ χρυσὸν ταμιεύεται, ἵν᾽ ἐσύστερον καὶ Ἴλιος ἔχῃ τὸν ἀνορθώσοντα καὶ τὸ λοιπὸν τοῦ γένους τὸν ζωπυρήσοντα. Δέχεται τὸν παῖδα ὁ Θρᾷξ, ὑποδέχεται τὸν χρυσὸν καί, τὸ τῆς μάχης ἀστάθμητον ὑφορώμενος, ἐπέχει τέως τῆς γνώμης τὸ βάρβαρον, ὑποκρύπτεται τὸ φιλόχρυσον, σχηματίζεται τὸ φιλόφιλον· τοιοῦτον γάρ τι χρῆμα ὁ βάρβαρος καί, τὴν δειλίαν οἰκονομῶν, ἔνθα πεφόβηται καί, τὸν φίλον πλαττόμενος, ἔνθα τὸ φανερῶς λυπεῖν οὐκ ἐθάρρησεν.

man. Thus Narcissus lives on after his death and no less than before blooms again in his beauty.

10

The Story of Polydorus

There was once a fear that Troy would fall, and Priam suspected that it would be captured. When he realized that disaster was imminent, he showed concern for his people and regard for his city, using the salvation of his son, the protection of his gold, and the friendship of a Thracian as a sort of counter-device against his ill fortune. He reviewed the assemblage of his sons, and he set the strongest of them against the Greeks, deploying them against his present trouble. But he kept Polydorus away from the war, since he was too young to fight, and turned him over to Polymestor, thus putting his son and his gold in trust against the impending disaster, so that in later times there would be someone to restore Ilium and revive the remnant of his people. The Thracian received the boy, welcomed the gold, and with a wary eye on the uncertainty of the war's outcome, for the time being held his barbarian mind in check, concealing his greed and posing as a true friend. For such a creature is the barbarian, managing his cowardice when he is afraid and pretending to be a friend when he does not dare to cause grief openly.

2   Ὡς γοῦν ἡ τύχη μετὰ καὶ τῶν Ἑλλήνων τῷ Πριάμῳ
ἐπέθετο, καὶ ὁ Πολυμήστωρ αὐτῷ ξυνεπιτίθεται· καὶ
κτείνει μὲν τὸν Πολύδωρον καὶ τὸ σῶμα νεκρὸν ἐπαφῆκε
πελάγεσι, προσαφαιρεῖται δὲ τὸν χρυσόν. Καὶ παρανομεῖ
τὴν φιλίαν τριπλάσια, μήτε περιόντα τὸν παῖδα οἰκτείρας
καὶ μετὰ τελευτὴν οὐ φεισάμενος καὶ χρυσοῦ μελετήσας
ἀφαίρεσιν, οὗ τὴν φυλακὴν ἐπιστεύετο.

3   Ἀλλ' ὅθεν ἠδίκει τὸν Φίλιον, ἐκεῖθεν αὖθις τὴν δίκην
ἀπέτισε. Χρυσὸς ἐκεῖνον ἀδικεῖν ἐδελέασε, χρυσὸς καὶ
πάλιν εἰς τὸ παθεῖν ὑπηγάγετο. Ἔγνω τὸν τοῦ Θρᾳκὸς
δόλον ἡ μήτηρ, ἐπέγνω τὸν τοῦ παιδὸς φόνον καὶ
μηχανᾶται τὴν ἄμυναν. Χρυσὸν καὶ πάλιν προβάλλεται καὶ
πιστεύει δῆθεν, ᾧ πάλαι καὶ χρυσὸν καὶ παῖδα ἐπίστευσε.
Πείθεται τούτοις ὁ Θρᾷξ, οὐχ ὑποπτεύει τὴν ἐπιβουλήν,
θαρρεῖ τὴν Ἑκάβην, εἴσεισι τὴν σκηνὴν καὶ θήραμα γίνεται
γυναικῶν καὶ χρημάτων ἐλπίσιν ἁλώσιμος. Οἷς μὲν γὰρ
ἀδίκοις ὀφθαλμοῖς εἶδε χρυσόν, τούτοις δικαίως τοὺς
ὀφθαλμοὺς αὐτὸς ἐξορύττεται· οἷς δὲ τοῦ παιδὸς ἀπαν-
θρώπως Ἑκάβην ἐστέρησε, τούτοις εἰκότως καὶ παίδων
πρὸς Ἑκάβης αὐτὸς ἀπεστέρητο.

Then, when fortune, along with the Greeks, attacked 2
Priam, Polymestor also made his move against him, killing
Polydorus and throwing his dead body into the sea, and seizing the gold as well. And so he transgressed his friendship
three times over: he took no pity on Polydorus while he was
still alive, did not spare his body after death, and schemed to
take money that had been entrusted to his protection.

But just as he offended the god of friendship, by the same 3
means he also paid his due: gold enticed him to commit a
crime, and gold in turn led him to suffer. The boy's mother
became aware of the Thracian's deceit, learned of her son's
murder, and plotted revenge. She offered gold once again, as
though she were entrusting it to the man to whom she had
previously entrusted both gold and her son. The Thracian
believed her words, not suspecting the scheme and having
no fear of Hecuba, and he entered her tent, where he became the prey of women and an easy catch because of his
hope for wealth. For just as he looked upon the gold with
unjust eyes, so also he himself justly had his eyes dug out,
and just as he inhumanely deprived Hecuba of her child,
so also he himself was fittingly deprived of his children by
Hecuba.

II

Τὸ κατὰ τὸν Δαίδαλον

Δαίδαλον σοφία μὲν καὶ τέχνη περιεσώσατο, Μίνως δὲ καὶ τοῦ παθεῖν ἐλπὶς τῆς πατρίδος ἀπήλασεν, οἷς ἔρωτος ἄθεσμον ἐσοφίσατο ξύμπνοιαν καί, σοφὸς ὢν ἐρωτικὴν ἀποσβέσαι πυράν, βασιλέως θυμὸν ὑπανάψας ἠγνόησεν. Ἐπεὶ γὰρ Πασιφάη μὲν ἤρα παράνομα, Δαίδαλος δὲ τὸν ἐπὶ ταύρῳ Πασιφάης οἶστρον ἐπλήρωσε, πληροῦται Μίνως θυμοῦ καὶ τῆς ἀνοίας μυσάττεται Δαίδαλον. Ὑφορᾶται τὴν δίκην ἐπὶ τούτοις ὁ Δαίδαλος καὶ τρόπον φυγῆς ἐπινοεῖται παράδοξον· ὅλας ἀετῶν ἐπεσώρευσε πτέρυγας καί, κηρῷ τὰ πτίλα συνδήσας, ταῖς χερσὶν ἐναρμόζεται. Οὕτω καὶ τὸν παῖδα πτερωσάμενος Ἴκαρον, τῆς Κρήτης ἀφίπταται.

2   Ἀλλὰ καί, τῷ παιδὶ τὸν Μίνω ξυναποδράς, οὐχὶ καὶ τὴν δίκην ἀπέδρασεν, ἀλλ᾽ οἷς τὸν ἀπὸ γῆς ὑπερίπταται πόλεμον, ἄλλον τρόπον οὐρανόθεν αὖθις ἐβάλλετο. Καὶ Μίνως μὲν οὐκ εἶχεν ὅπως ἀμύναιτο Δαίδαλον, Ἥλιος δὲ τοῖς πτεροῖς ἐπεβούλευε καί, ταῖς ἀκτῖσιν ὑπολυσάμενος τὸν κηρόν, κατὰ πελάγους ἠφίει τὸν Ἴκαρον. Καὶ δικαίως ἄρα Δαίδαλον εἰς παῖδα ἐζημίωσεν Ἥλιος, οἷς ταύρῳ τὴν Ἡλίου παῖδα Πασιφάην ἐζεύξατο, ἐντεῦθεν καὶ Δαίδαλος μὴ πάντη τέχνῃ θαρρεῖν ἐδιδάσκετο καὶ Δαιδάλου παῖς Ἴκαρος μὴ πάνυ τι πιστεύειν Ἡλίῳ κηρὸν ἐπαιδεύετο.

II

The Story of Daedalus

Daedalus's cleverness and artistic skill saved him from death, but Minos and his expectation of suffering drove him from his homeland because he had devised an illicit conspiracy of love, and although he knew how to extinguish the erotic flame, he had unknowingly kindled the anger of the king. For when Pasiphaë had conceived an unlawful love and Daedalus had fulfilled her mad desire for a bull, Minos was filled with rage and detested Daedalus for his foolishness. So Daedalus suspected that he would be punished for his actions and devised an unusual manner of escape. He collected entire wings of eagles and, having bound the feathers with wax, fit them together with his hands. Thus he flew away from Crete, after also attaching wings to his son, Icarus.

But he did not escape justice, even though he and his son 2 escaped Minos, because although he flew above the war that was waged against him on earth, he encountered another form of justice that came from the skies. Minos had no way to take vengeance on Daedalus, but the Sun conspired against his wings and, after melting the wax with its rays, hurled Icarus down into the sea. And justly did the Sun punish Daedalus through his child, because Daedalus had yoked Pasiphaë, the Sun's child, to a bull. And so Daedalus learned not to trust completely in his artistic skill, and Icarus, the son of Daedalus, was taught not to entrust wax to the Sun at all.

45

12

Τὸ κατὰ τὴν Πασιφάην

Ἔρως καὶ Πασιφάην εἰς ταῦρον οἰστρηλατεῖ καὶ τὸν πόθον ἦν ἀγαγεῖν εἰς πέρας ἀμήχανον· ἄνθρωπος ἦρα βοὸς καὶ γυναικὸς ἦν ταῦρος ἐρώμενος, ἔρως ἀπανταχόθεν ἀνόμοιος. Ἡ μὲν ἴσως που μαλακὴν ἠφίει φωνήν, ὁ δ᾽ οὐδὲν ἐπαΐων, ὡς ταῦρος, αἰνὸν ἐμυκήσατο. Λόγον ἀλογίᾳ ξυντρέχειν τὸ πάθος ἠνάγκαζε καὶ γυναικὸς ὄψιν βοείᾳ μορφῇ συγκεράννυσθαι καὶ ταύρῳ τὴν ἄνθρωπον ὑπο-ζεύγνυσθαι. Οὐκ εἶχε πείθειν οἷς θέλγουσιν ἄνθρωποι· ἂν ἐπαγωγόν τι προσεῖπεν, ὁ βοῦς οὐκ ἠσθάνετο· ἂν ἐρωτικὸν ἐμειδίασεν, οὐ φιλομειδὴς ὁ ταῦρος ἐδείκνυτο· ἂν δῶρα πρὸς Ἀφροδίτην προὔτεινεν, ἄδωρον τὴν Ἀφροδίτην ἡ φύσις τὸν ταῦρον ἐδίδαξεν. Ἔρως ἐντεῦθεν τῇ κόρῃ συνηγωνίζετο καὶ φύσις αὖθις ἐκεῖθεν ἀντέκρουε· παρεῖχεν Ἔρως, ἃ μὴ φύσις ἐβούλετο, καὶ φύσις ἐπεῖχεν, ἃ παρέχειν Ἔρως παρεβιάζετο· συνῆγεν Ἔρως, ἃ φύσις μακροῖς ὅροις διέστησε, καὶ ἡ φύσις οὐκ ἐδίδου τὰ μὴ πεφυκότα συνάπτεσθαι.

2 Ἔσαινε Πασιφάην τὸ κάλλος, ἀλλ᾽ ἐλύπει τὸ τοῦ ἔρωτος ἔκφυλον. Ὡς ἐπαφρόδιτον ὁρᾶν ἐγλίχετο καὶ ὡς θῆρα θυμικὸν ὑπεβλέπετο. Ηὔχετο καὶ βοῦς εἶναι δοκεῖν, ὡς ἂν τὸν ταῦρον ὑπέλθῃ τῷ σχήματι, ἀλλὰ θεοὶ μὲν οὐκ

12

The Story of Pasiphaë

Love also drove Pasiphaë mad for a bull, but it was impossible for her to consummate her desire. Though human, she loved a bull, and the bull became a woman's beloved. Their love was in all ways mismatched. She would perhaps at times speak softly, but he, understanding nothing because he was a bull, would bellow dreadfully. Her passion compelled reason to combine with irrationality, a female countenance to mingle with a bovine form, and a woman to be yoked with a bull. She could not persuade him with the charms that humans use: if she said something seductive, the bull did not perceive it; if she smiled longingly, the bull did not appear to enjoy her laughter; if she offered love gifts, nature taught the bull to resist them. And so Love contended with the girl, and nature struck back from the opposing side; Love supplied what nature rejected, and nature withstood what Love strove to supply; Love brought together what nature had banished to the far margins, and nature would not allow an unnatural union.

The bull's beauty was beguiling Pasiphaë, but the unnatu- 2 ral character of her love was causing her grief. She longed to gaze upon him because he was charming, but she cast her eyes warily upon him because he was a spirited beast. She prayed to take on the appearance of a cow, so that she might entrap the bull with her disguise, but the gods did

ἐπένευσαν, Δαίδαλος δὲ τοῦτο χαρίζεται καὶ γίνεται σοφώτερος Ἔρωτος, φιλανθρωπότερος φύσεως. Χαλκὸν εἰς βοῦν σχηματίζει καὶ μιμεῖται τοῦ ταύρου τὴν θήλειαν καί, τὴν βοῦν ἔνδον ὑπογλυψάμενος, ὑποβάλλει τὴν ἄνθρωπον. Ἐφέλκεται τὸν ταῦρον ἡ τέχνη, δελεάζει τοῦ χαλκοῦ τὸ πρὸς βοῦν ἐμφερὲς καί, μυκησάμενος ἔρωτα, τῇ Πασιφάῃ τὸν πόθον ἐπλήρωσε, καὶ τεραστίου γάμου τέρας ἀπογεννᾶται Μινώταυρος.

13

Τὸ κατὰ τὸν Ἴκαρον

Ἐνόσει Πασιφάη παράλογον ἔρωτα καὶ παστάδα παραλογωτέραν ἐπήξατο Δαίδαλος. Ἐπὶ τούτοις ὀργίζεται Μίνως καὶ σπεύδει τὸν Πασιφάης καὶ ταύρου νυμφοστόλον ἑλεῖν, ἀλλ᾽ ἦν ἄρα ἐκεῖνος καὶ πῦρ ἀφροδίσιον ἀποσβέσαι σοφὸς καὶ βασιλέως ἀναφθέντα θυμὸν ἀποδρᾶσαι σοφώτερος. Οὐ γὰρ οὐκ εὐπόρει μηχανῆς καὶ πάλιν ὁ Δαίδαλος, ἀλλὰ κἀνταῦθα τέχνη τὴν φύσιν ὑπερεβάλλετο· καί, ἃ φύσις οὐκ ἴσχυσε, Δαίδαλος ἐτεχνήσατο καί, τὴν φύσιν ἄνθρωπος ὤν, τὸν ὄρνιν ἐσχηματίσατο. Ἐπτέρωσε τῇ σοφίᾳ καὶ τὸν παῖδα Ἴκαρον, ἵν᾽ ὡς ἐκ μιᾶς μηχανῆς καὶ τὸ πατὴρ εἶναι μὴ ζημιωθῇ καὶ τὸ περιεῖναι κερδάνῃ·

not consent. Daedalus, however, granted this favor and became more clever than Love, more generous than nature. He shaped bronze into bovine form, imitated the female of the animal, and after hollowing out the cow on the inside, placed the woman within. His art attracted the bull, and the bronze imitation of a cow enticed it. Finally, the bull expressed his love with a bellow and then fulfilled Pasiphaë's desire. And a monster, the Minotaur, was born from this monstrous union.

13

The Story of Icarus

Pasiphaë suffered from a strange passion, and Daedalus built for her an even stranger bridal chamber. Minos grew angry at this and strove to capture the man who married Pasiphaë to the bull, but Daedalus was clever enough to extinguish the fire of love and was even more clever at escaping the inflamed anger of the king. For yet again Daedalus did not lack a device; rather, once more art overcame nature: what nature could not accomplish, Daedalus contrived by art, and though human by nature, he took on the appearance of a bird. By means of his ingenuity he also fit wings to his boy, Icarus, so that, through a single device, he might preserve his role as father and might gain his own survival.

φιλόστοργον γὰρ ὁ πατὴρ καὶ τὸ παράπαν ἀπολιπέσθαι τοῦ παιδὸς οὐκ ἀνέχεται.

2   Ἵπταντο γοῦν ἄμφω καὶ τὸν Μίνω ξυναπεδίδρασκον, ἀλλ' ὁ μὲν ἅτε σοφὸς καὶ τὴν μηχανὴν εἰδώς, ἐφ' ὅσον ἂν καὶ πτερύξαιτο, σύμμετρον τῷ σοφίσματι ποιεῖται τὴν πτῆσιν· ὁ δ' ὑπὲρ τὰ πτίλα καὶ τὸν κηρὸν καὶ τὴν τέχνην πτερύσσεται καὶ περιφρονεῖ μὲν τὸν Ἥλιον, πιστεύει δὲ ταῖς ἀκτῖσι τὸν κηρὸν καὶ τρυφᾶν ἐθέλει μᾶλλον ἢ πρὸς ἀσφάλειαν ἵπτασθαι. Τοιοῦτον γάρ τι χρῆμα νεότης· πρὸς ἡδονὰς ἀλόγιστα φέρεται καὶ τῆς χρείας ἐκφέρεται. Οὐ φέρει περιφρονούμενος Ἥλιος, ἐπιβάλλει τῷ κηρῷ τὰς ἀκτῖνας, ἀπελέγχει τὸν σοφιστήν, λύει τὸ σόφισμα καὶ ῥίπτει κατὰ πελάγους τὸν Ἴκαρον. Καὶ τοῦτο μιμεῖται Δαίδαλον Ἥλιος· ἐκ τῆς Ἡλίου παιδὸς Πασιφάης Μινώταυρον ἐκαινοτόμησε Δαίδαλος καὶ Ἥλιος ἐξ Ἰκάρου τοῦ Δαιδάλου παιδὸς Ἰκάριον πέλαγος ἀνθρώποις ἐγνώρισεν.

14

Τὸ κατὰ τὴν ἅλωσιν τῆς Τροίας

Ὁ τὴν ἅλωσιν τῆς Τροίας ἐπιζητῶν, ὅθεν γέγονεν, ἀνιστορείτω μοι τῆς Ἑλένης τὴν ἁρπαγήν· διὰ ταύτην γὰρ

For fathers are affectionate creatures and cannot bear at all to be separated from their sons.

So the two flew off and escaped Minos. But the father, 2 who in his wisdom understood how far his device could fly, made his flight according to the limits of his invention. Icarus, however, flew beyond the capacity of the feathers, the wax, and the artistry; he defied the Sun and entrusted the wax to its rays, wishing to indulge himself rather than fly safely. For such a creature is youth: it is driven irrationally toward pleasure and away from what it ought to do. The Sun did not tolerate this defiance. He attacked the wax with his rays; he repudiated the clever inventor and melted his invention; and then he cast Icarus down into the sea. And in this way the Sun imitated Daedalus, because Daedalus created a novel creature, the Minotaur, through Pasiphaë, the daughter of the Sun, and the Sun made the Icarian Sea known to humans through Icarus, the son of Daedalus.

14

The Story of the Fall of Troy

He who seeks to know how the fall of Troy came about, should, in my opinion, investigate the abduction of Helen. For on her account weapons were prepared, troops were

ὅπλων παρασκευαί, στρατευμάτων συναγωγαί, νηῶν
σύμπηξις, ἀχανοῦς πελάγους διαπεραίωσις, ἐν ἀλλοδαπῇ
στρατοπέδευσις, ἐν βαρβαρικῇ κατασκήνωσις, τάφρων
ὀρυγαί, σκολόπων παρορυγαί, ἐχθρῶν προσβολαί, ἑκατέ-
ρων μερῶν ἐξορμαί, ἀγωνιζομένων σφαγαί, αἱμάτων πη-
γαί, δακρύων ῥοαί, λειψάνων ταφαί, καταδρομαὶ πόλεων,
χρημάτων ἁρπαγαί, δεσμωτῶν οἰμωγαί.

2   Ὡς δὲ τὸ φρούριον ἀπόρθητον ἦν, ἐπλάσαντο τὴν
διάζευξιν καὶ Χερρόνησος εἶχε τοὺς Ἕλληνας. Τεχνασά-
μενοι δ᾽ ἵππον, ὑπογαστρίους ὁπλοφόρους ἄνδρας καὶ
χαλκάσπιδας φέροντα, ἔδοξαν τοῦτον καταλιπεῖν, ὡς τῆς
φάτνης ἀποσκιρτήσαντα. Ἄρτι δέ, τοῦ ἡλίου ὑπὲρ γῆν
ἀνακύψαντος, τὸν ἵππον ἰδόντες οἱ Τρῶες ὡς μὲν εὐμεγέθη,
ὡς δὲ περικαλλῆ τε καὶ πίονα, φριμασσόμενον χρεμετίζοντα,
τὼ πόδε πρὸς ὕψος ἐπαίροντα καὶ περικυρτοῦντα πάλιν
ὥσπερ ἐξ ἁρμογῆς, γαῦρον καὶ ἀτιθάσσευτον τῶν τῆς
πόλεως περιβόλων ἔνδον εἰσήγαγον. Περὶ δὲ νύκτα μέσην
οἱ ἐνεδρεύοντες, ἐξορμήσαντες, κατέσχον τὴν πόλιν καὶ
τοὺς μὲν ἀνεῖλον, τοῖς δὲ δεσμοὺς περιέθεντο καὶ πυρι-
καύστους τὰς οἰκίας εἰργάσαντο.

marshaled, ships were assembled, and the vast sea was traversed. There was a campaign in a foreign land, an encamp-
ment on barbarian soil; trenches were dug, and palisades
planted. Then followed attacks by the enemy, raids from
both sides, slaughters of combatants, fountains of blood,
and rivers of tears. Finally, there were burials of the dead,
sackings of cities, lootings of property, and lamentations of
prisoners.

And when the citadel proved unassailable, the Greeks 2
feigned their departure and hid themselves in the Chersonese. They fashioned a horse, which carried in its belly
men with weapons and bronze shields, and they seemed to
have left it behind, as though it had run away from its man-
ger. Then, when the sun had risen above the earth, the Trojans saw the horse: how great was its stature, how beautiful
and sleek. They saw it *snort and whinny,* lift its two front legs
high in the air and then in turn bend them as though they
were jointed. They led it, skittish and untamable, inside the
walls of the city. Around midnight, those hiding in ambush
leaped out and took control of the city. They killed some
people, put others into chains, and set the houses on fire.

15

Τὸ κατὰ τὸν Ὀδυσσέα

Εἶχεν Ἑλένην ἡ Τροία καὶ ἡ Ἑλλὰς ἐκεκίνητο καὶ Ὀδυσσεύς, εἰς ξυμμαχίαν καλούμενος, μανίαν ἐπλάττετο· καί ποτε δεῆσαν οὕτως ἱππάσασθαι, βοῦν ἵππῳ συμπνεῖν ἐβιάζετο καὶ πρὸς ἕνα ξυνῆγε ζυγόν, ἃ μήτε φύσις συνῆψε καὶ τέχνη διέστησε. Καὶ δειλὸς εἶναι λαθεῖν πειρώμενος, εἰς μανίαν ἐξέπιπτεν, ἀκουσίῳ δῆθεν κακῷ κακίαν ἐπικρύπτων αὐθαίρετον. Ὁρᾷ τὸ πλάσμα ὁ Παλαμήδης, εἰς νοῦν βάλλεται τὸ μηχάνημα καί, γνοὺς ὅ τι καὶ βούλεται τὰ τοῦ δράματος, ἀντιμηχανᾶται σοφώτερον· ἁρπάζει τὸν παῖδα Τηλέμαχον, εἰς μέσον ἄγει τῆς ἱππηλασίας καὶ δοκιμάζει τὸν πατέρα ἐλαύνοντα, ὡς· εἰ τῷ παιδὶ πάντως ἐπαφήσει τὸ ἅρμα, οὐκ ἔστιν Ὀδυσσεὺς ἐκεῖνος καὶ μέμηνεν· εἰ δὲ γνωρίσει τὴν φύσιν καὶ φείσεται τοῦ παιδός, ἐστὶν ἄρα Ὀδυσσεὺς ἐκεῖνος ὁ δόλιος καὶ τὸν εἰς Τροίαν ἀπόπλουν ὀκνεῖ καὶ παραπαίειν ἐσχηματίσατο. Καὶ δή, ξύμμαχον ἐπαγόμενος τὸ φιλότεκνον, ἀναρριπίζει τὸ τῆς φύσεως πῦρ, ὑπεκκάει τὰ σπλάγχνα, πολιορκεῖ τὴν ψυχὴν καὶ τὸν νοῦν αὐτόμολον ὡς ἀπὸ τείχους ἐξάγει τοῦ πλάσματος.

2   Οὕτω Παλαμήδης Ὀδυσσέα κατεστρατήγησεν, οὕτω, σοφῶς ἀργυρογνωμονήσας τὸν νοῦν, ἐθηράσατο καί,

15

The Story of Odysseus

Troy was holding Helen, Greece was mobilizing, and Odysseus, summoned to join the alliance, was feigning madness. And once, when he had to drive a chariot in this state, he forced an ox to team together with a horse, two animals which nature does not unite and which art keeps separate, and he put them under a single yoke. In attempting to hide his cowardice, he fell into madness, and he concealed his voluntary wickedness with an ostensibly involuntary evil. Palamedes detected the ruse, contemplated the contrivance, and having recognized what the performance was about, contrived something even more clever in response. He seized Odysseus's son, Telemachus, brought him into the path of the chariot, and tested the father as he was driving in the following way: if he drove the chariot without hesitation over the boy, then he was not Odysseus but had gone mad; if, however, he acknowledged his natural ties and spared the boy, then he was the deceitful Odysseus, who was avoiding the voyage to Troy and pretending to have lost his mind. And then, utilizing a father's love for his child as an ally, Palamedes reignited the fire of nature, inflamed Odysseus's heart, besieged his soul, and drew his treacherous mind out of its disguise as if from behind a wall.

Thus did Palamedes outwit Odysseus; thus, after cleverly 2 assessing the state of his mind, he set out to trap him, and

καθαρὸν εἶναι μαθὼν ὡς ὑπὸ γνώμονι, τῷ καινῷ τούτῳ πυρὶ τοῖς λοιποῖς ἀρίστοις τῆς Ἑλλάδος ἐγκρίνει. Οὐ γὰρ ἤνεγκε τὸ θέαμα Ὀδυσσεύς, ἀλλ᾽ ᾤκτειρε τὸν παῖδα καὶ τὸν ἔλεγχον οὐ διέδρασε, τὸ πατὴρ εἶναι τῶν ἐπὶ Τροίας πόνων ἀνταλλαξάμενος. Καὶ ξυνεμάχει τοῖς Ἕλλησι τοῦ λοιποῦ καὶ ψυχῇ πολυμηχάνῳ τοῖς Τρωσὶν ἐπεβούλευε καὶ κατὰ Παλαμήδους ἤσκει τὸ δόλιον.

16

Τὸ κατὰ τὴν Μύρραν

Μύρραν τὴν Θείαντος φύσις μὲν ἐχαρίτωσεν εἰς μορφήν, Ἔρως δὲ παρανομεῖν εἰς τὴν φύσιν ἠνάγκασεν. Εἶδεν ἐρωτικοῖς ὀφθαλμοῖς τὸν πατέρα καὶ τὸ κάλλος περιειργάσατο. Καὶ τὸ μὲν δοκεῖν ὡς πατέρα κατησπάζετο, τὸ δ᾽ ἀληθὲς ὡς ἐρώμενον περιεπτύσσετο. Οὕτως ἐπὶ ψυχῆς ἐθαλαμηπόλει τὸν Ἔρωτα· τὸ γὰρ εἰς φῶς ἀγαγεῖν οὐ μικρὸν ἠπείλει τὸν κίνδυνον.

2   Ὡς δ᾽ οὐκέτι τὸ τῆς Ἀφροδίτης ἔστεγε πῦρ, τολμᾷ τι καὶ πρὸς ἐπιβουλὴν τῷ πατρὶ καί, μεθύουσα Ἔρωτι, ξυνεῖδε μέθην ἄλλην ἐπίκουρον Ἔρωτος καί, Διονυσιακοῦ πυρὸς ὅλους ἀναψαμένη κρατῆρας, τὴν τοῦ Θείαντος ψυχὴν πυρπολεῖν μελετᾷ. Ὑπεμπίπλαται μέθης, ἐντεῦθεν

like an inspector judging his mind to be pure, through a unique test of fire he reckoned him among the other brave men of Greece. For Odysseus could not endure what he saw, but he took pity on his son and did not evade detection, receiving fatherhood in return for his labors in Troy. Thereafter he fought alongside the Greeks, plotted against the Trojans with his crafty soul, and exercised his treachery against Palamedes.

16

The Story of Myrrha

Nature bestowed beauty on Myrrha, daughter of Theias, but Love compelled her to transgress against nature. She gazed upon her father with desiring eyes and lavished too much attention on his handsome appearance, and while she pretended to hug him as a father, in reality she embraced him as a lover. Thus she played the maid to Love in the bedchamber of her soul, for bringing her feelings to light held out the prospect of no small danger.

But when she could no longer conceal the fire of Aphrodite, she dared to scheme against her father. Drunk with Love, she considered drunkenness to be another ally of Love, and having lit up whole mixing bowls with the fire of Dionysus, she set her mind to inflaming Theias's soul. Filled

RHETORICAL EXERCISES OF NIKEPHOROS BASILAKES

ὁ πατὴρ ἐραστὴς γίνεται καὶ ὡς ἐρωμένην τὴν παῖδα
προσίεται, οὐκ ἐλογίσατο τὴν φύσιν, οὐκ ἐσκέψατο τὸ
κακόν. Ἔρως γὰρ καὶ οἶνος αὐτῷ τὸν νοῦν ὑπεκύμαινον,
ἀνθρωπίνων ψυχῶν ἄμφω λῃσταί· ὁ μὲν ἡδὺς ὡς φίλος
ἐπιρρυείς, λάθρα τὴν κεφαλὴν ὡς προδότης ὑπέσειεν· ὁ δὲ
τὸν ὡς ἐν ἀκροπόλει τῇ κεφαλῇ φύλακα νοῦν βαθὺν ὕπνον
λήθης ἐκοίμιζε καί, τὰς τῆς ψυχῆς πύλας ἀναπεπταμένας
εὑρών, κατὰ σωφροσύνης ἔστησε τρόπαιον.

3   Ἀλλ' ἐπανῆκεν εἰς νοῦν αὖθις ἡ κόρη καί, τὴν ἀφροδίσιον
ἀποβαλοῦσα μέθην, συλλογίζεται τὸ μέλλον, ἀναλογίζεται
τοῦ πατρὸς τὸν θυμόν, προσδοκᾷ τὰ ἔσχατα πείσεσθαι καί,
πρὶν ἢ τῆς μέθης ἀνανῆψαι τὸν Θείαντα, θεοῖς ἐπεύχεται
μεταβαλέσθαι τὴν φύσιν. Καὶ θεοί, τὴν κόρην οἰκτείραντες,
εἰς φυτὸν μεταβάλλουσιν. Ἀλλ' οὐκ εἰς κενὸν ὁ Ἔρως
ἐξέπεσε, κἂν εἰς φυτὸν ἡ κόρη μετέπεσεν. Ὥρας γὰρ
ὠδίνων ἡκούσης, ἀναρρήγνυται μὲν ὁ φλοιός, ἐξαστράπτει
δέ τι χρῆμα κάλλους ἀμήχανον Ἄδωνις καὶ τὰ τῆς Ἀφροδίτης ἐντεῦθεν ἄρχεται παιδικά.

with drunkenness, her father became her lover and accepted his own daughter as his beloved. He did not consider natural ties, nor did he give thought to depravity. For Love and wine, both robbers of human souls, were overwhelming his mind. The latter, flowing sweetly like a friend, surreptitiously like a traitor began to make his head spin, while the former lulled his mind, which stands guard over the head as if on a citadel, into a deep, forgetful sleep and, finding the gates of the soul wide open, declared victory over self-control.

But the girl returned to her senses again, having cast off the aphrodisiac of drunkenness; she reflected on the future, considered her father's anger, foresaw that she would suffer the worst punishment, and, before Theias awoke from his drunken stupor, prayed to the gods to transform her nature. The gods took pity on the girl and transformed her into a myrrh tree. But Love did not go away empty-handed, even if the girl had been changed into a tree. For when the time for giving birth arrived, her bark split open and out flashed Adonis, an impossibly beautiful creature who soon became the darling of Aphrodite.

MAXIMS

I

"Εὐεργετῶν νόμιζε μιμεῖσθαι Θεόν"

Καὶ ἐξ ἄλλων μὲν πολλῶν ὁ πολὺς τὰ θεῖα καὶ μέγας Γρηγόριος ἐγνωρίζετο. Ἡ δὲ σοφία ἦν αὐτῷ τὸ ἐπίσημον, οὐ μόνον ἡ κάτω καὶ συρομένη καὶ στροφαῖς λέξεων καὶ λόγοις ἀποκρότοις κατακηλοῦσα τὰς ἀκοάς, ἀλλ᾽ ὅση καὶ πρὸς οὐρανὸν ἀνάγει τὴν ἀνθρωπίνην ψυχὴν καὶ τὸν κοσμοποιὸν ἐξαίρει Θεόν, καὶ τὸν ἄρρητον πλοῦτον τῆς αὐτοῦ ἀγαθότητος ἐκφαντορικῶς ἡμῖν παριστᾷ καὶ τὸ εὐσταλὲς καὶ κοῦφον καὶ εὔζωνον τῷ δεσπότῃ χαρίζεται νῷ, ὡς κατὰ τῆς σαρκὸς συμμαχοῦσα τῷ πνεύματι.

2   Ὅσα μὲν οὖν οὗτος περί τε φυσιολογίαν πνευματικὴν περί τε δογματολογίαν οὐράνιον καὶ περὶ τὰ χωριστὰ τῆς ὕλης ἐπόνησε καὶ τὸ μέγα τῆς Τριάδος μυστήριον καὶ τὸ τῆς ἐν ἀνθρώποις τοῦ Σωτῆρος ἀπόρρητον τὸ ἀπ᾽ αἰώνων καὶ γενεῶν κατὰ τὸν θεῖον κεκρυμμένον ἀπόστολον, τίς ἂν παραστῆσαι λόγος ἐφίκοιτο; Ἀλλά γε πρὸς τὸ προκείμενον ἡμεῖς τὸν λόγον ἰθύνωμεν καὶ θεωρητέον, τί περὶ τῆς εὐποιΐας ἡ τοῦ Πνεύματος σάλπιγξ ἐσάλπισεν ἡ πάντα περιηχοῦσα τὰ πέρατα· μέγα γάρ τι κέρδος ἐντεῦθεν ἐμπορευσόμεθα.

I

"In doing good, consider that you are imitating God"

Even among many others, Gregory was recognized as mighty and great in divine matters. He was distinguished for his wisdom, not only the worldly wisdom that is earthbound and charms the ears with turns of phrase and sonorous words, but also the sort that draws the human soul up toward heaven, exalts God as the creator of the world, manifestly furnishes us with the indescribable riches of his goodness, and gives the mind, our master, the gift of being well-equipped, lightly-armed, and well-girt, by allying with the spirit against the flesh.

So, as for how much this man labored in the investigation 2 of spiritual nature, the exposition of heavenly doctrine, nonmaterial things, *the* great *mystery* of the Trinity, and the ineffability of the Savior's incarnation among humans, which, as the divine apostle Paul says, *was hidden from eras and generations,* what speech would be able to express it? But let us direct our speech toward the subject set before us and examine what the trumpet of the Spirit, whose sound reaches to all the ends of the earth, trumpeted about doing good; for thereby we will gain a great profit.

3 Ὁ τῶν καταδεεστέρων, φησίν, ἐπιστρεφόμενος καὶ εὖ ποιῶν κατὰ διηνέκειαν μιμεῖται τὸν ἁπάντων δεσπόζοντα. Καὶ ταῦτα μὲν τῆς θεηγόρου γλώττης τὰ ῥήματα, ὅτι δὲ καὶ πρὸς ἀκρίβειαν ἰαμβοκρότοις λόγοις ταῦτα εἴρηκεν, ἡ τῶν λόγων ἀνάπτυξίς τε καὶ μεταχείρισις τρανώσει σαφέστατα.

4 Πάντα γὰρ ὁ Δημιουργὸς πρὸς εὐεργεσίαν τῶν ἀνθρώπων παρήγαγεν· ἥλιον πηγὴν τοῦ τῇδε φωτός, ἠρέμα πως τῷ ἀέρι κεραννύμενον καὶ προσηνῶς τοῖς ὄμμασι προσεμπίπτοντα, εἴτε ταῖς αὐγαῖς τοῦ πυρὸς καταπυρσεύοντα τὸ περίγειον· γῆν χλοηφόρον μυρίοις περιπυκαζομένην τοῖς ἄνθεσι καὶ καρποφόροις δένδροις βλαστάνουσαν· μυρία ζῷα ἐκ θαλάσσης, ἐξ ἀέρος, ἐκ γῆς· πηγὰς ναούσας γλυκερὰ καὶ διειδέστατα νάματα.

5 Ὁ γοῦν πρὸς τοσαύτας καὶ τηλικαύτας εὐεργεσίας τῆς πηγαίας χρηστότητος ἀφορῶν, καὶ ἑαυτὸν πάντα προϊέμενος καὶ ἐν ὑψηλῷ καὶ μεγάλῳ κηρύγματι προκαλούμενος, "Δεῦτε πάντες, ἐμὸν ἄρτον φάγετε καὶ πίετε οἶνον, ὃν ὑμῖν κεκέρακα. Ἀπολαύσατε τῶν ἐμῶν, ἢ μᾶλλον εἰπεῖν, τοῦ Θεοῦ δωρεῶν, ἀργύρου, χρυσοῦ, μαργάρων, διαυγῶν λίθων πολυτελῶν, περιβλημάτων λαμπρῶν, οὐδὲν ἐμοί," λέγων, "ἥδιστον, εἰ μὴ καὶ πρὸς κοινὴν ἀπόλαυσιν καὶ μετάληψιν πρόκεινται· οὐ γὰρ τῆς τῶν ἑτέρων ζωῆς τὴν οἰκείαν αὐτὸς προτίθεμαι."

6 Ἄγαλμα τοῦ Θεοῦ περικαλλὲς ἑαυτὸν περὶ τὸν χθόνιον τοῦτον χῶρον εἰργάσατο καί, παρ' αὐτοῦ παρηγμένος τῆς μὲν κατ' αὐτὸν οὐσίας διΐσταται, ἀπομιμεῖται δ' ὡς ἐφικτὸν

He who pays attention to the needy, he says, and does 3 good without ceasing imitates the Master of all. And these are the words of the divinely inspired tongue, but that he has expressed them accurately and poetically, my interpretation and treatment of his words will make very clear.

For the Creator introduced everything as a benefaction 4 to humans: the sun as the source of our light here, somehow gently mixing with the air and pleasantly falling on our eyes, or illuminating the earth with the rays of its fire; the land, bearing green leaves, thickly covered with countless flowers, and sprouting fruit-bearing trees; countless animals from the sea, the air, and the land; sweetly flowing springs and crystal clear streams.

And so the one who looks toward so many and such great 5 benefactions that come from the wellspring of goodness, abandoning himself entirely and summoning in a lofty and great pronouncement, says: "Come, all of you, and eat my bread and drink my wine, which I have mixed for you. Enjoy my (or, rather I should say, God's) gifts: silver, gold, pearls, radiant precious stones, shining robes. Nothing brings me any pleasure at all, unless they are set out for everyone to enjoy and share. For I do not put my own life before the lives of others."

He has made himself into a very beautiful image of God 6 in this earthly place, and, although as a creation of God he differs from God's essence, he emulates God to the best of

κατά γε τὸ ἐπιστρεπτικὸν καὶ προνοητικὸν καὶ
φιλάνθρωπον, ἅτε πᾶσι τὰ πρὸς χρείαν φιλοτιμούμενος,
δοτὴρ ἀγαθῶν καὶ αὐτὸς μετὰ Θεὸν καὶ ὢν καὶ θρυλούμενος
πανταχοῦ.

7 Ὁ δὲ συνέχων καὶ κατορύττων τὰ κάτω μένοντα καὶ
ἄνθεσιν ἴσα ῥέοντα καὶ μὴ δεδυνημένα πρὸς ἑτέραν λῆξιν
ἡμῖν, ἐντεῦθεν χωροῦσιν, ἐφέπεσθαι, τὸ κοινὸν ἀπαναι-
νόμενος ἀγαθὸν καὶ τὸ φύσει κοινωνικόν, μὴ τῆς τῶν
ὁμοφυῶν ἀπορίας ἐπιστρεφόμενος, μὴ τῆς ταλαιπωρίας
τῶν ὁμογενῶν προμηθούμενος, μόνης δὲ τῆς σφετέρας
ἐξεχόμενος ἀπολαύσεως, ἐκτρέχων τοῦ, πρὸς ὃν ἀφορᾶν
ἐπετράπημεν, ὡς εἰς προχάραγμά τι καὶ προκέντημα,
ἀποδιΐσταται τῆς ὑπερβαλούσης τοῦ Θεοῦ φιλανθρωπίας
καὶ ἀγαθότητος· ἐγγίζει γὰρ ὁ Θεὸς τοῖς ἐγγίζουσι καὶ
τῶν διϊσταμένων ἀφέστηκεν.

8 Ὅρα μοι τὸν φυτουργὸν τὸ τῆς φύσεως ἔργον ἀπο-
μιμούμενον· ἐκείνη, διὰ φλεβῶν ὡς διά τινων σωλήνων
πρὸς τὰ τοῦ σώματος μόρια τὸ αἷμα διαπορθμεύουσα,
τρέφει, ζωογονεῖ, συνιστᾷ· οὗτος, διά τινων συχνῶν ὀχε-
τῶν τὸ ὕδωρ πρὸς τὰς ἀμάρας ὀχετηγῶν, ποτίζει καὶ αὔξει
καὶ τὰ βλαστήματα γόνιμα δείκνυσιν. Ὡς οὖν οὗτος τὴν
ἐπιτροπεύουσαν φύσιν ἀπομιμεῖται, τῆς τῶν φυτῶν ἀρ-
δείας ἐπιμελόμενος, τῆς τῶν δένδρων προνοίας κηδόμενος,
οὕτω καὶ οὗτος, τὸ ἐπιστρεπτικὸν καὶ προνοητικὸν τοῦ
Θεοῦ παραζηλῶν καὶ φιλάνθρωπον, μιμεῖται τὸν πάσης
ὑπεριδρυμένον ὀντότητος.

9 Ἀβραὰμ καὶ Ἰωσὴφ καὶ οἱ φαιδροὶ τῆς ἐκκλησίας
φωστῆρες ἱκανοὶ τῷ λόγῳ πρὸς ἔνδειξιν, τοσοῦτον

his ability in his attentive, providential, and benevolent love of humanity, inasmuch as he lavished upon everyone whatever they needed, both being and having the reputation everywhere as being a giver of good things, after God.

But he who holds fast to and buries the things which re- 7 main here below, which pass away like flowers, and which cannot follow us to our other state when we pass away from here, rejecting the common good and our natural desire to share, paying no attention to the distress of his kinsmen, taking no thought for the misery of his fellow men, but clinging only to his own enjoyment and running away from Christ to whom we were instructed to look as a guide and model—this man is at odds with the extraordinary benevolence and goodness of God. For God draws near to those who draw near to him, and he withdraws from those who distance themselves from him.

Look, if you will, at the gardener imitating the work of 8 nature: nature, by transporting blood to the parts of the body through veins as if through pipes, nurtures, propagates, and supports life; the planter, by conducting the water to the trenches through continuous conduits, irrigates, increases, and renders the plants fruitful. And so, just as this man imitates our guardian nature by managing the irrigation of the plants and showing forethought for the trees, so also the benevolent man, by emulating God's attentive, providential, and benevolent love of humanity, imitates the one who transcends all existence.

Abraham and Joseph and the bright stars of the Church 9 are sufficient to demonstrate the saying, having been so

φιλοξενίας καὶ πτωχοτροφίας φροντίσαντες, ὡς οὐδενὸς
ἑτέρου τῶν ἀγαθῶν.

10 Ἀλλὰ καὶ σοφώτατος Σολομὼν καὶ Δαυίδ, ὁ προφήτης
ἅμα καὶ βασιλεύς, μακαριστὸν ἡγοῦνται καὶ ἔργον Θεοῦ
ἐργαζόμενον τὸν εὖ ποιεῖν προελόμενον καὶ τὸν ἱλαρὸν
δότην καὶ μὴ ἀνώμαλον βλέποντα.

11 Διὰ ταῦτα καὶ ὁ θεοφόρος οὗτος πατὴρ τὸ σοφὸν τοῦτο
καὶ συνέσεως πλῆρες ὑψηγόρησε λόγιον.

2

"Χάρις χάριν γάρ ἐστιν ἡ τίκτουσ' ἀεί"

Σοφοκλῆν ἐπαινέσαι προάγομαι, οἷς τοῦ μέτρου τὴν
χάριν ἐτήρησε καὶ γνωμολογεῖν οὐκ ἀπέλιπε. Μοιχείας
μὲν γὰρ καὶ γυναικῶν ἁρπαγὰς καὶ τὴν ἄλλην ἐκ τοῦ
μύθου φλυαρίαν ἀπέπτυσε, πρὸς μόνον δὲ τῆς ποιητικῆς
εἶδε τὸ χρησιμώτατον καί, γλῶτταν ἀσκῶν εἰς εὐσέβειαν,
οὐ κατεπαίρεται θεῶν, οὐκ ἐκτραχηλίζει τὴν νεότητα πρὸς
ἀσέλγειαν. Ἀλλά, τῶν ἄλλων μυθολογούντων, αὐτός, τὸ
τοῦ μύθου περιττὸν ἀποσκευασάμενος, διέξεισι μέν, εἰ
τύχοι, μοιχείαν Αἰγίσθου καὶ σφαγὴν Ἀγαμέμνονος, ἀλλ'
οὐκ ἀφῆκε τὸ κακὸν ἀτιμώρητον, ἀλλ' εὐθὺς ἐπὶ σκηνῆς
Ὀρέστης εἰσάγεται καὶ πίπτει μετὰ μοιχείαν Αἴγισθος, καὶ

concerned with hospitality and the care of the poor above all other good things.

But also the very wise Solomon and David, prophet and   10 king in one, both consider the man who has chosen to do good and who is revealed to be a consistent and *cheerful giver* as most blessed and as doing the work of God.

For these reasons this divinely inspired father Gregory   11 delivered this lofty saying, which is wise and full of intelligence.

2

"Kindness always gives birth to kindness"

I am prompted to praise Sophocles, because he preserved the charm of verse but did not neglect to deliver moral maxims. For he despised adultery and abductions of women and all the other nonsense from myth, and paid attention only to the most useful aspect of poetry, and, exercising his tongue in the cause of piety, he does not disparage the gods or pervert young men into licentiousness. Rather, while the others narrate myths, he alone, having removed what is superfluous in myth, does indeed narrate, if it so happens, the adultery of Aegisthus and the slaughter of Agamemnon, but he does not leave the evil unpunished; rather, Orestes is immediately brought on stage and Aegisthus perishes as a

ὁ θεατὴς ὁρᾷ τὸ ξίφος ἐπανατεινόμενον τοῖς μοιχοῖς καὶ τὸ κακουργεῖν οὐκ ἐθάρρησε.

2 Σωφρονίζει παρ' αὐτῷ καὶ μαινόμενος Αἴας τοὺς ὁμόφυλον ἐπὶ ψυχῆς μάχην ὠδίνοντας. Ἔχει τι παραμύθιον παρ' αὐτῷ καὶ δυστυχῶν ἄνθρωπος, κἂν ἴδῃ τὴν Ἠλέκτραν πενθοῦσαν, οὐ μόνος πενθεῖν ὑπολήψεται, οὐδ' ἔξω φύσεως νομιεῖται τὴν συμφοράν. Ὀρέστου δ' ἐπανήκοντος, κἀκείνη τὰ τοῦ πένθους οἰχήσεται καὶ θεατὴς δυστυχῶν οὐκ ἀτελεύτητον γνώσεται τὸ κακόν.

3 Οὕτως ἐγὼ τὴν Σοφοκλέους τραγῳδίαν καὶ δήμιον ἔννομον τίθεμαι καὶ τύχης ἀγνωμονούσης ὁρίζομαι παραμύθιον καί μοι δοκεῖ λέγειν ὡς ἀπὸ τῆς σκηνῆς, "Πενθεῖς; Ἔλπιζέ ποτε καὶ χαιρήσειν, ὅτι καὶ Ἠλέκτρα μετεβεβλήκει τὸ δάκρυον. Πλουτεῖς καὶ ἐπὶ τούτῳ μέγα φρονεῖς; Μὴ θάρρει—τὰ τῆς τύχης μένειν οὐκ οἶδε ῥεύματα, ἀλλ' οἴχεται θᾶττον καὶ μεταρρεῖ—καὶ σωφρονιζέτω σε μετὰ βασιλείαν ἐκπίπτων ἀλήτης Οἰδίπους. Ἀλλ' ἐπιμαίνῃ τῷ κάλλει καὶ συγχέεις γονὴν καὶ πρὸς τὸ τῆς μοιχείας καταφέρῃ κακόν; Ὅρα μοι τὸν Ὀρέστην μετὰ τοῦ ξίφους καὶ μητρὸς οὐ φεισάμενον."

4 Τοιαῦτα τὴν Ἀθηναίων πόλιν ὁ καλὸς οὗτος ποιητὴς ἐσωφρόνιζεν· ἡλίκον μὲν τὸ πάθος ἐπὶ σκηνῆς ἐχορήγησεν! Ὅσον δὲ τὸ ἦθος μετὰ γνωμολογίας τοῖς δράμασιν ἐγκατέμιξε! Καὶ τὸ τῆς ἐπωνυμίας σοφὸν ἔργοις αὐτοῖς ἐβεβαίωσε, τοῦτο τοῖς περὶ τραγῳδίας γενόμενος, ὃ τοῖς περὶ ποίησιν Ὅμηρος. Ἀλλ' ὅσῳ τοὺς ὁμοτέχνους τῷ περιόντι τῆς σοφίας αὐτὸς ἀπεκρύψατο, τοσούτῳ καὶ τῶν

consequence of adultery, and the spectator sees the sword being brandished against the adulterers and dares not do wrong.

Even Ajax, though being driven mad in Sophocles's play, brings to their senses those who are in anguish with the same sort of battle in their souls. Even a man afflicted with misfortune has some consolation in Sophocles's plays: if he sees Electra grieving, he will assume that he is not the only one to grieve, nor will he believe his misfortune is unnatural; but when Orestes returns, Electra's grief will depart, and our unfortunate spectator will realize that his suffering is not without end. 2

Thus I consider Sophoclean tragedy a legitimate public executioner, and I define it as a consolation for unfair fortune, and I think he is saying, as if from the stage, "Are you grieving? Have hope that you will someday rejoice as well, because Electra too has transformed her tears. Are you rich, and do you pride yourself on that? Do not be so confident— the streams of fortune do not know how to stand still; they move quickly and ebb and flow—and let the wanderer Oedipus, who went from kingship to exile, bring you to your senses. But do you go mad for beauty, confound paternity, and sink to the evil of adultery? Look, if you will, at Orestes with his sword, not sparing even his mother." 3

Thus this good poet brought the city of Athens to its senses. What great suffering he produced on stage! On the other hand, how much moral character he introduced into his plays through his maxims! And the Sopho- part of his name he confirmed by his very deeds, having become for tragedians what Homer was for poets. But to the degree that he eclipsed his fellow tragedians with the superiority of 4

λοιπῶν ἐκείνου γνωμῶν τὸ περὶ χάριτος γνωμολογηθὲν
χαριέστατον.

5 Ἐκ τοῦ καλῶς, φησί, δρᾶν τὸ καλῶς παθεῖν περιγίνεται
καὶ πάνθ᾽, ὁπόσα μήτηρ παιδί, καὶ χάρις ἀντὶ χάριτος
γίνεται.

6 Πρῶτον μὲν τὸν ποιητὴν ἐπαινῶ, οἷς καλῶς τὴν ἀν-
θρωπείαν φύσιν ἐσκέψατο καὶ ὡς χαρίζεσθαι· πεφύκαμεν
ἄνθρωποι μετὰ τὸ λαβεῖν καὶ δρῶμεν εὖ παθόντες. Ἔπειτα
καὶ τοὺς ἀγεννεστέρους τῶν ἀνθρώπων ἀπέσκωψεν, εἰ
στείραν οὕτως ἔχει τις τὴν ψυχήν, ὡς τὸ τῆς χάριτος
σπέρμα λαβοῦσαν μὴ τὸν τῆς εὐγνωμοσύνης ἀντιδοῦναι
καρπόν.

7 Εἰ δὲ τὴν ἀπὸ τῶν ἔργων μαρτυρίαν προσεπιθείημεν,
πολὺ δικαιότερον τῆς γνώμης τὸν ποιητὴν θαυμασόμεθα.
Τίς οὖν ἡ περὶ τῶν ἔργων ἐπιβεβαίωσις; Οὐ πάντα πᾶσιν
ἀρχῆθεν ἐφεύρηται, ἀλλ᾽ ἕτερα μὲν Ἑλλήνων σοφίσματα,
ἕτεραι δὲ Φοινίκων ἐπίνοιαι καὶ Περσῶν ἄλλα τεχνήματα.
Ἔχουσί τι καὶ Θρᾷκες οὔπω τοῖς ἄλλοις ἐλθὸν εἰς εὕρεσιν
ἐπιδείξασθαι, καὶ τῶν ἐθνῶν ὡς ἕκαστα διηρημένα τοῖς
γένεσι καὶ ταῖς ἐπινοίαις διήρηνται.

8 Ἀλλ᾽ ἧκεν ἡ χάρις κοινωνικόν τι χρῆμα καὶ φίλιον καί,
τὸ θηριῶδες ἐξελοῦσα τῆς γνώμης, πρὸς τὸ ἀνθρωπικώ-
τερον μετερρύθμισε καὶ νῦν παρὰ τοῦτο τῶν θηρίων
διενηνόχαμεν ἄνθρωποι. Ἐκεῖθεν ἡμῖν ἦλθε καὶ τὸ συν-
αγελαστικόν, ἐκεῖθεν καὶ τὸ τῆς φιλίας ἔχομεν ὄνομα καὶ
τὸ τὴν ἔνδειαν ἀναπληροῦν οὐκ ἄλλοθεν ἡμῖν προσεγένετο.
Ἔχει μὲν Ἰνδός, εἰ τύχοι, ἐλέφαντας, ὅπλα δὲ Λήμνιοι,

his wisdom, to the same degree his maxim about kindness is the most elegant of all.

The result of doing good, he says, is receiving good in re-   5
turn, and everything that a mother is to a child, kindness is for kindness in return.

First I praise the poet, because he observed human na-   6
ture carefully and found that we humans naturally show kindness after receiving it and do good when we have received good. Then he mocked baser men, if anyone has such a barren soul that when it receives the seed of kindness it does not produce the fruit of generosity.

But if we should also add the testimony from deeds, we   7
will much more justifiably admire the poet for his maxim. So then, what additional confirmation comes from deeds? Not everything was discovered by everyone from the beginning, but some things are clever devices of the Greeks, others are inventions of the Phoenicians, and still others are contrivances of the Persians. Even the Thracians can demonstrate something that has not yet been discovered by anyone else, and just as all nations are distinct in race, they are also distinct in their inventions.

But kindness has come as a common and beloved quality,   8
and having removed beastliness from the mind, it has reformed it to be more humane, and now in this respect we humans are superior to wild beasts. From there also came to us our social instinct; from there too we have the concept of friendship, and that which fulfills what we lack does not come to us from anywhere else. Indians, it so happens, had elephants, Lemnians had armor, Phoenicians had writing,

RHETORICAL EXERCISES OF NIKEPHOROS BASILAKES

γράμματα Φοίνικες, οἱ δ᾽ ἐξ Ἀθηνῶν ἵππους ὑπὸ ζυγὸν
ἀγαγεῖν ἐσοφίσαντο, ἀλλὰ πρὶν ἥκειν τὴν χάριν.

9   Οἷς οὐκ εἶχον, πρὸς εὐδαιμονίαν ἐλείποντο. Ἀλλ᾽
ἔγνωσαν ὅστις ὁ τρόπος τῆς χάριτος καὶ οὔτε τῶν παρ᾽
αὐτοῖς ἀπεστέρηντο καὶ τὰ παρ᾽ ἑτέροις ἐλάμβανον·
τεκτονεύειν τις εἰδώς, ἐδεῖτο μὲν τροφῆς τῆς ἡμέρου
ταύτης τῆς ἀπὸ σίτου, τῆς ἐκ σπερμάτων καί, πηξάμενος
ἅμαξαν, ἀπεδίδου τῷ περὶ γεωργίαν ἔχοντι καὶ σῖτον τῆς
τέχνης ἀντεκομίζετο. Ἱππεύειν τις τὴν ἀρχὴν ἐπεβάλετο
καὶ τὴν ἱππικὴν οὐκ ἦν ἐπιδείξασθαι, μὴ παρά του τὰ πρὸς
ἱππικὴν ξυνεργὰ κομισάμενος· ἐντεῦθεν εἶχε, τὸν χαλκὸν
καταβαλὼν αὐτὸς πρότερον, ὅτου καὶ προσεδέησε.
Πλουτεῖς καὶ δεῖ σοι λαμπροτέρας οἰκίας; Κατάβαλέ τι
τῶν χρημάτων τοῖς οἰκοδόμοις καὶ προσευδαιμονίσεις καὶ
τοῦτο τὸ μέρος. Περιπλέων ἐθέλεις ἔχειν καὶ θάλατταν; Ὁ
ναυπηγὸς ἀντιδώσει σοι τὸ ποθούμενον, εἰ πρότερον
αὐτὸς παρὰ σοῦ λήψεται.

10   Οὕτω καὶ τὴν ἀρχὴν ἡ χάρις ἐκυοφόρησε τὴν ἀντίχαριν
καὶ νῦν ἔτι τῆς καλῆς ταύτης κυοφορίας οὐ παύεται—
τοῦτο τὸ μέρος ἀγήρως ἡ φύσις οὐδὲν ἧττον ἢ περὶ
γένεσιν—οὐ δέχεται παρακμὴν τὰ τῆς ἀντιδόσεως, ἀλλ᾽
ὅλας πόλεις ὁσημέραι γεννᾷ, πᾶσαν μὲν γὰρ περιπλεῖ
θάλασσαν, πᾶσαν δ᾽ ἐπέρχεται γῆν καὶ παρὰ μέρος ἐστίν,
οὐ πολλάκις ἐκλείπουσα. Τὸ παντελὲς οὐκ ἐξέλιπεν·
ἀμβλώσκει μὲν γὰρ ἔσθ᾽ ὅτε καὶ χάρις καὶ τὸ βρέφος τὴν
ἀντίχαριν ἀρτίτοκον οὐκ ἀποδίδωσιν, ἀλλὰ ψυχῆς ἀγόνου
ταῦτα καὶ κύειν οὐκ εἰδυίας χάριν ἐστίν.

and Athenians contrived to put horses under the yoke, but all this occurred before kindness arrived.

They fell short in happiness because of what they did not 9 possess. But then they learned the ways of kindness, and so they both retained their own things and would get other things from others. Someone who knew how to do carpentry would lack cultivated food from grain and seeds; he would thus construct a wagon, give it in exchange to the man engaged in farming, and receive grain in return for his carpentry skill. In the beginning, someone would undertake to ride a horse, but he could not display prowess in horsemanship without acquiring the equipment for it from another man. Then, after first laying out the money, he would acquire whatever he needed. Are you rich, and do you need a more splendid house? Pay some money to the homebuilders, and you will be prosperous in this respect, as well. Do you wish to sail around and possess the sea too? The shipbuilder will give you what you desire in return, if he himself first gets something from you.

So also kindness generated reciprocal kindness from the 10 start, and even now it does not cease from this fine pregnancy—in this regard, no less than in respect to generation, nature never grows old—and the custom of kindness-in-return does not admit of decay, but daily generates entire cities, for it sails around the whole sea, goes to every land, and is everywhere in turn, only rarely failing to appear. And it has never failed entirely, for although there are times when even kindness miscarries and does not pay back a newly born infant, that is, reciprocal kindness, this is characteristic of a sterile soul, one that does not know how to conceive kindness.

11 Ἀλλ᾽ οὐκ ἤδη τὸ τῆς χάριτος ἄνθος ἀπέρρευσεν, ὅτι καὶ φύσις περὶ μὲν τήνδε ἢ τήνδε τῶν γυναικῶν οὐκ εὐστοχεῖ τὴν γένεσιν, ἐφ᾽ ἑτέρας δὲ τὸ γεννητικὸν ἄρτιον ἐφυλάξατο. Ὅσοις μὲν οὖν ἡ χάρις ξυνέστιος καὶ τὰ τῆς χάριτος οὐκ ἀμβλώσκεται—ἢ καὶ τὸ σπέρμα μὴ πρὸς ἄκανθαν μετατέτραπται—τούτοις δὴ κουροτρόφος εἰρήνη περιχορεύει τὰς πόλεις καὶ τὸ τοῦ μίσους δεινὸν ἐξωστράκισται καὶ τὰ τῆς ἀπεχθείας ἀπέωσται.

12 Ἐφ᾽ ὅσαις δὲ τῶν πόλεων μὴ τὰ τῆς χάριτος γόνιμα, ὅσος μὲν ὁ φθόνος ὑφέρπει! Ὅση δὲ ἡ ἀπέχθεια ἤδη καὶ πρὸς μάχην ἀνάπτεται! Καὶ ὁ τῶν πόλεων ἀνδραποδισμός, μὴ τικτούσης τῆς χάριτος, ἂν ἔχοι τὴν γένεσιν. Ἀλλ᾽ οὐδέ, μάχης ἠκούσης, εἰς τὸ παντελὲς ἐπιλέλοιπεν, ἀλλά, πρὸς μὲν τοὺς πολεμίους οὐδ᾽ ἂν ἴχνος ἴδοι τις χάριτος, τὰ δὲ πρὸς ἀλλήλους ξυνδεῖ μὲν εἰς ὁμόνοιαν, ἐπεγείρει δὲ εἰς συμμαχίαν καὶ στρατηγὸς ἄγει τὸ στράτευμα, μισθῷ τοὺς στρατιώτας εἰς ἀντίχαριν ἐπαγόμενος. Τὰ δ᾽ ὅπλα πόθεν ἔχουσιν οἱ στρατευόμενοι; Οὐκ ἀπὸ τῶν ὅσοι περὶ τὴν ὁπλοποιητικὴν ἐσπουδάκασι, πρότερον αὐτοὶ καταβαλλόμενοι χρήματα; Τοῦτο δὲ τί ἂν εἴη ἕτερον ἢ πάντως ἀντίχαρις; Καὶ σύ, ὦ παῖ, εἰ μὴ πρότερον πόνους ἀντιδοίης πολλούς, οὐκ ἄν ποτε τὸ τῶν λόγων χρῆμα κερδήσεις.

13 Τί δεῖ με πολὺν τὸν ἔξω τοῦ λόγου κύκλον ποιεῖσθαι καὶ μὴ ἀφ᾽ ἑστίας ἐπιχειρεῖν ἀπό γε τῆς φύσεως; Εἰ γὰρ μὴ πρότερον ἡ φύσις τὸ σπέρμα λήψεται, οὐκ ἂν ἀποδοίη βοῦν ἢ ἵππον ἢ ἄλλο τι τῶν <ζῴων> ὡς ἕκαστα. Εἰ γὰρ μὴ χάρις χάριν ἔτικτεν, οὐδ᾽ ἂν πόλεμον διεδέχετο πόλεμος,

But the flower of kindness has not already fallen away, be- 11
cause even nature does not grant successful reproduction to
each and every woman, but preserves the reproductive func-
tion perfectly in some of them, but not in others. So then,
all those for whom kindness is a close companion and the
custom of kindness is not miscarried—or the seed has not
turned into a thorn bush—for all these people, peace, the
nurturer of children, dances around their cities, dreadful hatred is banished, and enmity is expelled.

But in all the cities where the custom of kindness is not 12
fruitful, how much envy creeps in! How much enmity is already kindled even to the point of battle! The enslaving of
cities might be engendered if kindness fails to give birth.
But not even when battle comes has kindness failed entirely,
but while one would not see a trace of kindness shown toward the enemy, our relationship to each other binds us together in harmony and rouses us to fight as allies, and a general leads the army, inducing the soldiers with pay to show
reciprocal kindness. Moreover, from where do the soldiers
get their weapons? Is it not from those who have devoted
serious effort to the manufacture of arms, after the soldiers
have paid them money? What at any rate would this be
other than reciprocal kindness? And you, child, if you do not
first give much labor in exchange, you will never profit in
the currency of words.

Why must I circle widely around my topic and not make 13
a focused argument from nature? For if nature does not first
receive the seed, it will not produce an ox or a horse or any
other particular animal. For if kindness did not give birth to
kindness, war would not succeed war, violence would not

οὐδ᾽ ὕβρις ὕβριν μετήρχετο, ἀλλ᾽ εἶχεν ἄν τις ἐκ τῶν
ἐναντίων τἀναντία καρπούμενος.

14 Ὡς γὰρ ὁ σῖτος σῖτον οἶδε γεννᾶν καὶ ἵππος ἵππον καὶ
ἄνθρωπος ἄνθρωπον, οὕτω καὶ χάρις ἀντίχαριν.

15 Ὅρα μοι τῶν Ἀθηναίων τὸν δῆμον, τὸν πλεῖστα τῆς
Ἑλλάδος ἰσχύσαντα. Ἐπεὶ γὰρ ἐνέδει τροφῆς καὶ λιμὸς
τὴν Ἀττικὴν ἐπεβόσκετο, πρὸς Αἰγυπτίους ἀπήεσαν καί,
κομισάμενοι σῖτον, κατὰ Περσῶν ξυμμαχίαν συνέθεντο
καὶ Πλαταιεῦσι τῆς ἐπὶ Μαραθῶνος σπουδῆς τὴν Ἀθήναζε
πολιτείαν ἀντεχαρίσαντο. Κοινῇ μὲν οὖν καὶ πρὸς ὅλας
πόλεις οὕτω χάρις χάριν ἀπέτεκεν.

16 Ἰδίᾳ δὲ καὶ κάλλιστα Ἕκτορα μὲν ὁ μέγας Αἴας τοῦ
ξίφους ἠμείψατο, ζωστῆρα φοινικοῦν ἀντιδιδούς, Γλαῦκον
δὲ τῆς πανοπλίας ὁ τοῦ Τυδέως. Καὶ Τεῦκρον τῆς κατὰ
τῶν Τρώων εὐστόχου τοξικῆς Ἀγαμέμνων ἐθαύμασε καὶ
τὸν αὐτοῦ Τεύκρου πάλιν ἀδελφόν, μετὰ τὴν πρὸς Ἕκτορα
μονομαχίαν τῆς ἀριστείας τιμῶν, ἐπὶ τοῦ δείπνου νώτοισι
διηνεκέεσ<σ>ι γέραιρε.

17 Τὰ μὲν οὖν ἔργα τοιαῦτα τὴν μαρτυρίαν, καὶ οὕτως
ἐχόμενα τῆς τοῦ ποιητοῦ γνώμης. Δεῖ δὲ ἡμᾶς μηδὲ τῆς
ἀπὸ τῶν Μουσῶν ἀποσχέσθαι· εἴη δ᾽ ἄν, οἶμαι, Μουσῶν,
ὅσαπερ ἐπιπνοίᾳ Μουσῶν Ἡσίοδος ἀποφαίνεται. Καὶ τί
φησιν ἐκεῖνος ὁ Μούσαις κάτοχος γλῶτταν, μᾶλλον δὲ δι᾽
ἐκείνου αἱ Μοῦσαι· "Τὸν δὲ δεδωκότα τίς ἠμείψατο; Πρὸς
δὲ τὸν οὐκ εἰδότα χαρίζεσθαι οὐδείς ποτε, νοῦν ἔχων, τὴν
χάριν ἀνάλωσε."

18 Πῶς δ᾽ ἂν καὶ Πρόδικον τὸν σοφιστὴν παραλίποιμεν,
ἀξίως τῆς αὐτοῦ σοφίας ἀποφθεγγόμενον, "Δός τι καὶ λάβε

follow violence, but rather someone would reap opposites from opposites.

For just as grain can generate grain, and a horse generate a 14 horse, and a human generate a human, so also kindness can generate reciprocal kindness.

Look, if you will, at the people of Athens, the most pow- 15 erful state in Greece. For when they lacked food and a famine was consuming Attica, they went off to Egypt, and having obtained grain, they formed an alliance against the Persians. They also returned a kindness to the Plataeans for their zeal at Marathon by granting them Athenian citizenship. So then, kindness has thus given birth to kindness publicly and with regard to entire cities.

But also in the private and most splendid sphere: the 16 great Ajax repaid Hector for his sword, giving him a crimson belt in return, and Diomedes, the son of Tydeus, repaid Glaucus for his armor. Agamemnon admired Teucer for his well-aimed archery against the Trojans, and honoring in turn Ajax, the brother of Teucer himself, for his valor after the single combat with Hector, Agamemnon at the dinner *rewarded him with long slices from the back*.

Such is then the testimony that the deeds provide and in 17 this way they conform to the poet's maxim. But we must also not refrain from the testimony of the Muses; and such testimony would be, I suppose, whatever Hesiod declares by inspiration from the Muses. And what does that man, with his tongue possessed by the Muses, say, or rather what do the Muses say through him? "Who repaid the giver? No one with any sense has ever expended kindness on someone who does not know how to give kindness in return."

But how could we omit Prodicus the sophist, who worthy 18 of his wisdom says, "*Give something and receive something*"? He

τι," καὶ τὸ τῆς ἀντιχάριτος καλὸν αὐτόθεν ἀπὸ τοῦ συντρόφου σώματος παριστῶντα βεβαιότερον; "Ἃ δὲ χεὶρ τὴν χεῖρα νίζει" καὶ ἡ εὐώνυμος τῇ δεξιᾷ τῶν ἔργων ξυναίρεται καὶ νῦν μὲν αὕτη πρὸς ἐκείνης, νῦν δὲ ἐκείνη πρὸς ταύτης τῶν πόνων ἐπικουφίζεται.

19   Οὐκοῦν ἀποδεκτέον τῆς μὲν γνώμης τὸν Σοφοκλῆν, τοὺς δὲ χαριζομένους τῆς χάριτος· οὐ γάρ ἐστιν ὅπως ἑτέρως ἀγαθοὺς φίλους πλουτήσαιμεν, εἰ μὴ τὰς χάριτας διαμειβοίμεθα χάρισιν.

3

"Ἐχρῆν δ᾽ εὐθὺς εἶναι τήνδε τοῖς πᾶσιν δίκην, ὅστις πέρα τι τῶν νόμων πράσσειν θέλει κτείνειν· τὸ γὰρ κακοῦργον οὐκ ἂν ἦν πολύ"

Ἐμὲ δὲ εἴ τις ἔροιτο, τίνα δεῖ εἶναι τὴν τραγῳδίαν, κοινὴν ἂν εἴποιμι παιδαγωγίαν καὶ τούς γε ταύτην μετιόντας ἰατροὺς φαίην ἂν ἐγὼ πόλεων. Ταύτην δὴ τὴν ἰατρικὴν ὑπὲρ τοὺς ἄλλους ἐπησκήσατο Σοφοκλῆς· ὅσα μὲν προφυλακτικὰ τοῦ καλοῦ καὶ τῆς ἀρετῆς ξυνεκεράσατο φάρμακα! Ὅσα δ᾽ ὑπὸ φαυλότητος πεπονηκυῖαν ψυχὴν αὖθις ἀνεκαλέσατο! Αὐτίκα τὸ περὶ τῆς τοῦ

also demonstrates the inherent goodness of reciprocal kindness more securely on the analogy of cooperation in the body. *"Hand washes hand,"* and the left hand assists the right hand in its deeds, and now this one is relieved of its labors by that one, and now that one by this one.

Therefore one must praise Sophocles for his maxim and praise those who repay kindness with kindness. For there is no other way for us to be rich in good friends, except that we continually requite their kindnesses with our kindnesses. 19

3

"This just penalty should come immediately to everyone, that whoever wishes to act outside of the laws should be killed, for then there would not be so much wrongdoing"

If someone should ask me what tragedy ought to be, I would say that it ought to be an education for everyone in common and that its practitioners are the doctors of cities. This brand of medicine Sophocles practiced beyond all other tragedians. How many drugs he compounded to protect honor and virtue! How many of his drugs, in turn, have restored a soul afflicted with baseness! Moreover, in respect

κακουργεῖν ἐκτομῆς, ὅσην ἐφ᾽ ἑκάτερα κέκτηται τὴν ῥοπήν!

2 Ἐπεὶ γὰρ αὐξανόμενον ἑώρα τὸ κακὸν καὶ πάντα κακούργων μεστὰ καὶ δέος οὐδὲν τοῖς κακουργοῦσιν ἐπῆν, ἠγανάκτησε τῆς ὀλιγωρίας τῶν νόμων, ᾤκτειρε τῆς ἀτοπίας τὰς πόλεις, ὑπερήλγησε τοῦ καλοῦ καὶ τῆς δίκης καί, μέρος τι τῶν ἐν μύθοις ᾀδομένων ἀπολαβών, ὑφηγεῖται τὸ φάρμακον. Αἰγίσθου διηγεῖται μοιχείαν καὶ βασιλέως σφαγήν. Εἶτ᾽ ἐπιφέρει τὸν τοῦ πεσόντος παῖδα Ὀρέστην καὶ τιμωρεῖται μὲν τῆς μοιχείας Αἴγισθον, κολάζει δὲ Κλυταιμνήστραν τῆς ὕβρεως καί, παράδειγμα καλὸν ἀποδοὺς οἷς ἔδρασεν ἐπὶ τῆς σκηνῆς, ἀποδίδωσι καὶ λόγον ξυνᾴδοντα τοῖς εἰργασμένοις.

3 Εἰ γάρ, φησι, τοὺς καθ᾽ ἕκαστα κακοὺς ὡς νῦν ἐνταῦθα τὸν Αἴγισθον μετὰ τὴν κακουργίαν εὐθὺς τὸ ξίφος ἐδέχετο, οὐκ ἂν αἱ πόλεις οὕτω μικροῦ δεῖν κακουργούντων πόλεις ἐγίνοντο, οὐδ᾽ ἂν τὰ θεοῖς καὶ νόμοις ἀνειμένα χῶρος ἀσεβῶν ἐδόκει καὶ τὸ φαῦλον εἶχεν ἐπίδοσιν.

4 Ἐπαινετέος μὲν οὖν ὁ ἀνὴρ καὶ τῆς ἐπ᾽ Αἰγίσθῳ δίκης καὶ τῆς ἐπὶ Κλυταιμνήστρᾳ σφαγῆς, ἀλλ᾽ οὐδὲν ἧττον τοῦ καλοῦ τούτου παραδείγματος δίκαιος ἀγᾶσθαι καὶ οἷς, ὅπως δεῖ ἐκτέμνειν τὸ κακόν, οὐκ ἐσίγησεν. Εἰ γὰρ ἀνεῖλε μὲν Αἴγισθον, ἐσιώπησε δὲ τὴν κοινὴν τῆς κακίας τομήν, ἐπὶ μόνην ἂν ἐδόκει μοιχείαν ὁπλίζειν τὸν δήμιον.

5 Νῦν δ᾽ εἰς μέρος μὲν τὸν τῆς θεραπείας ἐπεδείξατο τρόπον, τὴν δὲ τούτου τοῦ φαρμάκου δύναμιν κατὰ πάσης ἄγει φαυλότητος καί, ὅσον ἔχει τὸ δραστήριον,

to the passage about the excision of wrongdoing, how great an influence he possesses in both kinds of remedies!

For when he saw evil increasing, everything full of wrong- 2 doers, and no fear hanging over them, he was annoyed at their contempt for the laws, he pitied the cities for the wickedness from which they suffered, he felt great pain on behalf of honor and justice, and so, selecting a sample of the stories sung in myths, he prescribed the drug. He narrated the adultery of Aegisthus and the slaughter of a king. Then he introduced Orestes, the dead man's son, and punished Aegisthus for his adultery and punished Clytemnestra for her violence, and, while he gave us a fine example in the actions depicted on stage, he also gave us a saying that harmonizes with those actions.

For if, he says, wicked men were in every instance to be 3 felled by the sword immediately after doing wrong, as Aegisthus is here and now, our cities would not have practically become cities of wrongdoers, nor would the places devoted to the gods and laws seem to have become the domain of impious men, and baseness would not have increased.

So then, Sophocles is to be praised both for the just pen- 4 alty inflicted on Aegisthus and for the slaughter inflicted on Clytemnestra, but he is rightly esteemed no less for this fine example and because he did not keep silent about the necessity of excising the evil. For if he had executed Aegisthus but kept silent about excising wickedness in general, he would have seemed to be arming the public executioner against adultery only.

But now he, in succession, has demonstrated the nature 5 of his treatment, introduced the power of this drug against every baseness, demonstrated how effective it was, and all

ἐπιδείκνυται, μονονοὺ καὶ ταῦτα προσεπιλέγει· "Γέμουσι κακῶν αἱ πόλεις καὶ νοσοῦσιν ἀθεράπευτα καὶ κάμνουσι μὴ παυόμενα καὶ δεῖ τοῦ φαρμάκοις στήσοντος τὸ δεινόν. Ἀλλ' οἶδα τὴν θεραπείαν ἐγώ· πρὸς γὰρ τῆς σοφίας τοῦτο τὸ καλὸν ἀπωνάμην. Κἂν οἱ τῶν πόλεων ἐπιστατοῦντες ἐθέλοιτε μαθεῖν, οὐ φθονήσω τῆς θεραπείας, οὐ καθέξω τὸ φάρμακον, ἐγγὺς τὸ παράδειγμα.

6   "Βαλλόμενος Αἴγισθος καὶ πίπτουσα Κλυταιμνήστρα, οὗτος ὑμῖν τῆς δίκης ἔστω κανὼν καὶ τοῦτον τῆς ὑγείας ὅρον τίθεσθε. Εἰ μοιχείας τις ἑάλω, μετ' Αἰγίσθου πιπτέτω, εἴ τίς τῳ θεῶν χεῖρας ἐπέβαλλε, κἀκείνῳ τὸ ξίφος ὁ δήμιος. Ἔφθασέ τις καὶ πρὸς τὸ τῆς ἀνδροφονίας δεινόν, αὐτὸ τιμωρὸν ἐχέτω τὸ ξίφος, ὅ, μηδὲν ἐγκαλεῖν ἔχων, ἐπέσεισεν· ἦλθέ τις καὶ ἐπὶ προδοσίαν πόλεως, ὡς κοινὸς ἀναιρείσθω πολέμιος.

7   "Λάμβανε καὶ κλοπῆς τιμωρίαν ὁ τοῖς νόμοις ἐφεστηκώς, κόλαζε καὶ τὸν ἐπ' ἀργύρῳ τὰς πρεσβείας ποιούμενον καὶ μὴ διαφυγέτω τὸν δήμιον μηδ' ὁ πρὸς χάριν ἐκκλησίας φθεγγόμενος. Ἀλλ' ὅπως τάχιον τὰ τῆς δίκης ἕψεται, μὴ δὴ ὁ περὶ τὴν τιμωρίαν διάμελε, μηδ' ἀναβάλλου τὴν ἐκτομήν—δεῖ σοι καὶ τάχους εἰς ἀναίρεσιν· ἐκφοβήσει καὶ τοῦτο τοὺς κακουργοῦντας οὐχ ἥκιστα—ὡς εἴγε λάθοις, ἀναβαλλόμενος, ἔλαθες καὶ τὸ κακὸν τιθεὶς γονιμώτερον." Τοιούτους χρὴ τοῦ ποιητοῦ νομίζειν εἶναι τοὺς λόγους, τὸ γὰρ εὐθὺς τάχος ὑφεῖται καὶ προσεπισπεύδει τὴν ἐκτομήν.

8   Τί δ' ἂν ἄλλο καὶ τὸ "θέλει" προσεπαγόμενον φαίη τις βούλεσθαι; Ἐμοὶ δοκεῖ τῇ βουλήσει μετρεῖν τὴν ἀναίρεσιν.

but added the following words: "The cities are full of evils, they suffer from untreated diseases, they are chronically ill, and they lack someone to stop their suffering with drugs. But I know the treatment; for by my wisdom I acquired this fine thing. And if you overseers of the cities wish to learn it, I will not deny you the treatment; I will not withhold the drug; the example is at hand.

"When Aegisthus is struck down and Clytemnestra falls, 6 let this be your standard for a just penalty, and consider this the definition of health. If someone is convicted of adultery, let him fall with Aegisthus. If someone lays his hands on one of the gods, let the public executioner also lay the sword on him. If someone goes so far as to commit the dreaded act of murder, let him have as avenger the very sword that he brandished against his victim, although he had no grounds to accuse him. If someone even commits treason against the city, let him be executed as a public enemy.

"Overseer of the laws, exact vengeance for theft; punish 7 the man who takes bribes as an ambassador, and do not let the unscrupulous demagogue escape the public executioner. But so that the just penalty will follow more quickly, you who oversee the punishment, do not examine it at length, and do not delay the excision—you must execute at once; this will frighten the wrongdoers more than anything—and even if no one notices that you are delaying, no one likewise notices that you allow evil to grow." One ought to regard such words as these as if they were the poet's, for he has immediately resorted to quick action and he hastens the excision.

But what else would someone say the addition of "wishes" 8 means? To me it seems to apportion the death penalty in

Κἂν οἷόν τε ξυνεῖναι, φησί, τῆς ἐπιβουλῆς πρὶν εἰς ἔργον ἐλθεῖν, ἐκθέριζε τὸ κακόν. Φυλοκρινοίη δ' ἄν τις καὶ οὕτω τὴν τοῦ φαρμάκου φύσιν· τῶν φαρμάκων τὰ μὲν προφυλάττει τὴν ὑγείαν καὶ μέλλουσαν τὴν νόσον φυλάττεται, τὰ δ' ἐπανακαλεῖται μεταπεσοῦσαν τὴν φύσιν καὶ γίνεται τῆς προφυλακῆς ἀπελεγχομένης ἀνόρθωσις.

9   Ὁ δὲ τοῦ καλοῦ τούτου ποιητοῦ καὶ τῆς ἐκείνου γνώμης καυτὴρ νεύει καὶ πρὸς ἑκάτερα καὶ προφυλάττει μὲν τὸ μὴ παθεῖν, οἷς οὐδὲν οὔπω τὴν ψυχὴν ἐλυμήνατο, ἀνορθοῖ δὲ τὴν δίκην καὶ πεσοῦσαν ἐπανακαλεῖται καὶ δέει τοῦ μὴ παθεῖν τούς γε, τὸν νοῦν ἔτι μὴ καὶ τὴν χεῖρα κλαπέντας, ὑπὸ κακίας φυλάξασθαι τὴν ἀπάτην ἠνάγκασε, καὶ ὅπως ἐντεῦθεν ἂν εἴη μαθεῖν, ἔπεσεν ὁ μοιχός, ἤκουσεν ὁ δεῖνα καί, τὴν πληγὴν ὑφορώμενος, τὸ κακουργεῖν ἐφυλάξατο· ὁ ταῖς ὁδοῖς ἐφεδρεύων, ἑάλω καὶ πέπτωκεν, εἶδεν ἕτερος ἐφεστὼς καὶ τὸν νοῦν αὐτὸν πεφόβηται μετὰ καὶ τῆς δεξιᾶς· κἂν ἔφθασέ τις αἵματος ἀνθρωπείου τὴν δεξιὰν γεῦσαι, κἂν ἀθέμιτον χεῖρα τοῖς ἱεροῖς ἐπέβαλε, κἂν ἄλλο τι τῶν οὐχ ὁσίων ἐτόλμησε καὶ τὸν τῆς Δίκης ποίνιμον ἔλαθεν ὀφθαλμόν, ἀλλ' ἐντεῦθεν διδάσκεται μηκέτι θηριώδη τόλμαν τρέφειν ἄνθρωπος κατ' ἀνθρώπου, μηδὲ θνητὸς ἀθανάτων κατεπαίρεσθαι, μηδ' ἄλλο τι σκαιωρεῖν ἐθέλειν παράλογον, ταχεῖαν οὕτω τὴν δίκην ἐφαλλομένην ὁρῶν καὶ μέχρι τοῦ θέλειν τὸ ξίφος ἀνατεινόμενον. Οὕτω πρὸς πάντας τὸ τοῦ Σοφοκλέους τοῦτο σοφὸν ἴσον φέρει τὸ δέος καὶ ἡ πόλις εὐνομεῖται καὶ τὴν δίκην ἔχει ξυνέστιον.

accordance with the criminal's intent. If it is possible to comprehend the plot, he says, before it comes to fruition, cut the evil down completely. And someone might carefully define the nature of the drug in this way: some drugs protect our health and fend off future illness, while others restore our nature when it has changed for the worse and rebuild our body's defenses when they are under attack.

But the cauterizing iron of this good poet and of his 9 maxim works in both directions: it defends us against suffering in that nothing corrupts the soul at all, and it restores justice and rebuilds it when it has failed, compelling those who have not yet had their minds and hands seduced by wickedness, out of fear that they might suffer, to guard against deceit; and so that it might be possible to learn from this: the adulterer falls, the average citizen hears about it, and, witnessing the deathblow, he guards against doing wrong himself; the man who ambushes travelers on the roads is caught and dies, and another man standing nearby sees it and is terrified in his very mind, as well as in his right hand. Even if someone managed to taste human blood with his right hand, even if he laid an unlawful hand on the sacred temples, and even if he dared to do any other unholy thing and escaped the notice of the avenging eye of Justice, even so, from this humans are taught no longer to nurture beastly audacity against other humans, and mortals no longer to disparage immortals or to wish to plot anything else unreasonable, when they see that the just penalty follows so swiftly and the sword is applied even for the intent to do wrong. Thus this wise saying of Sophocles inspires equal fear in everyone, and the city is well ordered and has justice at its core.

10 Εἰ δὲ μὴ μέχρι τοῦ θέλειν ἐπέθηγε τὸ ξίφος, πῶς ἂν
ἐκολάζετο τύραννος μετὰ τὴν τῶν νόμων κατάλυσιν καὶ
πόλεως δουλείαν καὶ ἀκροπόλεως ἅλωσιν; Καλῶς ἂν τὰ
τῆς τιμωρίας ἐλάμβανεν, οὐκ ὀλίγης τῆς τῶν δορυφόρων
ὑπούσης φρουρᾶς! Καίτοι τίς οὐκ οἶδεν ὡς, τυραννίδος
σκηπτοῦ δίκην ἐπεισπεσούσης ἐξ ἀκροπόλεως, ἐλευθερία
μὲν οἴχεται, τὰ δὲ τῆς δημοκρατίας ἔφθαρται καὶ
διαλέλυται, νόμων δὲ καὶ δίκης οὐδ᾽ ἴχνος τὸ παράπαν ἔτι
περίεστι; Τί δὲ ὁ τὴν θρεψαμένην καταπροέμενος ἀποίσεται
τὴν ἀξίαν τῆς ἐπιβουλῆς εἰς ἔργον ἡκούσης; Καὶ πῶς, ὑπὸ
τοῖς ἐχθροῖς γενομένης τῆς πόλεως; Ἐγὼ μὲν οὐκ ἂν
εἴποιμι.

11 Εἰ δὲ ταῦθ᾽ οὕτως ἔχει, δῆλον ὅτι καὶ πρὸς αὐτὴν
ἀντιτακτέον τῆς κακίας τὴν γένεσιν καὶ μηδὲ τὸ θέλειν
ἔστω τοῖς παρανομοῦσιν ἀνεύθυνον, ἀλλ᾽ ἐκτετμήσθω καὶ
βούλησις πονηρὰ καὶ τάχ᾽ ἂν οὕτω καὶ τὸ ἔργον συν-
εκτμηθήσεται. Εἰ δ᾽ ἐάσεις τὴν ἀρχὴν τῆς κακουργίας
ἀκόλαστον, ἥξει ποτὲ καιρὸς καὶ τομὴν οὐ δέξεται τὸ
πανούργευμα, τῶν νόμων αὐτῇ πόλει συνεκτριβέντων,
αὐτῷ βήματι.

12 Τίς δ᾽ ἂν ἔτι, τὰ μοιχῶν οὐχ ὁρῶν εὐθυνόμενα, οὐ συγ-
χέῃ γονήν, οὐ καταισχύνῃ μὴ προσήκουσαν εὐνήν; Ἢ
ποῖος, τὸν νυκτὸς τοῖς ἱεροῖς ἐπιθέμενον μὴ παραχρῆμα
τὴν ἀξίαν δεδωκότα μαθών, οὐ καταφρονήσει μὲν θεῶν,
ὑπερφρονήσει δὲ νόμων καὶ μετὰ πλείονος αὐτὸς
ἐπιθήσεται τῆς σπουδῆς; Οὐδ᾽ ἂν ὁ τυμβωρύχος ἀμελήσῃ
κατὰ τῶν κειμένων ἀνδριζόμενος, εἰ μηδεὶς εἴη τῆς τόλμης
ἐφέξων, οὐδ᾽ ἂν ἀνδροφόνος, οὐδ᾽ ἂν οἱ καθ᾽ ἕκαστα

But if Sophocles did not sharpen the sword to include 10 intent, how would a tyrant be punished for destroying the laws, enslaving the city, and capturing the acropolis? Surely he would accept his punishment when he has such a large cadre of bodyguards around him! And yet who does not know that, when tyranny strikes like a thunderbolt from the acropolis, freedom perishes, democracy is corrupted and dissolved, and not the slightest trace of laws and justice still remains? Why would the one who abandoned his native city get what he deserves when his plot has come to fruition? And how, if the city has come under the enemy's power? I at least could not say.

But if this is the case, it is evident that one must line up 11 for battle against the very origin of the wickedness and not let criminals escape being held accountable even for intent, but let wicked intent be excised, and perhaps in this way the deed will also be excised. But if you let the beginning of the wrongdoing go unpunished, a time will someday come when the villainy will not admit excision, when the laws have been utterly destroyed along with the very city and government.

But who, if he does not see adultery being censured, 12 would not still confound paternity and disgrace a bed not his own? Or what sort of person, upon learning that the man who attacked the temples by night did not immediately receive what he deserved, will not despise the gods, look down on the laws, and with greater zeal attack the temples himself? Neither would any tomb robber neglect to assault the dead, if there were no one to restrain him from this audacity or to bar him with laws as he is carried headlong into trou-

κακουργοῦντες, εἰ μήτις ὑπείη τὸ τῆς κακουργίας ῥεῦμα δίκη, καὶ νόμοις ἐμφράξων κατὰ πρανοῦς οὕτω φερόμενον· δεῖ γὰρ τὴν τῶν κακῶν ἀρχὴν καὶ τομῆς ἀρχὴν ποιεῖσθαι καὶ ἅμα ἐκλάμπειν τῆς γνώμης τὸ φαῦλον καὶ παραυτίκα τὸ τῆς εὐνομίας πῦρ ὑπονέμεσθαι τὰ φυόμενα.

13 Οὕτω καὶ γεωργὸς ἐκκαθαίρει τὸ λήϊον, ἔτι φυομένας τὰς ἀκάνθας ἐκριζῶν, πρὶν ἢ κατὰ γῆς ἐρριζῶσθαι καὶ χειρὸς ἁδροτέρας δεηθῆναι τὴν ἐκφοράν. Εἶδον ἐγὼ καὶ ἰατρὸν οὐκ ἀδόκιμον· ὁ δ᾽ ἅμα τι τῶν μελῶν ἔθνησκε καὶ τὸν σίδηρον αὐτὸς ἐπῆγε, συνθνήσκειν οὐκ ἐῶν τὰ λειπόμενα. Καὶ φυτουργός, εἰ κλάδον ὑπαίσθοιτο μαραινόμενον, τὸ πρὸς λύμην ἀφείλετο, δεδιὼς μὴ λάθοι τὸ κακὸν καὶ πρὸς τοὺς τῶν κλάδων ὑγιεστέρους ἐνσκήψαν καὶ ὅλον τὸ δένδρον αὐτίκα οἰχήσεται. Ἔστιν οὗ καὶ κυβερνήτης ὑφείλετό τι τῶν προτόνων καὶ τὰ ἱστία διέρρηξεν, εἰ τὸ πνεῦμα βιαιότερον ἐπεισφρήσειε καὶ καταδυομένην ἤδη τὴν ναῦν αὐτοῖς ἀνδράσιν ἐσώσατο.

14 Οὗ δὴ καὶ κακουργοῦντος, οὔκουν οὐδαμῶς ἀφεκτέον, εἰ μέλλοι τὸ λοιπὸν τῆς πόλεως σῴζεσθαι, ἀλλ᾽ ἐκκαθαρτέον τῆς τῶν ἐνοικούντων λύμης καὶ τοῦτο τὸ ἔμψυχον λήϊον· μὴ γάρ μοι μόνον χρησιμευέτω σίδηρος εἰς ἀναίρεσιν ἀκανθῶν, ἀλλὰ καὶ πρὸς αὐτῆς τῆς πόλεως ἀνακάθαρσιν.

15 Ἴδε μοι τὴν προὔχουσαν τῆς Ἑλλάδος πόλιν, τοὺς Λάκωνας. Παυσανίας, παυσάμενος λακωνίζειν, παρ᾽ αὐτοῖς ἔπιπτε καὶ ὁ τοὺς Μήδους καθελών, ὅτε τὰ Μήδων ἐφρόνησε, τὰ Μήδων ὑφίσταται. Τούτῳ φαρμάκῳ χρησαμένην οἶδα πρὸς θεραπείαν καὶ τὴν τῶν Ἀθηναίων πόλιν· παρεῖδον οἱ στρατηγοὶ τὸν ἐπὶ τοῖς πεπτωκόσι

ble, nor would a murderer or any other kind of wrongdoer hold back, without a just penalty to follow the flood of wrongdoing. For it is necessary to make the origin of the evils also the starting point for the excision, and, as soon as base intentions are revealed, immediately the fire of orderly governance must destroy the growing evils at their foundation.

In this way too a farmer clears out his field, uprooting the 13 thorny weeds while they are still growing, before they become firmly rooted in the earth and their removal requires a very strong hand. I have also seen a doctor of no small repute, who, when one of his own limbs was dying, applied the blade himself, thus preventing the rest of his body from dying along with it. And a gardener who observes a branch withering removes the corrupted part, fearing that the evil might spread to the healthier branches before he notices and the entire tree will immediately perish. Sometimes too if the wind should very violently sweep in, a helmsman removes one of the forestays, breaks down the masts, and saves the sinking ship along with its men.

When someone does wrong, we must in no way let it go, 14 if the rest of the city is to be saved; rather, this living field must also be cleared of the corruption that destroys its inhabitants. For let the blade be useful not only for the clearing of thorn bushes, if you will, but also for a cleansing of the city itself.

Look, if you will, at Sparta, the leading city of Greece. 15 Pausanias, having ceased to act like a Spartan, died at Sparta, and he who destroyed the Medes, when he began thinking like the Medes, suffered a punishment fit for Medes. I know that the city of Athens also used this drug as a cure. The generals disregarded the law applying to fallen comrades, and

νόμον καὶ ὁ δῆμος τῶν στρατηγῶν οὐκ ἐφείσατο, ἀλλ' οἷς οὐκ ἀνείλοντο τοὺς πεσόντας, δικαίως αὐτοὶ πρὸς τοῦ δήμου τὸ πεσεῖν ἐδυστύχησαν.

16 Τί δεῖ λέγειν Αἴγισθον ὡς μοιχὸν ἀναιρούμενον καὶ Παλαμήδην ὡς προδότην λιθολευστούμενον; Οὐκ ἐναριθμῶ τούτοις τὸν Σίσυφον, οὐ λέγω τὸν Τάνταλον, παρίημι τὸν Ἰξίονα, τὸν Τιτυόν, οὓς ὁ μῦθος ἐκόλασε, δέος ἡμῖν ἐντιθεὶς καὶ μετὰ τὴν ἐνθένδε ἀνάλυσιν καὶ τοῦ κακουργεῖν ὥσπερ ἐντεῦθεν ἐκκρούων.

17 Νοῦν δ' ἐχόντων, ἂν εἴη καὶ τὸν σοφὸν Εὐριπίδην ἄγασθαι, οὐ δεινὸν εἶναι τὸ τοὺς εἰργασμένους παθεῖν ψηφισάμενον. Ἐπαινετέος τῆς σοφίας καὶ Πυθαγόρας· εἰ γὰρ ἅ, φησίν, εἴργασται πείσεται, τοῦτ' ἂν εἴη νόμων θεσμὸς καὶ δίκης ἀντιταλάντωσις. Τί μὴ θαυμάζω κἀκεῖνον τὸν Λάκωνα, ὃς οὐ παντάπασι τὴν πονηρίαν ἀπεδοκίμασεν, ἀλλὰ πρός γε τοὺς πονηροὺς καὶ ταύτην ἔκρινεν εἶναι τῶν ὅπλων τὸ χρησιμώτατον;

18 Περιαιρετέον οὖν ἂν εἴη τῶν πόλεων ἅπαν ὅσον κακοῦργον καὶ τὸν ποιητὴν ἐπαινετέον τῆς γνώμης, οἷς οὕτω κακίαν δεόντως ἐκόλασεν.

the people did not spare the generals, but since the generals did not pick up the fallen, they themselves justly suffered the fate of falling at the hands of the people.

Why need I mention Aegisthus, who was executed as an 16 adulterer, and Palamedes, who was stoned as a traitor? I do not number among these men Sisyphus; I do not mention Tantalus; I pass over Ixion and Tityus, whom myth has punished, instilling fear in us, and because of the destruction that occurred in their situations, consequently driving us away from wrongdoing.

But sensible men might also cherish the wise Euripides, 17 who opined that it is not terrible for those who have done something wrong to suffer. Pythagoras should also be praised for his wisdom, for he says that if someone suffers the very wrongs he has done, this would be a law of laws and a weighing out of justice. Why should I not marvel also at that Spartan Lycurgus, who did not absolutely reject wickedness, but judged that against the wicked, at any rate, wickedness was the most useful of weapons?

So, then, one must remove every act of wrongdoing from 18 the cities and praise the poet for his maxim, because he so fittingly punished evil.

REFUTATION

Ὅτι οὐκ εἰκότα τὰ κατὰ τὴν Ἀταλάντην

Οὐ ζηλῶ τοῦ ψεύδους τοὺς ποιητάς, εἰ καὶ τῆς σοφίας τεθαύμακα· οἷς γὰρ οὕτω καλῷ χρήματι μὴ πρὸς ἀλήθειαν ἀπεχρήσαντο, οὐ μᾶλλον ἂν εἶεν ἄξιοι θαύματος, ἢ κακῶς ἀκούειν δίκαιοι. Ἐχρῆν γὰρ καὶ λόγους ὑποβαλέσθαι πρέποντας σοφίᾳ καὶ Μούσαις, εἰ Μουσῶν ὡς ἀληθῶς εἶχον ἐπίπνοιαν καὶ ἄσθμα δαιμόνιον. Οἱ δὲ τὰ μὲν ἔξω καὶ δὴ Μουσῶν ἄξιοι—κἂν ἴδῃς φράσιν καὶ σχῆμα καὶ τερατείαν καὶ τὴν ἄλλην τῆς ἀκοῆς ἐπήρειαν, φαίης ἂν αὐτὰς δοκεῖν ᾄδειν τὰς Μούσας καὶ τὴν γλῶτταν αὐτοῦ γε Ἀπόλλωνος οὐκ ἀποψηφιεῖ—τὰ δ᾽ ἔνδον οὕτως εἰσὶ φαῦλοι καὶ Θεοῦ μηδ᾽ ἴχνος ἐπιφερόμενοι, ὥσθ᾽ ἡ μὲν γλῶττα αὐτοῖς ὑψηλὴ καὶ περιηχὴς καὶ ὡς ἀπ᾽ οὐρανοῦ φέρεται, τὴν δὲ διάνοιαν ἀναπτύξας εἴποις ἂν μὴ ὅτι τῶν ἐν οὐρανῷ διαιτωμένων θεῶν, ἀλλ᾽ οὐδ᾽ αὐτῶν ἀνθρώπων τῶν γε μετριωτέρων εἶναι τούτους τοὺς λόγους.

2 Αὐτίκα γὰρ περὶ τῆς Οἰνέως Ἀταλάντης ἡλίκον αὐτοῖς ἡ σοφία τῆς ἀληθείας ἐξέπεσε! Γυναῖκα μὲν γὰρ πλάττουσι,

I

That the story of Atalanta is implausible

I do not esteem the poets for their falsehood, even if I admire their wisdom. For since they have abused such a fine talent and not employed it in the pursuit of truth, they would be less worthy of admiration than deserving of criticism. For they ought to have produced words befitting wisdom and the Muses, if they truly had the inspiration and divine breath of the Muses. But while some seem worthy of the Muses on the exterior—and if you see their style of expression, their bearing, their fanciful storytelling, and the rest of their insults to the ear, you would say that the Muses themselves seem to be singing, and you will not absolve the tongue of Apollo himself from responsibility—on the inside these men are so worthless and bear so little trace of God that although their speech is lofty, resounding, and, as it were, descended from heaven, once you have explicated their meaning, you would say not only that these words are not those of the gods who live in heaven, but also that they are not even those of humans themselves, or at least not the more temperate humans.

For example, concerning Atalanta, daughter of Oeneus, 2 see how far their "wisdom" has fallen short of the truth! For

τὰ δὲ τῆς γυναικὸς ἀφαιροῦνται καὶ θήλειαν μὲν εἶναι ξυγχωροῦσι, πρὸς δὲ τὰ τῶν ἀρρένων ἐπαίρουσι.

3   Καὶ τί φασιν οἱ σοφοὶ καὶ Μουσῶν ἔπιπνοι; Καὶ πόθεν ἡμῖν τὰ τῆς ἀπιστίας; Ἀταλάντη γεγένηται μὲν Οἰνέως, ἑλομένη δὲ παρθενεύειν, πρὸς ἀνδρείαν ἐτρέφετο· καὶ τὰ περὶ θήραν ἠσκεῖτο καὶ τόξον ἔτεινε καὶ ζῆλον εἶχεν Ἀρτέμιδος. Ἀλλ' ἧκεν ὥρα γάμου καὶ δρόμον ἐτίθει τοῖς ἐρασταῖς καὶ τῷ νικήσαντι ἑαυτὴν ἐδίδου τὸ ἄθλον. Ἐκάλει πολλοὺς ἐπὶ τὸν ἀγῶνα τὸ κάλλος, ἀλλ' ἀπράκτους αὖθις ἠφίει τὸ τάχος. Ἀλλ' ἦν Ἱππομένης καὶ τοῦ δρόμου καὶ τοῦ κάλλους ἡττώμενος, καὶ τοῖς ποσὶ μὴ θαρρῶν, χρυσοῖς μήλοις τὴν νίκην σοφίζεται. Ἐπεὶ δὲ καὶ εἶχεν ἄμφω τὸ στάδιον, ὁ μὲν ἤρχετο τοῦ σοφίσματος καὶ τῶν μήλων ἠφίει, ἡ δέ, μηδὲν ὑπιδομένη, ξυνέλεγε· καὶ ὁ μὲν προέβαινεν, ἡ δὲ περὶ τὴν ξυλλογὴν ἀπελείπετο· καὶ οὕτως Ἱππομένης σοφίᾳ μᾶλλον ἢ τάχει τῶν τῆς Ἀταλάντης ἔτυχε γάμων.

4   Τούτοις ἐκεῖνοι τὰς Μούσας ἐπιφημίζουσι, τούτοις αὐτὸς οὐ πείθομαι. Εἰ γυναικείαν Ἀταλάντη φύσιν εἶχεν, ἐκ τῆς τροφῆς ἐπιγνώσομαι· εἰ παρθενεύειν εἵλετο, καὶ θαλαμευομένην ὄψομαι. Εἰ δὲ τὰ γυναικῶν οὐκ ἐτρέφετο, καὶ τὸ γένος παρήλλαττε· βεβαιοῖ γὰρ τὸ γένος ἡ τροφὴ καὶ διαφόροις γένεσιν αἱ τροφαὶ παραπλησίως διάφοροι. Πατέρα μοι λέγεις Ἀταλάντης Οἰνέα καὶ δέχομαι. Παρθένον ὑποτίθης καὶ πείθομαι. Ἀπόδος καὶ τροφὴν παρθένοις προσήκουσαν. Ὡς νῦν γε πλάττεις, φύσιν μὲν

they make her out to be a woman, but they rob her of the characteristics of a woman, and although they agree that she is a female, they praise her for her masculinity.

And what do they say, these men who are wise and in- 3 spired by the Muses? And why do we not believe them? Atalanta was born to Oeneus, and although she chose to remain a virgin, she was raised to be manly. She trained in hunting, shot the bow, and emulated Artemis. But when the time for marriage came, she set up a running race for her suitors and offered herself as the prize to the victor. Her beauty summoned many to the contest, but her speed sent them away again unsuccessful. But Hippomenes was discomfited by both the race and her beauty, and lacking confidence in his feet, he devised a trick to win his victory with golden apples. And when the two contestants started the race, he began his trick: he would throw out the apples, and she, suspecting nothing, would gather them up; he would pull ahead, while she fell behind as she gathered them. And in this way Hippomenes won his marriage to Atalanta by cleverness rather than by speed.

The poets attribute these stories to the Muses, but I my- 4 self do not believe them. If Atalanta had a womanly nature, I should recognize it from her upbringing. If she chose to remain a virgin, then I should see her confined to the women's quarters. But if she was not raised in the ways of women, then she also transposed her gender. For one's upbringing confirms one's gender, and for the different genders the ways of upbringing are correspondingly different. You tell me that Atalanta's father is Oeneus, and I accept that. You posit that she is a girl, and I believe you. Then you should also restore to her an upbringing befitting a girl. As you are

θήλειαν, τρόπον δὲ ἄρρενα, καὶ τὸ τῆς τροφῆς παράδοξον ἀμφίβολον ποιεῖται τὴν γένεσιν· σκοπητέον γὰρ τίνες γυναιξὶν αἱ τροφαὶ καὶ ὅπως αἰδοῦς ἔχουσι, καὶ τίς Ἀταλάντης ὁ τρόπος καὶ ὅπως τὰ τῆς τροφῆς παραλλάττονται.

5　Οὐκοῦν, ἅμα τίκτεται βρέφος, γυνὴ καὶ προῆλθεν εἰς φῶς ἅμα καὶ θάλαμον, καὶ μετὰ τὴν τεκοῦσαν νηδὺν οὐδὲν οἶδε πλέον θαλάμου γυνή. Ἐπὶ τούτοις ὑπὸ ταῖς τῆς μητρὸς χερσὶν ἐκπαιδεύεται τὰ παρθενικά· αἰδεῖται μέχρι καὶ βλέμματος· εἰς ἀρρένων ὄψιν οὐκ ἔρχεται. Ἐπὶ τοσοῦτον ἦλθεν αἰδοῦς τὸ τῶν παρθένων χρῆμα· μόνης οἶδε παρθενίας ἐξέχεσθαι· ὑπὸ τῇ ταλασίᾳ διαπονεῖται· περὶ τὴν γυναικωνῖτιν οἰκουρεῖ· ταῖς θεραπαινίσι συνεξετάζεται. Ταῦτα γυναικὸς σωφρονούσης ἔργα, ταῦτα παρθένων παιδεύματα.

6　Τὴν δέ γε τῶν ποιητῶν Ἀταλάντην ταύτην τόξον εἶχε καὶ λόφοι καὶ θῆραι καί, θῆλυς οὖσα, τὴν φύσιν ἠνδρίζετο. Ἦπου καὶ περὶ τοξικὴν ἤριζε καὶ τὸ παρθενικὸν οὐκ ᾐσχύνετο, ὡς ἔγωγε οὐχ ὁρῶ, πῶς ἄν τις ταῦτα καὶ πείθοιτο. Κἂν γὰρ τὴν κόρην ἔχειν οὕτω φύσεως δώσομεν, ἀλλ᾽ ἥ γε μήτηρ—εἰ μὴ τὴν κλῆσιν ἐψεύδετο—πῶς ἂν ἀφῆκεν ἔξω τοῦ θαλάμου καὶ προσαπέλυσε τῆς χειρός, ἣν μέχρι καὶ γάμων ἔδει παιδαγωγεῖν; Κἂν ἡ μήτηρ τοῦτο τὸ μέρος οὐκ ἐφρόντισε τῆς παιδός, ἀλλά γε πρὸς τοῦ πατρὸς ἤκουσεν ἄν, ὁπόσα πρὸς Διὸς Ἀφροδίτη, "Ὦ τέκνον, οὔτι τοι πολεμήϊα ἔργα δέδοται," ἔπειτα θήλεια μὲν θεὸς πολέμου

making her out to be now, female in nature, but male in behavior, then also her paradoxical upbringing throws her gender into doubt. Just consider what ways of upbringing women have and how these entail modesty, and what the behavior of Atalanta is and how the elements of her upbringing are transposed.

As soon as a female infant is born, she is a woman; she   5
sees the light of day and simultaneously enters the women's quarters, and after her mother's womb a woman knows nothing beyond these quarters. And so she is trained by her mother's hands in virginal conduct. She is shy and this extends even to her glance. She does not come within sight of males. To such a height of modesty do virgins come. She knows how to cling to maidenhood alone. She labors at spinning wool. She does the housekeeping in the women's quarters. She is reckoned as one of the maidservants. These are the deeds of the chaste woman, these the lessons learned by young girls.

But a bow and hills and hunting occupied this Atalanta of   6
the poets and, although she was female, she had a manly nature. I suppose she both competed in archery and was not ashamed of her maidenhood—no, for my part I do not see how anyone would believe this. For even if we grant that the girl was like that by nature, surely how would her mother—if she did not give the lie to that name—have let her outside the women's quarters and also have released her from her hand, the girl whom she was supposed to train right up to her wedding day? Even if her mother took no thought for her daughter in this respect, still she would have heard from her father what Aphrodite heard from Zeus, *"My child, the deeds of war are not granted to you,"* and thereafter the female

φέρει τὰ δεύτερα καὶ θνητὴν οὐκ ἤνεγκε δεξαμένη πληγήν.

7   Ἀταλάντη δ᾽ ἐπεβάλλετο πολεμεῖν καὶ θνητὴ θήλεια
μεῖζον ἴσχυσεν Ἀφροδίτης· μὴ γὰρ δὴ τὴν θήραν νομιστέον
ἀπόλεμον, ἀλλ᾽ εἰσὶ θῆρες ὁπλιτῶν φοβερώτεροι. Αὐτίκα
πρὸς ἕνα θῆρα μόλις Αἰτωλῶν πόλεις ὅλαι διήρκεσαν. Κἂν
θηρατικὴν εἶναι τὴν κόρην δοίη τις, ἀλλά γε τὸ καλὴν
εἶναι πάντως ὑφείλετο. Ἀγρότις ἦν, τὰ πολλὰ ἐν ὄρεσι
διέτριβεν, ἐφ᾽ ὑψηλῶν τῶν λόφων διῆγεν, ὑφ᾽ ἡλίου ἐβάλλετο, τὸ δ᾽ ἄρα καὶ μελαίνει τὴν ὥραν καὶ τὸ πολὺ τοῦ
κάλλους ἂν ἴσως παρείλετο. Καὶ τὸ τῶν Αἰθιόπων γένος
ἡλίου ἔργον ἂν εἴη βάλλοντος ἄκρατα καὶ τῶν γυναικῶν
λευκοτέρας ἄν τις ἴδῃ τὰς ἀστικὰς ἤπερ τὰς ὀριτρεφομένας,
τὰς ἐν ἀγροῖς.

8   Ἀλλ᾽ ἔστω καλὴ μὲν ὡς κόρη, πολεμικὴ δὲ ὡς ἀνήρ.
Πόθεν δὲ καὶ ταχυτῆτος ποδῶν, τὸ γυναικῶν ἀλλοτριώ-
τατον, εὕρατο; Εἰ γὰρ ὅτι καλὴ διὰ τοῦτο καὶ τοὺς πόδας
πτηνούς, ὥρα καὶ πᾶσαν εὐπρεπῆ κόρην εἰς τάχος ὑπερ-
φέρειν τῶν ἄλλων. Εἰ δὲ τῷ κάλλει καὶ ταχυτὴς ἕψεται, καὶ
ταχὺς ἅπας ἂν εἴη τὴν ὄψιν καλός. Εἰ δὲ πρὸς ἀνδρείαν
τίθης καὶ τοῦτο, ἀλλ᾽ οὐκ ἀνδρείᾳ τὸ τάχος συνέζευκται·
πολλοὶ γὰρ τοὺς μὲν πόδας κοῦφοι, τὰς δὲ χεῖρας οὐ
θαυμαστοί. Κἂν γοῦν τὰ γυναικῶν ἐβιάζετο, ἀλλ᾽ εἰς ἀνδρὸς ἀρετὴν οὐκ ἂν τοὺς ἄνδρας ὑπερεβάλλετο.

9   Παρθένος ἠγωνίζετο καὶ ἀνὴρ ἀπελείπετο· ἀνδρῶν
ἐκράτει γυνὴ καὶ πρὸς γυναικὸς ἄνδρες ἠλέγχοντο. Ὅλως
δὲ τίνα λόγον εἶχεν ὁ τοῦ τάχους ἀγών; Εἰ μὲν ἦλθεν εἰς

god played a secondary role in the war and did not endure receiving a blow like a mortal.

But Atalanta devoted herself to war, and though a mortal 7 woman she was stronger than Aphrodite. For one should not suppose that hunting is unwarlike; rather, wild beasts are more fearsome than armed soldiers. For example, entire cities of Aetolians were scarcely a match for one beast. Even if someone should grant that the girl was skilled at hunting, still she could not have been beautiful. She was a hunter; she spent most of her life in the mountains; she passed her time on lofty hills; and she was continually struck by the sun's rays, which darken youthful good looks and perhaps would have seriously diminished her beauty. The Ethiopian race is the result of the sun's rays striking people excessively, and one sees that women from the city are whiter than the mountain-bred women in the countryside.

But let us grant that she was beautiful, like a girl, and a 8 warrior, like a man. From where did she get the swiftness of her feet, the attribute most alien to women? For if because she was beautiful she therefore also had winged feet, then of course every good-looking girl should surpass the rest in speed. But if speed accompanies beauty, then every swift man would also be beautiful in appearance. You might attribute this too to manliness, but still speed does not correspond to manliness, for many men are nimble-footed but unremarkable in their hands. And so even if she utterly ignored the ways of women, still she would not outdo the men in a man's area of excellence.

A girl competed, and a man was left behind; a woman 9 mastered men, and men were tested and found wanting by a woman. What reason was there in fact for the contest of

ἔρωτα, τί μὴ τὸν ἐρώμενον ἤγετο; Εἰ δ᾽ οὔπω τὴν ψυχὴν ἐξ ἔρωτος ἔπαθε, τί μὴ τὸ παρθενεύειν ἐφύλαττεν; Εἴτε τις ἐρῶσαν ταύτην ὑπόθοιτο, εἴτε μὴ ξυγχωροίη τὸ πάθος, οὐδένα λόγον εἶχεν ἡ πρόκλησις, οὐδ᾽ ἐχρῆν ἀγωνίζεσθαι.

10 Ἀλλ᾽ ἴδωμεν, εἰ δοκεῖ καὶ τὸ κήρυγμα. Κοινὸν ἐκήρυξε τὸν ἀγῶνα, οὐκ ἀπέκλεισεν οὐδενὶ τὸ στάδιον, πᾶσιν ἀνεπέτασε τὸ γυμνάσιον. Κἂν φαῦλος τὴν ὄψιν ὑπερβάληται, κἂν ἐνδεὴς ἀπὸ τύχης, κἂν οὐχ ὑψηλὸς ἀπὸ γένους; Μετὰ τὴν νίκην τὸ ἆθλον ἀποίσεται καίτοι γυναικὶ μεῖζον τούτων εἰς ὄνειδος. Ἀλλ᾽ οὐχὶ κοινόν, οὐδὲ πρὸς πάντας τὸν ἆθλον ἀνείλετο. Καὶ τίνα ταχυτῆτος εἶχε δόξαν τὸ μὴ πάντας ἐπίσης θαρρεῖν, ἀλλὰ τὸν μὲν ὡς νωθρὸν ὑποπτεύειν καὶ δέχεσθαι, τὸν δὲ τὸ τάχος ὑφορᾶσθαι καὶ τὸν ἀνταγωνιστὴν μὴ προσίεσθαι;

11 Τίς δ᾽ οὐκ ἂν τὴν κόρην ὑπώπτευσε, εἰ τὴν προτέραν τροφὴν ἐλογίσατο; Ἀνδράσι συνδιῆγε καὶ τὸ χρῆμα παρθενίᾳ πολέμιον. Ἅμα τις εἶδε παρθένον, καὶ πρὸς τὸ κάλλος ὅλους ἀφῆκε τοὺς ὀφθαλμοὺς καὶ τὸ ἐντεῦθεν λόγος καὶ πεῖρα καὶ δῶρα πρὸς Ἀφροδίτην. Ἔστιν οὗ καὶ βίαν ἔρως ἐπήγειρε. Τὸ γοῦν ἐπὶ τῇ τροφῇ πρὸς ἀνδρῶν ὁμιλίαν τοῖς ἐρασταῖς διεβέβλητο καὶ παρθένος οὐκ ἦν ἀνενδοίαστος. Εἰ δ᾽ οὐκ ἔχει παρθενίαν, ὁ γάμος ἀβέβαιος· εἰ δ᾽ ἦν τῇ κόρῃ τὸ παρθενεύειν ἀμφίβολον, πολλοὺς ἂν οὐκ εἶχε τοὺς ἐραστάς. Εἰ δ᾽ οὐκ εἰς πλῆθος ἐπαφῆκε τὸν ἔρωτα, τί λοιπὸν ἔδει κηρύγματος;

speed? If she fell in love, why did she not marry her lover? If she did not yet feel the passion of love in her heart, why did she not preserve her maidenhood? Whether one supposes that she was in love or does not concede that she felt passion, there was no reason for the challenge, and she should not have competed.

But let us see if even the proclamation seems reasonable. 10 Let us suppose that she proclaimed a public contest, that she did not bar anyone from the racetrack, and that she opened the doors of the gymnasium to all. What if a man of base appearance, or an indigent man, or a man of low birth should beat her? After the victory he would carry off the prize, and yet that is an even greater insult to a woman than this. Let us then suppose that the contest she took on was not public and not for everyone. What fame on account of her speed would then arise if she was not equally confident against everyone, but rather, if she suspected someone was slow, she welcomed him, while, if she was wary of another because of his speed, she did not admit him as a competitor?

Who would not have been suspicious of the girl, if he 11 took into account her prior upbringing? She spent time with men, and this lifestyle is hostile to virginity. For as soon as one sees a girl, he casts his eyes entirely upon her beauty, and from that point on there is talking and wooing and love gifts; sometimes love even excites violence. Thus as far as her upbringing was concerned, she had been slandered to the suitors for having been in the company of men, and her virginity was not unquestionable. If she did not have her virginity, marriage was unlikely. If the girl's virginity had been in doubt, she would not have had many suitors. If she had not made her love available to a large number of men, what need was there for a proclamation?

12 Ἀλλὰ δεδόσθω καὶ πλῆθος ἐραστῶν καὶ κήρυκες δρόμου καὶ γυναικὸς νίκη καὶ ὕβρις ἀνδρῶν. Ὁ δὲ σοφὸς Ἱππομένης πόθεν εἰς νοῦν ἔλαβε τὸ μηχάνημα; Καὶ πῶς ἀπὸ χρυσοῦ τὴν ὀπώραν ἐσκεύαζεν; Εἰ χρυσῷ τὴν κόρην ἀπατήσειν ἐνόμισε, διατί μὴ τὸν χρυσὸν ὡς ἕδνα ἐκόμισεν; Εἰ δέ, χρυσὸν διδούς, οὐκ ἔπειθε, πῶς ἡ κόρη μετὰ τῆς ἀπάτης ἐδέχετο, ἐξὸν καὶ πλείω τὰ ἕδνα λαβεῖν καὶ μὴ προσαπολαβεῖν ἧτταν καὶ γνώμης δόξαν οὐ σταθηρᾶς; Πότερον δὲ πλείω τὰ μῆλα ὁ σοφιστὴς ἐκεῖνος, εἴτουν ἐραστής, ἐπεφέρετο; Καὶ πῶς ἦν ἀγωνίσασθαι τοσοῦτο βάρος ἐπιφορτισάμενον, ὅπου καὶ τὰ περιττὰ τῶν χιτωνίων ἐχρῆν ἀποδύσασθαι; Εἰ δὲ μικρὸν ἦν εἰς ἀριθμὸν τὸ σόφισμα, βραχὺν ἂν ἡ κόρη χρόνον εἰς συλλογὴν ἀπησχόλητο καὶ τὸν χρυσὸν ἂν ἐκεῖνος προσαπωλωλέκει, μηδὲν τῆς σοφίας προσαπονάμενος.

13 Τί δὲ προήλατο τὴν ἀρχὴν καὶ τῆς κόρης μᾶλλον εἰς δρόμον προέκοπτε καὶ τί λοιπὸν ἐδεῖτο τῶν μήλων καὶ τὴν νίκην ὑπέκλεπτεν, εἰ τοῖς ποσὶν εἶχε κρατεῖν καὶ δίχα σοφίσματος; Ἀλλ' ἐξ αὐτῆς βαλβίδος, τὸ τάχος λειπόμενος, ἐπὶ τὸ σόφισμα ἔβλεψε καὶ παρὰ τὴν ἀρχὴν ἡ κόρη προέβαινε. Καὶ πῶς εἶδε τὰ μῆλα ῥιπτούμενα; Συλλέγειν οὐκ ἦν, εἰ μὴ βλέπειν εἶχε βαλλόμενα· οὐ γὰρ δήπου πάντως τὴν κόρην ἠκροβολίζετο.

14 Ταῦτα καὶ λέγειν οὐκ ἀληθῆ καὶ πιστεύειν οὐ δίκαια· τό τε γὰρ ψευδολογεῖν οὐκ ἐπαινετὸν καὶ τὸ πάντα πείθεσθαι πρὸς ἀνδρὸς οὐκ ἔχοντος νοῦν.

But let us grant the crowd of suitors, the heralds of the 12
race, the victory of a woman, and the humiliation of men.
Where did the clever Hippomenes get the idea for his trick?
And how did he make the fruit from gold? If he thought that
he would deceive the girl with gold, why did he not bring the
gold as a wedding gift? But if, after giving her the gold, he
did not persuade her, how did the girl accept him along with
the deceit, since she could have gotten more gifts without
also accepting defeat and acquiring a reputation for being
fickle? And did that clever trickster—that is to say, lover—
bring more apples? Then how was he able to compete after
loading himself down with so much extra weight, when he
should have removed even any unnecessary clothing? If the
trick involved a small number of apples, the girl would then
have been detained for only a short time in gathering them,
and he would have lost the gold as well, having derived no
benefit from his trickery.

And how did he at first take the lead and get ahead of the 13
girl on the racecourse, and why then did he need the apples
to steal the victory, if he was able to win with his feet and
without a trick? Rather, from the very starting line, lacking
in speed, he looked to trickery, and from the very beginning
the girl was ahead of him. Then how did she know that the
apples were being tossed? She could not pick them up, unless she could see them being thrown; surely he did not hurl
missiles at the girl from behind.

These things are both untrue to say and unjust to believe. 14
For telling lies is not praiseworthy, and only a man with no
sense believes everything.

CONFIRMATION

I

Ὅτι εἰκότα τὰ κατὰ τὴν Ἀταλάντην

Εἰ μᾶλλον τῶν ἄλλων ἀνθρώποις γε οὖσι περιποιητέον ἀλήθειαν, πρὸ τῶν ἄλλων αὐτὴν ἐπαινετέον τὴν ποίησιν. Μούσαις μὲν γὰρ ἐπιπνεῖται, Μουσῶν δὲ ἄξια φθέγγεται, καὶ γλώττῃ θνητῇ τὰ θεῶν εἰς ἡμᾶς τὸ τῶν ποιητῶν γένος μετοχετεύει καί, Μουσῶν γενόμενοι κάτοχοι, τὰ Μουσῶν ἀναφαίνουσι. Θεῶν δὲ πάντων καὶ Μουσῶν αὐτῶν τἀληθῆ λέγειν, οἷς δὲ χρῶσι τὰ Μουσῶν ποιηταί, καὶ τὸ πρὸς ἀλήθειαν ᾄδειν ἐφέλκονται.

2   Ἀλλ᾽ ὅμως εἰσί τινες, οἳ πρὸς τοσοῦτο μανίας ἥκουσιν, ὡς προσχήματι μὲν κατηγορεῖν τῶν ποιητῶν, τῇ δ᾽ ἀληθείᾳ Μουσῶν καί, τὸ τῆς ποιήσεως προσωπεῖον περιρρηγνύντες, λελήθασιν, εἰς αὐτὰς τὰς ὑποκρινομένας θεὰς τὴν ὕβριν προσάγοντες. Τῆς οὖν τούτων γλώττης καὶ τῆς πρὸς πάντα δυσπιστίας καὶ Ἀταλάντη μετὰ Μουσῶν ἀπώνατο· οὐ γάρ φησι τοιαύτην γεγενῆσθαι τὴν Οἰνέως, οἵαν ἡ ποίησις βούλεται, ἀλλ᾽ εἶναι πάντα μῦθον καὶ πλάσματα, οὕτως ἁπλᾶ ῥήματα. Οὐ περιοπτέον οὖν ἂν εἴη καὶ ποιητὰς κατηγορουμένους καὶ Μούσας περιυβριζομένας, ἀλλ᾽ ὑπερμαχητέον τῆς ἀληθείας ὡς οἷόν τε.

I

That the story of Atalanta is plausible

If we, being human, must be concerned with the truth above all, then we must indeed praise poetry above all. For poetry is inspired by the Muses and utters words worthy of the Muses; by human language the race of the poets channels to us what comes from the gods, and being possessed by the Muses, they bring to light what comes from the Muses. It is typical of all the gods and especially the Muses to speak the truth, and since poets proclaim what comes from the Muses, they are also compelled to sing truthfully.

But nevertheless there are some who have reached such ₂ a point of insanity that under the pretext of accusing the poets they actually accuse the Muses, and having stripped away the mask of poetry, they surreptitiously insult the very goddesses whom the mask represents. And so Atalanta, together with the Muses, has endured the verbal abuse and total disbelief of these men. For a critic denies that the daughter of Oeneus was such a girl as poetry suggests; rather, he says that she is a complete myth and a fabrication, mere words. One should therefore not ignore poets who are being accused and Muses who are being grossly abused; rather, one must fight for the truth as well as one can.

3   Τί γὰρ ἄπιστον, εἰ πατὴρ ἤκουσεν Ἀταλάντης Οἰνεύς, τοῦ γάμου ταύτην ἔχοντος φύσιν; Εἰ δὲ καὶ κάλλος εἶχεν ἡ παῖς; Θεῶν ἦν ἀπόγονος καὶ θειοτέραν εἶχε μορφήν, καὶ τὴν τοῦ προσώπου ὀπώραν ἔβαλλε μὲν πυρωδέστερον ἥλιος, ὁπότε φοιτῴη πρὸς θήραν, οὐκ ἐπέφλεγε δὲ ὅτι καὶ Ἀχιλλεὺς περί που τὸ Πήλιον ἐθήρα μέν, τὸ δέ γε τῆς ὄψεως ἄνθος οὐδὲν ἧττον αὖθις ἐπέλαμπεν.

4   Ἀλλὰ πρὸς ἀνδρείαν ἐτρέφετο καί, τὴν οἰκουρὸν ἀπολιποῦσα τροφήν, τὰ παρὰ φύσιν ἠλαζονεύετο. Καὶ τί κατηγόρημα φύσεως, εἰ καὶ πρὸς γυναῖκά ποτε γέγονεν ἀνδρείας φιλότιμος; Πρῶτον μὲν γὰρ οὐ πανταχῇ τὸ θῆλυ τοῦ γένους τότε εἰς ῥώμην ἦκον ἀποδοκιμαστέον. Κἂν εἰς τοὺς θῆρας ἐξιχνεύσῃς καὶ θήλειαν ὄψει δύσμαχον, καὶ μᾶλλον, εἰ τύχοι, θαρρήσεις τοὺς ἄρρενας. Ἔπειτα, εἰ τοῖς ἀνθρώποις ὁ πρὸς τὰ θηρία δέδοται πόλεμος, εἴη ἂν καὶ τὴν Οἰνέως οὖσαν ἄνθρωπον τὰ πρὸς θήραν ἀσκήσασθαι.

5   Εἰ δὲ τῆς ἀνδρείας τὸ γυναικεῖον φῦλον ἀπέκλεισας, ὅρα καὶ τῶν ἀνδρῶν μηδένα λέγειν ἀπόλεμον· εἰ δ᾽ ἔστιν οὗ καὶ τὸ ἄρρεν εἰς ἀνδρείαν ἐμέμψω, καὶ τὸ θῆλύ ποτε πρὸς ἀνδρείαν θαύμασαι. Εἰ μὲν γὰρ ἁπάσας γυναῖκας ἡ ποίησις ὥπλισεν, εἶχεν ἂν λόγον δυσπιστεῖν τὸ παράλογον· εἰ δὲ τὸ χρῆμα σπάνιον, οὐκ ἄπιστα τὰ τοῦ θαύματος.

6   Ἀκούεις δὲ καὶ τὰς Ἀμαζόνας γυναῖκας, ὅλον ἔθνος, ὅπως ἔργον εἶχον τὸν πόλεμον καί, ἄνδρας ὄντας, οὐκ

For why is it unbelievable if Oeneus was called Atalanta's ₃ father, considering the nature of her marriage? And why is it unbelievable if the girl was beautiful too? She was descended from the gods and her appearance was quite divine. The sun's fiery rays did strike the youthful beauty of her face more fiercely when she roamed around hunting, but they did not burn her, because Achilles too hunted in the region of Mount Pelion, and still the bloom of his beauty shone no less brightly afterward.

But, the critic says, she was raised to be manly and, reject- ₄ ing an upbringing at home, she boasted of what was unnatural behavior. And why is it an accusation against nature, if the pursuit of manliness was ever desirable for a woman too? For, first of all, one must not completely reject the idea of the female of the species being strong in those days. If you search even among wild animals, you will see that the female is also hard to fight, and it may be that you will be more courageous against the males. Second, if humans have been given the ability to fight wild animals, it would also be possible for the daughter of Oeneus, being human, to go hunting.

If you exclude the female gender from manliness, make ₅ sure that you also call no man unwarlike. But if you ever faulted the male for his lack of manliness, make sure that you occasionally admire the female for her manliness as well. For if poetry turned all women into soldiers, it would be reasonable to mistrust this unreasonable depiction, but if the phenomenon is rare, the fact that it is surprising does not make it unbelievable.

You also hear how the Amazon women, an entire nation, ₆ had war as their occupation and did not fear the Greeks

ἐδεδίεσαν Ἕλληνας, οὓς οἱ περὶ Τροίαν, ἄνδρες ὄντες, οὐκ
ἔφερον. Πενθεσίλεια δὲ καὶ τὴν Ἀχιλλέως μελίαν ἐπιοῦσαν
οὐκ ἔτρεσε καὶ ὁ ἥρως τὴν ἀπὸ γυναικὸς μάχην μᾶλλον
ὑπώπτευσεν Ἕκτορος. Εἰ δ᾽ ἐκείνας τίθης ἐξ Ἄρεος, καὶ
τὴν Ἀταλάντην ἐκ Διὸς ἐγώ, πρὸς ὃν τὸ γένος ἀνέφερεν.
Οὐ δὴ πατέρα μὲν λογιστέον τὸν Ἄρην φιλότιμον, τὸν δὲ
Δία πρόγονον ἀφιλοτιμότερον θετέον τοῦ Ἄρεος.

7   Ἥρως ἦν ὁ πατήρ, τὸ δὲ τῶν ἡρώων γένος οἶσθα ὡς
ἔφθασε πρὸς αὐτὸ τὸ τῆς ἀνδρείας ἔσχατον. Εἰ γοῦν
Ἀταλάντη καὶ πλέον τι παρὰ τὰς ἄλλας ἴσχυσε, τοῦ πατρὸς
ἦν ἡ παῖς κατὰ τὴν παροιμίαν, καὶ τοῖς ἔργοις ἐδήλου τὸν
φύσαντα. Ἀνδρῶν ἐκράτει πατὴρ καὶ παῖς παρὰ τὰς ἄλλας
ἠνδρίζετο, εἰ δ᾽ ὁ πατὴρ οὐκ ἐδίδου τῷ θαλάμῳ τὴν παῖδα
καὶ πρὸς θήραν ἔχειν ἐπέτρεπε, Δία πρόγονον ἐμιμήσατο
καὶ πρὸς τὸν τῆς ἐκείνου παιδὸς ζῆλον Ἀθηνᾶς καὶ αὐτὸς
τὴν παῖδα ὥπλιζεν. Οὔτε δὲ Ζεὺς Ἀθηνᾶν τὸ "οὔτι σοι,
τέκνον, πολεμήϊα ἔργα δέδοται" προσαπέσκωψεν, οὔθ᾽ ὁ
τοῦ Διὸς Οἰνεὺς ἀνδριζομένην τὴν παῖδα ἐπέπληξε.

8   Μὴ θαυμάσῃς, εἰ τὴν παῖδα ὄρεσι καὶ λόφοις ἐπίστευσεν,
οὐδὲ γὰρ ἤδη καὶ παρῆκεν ἀπαιδαγώγητον, ἀλλ᾽ ὡς μὲν
ἀρρενωπὸν τὴν ἀνδρείαν εἰς θήραν ἐστέλλετο, ὡς δὲ
χαροπὸν τὴν ὄψιν παιδαγωγοῖς ἐφυλάττετο· οὐ γὰρ δήπου,
βασιλέως γε οὖσαν παῖδα, τὴν πρέπουσαν παρθένοις
φυλακὴν ἀφαιρήσομαι, ἀλλ᾽ εἶχε πολλοὺς τοὺς ἑπομένους
τοὺς αὐτοῦ καὶ πρὸς θήρας μελέτην καὶ πρὸς ὥρας
φυλακήν. Ἤιδει πρὸς τούτοις ὁ πατήρ, ὡς ὀρειφοιτᾷ μὲν

even though they were men—the same Greeks whom the Trojans, who were also men, could not endure. Penthesilaea did not flee the approach of Achilles's ashen spear, and the hero was more leery of the battle with a woman than of the one with Hector. But if you point out that the Amazons were descended from Ares, I will point out that Atalanta was descended from Zeus, to whom she traced her lineage. One must not reckon that the Amazons' father Ares was ambitious in the pursuit of honor, and yet posit that Atalanta's ancestor Zeus was any less ambitious than Ares.

Her father was a hero, and you know how the race of heroes was the first to reach the very pinnacle of manliness. If Atalanta was somewhat stronger than other women, then she was her father's child, as the proverb goes, and by her deeds she made clear who fathered her. Her father ruled over men, and his child, unlike the other girls, acted like a man. If her father did not keep his child locked away in the women's quarters but permitted her to hunt, he imitated his ancestor Zeus and, jealous of Zeus's daughter Athena, he too armed his child. Neither did Zeus jeer at Athena, "*My child, the deeds of war are not granted to you,*" nor did Zeus's son Oeneus rebuke his child for acting like a man. 7

Do not be surprised if he entrusted his child to the mountains and hills, for he did not then leave her without the guidance and protection of attendants; rather, since she was manly in her courage, he prepared her for hunting, but, since she had a radiant countenance, he also protected her with attendants. For of course I will not deprive her, being the child of a king, of the protection befitting a virgin; rather, she had many of his attendants both to train her in hunting and to protect her youthful beauty. In addition, her 8

115

καὶ Ἄρτεμις, ἀλλ᾽ οὔτ᾽ αὐτὸς ὁ Πάν, οὔτ᾽ ἄλλος τῶν δαιμόνων τῆς θεοῦ τὴν βίαν ἐθάρρησεν. Εἴ τις ἐπέθετο, τὸ τόξον ἤρκει πρὸς ἄμυναν, παρῆν καὶ νικωμένην ἱππάσασθαι καὶ τὴν βίαν διαφυγεῖν.

9 Τὸ δ᾽ αὐτὴν εἰς ἔρωτα πεσεῖν, τοῦτο δὴ γνώμης φαυλοτέρας ἐνόμισε καὶ ἅμα τοῦ γένους ἀνάξιον, τὴν ἐξ Οἰνέως, τὴν ἀπὸ Διὸς ἄτιμον ἀνθελέσθαι γάμον καὶ καταισχύναι γένος ὑψηλὸν οὕτω καὶ μέχρι θεῶν ἀναγόμενον. Ἐπ᾽ αὐτῇ δὲ ἦν, κἂν ἔπαθέ τι τοιοῦτον, πρὸς τὸ τοῦ γάμου σεμνόν, ὅτε καὶ βούλοιτο, μετασκευάσαι· οἷς <δ᾽> οὖν καιρὸν εἶχε τοῦ γάμου, τὴν βούλησιν Ἔρως καιρὸν οὐκ ἐδέχετο.

10 Εἰ γὰρ δὴ μὴ τοιαύτην εἶναι δώσομεν, κἂν ἐπ᾽ οἴκου, τὸ κακὸν οὐκ ἀπώκνησεν, ἀλλ᾽ ἔλαθεν ἂν καὶ μητρὸς ὀφθαλμοὺς καὶ τῶν θεραπαινίδων τὰς θαλαμηπόλους ῥᾳδίως ἂν ἠπάτησεν. Ὥστε τί πλέον ἂν εἰς φυλακὴν ἴσχυσε θάλαμος; Ἔστιν ἄρα, καὶ θαλαμευομένην, οὐ σώφρονα κόρην ἐξ Ἀφροδίτης παθεῖν καὶ πρὸς θήραν ἐξιοῦσαν τήν γε σωφρονοῦσαν φυλάξασθαι.

11 Τὸ δὲ τῶν ποδῶν τάχος οὐ χρὴ θαυμάζειν. Ὡς ἐπίπαν μὲν γὰρ ἕπεται τῷ τάχει καὶ κάλλος, καὶ τοῦτ᾽ ἂν εἴη φύσεως εὐστοχία καὶ κόσμος ἐπιπλεκόμενος. Οὐ γὰρ δὴ τὸ κάλλος ἔδοξε τῇ φύσει ἀρκεῖν, ἀλλὰ καὶ δρόμον προσεχαρίζετο· ἔδει γὰρ ὡς τὰς χεῖρας τῶν ἄλλων διέφερεν, οὕτω καὶ τοὺς πόδας ἔχειν τι πλέον φιλοτιμήσασθαι. Ἀνδρεῖος ἦν Ἀχιλλεύς, ἀλλὰ καὶ ταχὺς οἷος δοκεῖν

father knew that Artemis also roamed the mountains, but that neither Pan himself nor any of the lesser divinities would dare to assault the goddess. If someone did attack, the bow was sufficient for self-defense, and if defeat was imminent, she could ride her horse and escape the assault.

As for the fact that she fell in love, our critic thought that 9 this was reflective of a baser character and at the same time unworthy of her lineage—that a girl, descended from Oeneus and Zeus, should prefer a dishonorable marriage and shame a lineage that was so lofty and that extended all the way back to the gods. Yet even if she felt some such passion, she could transform it into holy matrimony whenever she wished, but since Love found an opportunity for marriage, he did not wait for her willingness to become his opportunity.

For if we will not grant that she was like this, then even 10 if she was at home she would not have avoided the evil, but instead she could have escaped her mother's watchful gaze and easily deceived the servants who were her chambermaids. As a result, how could the women's quarters have protected her any more effectively? It is possible, then, that although kept in the women's quarters, an imprudent girl might feel the passion of love, and a chaste girl, in fact, might protect herself even though she went out to hunt.

One ought not be surprised at the swiftness of her feet. 11 For beauty generally accompanies speed, and this is a mark of the shrewdness and intricate design of nature. For nature did not think beauty was sufficient, but it also blessed her with the ability to run. For just as she must have excelled the others with her hands, so also she must have been able to take even greater pride in her feet. Achilles was manly, but

ἵπτασθαι· καλὸς ἦν Ἀντίλοχος, ἀλλ᾽ εἶχε καὶ ποδῶν ὀξύτητα· πρὸς μάχην ἕτοιμος ὁ Λοκρός, ἀλλὰ δραμεῖν ἑτοιμότερος. Ὡς τὰ πολλὰ μὲν οὖν ἡ φύσις ἀρετὴν ἀρετῇ παραζεύγνυσι, καί τις καλὸς εἶναι δοκῶν εἰς τάχος οὐ λείπεται.

12 Εἴη δ᾽ ἂν παιδευτικὸν δρόμου καὶ τὸ γυμνάσιον. Ἡ δὲ πρὸς θήραν εἶχε τὸ στάδιον καὶ τοὺς πόδας τοῖς ὁσημέραι δρόμοις ἐκούφιζεν. Ἢ γὰρ πόθεν ἡ τοῦ μύθου χελώνη τὸν ἵππον ὑπερεβάλετο; Οὐκ ἀπὸ μελέτης, οὐκ ἀπὸ γυμνασίου, ἤγουν φύσεως;

13 Φιλοτιμίαν καὶ τοῦτο λογιστέον ἢ θετέον εἰς ἄσκησιν. Ἀλλ᾽ ἦκεν ὁ τοῦ γάμου καιρός, ἡ δὲ οὕτω τοι πρὸς ἀρετὴν ἤσκητο, ὥστε ἕδνων μὲν ὀλίγα ἐφρόντιζε, γένους δὲ οὐ περιείχετο, μορφῆς δὲ λόγον ἐποιεῖτο βραχύν, πρὸς μόνον δὲ τὸ τάχος ἔβλεψε, τοῦτο μὲν ὡς ἀπὸ τῆς θήρας θαυμάζουσα, κἀκεῖ γὰρ ἑώρα τὸ χρῆμα τοῦτο, ὁπόσα ξυναίρεται, τοῦτο δὲ καὶ ὡς ἀπὸ τῶν ποδῶν τὰς χεῖρας φυλοκρινήσασα, ἢ καὶ πρὸς αὐτὸν Ἔρωτα, πτηνὸν ὄντα, πτηνοὺς καὶ αὐτὴ τοὺς πόδας ἀντεπεδείκνυτο. Ἴσως δ᾽ ἂν καί, παρθενεύειν ἑλομένη μέχρι παντός, οὕτω σοφῶς τὸν γάμον ἤλπιζε φεύξεσθαι.

14 Σὺ δὲ τί ποιεῖν ἐβούλου τὴν ἐξ Οἰνέως, τὴν ἀπὸ Διός; Ὡς μίαν τῶν ἄλλων ἄγεσθαι; Ἀλλ᾽ οὐκ ἦν ἁπλῶς παρθένος. Ἀλλ᾽ ἕδνα δέχεσθαι; Κόρης ἂν ἦν ταῦτα σκιατραφουμένης, μὴ πρὸς ἀνδρείαν τραφείσης. Ἢ τοὺς μὲν ἐραστὰς ἀγωνίζεσθαι, τὴν δ᾽ ἑστάναι καὶ μένειν, ὅστις αὐτὴν ὡς ἄθλον μετὰ τὴν νίκην ἄξεται, ὥσπερ εἰ μὴ χεῖρες ἦσαν αὐτῇ καὶ πόδες παρ᾽ οὐδὲν ἐκείνων λειπόμενοι; Ἀλλὰ

he was also so swift that he seemed to fly. Antilochus was handsome, but he also had swift feet. Locrian Ajax was ready for battle, but even more ready to run. And so in general nature joins virtue with virtue, and someone who appears beautiful is not lacking in speed.

Her athletic training too would have taught her to run. 12 She had the racecourse to train her in hunting and she made her feet light with daily races. For how did the tortoise in the fable surpass the horse? Was it not from exercise, not from athletic training, rather than from nature?

One must either reckon this as ambition or attribute it 13 to practice. But when the time for the marriage came, she was so practiced in virtue that she thought little of wedding gifts, did not cling to her lineage, gave little thought to her appearance, and counted on her speed alone, marveling at her speed because of her hunting, for there she observed it as an advantage whenever she took part in the chase, and relying more on her feet than her hands — or, alternatively, she was demonstrating to Love himself, who was winged, that she herself had winged feet too. Perhaps also having chosen to remain a virgin to the very end, she hoped to avoid marriage in this clever way.

What did you want the descendant of Oeneus and Zeus 14 to do? To be married off, like an ordinary girl? But she was not simply a virgin. Or to accept wedding gifts? These would have been the actions of a girl raised indoors, not one brought up in manliness. Or for the suitors to compete, while she stood by and waited for the one who would lead her away like a prize after the victory, as if she had no hands and her feet were utterly inferior to theirs? Rather, you

κηρύττειν τὸν ἀγῶνα καὶ ἅμα αὐτὴν ἄθλον εἶναι καὶ
ξύναθλον, καὶ μὴν τοῦτο καὶ αὐτ<ὴ> ποιεῖ.

15   Καὶ ἀποδύσασθαι μὲν εἰς πάλην οὐκ ἐδοκίμαζεν ἀπρε-
πὲς γάρ, ἐλθεῖν δὲ εἰς χεῖρας ἐν ὅπλοις οὐκ ἐβούλετο—
ἀρρενωπότερον γάρ—. Ἄλλως τε καὶ φονικὰ ταῦτα καὶ
Ἐριννύος μᾶλλον ἢ κόρης ἔργα ἐνόμισεν, εἰ τοὺς ἐραστὰς
αὐτὴ μετὰ ξίφους δέχεται καὶ φόνου ποιεῖται τὴν γάμων
ὑπόθεσιν καὶ τοῦ καλλίστου πρὸς φιλίαν κτήματος, τὸ
δεινότατον, εἰς ἀπέχθειαν προβάλλεται πόλεμον. Οἷς μὲν
οὖν ἔτι παρθένος ἦν, τὰ παρθένων δηλαδὴ τὸν γάμον
ἐκήρυττεν, οἷς δὲ τῶν ἡρωΐδων ἦν τὸ κεφάλαιον, καὶ τῆς
ἀνδρείας ἀδελφὸν ἐζήλου Μελέαγρον καὶ τὸν ἐς τάχος
ἀγῶνα τῷ κηρύγματι προσεπέθηκε.

16   Μικροῦ καὶ τοιαῦτα λέγειν ὡς ἀπὸ τοῦ κηρύγματος τὴν
παρθένον μαντεύομαι· "Οἰνέως εἰμὶ παῖς, εἰς αὐτὸν ἀνα-
φέρω Δία τὸ γένος, ἀδελφὸν ἔχω Μελέαγρον. Πρὸς
ἀνδρείαν ἐτράφην καὶ φέρω τρόπον ἄρρενα, κἂν τὴν φύσιν
ἔχω θήλειαν. Καὶ δεῖ με λοιπὸν καὶ ὡς γυναῖκα τὰ γυναικῶν ὑποίσειν, ὅτι καὶ φύσις τοῦτο βούλεται καί, ὡς κατ'
ἄνδρα τραφεῖσαν, καὶ γάμον λαβεῖν ἀνδρικώτερον." Οὕτω
νομίζω τὴν ἡρωΐδα ταύτην ξυλλογίσασθαι καὶ ἡ ἐπὶ τῷ
τάχει πρόκλησις τῶν ξυλλελογισμένων τούτων ἂν εἴη συμ-
πέρασμα.

17   Ἐπὶ τούτοις ᾔδει καὶ τὴν ἀδελφὴν Δηϊάνειραν, ὡς
πλείους εἶχε τοὺς ἐραστὰς καὶ ἡ μὲν ἄθλον ἐτίθετο, οἱ δὲ
τῶν ἄλλων μείζους Ἀχελῷος καὶ Ἡρακλῆς ὡς ἐπ' ἄθλῳ τῇ
κόρῃ διεπυκτεύοντο. Ταύτην, οἶμαι, τὴν ἀδελφὴν καὶ
Ἀταλάντη τοῦ ἄθλου μὲν ἐζήλωσε, τὸ δ' ὡς ἄθλον κεῖσθαι

should expect her to announce the contest and at the same time announce that she was both the prize and a contestant. And indeed this is exactly what she did.

And she did not see fit to disrobe for battle, for that 15 would have been inappropriate, nor did she wish to come to blows with weapons, for that would have been too masculine. Most of all, she believed that these actions would be bloody and more characteristic of a Fury than of a girl, if she welcomed the suitors with a sword and turned an occasion for marriage into a pretext for murder and started a war, which would replace the finest opportunity for love with hatred, a most terrible development. To the extent that she was still a virgin, she proclaimed what a virgin would proclaim, namely marriage; to the extent that she was the best among heroines, she emulated her brother Meleager in his manliness and added to her proclamation the contest in speed.

I almost divine that in the proclamation the girl was say- 16 ing something along these lines: "I am the child of Oeneus; I trace my lineage to Zeus himself; I have a brother Meleager. I was brought up in manliness and I engage in masculine behavior, even if I have a feminine nature. And now as a woman I must submit to the ways of women, because nature also wishes this, and, since I was raised like a man, I should arrange a marriage in a more manly fashion." Thus I believe this heroine reasoned, and her challenge for speed would be the logical conclusion of this reasoning.

Moreover, she knew that her sister Deianira also had 17 very many suitors; she had set herself up as the prize, and Achelous and Heracles, who were greater than the rest, had sparred for the girl as if for a prize. Atalanta, I suppose, admired this sister for being a prize, but did not see fit to be

τοῦ ἀγῶνος οὐκ ἐδοκίμασεν, ἀλλ᾽ αὐτὴ καὶ ἆθλον εἶναι καὶ ἀθλητὴς ἠβούλετο καὶ τὸν ἀγῶνα τοῦτο τὸ μέρος πρὸς τὴν ἀδελφὴν διηλλάττετο, ὅτι καὶ τὴν τροφὴν πρότερον.

18 Εἰ δὲ καὶ κοινὴν ἀκούεις τὴν πρόκλησιν, συλλόγισαι ὡς κοινὴ μὲν ἦν, ἀλλὰ πρὸς βασιλεῖς, ἀλλὰ πρὸς ἥρωας, ἀλλὰ πρὸς τοὺς ἀπὸ Διός, οἳ καὶ τύχης ἱκανῶς εἶχον καὶ πρὸς τὸ ἀνδρεῖον, θεοὺς προγόνους ἔχοντες, οὐκ ἐλείποντο. Περιῆν δ᾽ ἂν αὐτοῖς καὶ κάλλους, οἵου καὶ θεοὺς προγόνους ἐμφῆναι, ὥστ᾽ εἶχον ἂν καὶ τῆς κλήσεως τὸ θεοείκελον. Πρὸς τούτους κοινὰ τὰ τῆς προκλήσεως λόγισαι, εἰ γὰρ μὴ τὸ γένος εἶχον ἀπὸ Διός, εἰ μὴ παῖδες ἦσαν κρατούντων, εἰ μὴ τοῦ τῆς κόρης κάλλους ἄξιοι, τούτοις δ᾽ οὐδ᾽ ἂν τὴν ἀρχὴν οὐδ᾽ ἐπὶ σμικρὸν ὑπανεῴγει τὸ στάδιον. Τότε γὰρ τὴν ἀπὸ Διὸς τοὺς κάτω τῶν ἀνθρώπων ὑπερβάλλειν οὐκ εἶχέ τι θαύματος, καὶ τὸ ἡττηθῆναι μέγα πρὸς ὄνειδος.

19 Καὶ δὴ τῶν ἄλλων μὲν ἐκράτει τῷ τάχει, μόνος δὲ ταύτην Ἱππομένης παρῆλθε, σοφίαν τῷ δρόμῳ συγκαταμίξας. Οἷς μὲν γὰρ τοῦ κάλλους ἑάλω, τὸν ἀγῶνα δέχεται, οἷς δ᾽ οὐκ ἐπίστευε τοῖς ποσί, τὴν νίκην σοφίζεται. Εὖ μὲν γὰρ ἐπεφύκει τοὺς πόδας, ἀλλ᾽ ἦν ἔτι τὰς τοῦ κρατεῖν ἐλπίδας ἀμφίβολος, ἐξ ὧν τὸ κρατεῖν ἡ κόρη τοὺς ἄλλους παρείλετο. Οὐκοῦν σοφία τὸ τοῦ τάχους λειπόμενον ἀνορθοῖ καὶ γίνεται σοφὸς ἐραστὴς πρὸς Ἀφροδίτην· ὁρᾷ τὴν παῖδα, ἱκετεύει Ἔρωτα, ζητεῖ τὴν ἐπικουρίαν καὶ τὸ ἐντεῦθεν, ἐπιπνεύσαντος Ἔρωτος, εἰς νοῦν λαμβάνει τὸ

CONFIRMATION

set out as a prize in her contest; rather, she wanted to be both prize and contestant herself, and in this respect, in contrast to her sister, she changed the nature of the contest, because she had also previously changed the nature of her upbringing.

But if you hear that the invitation was open, consider 18 that it was in fact open, but open only to kings and heroes and descendants of Zeus, who were of sufficient fortune and who, with gods as their ancestors, were not lacking in manliness. They would also have excelled in such beauty as to indicate that their ancestors were gods, so that they would have the word "godlike" in their names. Toward such men, you should consider that the invitation was open; for if they did not have their lineage from Zeus, or if they were not the sons of rulers, or if they were not worthy of the girl's beauty, she would not have allowed them on the racecourse at all, not even briefly. For, in that case, it would not have been surprising if the descendant of Zeus won against lower-class men, but for her to have been defeated would have been a great insult.

Well, she overcame the rest with her speed, but Hippo- 19 menes alone outstripped this girl by combining cleverness with his running. Since he was captivated by her beauty, he accepted the challenge, but since he did not trust his feet, he devised a trick to win his victory. For he had swift feet by nature, but he was nonetheless doubtful about his chances of winning because the girl had deprived the others of victory. Therefore cleverness compensated for what he lacked in speed, and he became a clever suitor thanks to Aphrodite. He saw the girl, asked for Love's help, sought assistance, and then, with Love's inspiration, got the idea for a trick: taking

123

σόφισμα καί, χρυσὸν λαβών, εἰς ὀπώραν μετασκευάζει καὶ ἡ ὀπώρα Ἔρωτος ξύμβολον, Ἀφροδίτης ἀνάθημα.

20 Ταύτην δὴ τὴν χρυσῆν ὀπώραν τὰ μῆλα λαβών, προκαλεῖται τὴν κόρην εἰς δρόμον καὶ ἅμα ἐξήλλοντο καὶ τῶν χρυσῶν μήλων Ἱππομένης ἠφίει, ἡ δὲ κόρη, τὸ καινὸν τῆς μηχανῆς οὐκ ἔχουσα ξυνιδεῖν, ξυνέλεγε τὸ μέντοι, καὶ τοῦ ξυναθλοῦντος ἴσως ποιουμένη κατάγελων. Εἰ χρυσὸν οὕτως ἐπιρριπτεῖ, δέον τοῖς ποσὶν ἀγωνίσασθαι, τόδε τι θαρροῦσα, καὶ μετὰ τὴν συλλογὴν προφθῆναι καὶ δρέψα- σθαι νίκην χρυσῆν. Ὤιετο γὰρ ἂν οὕτω διάδηλα μᾶλλον τὰ τοῦ τάχους ἔσεσθαι, εἰ καὶ παραδράμοι, ξυλλέγουσα, ἐντεῦθεν ἠφίει μὲν Ἱππομένης, ἡ δὲ κόρη ξυνέλεγε καί, πρὸς τὸ συλλέγειν ἀποτείνασα, τὸν λογισμὸν Ἱππομένους ἐλείπετο.

21 Ἧκεν ἡ κόρη πάλιν ἐγγύτερον, ὁ δὲ τὸν δόλον προύβάλλετο, κἀκείνη πρὸς συλλογὴν ἀπησχόλητο, ἀλλ᾽ ἐπέτεινεν αὖθις ἐκείνη τοὺς πόδας καὶ ὁ Ἱππομένης τὰ χρυσᾶ μῆλα κατὰ γῆς αὖθις ἔβαλλεν, ἡ δ᾽ ἀπεδρέπετο τῆς ἀπάτης καὶ τοῦ χρυσοῦ. Οὔτε γὰρ πάντως τοὺς πόδας Ἱππομένης ὑστέριζε καὶ τὸ ταχὺ τῆς κόρης ὁ δόλος ἐπεῖχεν ἐντεῦθεν, οὔτε τὰ τῆς ἐπινοίας ἀνόνητα, οὐ γὰρ ἂν εἰς τέλος ἡ ταχύτης ἐπήρκεσεν. Οὔτ᾽ αὖθις ἔδει τὴν κόρην ἀκροβολίζεσθαι, ἀλλ᾽ ἅμα τῆς βαλβίδος ἐξήλλοντο καὶ ἡ μὲν ξυνέλεγεν, ὁ δὲ προέβαινε καί, τῆς κόρης ἠκούσης ἔγγιον, ὁ μὲν αὖθις ἐπιρρίπτει τῶν μήλων μικρὸν τὴν δεξιὰν προτεινάμενος, ἡ δὲ καὶ πάλιν ξυνέλεγε.

22 Οὕτω καὶ Μήδειαν λαβεῖν Αἰήτης οὐκ ἴσχυσε, τοῦ γὰρ παιδὸς Ἀψύρτου τὰ μέλη προσεπιρρίπτει τῷ πατρί, κατόπιν ἥκοντι. Ὁ δ᾽ ἐπεκλᾶτο πρὸς τῆς φύσεως καὶ τῶν μελῶν

some gold, he fashioned it into the shape of fruit, and the fruit was the symbol of Love, an offering to Aphrodite.

Taking this golden fruit, the apples, he challenged the girl   20
to a race, and as soon as they leaped forth, Hippomenes threw the golden apples, and the girl, unable to comprehend the novelty of the trick, nevertheless gathered them up, perhaps mocking her competitor. If he was thus throwing gold at her (she thought) when he should have been running against her, she was quite confident that, even after stopping to collect the apples, she would both come in first and reap a golden victory. For she believed that in this way her speed would be more obvious, even if he should run past her while she was gathering them up. Therefore Hippomenes threw the apples, and the girl gathered them, but in her effort to gather them, she fell short of Hippomenes in her reasoning.

The girl again drew near him, and he tossed out his trick-   21
ery and she lost ground while gathering. Again she put on a burst of speed and Hippomenes again threw the golden apples on the ground, and she reaped the deceitful gold. For it is absolutely not the case that Hippomenes was lagging behind as a runner and only his stratagem served to check the girl's speed, nor was his scheming pointless, for in the end his speed alone would not have been sufficient. Nor again did he have to hurl missiles at the girl from a distance; rather, as soon as they leaped forth from the starting line, she started gathering, and he went ahead, and as the girl closed the gap, he again threw the apples, extending his right hand a little, and she again picked them up.

So also Aeëtes was unable to catch Medea, for she threw   22
the limbs of his son Apsyrtus at their father as he came along behind. And he was moved to pity by his natural ties, and he

περιείχετο καὶ τοῦτο, πολλάκις γινόμενον, τὸν μὲν ὑστερίζειν ἐποίει, τὴν δ᾽ οἴχεσθαι δραπετεύουσαν. Ὁ γοῦν ἀνὴρ πρὸς γυναικὸς εἰς δόλον ἡλίσκετο, τοῦτο γυνὴ πρὸς ἀνδρὸς πάλιν ἡπάτηται.

23 Καὶ μή μοι λεγέτω μηδεὶς ὡς "Εἰ τῇ κόρῃ χρυσὸς ἦν τὸ ποθούμενον, τί μὴ τὰ ἔδνα ἐδέχετο;" Ἀπάτη γὰρ ἦν, οὐ πόθος εἰς συλλογὴν καὶ κόμπος εἰς τάχους ὑπερβολήν, οὐκ ἔργον χρυσοῦ. Εἰ δὲ καὶ τῶν χρυσῶν μήλων ἥττηται, τὴν ἧτταν οὐκ ἂν ἐδυσχέραινεν; Ἀλλ᾽ ἔχαιρε παρ᾽ Ἱππομένους ὡς Ἀφροδίτη πρὸς Ἀλεξάνδρου τὴν χρυσὴν ὀπώραν δεχομένη, κάλλους ἔπαθλον.

24 Ἔγνω δ᾽ ἂν ἴσως καὶ θερμότερον ἐραστήν, ὡς μετ᾽ Ἀφροδίτης αὐτῇ τὸ καλὴ δοκεῖν ψηφιζόμενον; Εἰ δὲ καὶ "τῇ καλῇ" τὸ μῆλον ἐκεῖνος ἐπέγραψε, τοῦ τάχους ἂν τὴν κόρην ἐξέλυσε; Πολλοὶ γάρ, οἷς πρὸς ἔριν οὐ λείπονται, τούτοις πρὸς χάριν ὑπείκουσι θαυμαζόμενοι. Κόρη δὲ καὶ μᾶλλον ἐπαίνοις εὐάλωτος, κἂν εἰς κάλλος θαυμάσῃς, ἡπάτησας. Τί δ᾽ ἂν Ἀφροδίτης ἐπιτερπέστερον ὄνομα; Ἢ τί πρὸς εὐφημίαν κόρης μᾶλλον ἁλώσιμον;

25 Ταῦτα καὶ Μουσῶν ἐπιπνοίας ἄξια τίθεμαι καὶ τούς γε μὴ θαυμάζοντας τῆς τῶν ῥημάτων ἁπλότητος τῆς παρὰ τὸ προσῆκον ἀπειθείας αὐτὸς οὐκ ἐθαύμασα· ἀλλ᾽ ἰσχυρισαί-μην ἂν ταὐτὰ τοῖς μαινομένοις νοσεῖν, οἳ καὶ πρὸς αὐτὴν αἴσθησιν ἀπομάχονται, φλέγειν, οὐ τρέφειν τὸν ἄρτον ἰσχυριζόμενοι.

clung to the limbs, and this, happening over and over, made him lag behind and allowed her to run away and escape. At any rate, just as in the one case a man was bested by a woman through deceit, in the same way a woman was in turn deceived by a man.

And let no one say to me, "If what the girl longed for was gold, why did she not welcome the wedding gifts?" For it was a deception, not a longing to gather them, and it was a boast about her superior speed, not an effort expended only for the sake of gold. But if she was defeated by the golden apples, would she not have been disgusted at her defeat? Instead, she rejoiced because of Hippomenes, just as when Aphrodite received the golden apple from Alexander as a prize for beauty. 23

Would Atalanta have perhaps judged Hippomenes a rather impetuous suitor because he cast his vote in favor of her beauty, just as happened to Aphrodite? And if he had inscribed the apple "for the beautiful one," would he have deprived the girl of her speed? For many people, when admired, yield and grant favor to people to whom they are not inferior in competition. But a girl is even more easily captivated by compliments, and as soon as you express your admiration for her beauty, you deceive her. And what name would be more delightful than that of Aphrodite? Or who is easier to capture with praise than a girl? 24

I regard these things as worthy of the inspiration of the Muses, and as for those who are not amazed by the simplicity of the words, I myself am not amazed by their inappropriate disbelief; rather, I would maintain that they are suffering from the same illness as madmen, who fight against their very senses, maintaining that their bread is burning them, not nourishing them. 25

ENCOMIUM

I

Οὐ δειλιάσω τὸν Μῶμον οἷς ἐπαινέσαι τὸν κύνα προήρημαι· οὐδὲ γὰρ οὕτω κἀγὼ πρὸς τὴν Διονύσου μανίαν ἐκκυλισθήσομαι, ὡς καὶ θεὸν αὐτὸν ἀπεργάσασθαι. Εἰ γάρ τις ἐπαινέσαι τι προαιρούμενος, καὶ τοῖς ἀδυνάτοις ἐγχειροίη κατασεμνύνειν, ἀπίθανα καὶ τὰ προσόντα πάντως ἐργάζεται. Τοὺς τοιούτους ἐπισκώπτων οἶμαι κἀκεῖνος ὁ σοφιστής, ὁ Σύρος ὁ γελοιαστής, ὁ φιλοπαίγμων ὁ κωμικός, εἰς οὐρανοὺς ἀναγαγόντα Διόνυσον τὸν κύνα τῆς ἐρωμένης ἐπλάσατο, καὶ Μῶμον εἰρωνευόμενον ἐπ᾽ αὐτῷ. Ἐγὼ δ᾽ ἀλλ᾽ ὅτι μὲν θεὸς αὐτός ἐστιν οὐκ ἐρῶ, θεοῖς δὲ τοῦτον φίλον ἀποφηνάμενος, συμμαρτυροῦσαν πάντως ἔξω καὶ τὴν ἐνέργειαν. Ἐπιφέρεται μὲν γὰρ καὶ τόξον καὶ φαρέτραν ἡ Ἄρτεμις, ἀλλὰ καὶ κύνας ὀπαδοὺς προσεπάγεται, κἀντεῦθεν τὸ τῆς κυνηγεσίας ὄνομα προσεκτήσατο. Ἐπεὶ δ᾽ ἐκ θεῶν ἀνθρώποις τὰ κάλλιστα, καὶ εἰς αὐτοὺς τὸ πρᾶγμα μεταπεφοίτηκε, κάλλιστον οἶμαι πάντων ὅσα μετὰ τὸν ἄνθρωπον.

2   Βασιλεῦσι μὲν ἀκραιφνεστάτην ἀφοσιοῦται τὴν ἡδονήν, ἵνα μὴ λέγω καὶ τοῖς λοιποῖς ὁπόσοις ἔργον κυνηγεσία· καὶ κατατρέχει μὲν ἐλάφων καὶ λαγωῶν καὶ τῶν λοιπῶν κνωδάλων τῶν ἐπὶ γῆς, ἐξ ὧν ἑτοιμάζει βασιλικῇ τραπέζῃ τὸ ἁβροδίαιτον, τὸ δέ γε καινότατον, ἐνεργοῦσαν ἔχει τὴν

I

I will not fear the criticism of Momus because of the manner in which I have chosen to praise the dog; for I will not plunge so recklessly into the madness of Dionysus as to turn the dog into a god. For if someone chooses to praise something and tries to glorify it with impossible qualities, he makes even the qualities it does possess completely improbable. It was in mocking such encomiasts as these, I suppose, that even that famous sophist, the Syrian jester, the fun-loving comedian Lucian, depicted Dionysus leading his girlfriend's dog up to heaven and Momus mocking him for it. I, on the other hand, will not say that the dog is a god, but in declaring that he is dear to the gods I will surely also have the gods' own actions to testify in my favor. For Artemis carries both a bow and a quiver, but she also leads a pack of dogs; for this reason she has even acquired the epithet "dog-leading." Since the finest things come to humans from the gods, and this creature has been passed down to humans, then the dog is the finest of all things, I suppose, after the human being.

The dog offers the purest pleasure to kings, not to mention all the other people engaged in hunting. The dog chases down deer and rabbits and all the other wild animals upon the earth, from which he prepares a luxurious feast for the king's table. Strangest of all, he has a sense of smell as

ὄσφρησιν, ὁπόσα δὴ καὶ τὴν ὅρασιν. Ἐκρύβη γάρ τι τῶν ὀφθαλμῶν, καὶ περὶ μέσην λόχμην ἐκπέφευγεν, ἀλλ' οὗτος προβάλλεται μὲν ἑτέραν δύναμιν ὀφθαλμῶν, διὰ δρυμὰ πολλὰ καὶ ὕλην ἐρχόμενος, κἀξιχνοσκοπούμενος καὶ ῥινηλατῶν ὡς εἰπεῖν. Ἤδη δέ που καὶ τὸν δραπέτην αὐτοῖς ἐκγόνοις κατέλαβε, καὶ πάνθ' ὁμοῦ ληϊσάμενος μέγα τι κυδιόων πρὸς τὸν δεσπότην ἠγάγετο. Εἶδον ἐγὼ καὶ τὴν φύσιν αὐτὴν αὐτὸν βιαζόμενον, καὶ ταῖς πτηνῶν ἀ<γέ>λαις ἐπιτιθέμενον. Οὐκ οἶδε πόνος ἔχειν τὸν θηρευτὴν ἀνέστιον εἰληθερούμενον πανημέριον· "Τερπωλὴ γὰρ ἕπεται θήρῃ πλέον ἠέπερ ἱδρὼς" κατὰ τὸν Κίλικα ποιητήν, ὅπου δὲ κέρδος μεθ' ἡδονῆς, ἐκεῖθεν ἐκποδὼν καὶ πόνος καὶ κάματος.

3   Βούλει καὶ ὡς ἐν πίνακι τῷ λόγῳ τὰ τῆς θηρευτικῆς διαγράψω σοι. Φέρεται μὲν ὁ θηρευτὴς ἱππαζόμενος, ἐπιθωΰζων τὰ κυνηγετικά, κύκλῳ δ' ἀμφ' αὐτὸν οἱ κύνες παρομαρτοῦσιν, οἷα περὶ στρατηγόν τι στρατόπεδον ἑτοιμαζόμενον εἰς παράταξιν· ὁπηνίκα τὸν μὲν ἴδῃς περὶ τοὺς πόδας αὐτοῦ κυλινδούμενον, καί τι θωπευτικὸν προσκνυζώμενον· τὸν δ' αὖθις τοὺς πόδας γυμνάζοντα καὶ πρὸς ἑτέρους περὶ τάχους ἀνθαμιλλᾶσθαι φιλοτιμούμενον· ἕτερον τοῖς περὶ τὸν τράχηλον ἀναδέσμοις ἐπαγαλλόμενον καὶ ταῖς ψηφῖσι γαυρούμενον καὶ τοῖς χρυσοειδέσι ῥυτῆρσιν ἐναβρυνόμενον, ἡδεῖαν ὄψιν τοῖς θεωμένοις εἰ μή πού τις ἐξ ἀδάμαντος τὴν καρδίαν κεχάλκευται, γλαυκή τε τοῦτον ἔτεκε θάλασσα. Ἐπὰν δὲ καὶ πρὸς αὐτὸν τὸν τῆς θήρας τόπον ἀφίκωνται, πεδιάδα τινά φημι θηροτρόφον ἤ που τυχὸν καὶ ἀκρώρειαν, ἵστησι μὲν περὶ αὐτὸν τοὺς πάντας ὁ θηρευτὴς μάχης ἀκόρητον ἐνορῶντας· ἔπειθ' ὡς ἐκ

powerful as his vision. For when an animal is hidden from the dog's eyes and escapes into the midst of a thicket, the dog employs a power other than vision as he goes through thick woods and forest, both *tracking it down* and *sniffing it out,* so to speak. Occasionally, the dog somehow catches its prey along with its very offspring, and seizing them all at once, he very proudly takes them to his master. I have even seen a dog challenging nature itself and attacking *flocks of birds.* Labor cannot keep the hunter away from home and out in the sun all day long, *"for delight follows the hunt more than sweat,"* as the Cilician poet Oppian says, and wherever profit is accompanied by pleasure, both labor and weariness make way.

You also wish for me to describe for you in words, as if in a painting, the practice of hunting. The hunter rides around on horseback, urging on the hunt, and the dogs gather around him in a circle, like an army around its general as it readies for battle. At any given time you could see one dog rolling around at the hunter's feet, whining in a fawning manner, and another exercising his legs and eagerly competing against others in a race, and still another glorying in the collar on his neck, reveling in the gems and taking pride in the golden leash: a pleasant sight for onlookers, unless someone has a *heart forged of adamant* and *the gray sea bore* him. When they arrive at the actual location of the hunt, by which I mean a plain that nourishes wild beasts or perhaps even a mountain ridge, the hunter stations the dogs all around him as they avidly watch for battle. Then, as though

βαλβῖδος ἀφειμένοι τινός, ἄπαντες ἀολλέες περὶ τὴν ὕλην ἐμπίπτουσιν.

4 Ἀλλὰ γὰρ ὅλοις μοι τοῖς ὀφθαλμοῖς πρὸς τὴν γραφὴν ἐνατένιζε· εἰ δὲ καὶ μὴ Ἀπελλῆς τις ἐστὶν ἢ καὶ Πραξιτέλης ὁ ζωγραφῶν, κἀντεῦθεν αὐτὸς μηδέν τι τῶν χρωμάτων καὶ τῆς γραφῆς ὡς ἀτέχνου πρὸς εὐφροσύνην ἀπόναιο, τὸ γοῦν τῆς ἱστορίας σοι γλαφυρὸν οὐκ ἀμυδρὰν εὑρήσεις τὴν ἡδονὴν προτεινόμενον. Ὅρα λοιπὸν τοὺς μὲν ἐλάφοις ἐπεισπεσόντας, καὶ κεραΐζομένους ταύτας οὐκ ἀγεννῶς, ἕτερον ὅλην φάλαγγα λαγωῶν στυφελίζοντα, καὶ τὸν ὀπίστατον αἰὲν ἀποκτείνοντα, ἕτερον κάπρῳ κρυερῷ πρὸς βίαν ἐπιτιθέμενον, καὶ τοῖς ὀδοῦσιν ὡς δόρασιν ἀπανταχό- θεν καταδαρδάπτοντα, ἕτερον ἑτέροις ὡς ἔτυχε συμπλε- κόμενον. Ἐπὰν δέ ποτε καὶ καταλῦσαι δέοι τὸν μαχησμὸν κεκορημένους δηϊοτῆτος, ὅρα τὸ τηνικαῦτα θέαμα ἥδιστον· οὐδένα κενὸν ἐπανιόντα καὶ ἄπρακτον, ἀλλ' ἅπαντα τὸ θηραθὲν ἐφελκόμενον καὶ πρὸς αὐτὸν τὸν δεσπότην ὡς φορολόγον ἐπάγοντα. Οὕτω πάντα λαμπρὰ καὶ χαρίεντα, κἂν μόνον εἰς ἀκοὴν μὴ καὶ τὴν ὄψιν αὐτὴν γενήσονταί τινι τὰ τοῦ πράγματος· ὅλας ἱμέρου πηγὰς καὶ μόνον ἀναστομοῖ τὸ διήγημα. Καὶ ταῦτα μὲν τὰ δημόσια κἀν τοῖς ὑπαίθροις γινόμενα, τὰ δὲ κατ' οἴκους τίς μὴ θαυ- μάσεται καὶ ταῦτα μηδὲν τῶν ἔξω πρὸς ἡδονὴν ἀποδέοντα;

5 Ἤδη μὲν οὖν προφθάσας ἐδήλωσα, <οὐ>δενὸς ἁπάντων ὅσα μετὰ τὸν ἄνθρωπον, τὸν κύνα τοῖς προτερήμασιν ἐλαττοῦσθαι· τὸ δέ γε νῦν ῥηθησόμενον οὐ μόνον ἀκριβεστέραν τὴν περὶ τούτου πίστιν ἐργάσεται, ἀλλ' ἤδη τι καὶ θάμβος τοῖς ἀκρωμένοις προσεπαφήσει. Πάντων

released from a starting gate, they all burst into the forest in a mob.

Now look upon the painting with your full attention. 4 Even if the artist is not an Apelles or a Praxiteles, and you would therefore derive no happiness at all from the colors and the painting because they are amateurish, at least you will find that the elegant depiction of the story offers you no faint pleasure. Visualize, then, the dogs attacking deer and nobly slaughtering them; one dog striking at an entire phalanx of rabbits and *always killing the hindmost;* another ferociously attacking a terrifying boar and with spear-like teeth devouring it from all sides; and still others tangling with various other animals. When at last, glutted with the killing, the dogs must end the battle, visualize the very pleasant spectacle that happens then: no dog comes back empty-handed and unsuccessful, but each and every one comes dragging his quarry and bringing it to the master himself as if he were a tax collector. Thus everything is splendid and lovely, even if the details of the event can only be heard with one's ears and not actually seen. May even this narrative on its own open up all the fountains of your longing. These activities are public and take place in the open, but as for indoor activities, who will fail to be surprised that these too offer no less pleasure than those that occur outdoors?

I have already made it clear that in its advantages the dog 5 does not fall short in comparison to any creature after human beings. The topic that I will now discuss will not only make the proof of this more precise, but in fact will also strike my audience with some astonishment. For although

γὰρ τῶν ἀλόγων ἀξύμβατον πάντη τὴν ἀλογίαν δυστυχη-
σάντων, τῇ λογικότητι μόνος ὁ κύων—ἀλλὰ μὴ ταραχθῇς
πρὸς τὴν ἀκοήν—ἐφεύρηταί τι κἀνταῦθα πλεονεκτῶν·
ἵππος μὲν γὰρ χρεμετίσας καὶ μυκησάμενος βοῦς, καὶ
βληχησάμενος ἀρνειός, ἀλόγως οὑτωσὶ τὸν ἀέρα πλήττειν
νομίζονται τῷ τῆς φωνῆς ἀσημάντῳ καὶ περιττῷ· τοῦ δὲ
κυνὸς ὑλακτήσαντος προσυπεσήμαινέ τι τὸ φώνημα, καὶ
παρουσίαν ξένων ἐδήλωσεν, ὡς εἴ γε καὶ διηρθρωμένα
λέγειν ἠδύνατο, τάχα καὶ "Τίς πόθεν εἶς;" ἕκαστον προσ-
επήρετο. Τοιαῦτα δ᾽ ἂν οἶμαι καὶ πρὸς αὐτὸν τὸν δεσπότην
ἐφθέγξατο· "Τίς ἡ τοσαύτη σοι τῶν πέριξ τουτωνὶ φραγμῶν
ἐπιμέλεια, δέσποτα; Τίς ἡ τῶν πυλῶν προσοχή, καὶ τῶν
κλειδῶν ἡ φροντίς, καὶ τὸ πρὸς ταῦτα δαπανηρόν; Μηδέν
σοι τούτων μελέτω· ἐγώ σε καὶ ὡς πυλωρὸς φυλάξω καὶ
ὡς δορυφόρος περιφρουρήσω." Τοιαῦτά σοι τὰ τοῦ κυνὸς
προτερήματα, ξύμμικτον ἡδονῇ καὶ τὴν ἔκπληξιν τοῖς
τέως αἰσθανομένοις ἐπάγοντα. Οὗτος καὶ ποίμνας προβά-
των καὶ βοῶν καὶ ἵππων ἀγέλας φυλάττειν οὐκ ἀμαθής,
καὶ θηριομαχεῖν οὐκ ἀπαίδευτος.

6   Τί μὴ λέγω τὸ πάντων καινότερον, ὡς καὶ τυφλοὺς
ὁδηγεῖ καὶ ὀφθαλμὸς ἐκείνοις ἕτερος γίνεται, καὶ περιάγει
μὲν ἀπανταχόσε περὶ τὰς θύρας ἄρτον αἰτήσοντας, αὖθις
δὲ καθοδηγεῖ περὶ τὸ κατάλυμα; Τί ταυτησὶ τῆς εὐνοίας
μεῖζον γένηται πρὸς θεῶν; Ὁ γὰρ μηδὲ πρὸς ἀλλήλους
ἄνθρωποι πράττειν ἀνέχονται, τοῦτο δὴ τὸ τὴν ἀλογίαν
λαχὸν πρὸς τοὺς ἀνθρώπους ἐργάζεται· καθυποκλίνει μὲν
γὰρ τὸν αὐχένα τοῖς βουλομένοις μετ᾽ εὐλαβείας οἷον καὶ

all the irrational animals are cursed with an absolutely irreconcilable inability to reason, in terms of his rationality the
dog alone—do not be disturbed at hearing this—has been
found to have an advantage here, too. For when a horse
neighs and an ox bellows and a ram bleats, we believe that
they are senselessly striking the air with unintelligible and
superfluous sounds. But when a dog barks, the sound has an
additional underlying meaning; it reveals the presence of
strangers, just as if the dog were able to use articulate
speech, and perhaps he is also asking each visitor, "Who are
you? Where did you come from?" He would utter words
along the following lines, I suppose, to the master himself:
"Why are you so diligent in putting up these fences all
around you, master? Why are you so attentive to the gates
and so concerned over the locks, and why do you spend so
much money on all this? Let none of these things concern
you. I will guard you like a gatekeeper and protect you on all
sides like a bodyguard." Such are the advantages of the dog
to you, which bring astonishment combined with pleasure
to those who already understand them. This animal is also
not ignorant of how to guard flocks of sheep and herds of
oxen and horses, and he is not untrained in fighting wild
beasts.

Why do I not mention the most unusual characteristic 6
of all, that he leads the blind and becomes another eye for
them, and that he leads them around everywhere to beg for
bread at people's doors, and then leads them back again to
their lodging? What goodwill from the gods could be greater
than this? For something that humans do not even tolerate
doing for each other is precisely what this irrational animal
does for humans. For he reverently and humbly bends his
neck in submission to anyone who wishes, and he skillfully

ταπεινότητος, ἐπιτεχνᾶται δέ τι καὶ βάδισμα ξύμμετρον ὡς μὴ πρὸς βίαν ἕλκειν δοκοίη τὸν ὁδηγούμενον, καίτοι τί ποτ᾽ ἂν ἐμποδών, εἰ μόνον ἠθέλησε, προσεγένετο καθυλακτῆσαι μὲν τοῦ δεσπότου, τὸν δὲ δεσμὸν διαρρῆξαι καὶ ἀποδρᾶναι; Ἀλλ᾽ οὗτος καὶ τυπτόμενος φέρει καὶ διωκόμενος οὐκ ἀποδιδράσκει· θᾶττον γὰρ ἂν ἐκπνεύσῃ τυπτόμενος, ἢ τοῦ δεσπότου μικρὸν ἀποστήσεται. Πλουτεῖ γὰρ μετὰ τῶν λοιπῶν καὶ τὴν εὔνοιαν, οὐκ ἀγεννές τι φύσεως φιλοτίμημα, καὶ τοῦτο κάλλιστα ποιῶν ὁ μυθοποιὸς παρεγύμνωσεν, ἐν οἷς τὴν κύνα μᾶλλον ἢ τὴν κυρίαν εὐνοοῦσαν εἶναι πρὸς τὸν δεσπότην διϊσχυρίσατο, πολύ τι καὶ τοῦ παιγνίου προσεγχεάμενος τῷ σπουδάσματι.

7 Συμμαρτυρεῖ μοι τὸ πρᾶγμα καὶ τὸ περὶ τὸν Νικίαν ἐκεῖνον τὸν κυνηγέτην συμβεβηκός. Ἐπεὶ γὰρ ἐκεῖνος ἀπροόπτως οὕτω φερόμενος εἰς ἀνθρακιὰν πυρὸς αὐτόματος ἔπιπτεν, ὅρα κἀνταῦθα τοῦ ζώου τὸ φιλοδέσποτον· ἐθρήνησε μὲν ὡς ἡ φύσις ἐδίδου τὰ πρῶτα, κύκλῳ περὶ τὴν κάμινον διατρέχον καὶ τὸν δεσπότην ἐπιζητοῦν· ἐπεὶ δὲ μηδέν τι καὶ δράσειν ἴσχυσε πρὸς τὴν συμφοράν, ἐπικουρίας ἀνθρωπίνης εἶναι τὸ πάθος ἐνόμισεν ἄξιον καὶ τοὺς παριόντας τῶν ἱματίων <ὁδ>ὰξ ἐφελκόμενος περὶ τὴν κάμινον ἦγε καὶ τὴν συμφορὰν ἀνεδίδασκεν. Οὕτω φιλανθρωποτάτης ψυχῆς τὸ ζῶον καὶ μηδέν τι τῆς <ἀρετῆς ἀ>ποδεούσης ἐστί.

8 Τὸν δὲ γηραλέον ἐκεῖνον κύνα τὸν Ἰθακήσιον ποῦ θήσομεν, ὃς ἐκ τῆς τοῦ γήρως ταλαιπωρίας πάντη μένων ἀκίνητος, ἀλλ᾽ ὅμως μετὰ τὸν εἰκοσαετῆ χρόνον ἐκ Τροίας ἐπανήκοντα τὸν δεσπότην ἐγνώρισε καὶ τότε μόνως

keeps in step so that he may not seem to be forcefully dragging the one who is leading him. And yet what would pre-
vent him, if only he wanted to, from barking at his master,
breaking his leash, and running away? To the contrary, even
when being beaten, this animal endures it, and when being
chased, he does not run away. For when he is being beaten,
he would sooner die than move away from his master even a
little. For along with all his other qualities he abounds in
goodwill, a noble aspect of his nature on which he prides
himself. The fabulist Aesop has revealed this in a very fine
story, where he confidently affirms that the female dog
shows more goodwill to her master than her mistress does,
instilling a good bit of humor into his serious point.

The experience of Nicias the famous hunter also sup- 7
ports my testimony. For when that man unexpectedly lost
his balance and accidentally fell into the hot coals of a fire,
you may see here too the animal's love of his master. At first
the dog wailed, as nature dictated, running in a circle around
the charcoal pit and searching for his master. But when he
was unable to do anything about the calamity, he decided
that the man's suffering required human help, and using his
teeth to drag passersby by their cloaks, he brought them up
to the charcoal pit and informed them of the disaster. So
very benevolent is the soul of this animal, a soul lacking no
part of virtue at all.

Where shall we place that famous old Ithacan dog Argus, 8
who, though reduced to total immobility from the burden
of old age, nevertheless after the passage of twenty years
recognized his master Odysseus when he returned from

ἀνέστη καὶ τοὺς ἐκείνου πόδας ἠσπάζετο; Θάμβους ὄντως τὸ πρᾶγμα καὶ πολλῆς ἐκπλήξεως ἄξιον! Τούτων τὸ τάχος παραγυμνοῦν βουλόμενος Ὅμηρος "ἀργοὺς" κατονομάζει τούτους εἰρωνικώτερον. Τί δ', οὐχὶ καὶ Τηλέμαχος κύνας περὶ τὴν ἀγορὰν ὡς φύλακας προσεφείλκετο; Εἰκότως ἄρα καὶ Πλάτων στρατιώτας τούτους ἐκάλεσε, τοῖς μὲν οἰκείοις φυλακτικοὺς καὶ μειλιχίους, τοῖς δ' ἀλλοτρίοις ἀναιδεῖς τε καὶ φοβερούς.

9 Εἶτά μοι βόας καὶ ἵππους τολμᾷ τις ἐγκωμιάζειν, τοὺς ὑπὸ κυνὸς ὡς ὑπὸ φρουρίου φυλαττομένους, ὡς μὴ θηρῶν κρεῖττον εἶναι φήσῃ τὸ φυλάττον; Εἰ μὴ τῶν Μελιτίδου σπαράγματα γένοιντο, καὶ τίς ποτ' ἂν τοῦ φύσαντος φρενῶν τυγχάνει διάδοχος, καὶ τῆς Κοροίβου μωρίας ἀνάπλεως; Ὡς ἔγωγε θαρρούντως ἀποφηναίμην μηδέν τι τῶν παρ' ἀνθρώποις εἶναι τιμίων ὅσα ψυχῆς εὐγενοῦς τυγχάνει γνωρίσματα, ἐφ' ᾧ μὴ καὶ κύνες φιλοτιμήσονται.

Troy and only then stood up and licked that man's feet? This deed is truly worthy of wonder and great astonishment! Wishing to reveal the speed of these animals, Homer rather ironically calls them "*lazy*." What about the fact that Telemachus also took dogs with him to the assembly for protection? Plato too reasonably called them soldiers, since they are protective and gentle to friends, but ruthless and formidable to strangers.

Then does someone dare to praise to me oxen and horses, 9 which are guarded by a dog as if by a garrison, in order to claim that what does the guarding is no better than beasts? No one would, unless he was a descendant of the sons of Melitides. But who today is heir to the brains of that ancestor or full of the foolishness of Coroebus? Thus I would confidently declare that among the things valued by humans that are signs of a noble soul, there is not one to which dogs will not also aspire.

ETHOPOEIAE

I

Τίνας ἂν εἶπε λόγους ὁ Ἰωσήφ, ὑπὸ τῆς Αἰγυπτίας γυναικὸς κατηγορηθεὶς καὶ εἰς εἱρκτὴν ἐμβληθείς

ὡς ἐπὶ δυστυχίᾳ γεγένημαι καί, μηδὲν ἀδικῶν, δοῦλος γίνομαι καί, σωφρονῶν, παρὰ τοῦτο κολάζομαι. Ἐπ᾽ ἐμοὶ καὶ χορὸς ἀδελφῶν τὴν φύσιν ἐψεύσατο καὶ δεσπότις γυνὴ τὰ σωφρόνων γυναικῶν οὐκ ἐτήρησε. Φθόνος με καθεῖλεν ἀδελφῶν τὰ πρῶτα καὶ νῦν αὖθις ἔρως κατεστρατήγησεν· ἀπόλωλα καὶ φθόνῳ καὶ ἔρωτι. Ὢ δυστυχὴς ἐγὼ καὶ μισούμενος καὶ φιλούμενος!

2 Ἦν μοι πατὴρ εὐδαίμων καὶ πλῆθος ἀδελφῶν καὶ πάντα λαμπρά. Ἐπ᾽ ἐμοὶ παρὰ τοὺς ἄλλους προσεῖχε τὸν νοῦν ὁ πατήρ, ἐμοὶ καὶ τὰς χρηστοτέρας τῶν ἐλπίδων ἐσάλευεν. Ἐπὶ τούτοις μέγας ἐγὼ τὰ ἐνύπνια καὶ γίνομαι λαμπρὸς ὄναρ, ὃν ὕπαρ εἰς δουλείαν φθόνος κατήνεγκεν. Ἔχαιρον, ὑφ᾽ ἡλίῳ καὶ σελήνῃ προσκυνούμενος, ἤκουσα καὶ τῶν λοιπῶν ἀστέρων δεσπότης. Θέρους αὖθις ἐδόκει καιρὸς καὶ τοὐμὸν δράγμα πάνθ᾽, ὁπόσα καὶ δεσπότης πρὸς δούλων, τοῖς τῶν ἀδελφῶν εἶχε δράγμασι. Ταῦτα τοὺς

I

What Joseph would say after being accused by the Egyptian woman and thrown into prison

Surely, I was born for misfortune! Though committing no wrong, I have become a slave, and, though being chaste, I am nonetheless being punished! A band of my brothers has betrayed our natural ties, and my mistress, though a woman, has not observed the ways of chaste women. First, the envy of my brothers destroyed me, and now in turn love has taken the field against me; I am undone both by envy and by love. Alas, how unlucky I am, both when I am hated and when I am loved!

I had a prosperous father and a multitude of brothers and ^{2} everything that is splendid. To me my father devoted more attention than to the others, and on me he anchored his most auspicious hopes. And so I became great and magnificent in my dreams, but in real life envy has reduced me to slavery. I used to rejoice, being revered by the sun and the moon, and I was known as the master of the other stars. On one occasion it seemed to be summertime, and my sheaf dominated the sheaves of my brothers, just as a master does his slaves. These blessings kindled my brothers' envy; be-

ἀδελφοὺς εἰς φθόνον ἐξέκαυσεν, ἀπὸ τούτων τὸ τοῦ γένους ἐλευθέριον ἐγὼ περιήρημαι.

3   Ἐντεῦθεν ἔπιον τοῦ Νείλου, εἶδον τὴν Αἴγυπτον, ἐπέγνων τὰ δούλων ἔργα καὶ τὸ δυστύχημα ἔφερον. Ἀλλ' ὢ τῆς μετέπειτα ἐπηρείας! Ὢ τοῦ δευτέρου κλύδωνος, ὅν μοι τὸ κάλλος ἐπήγειρεν! Ἐλάνθανον ἐπὶ τοῦ προσώπου φέρων τοῦ κακοῦ τὴν ἀρχήν, ἠγνόουν ὡς καὶ σωφρονῶν τις κολάζεται, δεσπότιν ἔλαχον ἀκόλαστον γύναιον. Ἔδοξα τὴν ὄψιν καλός, ἐθαυμαζόμην τὴν ὥραν. Ἡ δὲ ἀλλ' εἶδεν, ἐθαύμασε καὶ τὴν θέαν οὐ μέχρι θαύματος ἔστησεν. Ἀλλ' ἔπαθε πρὸς ἔρωτα καὶ τῇ γνώμῃ δουλεύειν οὐκ ᾐσχύνετο, δεσπότις οὖσα τῷ σώματι. Εἰς πειθὼ τὸ πρῶτον ἔβλεψεν, ἐγὼ δ' οὐκ ἐπένευον. Ὁπλίζεται λοιπὸν εἰς ἀναίδειαν, ἐφείλκετό με τοῦ χιτωνίου, ἐγὼ δ' ἀντέτεινον. Καὶ ἦν ἀγὼν ἔρωτος ἀκολάστου καὶ γνώμης σώφρονος. Ἡ μὲν ἤρα τῆς τοῦ σώματος ὥρας, ἐγὼ δὲ τοῦ τῆς ψυχῆς κάλλους. Ἀλλὰ τότε μὲν ἐκράτησεν ἔρως οὑμὸς καί, τὸ χιτώνιον ἀποδύς, εὐθὺς ἀπεπήδησα.

4   Ὁ δὲ λοιπὸς ἐκείνης ἔρως ἀγανακτεῖ τὴν ἧτταν, ἐπιστρατεύει τὸ δεύτερον καί, τῆς βίας λάφυρον ἐπαγόμενος τὸ χιτώνιον, συγκροτεῖ πρὸς ἐπιβουλὴν πόλεμον ἕτερον. Ἀναστρέφει τὰ πεπραγμένα καὶ βίαν ἐπεγκαλεῖ καὶ γνώμην ἀκόλαστον τῷ σωφρονοῦντι, τῷ βεβιασμένῳ, τῷ πεπονθότι. Προσεπιδείκνυσι καὶ σύμβολον, ὅπερ ἐγὼ πρὸς σωφροσύνην ἀπέλιπον. Ἐπὶ τούτοις δεσμώτης γίνομαι καὶ νῦν τὰ τῶν κακούργων ὑπέχω, μηδὲν κακουργίας μετειληφώς, καὶ δίκας, ὧν οὐ πεπονήρευμαι, δίδωμι.

cause of them I was stripped of the freedom that belongs to my family.

Thereafter I drank of the Nile; I saw Egypt; I came to 3 understand the work of slaves and endured my misfortune. But alas, the spiteful treatment that followed! Alas, the second wave of adversity, which my beauty awakened! Unbeknownst to me, I bore the origin of my woes in my face; I was unaware that even a chaste man could be punished; I was allotted as my mistress a licentious wench. I was considered handsome in appearance; I was admired for my youthful beauty. But she saw, she admired, and she did not limit her looking to mere admiration. She was afflicted with love, and though a mistress in body she was not ashamed to be a slave in mind. At first she tried persuasion, but I would not consent. Then she armed herself for shamelessness; she pulled me toward her by my tunic, but I resisted. A struggle ensued between a licentious love and a chaste mind. She was in love with the youthful beauty of my body, but I loved the beauty of my soul. But then my love won out, and having cast off my tunic, I immediately ran away.

But the love that remains in her is angry at its defeat; 4 it marches out a second time, and presenting the tunic as spoils from the rape, it cobbles together another sort of battle to augment the scheme. She turns what happened upside down, and brings charges of rape and a licentious intent against one who is chaste, one who has been violated, one who has suffered. She exhibits as evidence what I left behind to preserve my chastity. After this, I became a prisoner and now am suffering the fate of criminals, though I have engaged in no crime, and I am paying the penalty for wicked acts that I have not committed.

5 Ὦ φθόνε καὶ δουλεία καὶ ἔρως καὶ εἱρκτὴ καὶ πάντα παράλογα! Ἔρως ἐπ' ἐμοὶ ταὐτὰ φθόνῳ δεδύνηται καὶ πάνθ', ὁπόσα φθονούμενος πρότερον, ταῦτα καὶ νῦν ἐρώμενος δεδυστύχηκα. Φθόνος ἀδελφῶν ἀφείλετό μου τὴν ἐσθῆτα τότε καὶ νῦν γυναικὸς ἔρως ἐγύμνωσε. Λάκκος εἶχε τότε τὸν μηδὲν ἀδικήσαντα καὶ νῦν εἱρκτὴ καὶ δεσμὸς τὸν μηδὲν κακουργήσαντα. Νικῶ σε, πάτερ, ταῖς συμφοραῖς καὶ τοῦτο μόνον εὐτυχὴς ἐγώ. Φθόνον ἔπαθον συγγενῆ καὶ τοῦτο μόνον ἔχω τῷ τεκόντι παρόμοιον. Μᾶλλον μὲν οὖν ὑπερβαίνω καὶ τοῦτο τὸ μέρος· ὃ γὰρ ὑφ' ἑνὸς ἐκεῖνος ἁπλοῦν ἐδυστύχησε, τοῦτο πρὸς πολλῶν ἐγὼ πολλαπλάσιον.

6 Ὦ λαμπρότης ἐνυπνίων ἐκείνων, ὦ προσκυνῶν ἥλιε καὶ ἀστέρες ὑποκλινόμενοι καὶ δουλεύοντα δράγματα, ὕπνος ἄρ' ἦτε σαφὴς καὶ τῶν εἰσέπειτα κακῶν τούτων κατάγελως.

O envy and slavery and love and prison and all things be- 5 yond expectation! Love has had the same power over me as envy, and in all the ways that I was unfortunate previously because I was envied, I am also unfortunate now because I am loved. My brothers' envy robbed me of my clothing then, and now a woman's love has stripped me naked. A pit held me then, though I had done no wrong; a prison and chains hold me now, though I have committed no crime. I am out-doing you, father, in misfortunes, and in this alone am I win-ning. I suffered from an envy akin to his, and in this alone I am similar to my father. Rather, I actually surpass him in this regard, as well; for the misfortune that he suffered a sin-gle time at the hands of one person, I suffered many times over from many people.

O magnificence of those former dreams; O sun bowing 6 and stars bending down and sheaves working as slaves! You were clearly a sleeping dream and a mockery of these evils to come.

2

Τίνας ἂν εἴποι λόγους ὁ Ἰωσήφ, τῆς εἱρκτῆς ἐκβληθεὶς καὶ κρίνας τῷ βασιλεῖ τοὺς ὀνείρους καὶ τὴν ὅλην Αἴγυπτον οἰκονομεῖν ἐγχειρισθείς

Οὐκ ἦν ἄρα τὴν δίκην εἰς τέλος ἀπολιπεῖν, οὐδ᾽ εἰς τὸ παντελὲς κατηγορίαν ἰσχῦσαι καὶ φθόνον ἄδικον. Φθόνος με τὰ πρῶτα ξενηλατεῖ καὶ τοῦ γένους ὑπερορίζει καὶ τῆς ἑστίας γένους ἀπέχθεια καὶ μῖσος ἐφέστιον. Ἔπειτα πάλιν ἔρως ἐπιστρατεύει καὶ δεσμώτην εἷλεν ἐπιβουλὴ γυναικός, ὃν ἔρως οὐκ ἴσχυσεν ἑλεῖν δέσμιον. Οὕτως ἐδυστύχουν ἐγὼ τὰ ἀνέλπιστα, ἐπὶ τούτοις ἔμενον τὴν δίκην. Προὐκαλούμην σύμμαχον τὴν ἀλήθειαν, Θεὸν ἐπεβοώμην τὸν πάτριον, ὁ δ᾽ οὐκ ἐμέλλησεν, ἀλλ᾽ ἧκεν, ἐπήμυνε καὶ τῆς σωφροσύνης ἠμείψατο. Καὶ νῦν οὐκέτι δοῦλος ἐγὼ καὶ τὰ κακούργων ἐκπέφευγα.

2   Ὦ πάντα μοι φανέντα παράλογα! Καὶ φθόνος πρώην οὐκ ἐλπιζόμενος καὶ δεσμός, οἷς ἐσωφρόνουν, μὴ προσδοκώμενος, καὶ νῦν φῶς ἐλευθέριον καὶ κακῶν ἀπαλλαγὴ καὶ λύσις δεσμῶν. Ὡς καλόν γε τὸ τῆς σωφροσύνης φυτὸν καὶ καλοὺς τοῖς δρεπομένοις ἀποδίδωσι τοὺς καρπούς, οὐκ ᾔσχυνε τὸν ἑαυτῆς ἐραστὴν ἐμέ, οὐ προὔδωκεν οὐδ᾽ ἡ ταύτης ἀδελφὴ ἡ Δίκη τὸν οὕτω παθόντα τὰ ἀδικώτατα. Ἀλλ᾽ ἧκεν ὀψὲ μὲν καὶ μετὰ πολλοὺς τοὺς κινδύνους, ἀλλ᾽

2

What Joseph would say after being released from prison, interpreting the dreams for the king, and being entrusted with the administration of all of Egypt

It was impossible, then, for justice to abandon me completely, and for accusations and unjust envy to prevail entirely. First, envy banished me, and both the enmity of my family and hatred at home drove me away from home and family. Then love marched against me again, and though love was unable to take me captive, a woman's scheme took me prisoner. Thus I suffered unanticipated misfortunes, and so I awaited judgment. I called on truth as my ally; I cried out to the God of my fathers, and he did not delay, but he came, he defended me, and he rewarded me for my chastity. And now I am no longer a slave, but have escaped the plots of the wrongdoers.

Oh, all the things that have unexpectedly happened to me! There was both the recent envy that I did not anticipate, and the prison—because I was chaste—that I did not foresee, and now there is the light of freedom and deliverance from my ills and a release from my chains. How fine indeed is the tree of chastity, and how fine the fruits she returns to those who pluck them! Chastity did not disgrace me, her lover, nor did her sister Justice betray the one who thus suffered the greatest injustices. Rather, she came—yes,

RHETORICAL EXERCISES OF NIKEPHOROS BASILAKES

ἀπέδωκε πάντα σὺν τόκῳ καὶ τὰς ἐλπίδας ὁ πολὺς οὐκ ἀπήλεγξε χρόνος. Ἐξείλετο δεσμῶν, συνεξείλετο δουλείας, σοφίας ἐνέπλησε, βασιλεῦσιν ἐπέδειξε καί, τὸ δὴ μεῖζον, ὅλην Αἴγυπτον ἐχαρίσατο. Τοῦτο νῦν ἔχω τοῦ φθόνου τόκον καὶ τῆς εἱρκτῆς καὶ τὴν δίκην τῆς μακρᾶς ἀναβολῆς ἐκείνης οὐ μέμφομαι.

3   Τίς εἶδέ ποτε τηλικαύτην τύχης καινοτομίαν; Τίς ἤκουσεν ἐπιπλοκὴν πραγμάτων οὕτως ἀνέλπιστον; Οὐκ ᾔδειν ἐξ ἐναντίων τἀναντία καρπούμενος· ὅτε καλῶς ἔχειν ἐδόκουν, τὰ δεινότατα ἔπασχον καί, φαινομένων κακῶν, κερδαίνων ἐλάνθανον καί, ῥόδα μέλλων τρυγᾶν ἐξ ἀκανθῶν, οὐκ ἐγίνωσκον. Κατεκρινόμην δουλείαν, ὅτε βιοῦν ἐδόκουν τὰ ἐλευθέρια, καὶ νῦν, ὅτε μηδ᾽ ἐλπὶς ἐλευθερίου τροφῆς ὑπελείπετο, τὴν φίλην ἐλευθερίαν αὖθις ἀπέλαβον. Ἐδυστύχουν τὰ κακούργων, ὅτε μηδὲν ἠδίκουν, καὶ νῦν, ὅτε κακουργεῖν ἐκρινόμην, τῆς εἱρκτῆς καὶ τῶν δεσμῶν ἠλευθέρωμαι.

4   Ὦ σὺ τότε συνδεσμῶτα καὶ ταῦτα δυστυχῶν καὶ νῦν τὰ μεγάλα συνευτυχῶν, ἱκανῶς με τῆς σοφίας ἠμείψω, πρέπουσαν τὴν χάριν ἀπέδωκας, ἔλυσας τῶν δεσμῶν τὸν πρὸ τοῦ σοι τὴν λύσιν ἐπαγγειλάμενον. Ἄμφω τῆς εἱρκτῆς συμμετείχομεν, ἄμφω καὶ νῦν τῶν βασιλείων συμμετεσχήκαμεν. Ἀλλ᾽ ὦ τῶν ἐνυπνίων ἐκείνων, ἃ σὺ μὲν προὔτεινες, ἐγὼ δ᾽ ὑπέλυον! Ὦ τῶν ἐπὶ τούτοις λαμπροτέρων, ἃ βασιλεὺς μὲν προὔβάλλετο, ἐγὼ δ᾽ εἰς τὸ σαφὲς ὑπανέπτησον! Ὡς ἦν ἄρα καὶ πάλιν ἐνυπνίῳ τὴν ἐλευθερίαν κομίσασθαι τὸν χάριν ἐνυπνίων ὑπὸ φθόνου δουλεύσαντα. Ἐξ

152

late and after these many dangers, but she repaid everything with interest, and the long wait did not refute my hopes. She set me free from my chains, helped set me free from slavery, filled me with wisdom, exhibited me before kings, and— best of all—granted me all of Egypt. This I now have as a payment of interest for the envy and the prison, and I find no fault with justice for that long delay.

Who ever saw such a novelty of fortune? Who ever heard 3 of such an unexpected and complex chain of events? I did not know that I was reaping opposites from opposites; when I thought things were going well, I suffered most terribly, and when evils were manifest, I profited unawares, and when I was about to gather roses from thorn bushes, I did not realize it. I was condemned to slavery when I thought I was living a life of freedom, and now, when not even the hope of a free man's food remained, I have recovered my own dear freedom again. I suffered the fate of wrongdoers, when I was doing no wrong, and now, when I was judged to be a wrongdoer myself, I have been freed from prison and my chains.

O you, chief cupbearer, who were then my fellow pris- 4 oner, who suffered these misfortunes and now share great good fortune with me: you fully compensated me for my wisdom, you gave fitting thanks in return, you released me from my chains, as you had previously promised to do. We both shared in the prison together; now we have both shared the palace together, as well. Oh, those dreams which you put forward, but which I explained! Oh, the more magnificent ones that came later, which the king proposed as problems, and which I clearly explicated! Thus, a dream was able to restore freedom to one who was enslaved by envy for

ὀνειράτων δοῦλος εἶδον τὴν Αἴγυπτον, ἐξ ὀνειράτων καὶ νῦν τῶν Αἰγυπτίων ἐκράτησα.

5 Ἤκουσιν οἱ τῶν βοῶν πίονες, οἱ τῶν ἐνιαυτῶν εὐφορώτατοι· τοῦτον ἐγὼ τὸν κόρον καλῶς διαθήσομαι, ὅλον ἀποταμιεύσω τὸν σῖτον, εἰς μάτην οὐδὲν ἀναλώσομαι. Ἥξουσι μετ' οὐ πολὺ καὶ βόες ἰσχνοὶ τὰ σώματα, χρόνος ἕτερος, παρ' ᾧ λιμὸν ἐπαπειλεῖ τὰ ἐνύπνια· καὶ σιτοδοτήσω καὶ θρέψω τὴν Αἴγυπτον, εἰς καλὸν ταῖς προτέραις εὐφορίαις ἀποχρησάμενος. Μᾶλλον μὲν οὖν κοινὸν ἔσται πρὸς πᾶσαν γῆν τὸ κακὸν καὶ τῆς σιτοδοσίας κοινώσομαι.

6 Τοῦτο ἦν ἄρα τὰ δράγματα, τοῦτο προσκυνῶν ἥλιος καὶ ἀστέρες ὑποκλινόμενοι, ὅτι πᾶσαν δεῖ με θρέψαι τὴν ὑφ' ἥλιον καὶ πάντες, ἐφ' ὅσοις τὸ τῶν ἀστέρων ἔφθασε φῶς, προσπεσοῦνται σιτοδοτοῦντι καὶ τῆς ἐμῆς οἰκονομίας δεήσονται. Οἶμαι δ' ὅτι καὶ αὐτοὺς ὄψομαι τοὺς ἀδελφοὺς προσπίπτοντας ἐπὶ δράγμασι καὶ θεάσονται δεσπότην, ὃν δουλεύειν ἐνόμισαν. Τούτους ἀστέρας ἐγὼ τίθεμαι τοὺς ἀπὸ Σάρρας, τοὺς ἐξ Ἀβραάμ· τούτῳ γὰρ καὶ Θεὸς ὑπὲρ τοὺς ἀστέρας πληθῦναι τὴν γονὴν ἐπηγγείλατο. Καὶ γένοιτό μοι τοὺς ἀστέρας τούτους ἰδεῖν καὶ προσεποψοίμην τὸν πατέρα, τὸν ἥλιον.

the sake of his dreams. Because of my dreams, I saw Egypt as a slave; because of my dreams, I have now become master of the Egyptians.

The fat cattle have come, and the most productive of the 5 years. I will oversee this surplus well; I will manage all the grain wisely; I will expend nothing in vain. There will also come, in the near future, cattle with emaciated bodies, a second period in which the dreams threaten famine; I will distribute grain and feed Egypt, making good use of the abundant produce from before. Moreover, the suffering will be shared by the whole world, and I will share and distribute our grain.

This, then, is what the sheaves portended; this was the 6 sun bowing and the stars bending down—that I must feed the whole world under the sun and that everyone on whom the light of the stars ever shone will prostrate themselves before me as I distribute the grain, and they will beg for my stewardship. I suppose that I will see even my very brothers prostrating themselves for sheaves, and they will see as their master the one whom they believed to be a slave. These stars I regard as the ones born of Sarah, the ones born of Abraham; for God also promised him that he would multiply his offspring beyond the number of the stars. And may I be able to see these stars and look upon my father, the sun.

3

Τίνας ἂν εἶπε λόγους ὁ Σαμψών,
αὐξηθείσης τῆς τριχός,
μέλλων ἐπικατασεῖσαι τὸν οἶκον τοῖς
ἀλλοφύλοις ἀθρόον μετὰ τῆς Δαλιδᾶς
συμποσιάζουσιν

Ὦ χεῖρες, εἰς οἶον ὑμῖν πέρας ἥκει τὰ τῆς ἀνδρείας!
Μύλων ὑμᾶς διεδέξατο καὶ δουλεία πρὸς ὕβριν καὶ ὄνων
ἔργα νῦν ὑπέχετε, ἃς ὄνου σιαγὼν ὥπλιζε πρότερον, καὶ
τῶν ἀτυχημάτων μείζων ἐφ᾽ ὑμῖν ὁ κατάγελως. Ὁ πρὶν
γενναῖος ἐκεῖνος ἐγώ, ὁ καὶ γυμνὸς ὁπλίτας φοβῶν καὶ
πολλοὺς εἰς ἀναιρῶν, αἰχμάλωτος γέγονα γυναικὸς καὶ
νῦν γέλως πρόκειμαι τοῖς ἐχθροῖς καὶ δουλεύω τὰ ἀτι-
μότατα. Ὦ γυναικῶν γένος ἐπάρατον! Ὃν ἐφίλει, περι-
ειργάζετο καί, ὃν τῆς ῥώμης ἐθαύμαζε, τοῦτον τὰ ὅπλα
παρείλετο. Ὦ κακῶς ἰδόντες ὀφθαλμοὶ καὶ παρὰ τοῦτο
νῦν ἔτι βλέπειν οὐκ ἔχοντες! Οὐκ εἰς καλὸν ἀπεχρήσασθε
τῷ βλέπειν, τοιγαροῦν δικαίως ἀφῄρησθε.

2   Ὦ τῆς πρώην σωφροσύνης ἐκείνης! Ὦ τῶν ἀπὸ ταύτης
ἀριστευμάτων! Ἐσωφρόνουν καὶ προὔβαινέ μοι τὰ τῆς
ἀνδρείας. Ἐφυλαττόμην μέθην καὶ λέων ἡλίσκετο. Οὐκ
ἠσέλγαινον καὶ δυσμενεῖς ἐπεφρίκεσαν. Ἐτήρουν τὰ τῆς

3

What Samson would say when, as his hair begins to grow back, he is about to shake to the ground the house that is packed with Philistines drinking with Delilah

O hands, to what an end have your feats of courage brought you! A millstone and insulting slavery are now your lot, and you, once armed by the jawbone of an ass, now endure the work of asses, and greater than these misfortunes is their mockery of you. I, the former noble one, who, though unarmed, routed armed men and who, though alone, destroyed many, have become a woman's captive and now stand before my enemies as an object of ridicule, and I perform the most dishonorable services. O accursed race of women! This man whom she loved, took special care of, and admired for his strength, she has now robbed of his weapons. O eyes, which once looked with wicked intent, but now by contrast are unable to see at all! You did not use your sight for good purposes, and so you have justly been destroyed.

Alas, my former chastity! Alas, my brave deeds that arose 2 from it! I behaved chastely, and my courage brought me success. I guarded against drunkenness, and a lion was defeated. I did not behave licentiously, and my enemies shuddered

ἐπαγγελίας καὶ χρυσῆν κόμην ἐπὶ κεφαλῆς εἶχον ὅπλον ἀσίδηρον. Ἐκράτουν σιαγόνος καὶ πλησμονῆς ἀλόγου καὶ σιαγὼν ὄνου τὰ τῶν ὅπλων ἐπλήρου μοι. Τὸ δὲ δὴ μεῖζον, καὶ δίψαν ἴστη καὶ τρόπαιον, τὸ μέν, ὅτε τοὺς πολεμίους συνέθλιβε, τὸ δ᾽, ὅτε συνθλιβομένῳ μετὰ τὴν μάχην ὕδωρ ἐπήγαγεν.

3 Ἀλλ᾽ ἐξέπεσον εἰς ὕβριν, τοιγαροῦν περιύβρισμαι τὰ δεινότατα. Αὐτὸς ἐμαυτῷ τὴν συμφορὰν ταύτην ἐπήγειρα, αὐτὸς κατὰ τῶν ὀφθαλμῶν μόνον οὐκ ἐπήνεγκα τὸ σιδήριον. Οὐκ ἔξωθεν ἀλλ᾽ οἴκοθεν βέβλημαι· παρεῖδον τὴν ἐκ παιδὸς σωφροσύνην· παρέβην τὰ τῆς ἐπαγγελίας, ἐφ᾽ ᾗ γεγέννημαι. Εἰς ἕν μοι τὰ τῆς ἰσχύος ἔκειτο. Εἰς τρυφὴν ὑπήχθην, κάλλος ἐθαύμασα, γυναικὸς ἑάλων, τῇ δὲ καὶ γνώμη καὶ γένος καὶ τὰ πάντα ἀλλόφυλα. Εἰς τοσοῦτον ἐμαυτὸν ὤθησα τὸ κακόν, τοιγαροῦν ἑάλων καὶ δίκας ἔδωκα τῆς πρώην ἀνδρείας ἅμα καὶ τῆς εἰσέπειτα παροινίας, ἐκεῖνο τοῖς ἀλλοφύλοις, ὧν τοὺς τραυματίας ἐπλήθυνα, τοῦτο Θεῷ τῷ πατρίῳ. Θεὸν γὰρ ἠθέτουν, ὅτε τὰ τῆς ἐπαγγελίας ᾔσχυνον.

4 Ἀλλ᾽ οἴμοι! Τὰ τῶν προγόνων δυστυχῶ καὶ βεβαιῶ τὸ γένος τῇ συγγενείᾳ τῆς συμφορᾶς. Μαδιανίτας ἐπόρθουν καὶ τὴν ἐκείνων ἰσχὺν ἔφερεν οὐδέν, ἀλλ᾽ ἔπιπτον αὐτοῖς ὁπλίταις αἱ πόλεις καὶ ἦν τὸ δεινὸν ὡς ἀμήχανον.

5 Ἀλλ᾽ ἧκε τοῖς πολεμίοις, οὐκ οἶδ᾽ ὅθεν, εἰς νοῦν καὶ κάλλος γυναικῶν ἐφοπλίζουσι καὶ οἱ πρὸ τοῦ βάλλοντες ἔπιπτον καὶ γυναικῶν γεγόνασιν ἔργον, οὓς πρότερον

with fear before me. I abided by the command and kept the golden hair on my head as a weapon not made of iron. I mastered my jaws and an irrational need to fill my belly full, and the jawbone of an ass fulfilled my need for weapons. What is more, it put a stop to my thirst and brought me victory, in the latter case when it distressed the enemy, in the former when it supplied me with water in my distress after the battle.

But I fell into arrogance, and so I have been treated most 3 arrogantly and terribly. I brought this misfortune on myself; I all but brought the blade against my own eyes. I have been struck not from without but from within. I disregarded the chastity practiced from my youth. I violated the terms under which I was born; my might was dependent on one thing. I was seduced by luxury; I was amazed at beauty; I was defeated by a woman, whose mind and race and everything were Philistine. I thrust myself into such a great evil, and so I was defeated and paid the penalty both for my former courage and for my drunken violence thereafter, paying the first penalty to the Philistines, the number of whose wounded men I multiplied, and paying the second to the God of my fathers, for I rejected God when I disgraced the command.

But alas! I am cursed with the sufferings of my ancestors, 4 and I confirm my lineage with a misfortune akin to theirs. They sacked the Midianites and nothing could withstand their strength, but their cities fell together with their armed men and the suffering was almost impossible to bear.

But the enemy got the idea—I do not know from where 5 —to use women's beauty as a weapon, and those who formerly hurled their weapons have fallen, and those whom

ἄνδρες οὐκ ἔφερον. Ταύτην δίδωμι τῆς ἀσελγείας δίκην κἀγώ, ὑπὸ τοιαύτης ἁλίσκομαι παρατάξεως, τοιοῦτον ἥττημαι πόλεμον. Ἐπίστευσα ἐμαυτὸν ἔρωτι, προΰδωκα τὰ τιμιώτατα γυναικὸς πόθῳ καὶ ἀσελγείας ὑπερβολῇ.

6 Ὦ πάντα ἁπλοῦς ἐγὼ καὶ μηδὲν ὀκνῶν χαρίζεσθαι πρὸς ἔρωτα! Ἥρετό μου τὴν ἰσχύν, ἐγὼ δ' ὑπέκρυπτον καλῶς γε τὰ πρῶτα. Ἐσχηματίζετο λύπην καὶ πάλιν ἠπάτησα, ἡ δ' ἀπεπειρᾶτό μου τῶν χειρῶν καί, γνοῦσα τὴν ἀπάτην, αὖθις ἤσχαλλεν, ἐδυσφόρει καὶ ἅμα δακρύειν ἐπλάττετο. Ἐνταῦθα ἐμαλακίσθην ὁ γενναῖος ἐγὼ καὶ δακρύουσαν οὐκ ἤνεγκα κόρην, τοιγαροῦν δακρύειν μοι περιλείπεται. Ἐπέδειξα τὸ χρυσοῦν ἐπὶ κεφαλῆς ὅπλον, ἡ δ' οὐκ ἐφείσατο, ἀλλ' ἅμα τε τὸν βόστρυχον ἐκείνη καὶ τοὺς ὀφθαλμοὺς ἐξέκοπτον οἱ πολέμιοι.

7 Ἅμα τὰ τῆς ἐπαγγελίας παρεώραται καὶ σίδηρος ἐπὶ τὴν δυστυχῆ ταυτηνὶ κεφαλὴν ἀναβέβηκε καὶ πρὸς αὐτοὺς ὀφθαλμοὺς ἔφθασε τὸ δεινόν. Ὦ τοῦ γέλωτος! Ὦ τῆς ὕβρεως! Χεὶρ ἀπήλεγξε γυναικὸς χεῖρας ἐκείνας, ὑφ' ὧν λέων ἔπιπτε καὶ πολλαὶ χεῖρες ὁπλιτῶν ἀπηλέγχοντο. Οἱ δέ—ἀλλ' ὦ τῆς περινοίας!—εἰς τοὺς ὀφθαλμοὺς εὐθὺς ἔβλεψαν, ἐπ' αὐτοὺς ὅλον ἐξεκένωσαν τὸν θυμόν, ἵν' ἐπὶ μᾶλλον ἐφυβρίζειν ἔχοιεν καὶ δοῦλος ἀλλοφύλων βιώσομαι.

8 Ἀλλ' εἰς καιρὸν ἡμῖν ἐπανῆκε τὸ ὅπλον, ἤδη μοι τῆς ἀνδρείας ὁ στάχυς ἀνέβλαστεν, αἰσθάνομαι τῆς ῥώμης ἐπανθούσης. Σαμψὼν ἐκεῖνος ἐγὼ πάλιν ὁ πρότερον, οὐκέτι μοι καθ' ἕνα τὰ τῆς ἰσχύος, ἀλλ' ἐξέφυ τῆς κεφαλῆς ὡς ἀπὸ ῥίζης ὁ βόστρυχος καὶ χεῖρας ἔχω πρὸς ὅλον ἀρκούσας στρατόπεδον. Μικροῦ καὶ χάριν οἶδα τοῖς

men were once unable to withstand have become victims of women. I too pay this penalty for my licentiousness; I am defeated by such a battle line; I have lost such a war. I entrusted myself to love; I surrendered the most honorable things to my desire for a woman and to excessive licentiousness.

Alas, what a complete fool I have been, not hesitating to 6 grant any favor when it came to love! She asked me about my strength, and at first I hid it from her well. She pretended to grieve and again I deceived her, but she tested my hands and, upon discovering my deception, became upset again; she took it hard and pretended to cry. Then, being noble, I was softened and could not endure a girl crying, and so now crying is all that is left for me. I revealed the golden shield on my head, and she showed me no mercy but cut off my locks, and the enemy put out my eyes.

As soon as the command was disregarded, a blade reached 7 this unlucky head, and the horror reached my very eyes. Alas, the mockery! Alas, the insult! A woman's hand vanquished those hands by which a lion fell and by which many hands of armed men were vanquished. And they—but alas, their craftiness!—immediately looked to my eyes; they emptied out all their wrath upon them, so that they could abuse me even more, and now I will live as a slave to Philistines.

But my shield has returned to me in good time; already a 8 sprout of my courage has regrown; I can feel my strength blooming; I am once again the Samson that I was before; no longer is my strength that of a mere individual, but the locks have grown from my head as if from a root and I have hands capable of taking on an entire army. I am almost grateful to

ἀλλοφύλοις, ὅτι μου τοὺς ὀφθαλμούς, οὐ τὰς χεῖρας ἐξέκοψαν, ὡς νῦν γε καιρὸς ἀμύνασθαι τοὺς ἐχθρούς.

9   Οἱ δέ που χαίρουσι τὰ ἐπινίκια καὶ προσεπεντρυφῶσι τῇ καθελούσῃ τὸν πολέμιον κόρῃ, τάχα με καὶ προσεπισκώπτουσιν, ὅπως ἐμαυτὸν ἀλλοφύλῳ προὔδωκα γυναικὶ καὶ τὸν ὄντως ἔκφυλον ἐθάρρησα ἔρωτα. Οἶμαι δ' ὅτι μετά γε τὸν πότον καὶ τὴν πολλὴν μέθην προσεπικαλέσονται καὶ τὸν Σαμψὼν ἐμὲ καὶ προσεπιχλευάσουσιν, ἐγὼ δὲ ἅλις ἔχω καταγελώμενος, οὐκ ἀνέξομαι πολεμίας φωνῆς, προσεπιταττούσης καὶ προσεπορχεῖσθαι τοῖς σκώμμασιν.

10   Ἀλλ' εὖγε τῆς ἑορτῆς! Εὖγε τῶν ἐπινικίων! Καιρὸν ἔχει μοι τὰ τῆς ἐπιβουλῆς· οἱ μὲν ἄνω που τρυφῶσιν ἀθρόοι παρὰ τὰ μετέωρα, ἐγὼ δὲ κάτω πρὸς αὐτὰ τὰ τὴν οἰκίαν ἑδράζοντα. Ἄγε περιήγησαί μοι, ὦ παῖ, γενοῦ μοι πρὸς μικρὸν ἀντὶ τῶν ὀφθαλμῶν, ἀναπλήρωσον ταῖς χερσὶ τὸ λειπόμενον. Ἐπίδειξον μόνον τοὺς κίονας τῇ χειρί, τὸ δ' ἀπὸ τοῦδε τῆς οἰκίας ἔξιθι· δεῖ γάρ σε ζῆν ἔτι καὶ περιεῖναι, ὅτι διὰ σοῦ μοι δώσουσι δίκην οἱ δυσμενεῖς. Ὡς ἐγὼ συντεθνήξομαι καλῶς τοῖς ἐχθροῖς, ἐπεὶ τὸ σὺν ἡδονῇ ζῆν ἀφήρημαι.

the Philistines for cutting out my eyes rather than cutting off my hands, because now it is time to avenge myself on the enemy.

They are probably celebrating their victory and taking delight in the girl who brought down their enemy, and perhaps they are also mocking me for how I entrusted myself to a Philistine woman and felt confident in a love that was truly alien. I suppose that after the drinking and the great drunkenness they will again summon me, Samson, and ridicule me, but I have had enough of being mocked; I will not tolerate the enemy's voice ordering me also to dance to their jeers.

But hurray for the banquet! Hurray for the victory celebrations! Now is the time to carry out my plan. Above they are probably reveling in a crowd high above the ground, while below I am standing next to the house's very supports. Come on, boy, and describe them to me; for a short time be a substitute for my eyes; supply what is missing to my hands. Just show me the columns with your hand, and then leave this house. For you must go on living and survive, because through you my enemies will pay the penalty that they owe me. Thus I will die well along with my enemies, since I have been robbed of living pleasurably.

4

Τίνας ἂν εἴποι λόγους ὁ Δαυίδ,
διωκόμενος ὑπὸ τοῦ Σαοὺλ καὶ
κρατηθεὶς ὑπὸ τῶν ἀλλοφύλων καὶ
μέλλων ἀποσφαγῆναι

Εὖγε τῆς τῶν ὁμοφύλων εὐνοίας! Εὖγε τῆς περὶ τὸν
ἀριστέα προθέσεως! Ὡς καλήν γε τῆς ἀριστείας ἀντι-
λαμβάνω τὴν δωρεάν! Μετὰ τρόπαιον δραπετεύω, μετὰ
νίκην ἐλαύνομαι καὶ γίνεταί μοι πολέμου τελευτὴ μάχης
δευτέρας ἀρχὴ καὶ τὰ τῆς ἀριστείας εἰς φυγὴν ἀποτελευτᾷ.
Γολιὰθ μὲν ἐκεῖνος, Θεοῦ ζῶντος ἐξονειδίζων παράταξιν,
πέπτωκε μετὰ καὶ τῶν αὐτοῦ θεῶν καὶ τὸ δὴ μεῖζον, οἷς
ὥπλιστο καθ᾽ ἡμῶν, τούτοις παρ᾽ ἡμῶν ἀπεσφάττετο. Καὶ
γέγονεν ἔργον μαχαίρας μὲν τῆς αὐτοῦ, δεξιᾶς δὲ ταυτησὶ
τῆς ἐμῆς, τὸ δ᾽ ἄλλο πᾶν ὅσον ἀπερίτμητον ᾤχετο.

2   Τίνα γοῦν μοι τὰ γέρα; Τίνες αἱ τῶν τροπαίων μοι
ἀμοιβαί; Ὁμόφυλος μάχη μετὰ μάχην ἀλλόφυλον, οἰκείων
φυγὴ μετὰ φυγὴν δυσμενῶν. Πόλεμον ἐκράτησα γνωρι-
ζόμενον καὶ φεύγω πόλεμον ἄλλον ἀνέλπιστον, ὃν οὔτε
κρατεῖν εὐσεβές· τὸ γὰρ δυσμεναῖνον ὁμόφυλον οὔτ᾽ αὖθις
ἁλίσκεσθαι δίκαιον, τὸ γὰρ ἐξ ὁμοφύλων πεσεῖν οὐ καλόν.

3   Τί ταῦτα Σαούλ; Διώκεις, ὃν ἐν ὅπλοις ἐθαύμαζες. Ὃν

4

What David would say when, being pursued by Saul, he is held captive by the Philistines and is about to be killed

Bravo for the affection of my people! Bravo for the good-will toward the hero! What a fine gift do I receive in return for my heroism! After a triumph I run away; after a victory I am driven off; the end of a war becomes the beginning of a second battle for me, and my heroic deeds culminate in flight. The famous Goliath, *scorning the army of the living God,* has fallen along with his gods, and what is more, by the same weapon with which he armed himself against us, he was slaughtered by us. And he fell victim to his own sword, but it was wielded by this right hand of mine, and all the rest of the uncircumcised perished.

What, then, were my prizes? What were the rewards for 2 my triumphs? A battle against my own people after a battle against Philistines, and a flight from my friends after an escape from my enemies. I won a conventional war, and I flee another unexpected war that would be impious to win. For it is not just for one's own tribesman, though hostile, even to be captured; for it is not right for one to be killed by the hands of his own tribesmen.

What does this mean, Saul? You are pursuing the one 3 whom you admired in arms. The one whom you joined to

εἰς γένος συνῆπτες, τοῦτον τοῦ γένους ἀποδιϊστᾷς. Ἀπελαύνεις, ὑφ' οὗ τὸ πολέμιον πρότερον. Μανίας ἔργα ταῦτα καὶ πνεύματος πονηροῦ. Ἦπου καὶ πάλιν μέμηνας; Ἄγχει τάχα καὶ πάλιν σε τὸ δαιμόνιον; Ἀπελήλαται μεθ' ἡμῶν καὶ τὰ κρούματα, ὑφ' ὧν σοι τῆς ψυχῆς τὸ μαινόμενον ἐξεκρούετο, καὶ νῦν ἐπεισπηδᾷ σοι σφοδρότερον. Ἐκείνου τοῦ πονηροῦ πνεύματος τοῦτον ἐγὼ κρίνω τὸν πόλεμον, ἐκεῖθεν εἶναι ταῦτα νομίζω τὰ τραύματα. Ἐπλήττετο παρ' ἡμῶν τοῖς τῆς κιθάρας κρούμασιν. Ἔφευγεν, ἐδραπέτευεν, ἤλγει, τῆς σῆς ψυχῆς ὥσπερ τινὸς οἰκίας ἀπελαυνόμενον. Εἶτ' αὖθις παλινοστεῖ καὶ χεῖρα μανικὴν πρὸς μουσικὴν ἀνθώπλισε δεξιάν. Ἵν' ἢ πεσοῦμαι, φεύγων, καὶ δίκην λήψομαι τῶν κρουμάτων, ἢ καὶ κρατήσω, μαχόμενος, καὶ τὰ τῆς νίκης μεταπεσεῖταί μοι πρὸς ἀσέβειαν. Ὡς ἔμοιγε κρεῖττον πεσεῖν, ἢ πρὸς ὁμοφύλους βάψαι τὸ δόρυ καὶ τρόπαιον ἐξ ἀσεβείας λαβεῖν.

4   Ἀλλ' οἴμοι! Τίνα τοῦτον ὁρῶ πόλεμον ἕτερον; Ἐχθροὺς ἀλλ' ὁμοφύλους ἐκπέφευγα καὶ δυσμενέσιν ἀλλοφύλοις ἐμπέπτωκα. Πόλεμος ἐπ' ἐμοὶ τίκτειν οἶδε πόλεμον καὶ πόλεμον δυσμενῶν ὁμοφύλων διαδέχεται πόλεμος καὶ δυσμενεῖς ὁμοφύλους αὖθις ἄνδρες πολέμιοι. Ἐγὼ καὶ νικῶν ἐλαύνομαι καὶ φεύγων ἁλίσκομαι. Τί δράσω; Τί χρήσομαι τοῖς παροῦσι; Μέσος πολεμίων ἕστηκα. Ἤδη μου τὴν μορφὴν ὑποπτεύουσιν, ἤδη μου περιεργάζονται τὴν δεξιάν. Ἀμήχανον τὸ κακόν, βάρβαρος ὄχλος Γολιὰθ τοῦ πεσόντος ὑφ' ἡμῶν ὁπλίζεται, γένος ὅλον ὑπ' ἐμοῦ τὸν στρατηγὸν ἀφῃρημένοι, τηλικαύτην ἐν πολέμοις περικεκομμένοι δεξιάν.

your family, you are separating from your family. You are driving away the one by whom you formerly drove away the enemy. These actions are the result of madness and an evil spirit. Have you perhaps gone mad again, and is the demon perhaps choking you again? The plucking of the lyre that expelled the madness from your soul has been driven off along with us, and now the madness is attacking you more violently. I judge this to be the war of that evil spirit, and I believe these wounds come from it. I wounded it by plucking on the lyre. It fled, it ran away, and it felt pain, being driven out of your soul as if from a home. Then it returned again and armed your insane right hand against my music. So either I will fall, fleeing, and pay the penalty for my music, or I will triumph, fighting, and my victory will result in impiety. Thus it is better for me to fall than to bloody my spear against my own people and win a victory as a result of impiety.

But alas! What is this new war I see? I have escaped the 4 enemy—my own people—and have fallen in with hostile Philistines. War knows how to beget war on me, and a war against my own people follows a war against hostile men, and military enemies in turn follow hostile men from my own people. I am persecuted when I am victorious, and I am captured when I flee. What will I do? How will I manage my present circumstances? I stand in the midst of the enemy. Already they are suspicious of my appearance; already they are scrutinizing my right hand. The evil is impossible to bear; I killed Goliath, and his barbarian mob is up in arms; an entire race has been deprived of their general by me and has had so great a right hand cut off in war.

5 Ἆρα δακρύσω; Ἆρα τὴν συμφορὰν ἀποκλαύσομαι; Προβαλοῦμαι νόμον πολέμου καὶ συγγνώσονται, ὡς ἦν ἐν ὅπλοις ἀγὼν καὶ μαχομένῳ δυσμενεῖς βάλλειν ἐπὶ μάχης ἀφεῖται, νῦν δ' ἀλλ' ἱκέτης ἥκω καὶ γίνομαι ξύμμαχος. Ἀλλ' οὐκ οἶδε τὸ βάρβαρον σπένδεσθαι, ἀλλ' οὐκ οἶδεν ἱκεσίας αἰδῶ, οὐ πρὸς οἶκτον μαλάσσεται. Εἰς οὐδέν μοι τοιγαροῦν πεσεῖται τὰ δάκρυα. "Γενναῖος εἶ," φήσουσι, "δίκας ἡμῖν ὀφείλεις· πέπτωκεν ὑπὸ σοῦ Γολιάθ, πίπτε καὶ σὺ παρ' ἡμῶν."

6 Ἀλλ' εὖγε τῆς ἐπινοίας, ὀψὲ μέν, συνῆκα δ' οὖν. Ἀνοίας προσωπεῖον ὑποδύσομαι καὶ φρενῶν ὑποκρινοῦμαι παραφορὰν καὶ σκηνοβατήσω τὰ μανικά. Οὕτως οἶμαι τὸ τοῦ πάθους ὑπερβάλλον καὶ τὸ βάρβαρον καταιδέσει καὶ Σαοὺλ ἴσως εἰς οἶκτον ἐφέλξεται· αἰδεσθήσεται γάρ, εἰ δι' ἐκεῖνον αὐτὸς μέμηνε, δι' ὃν μαινόμενος πέπαυται.

Should I cry? Should I bewail my misfortune? I will cite 5
the law of war in my defense, and then they will pardon me
on the ground that it was a contest of arms, and a combatant
is allowed to strike down his enemy in battle, but now I have
come as a suppliant and am becoming their ally. But no, barbarians do not know how to make treaties, and they show
no respect for supplication, nor do they relent out of pity. In
vain, therefore, will my tears fall. "You are noble," they will
say, "and you must pay the penalty; Goliath has fallen by
your hand: now you too will fall by ours."

But bravo for my clever thought. The thought may have 6
come late to me, but nevertheless it did come: I will put on a
mask of idiocy, act deranged, and make a pretense of madness. Thus I think even the barbarians will respect my excessive suffering, and perhaps Saul will be moved to pity. For
he will be ashamed, if he himself has gone mad over the very
man who put an end to his madness.

5

Τίνας ἂν εἴποι λόγους ὁ Δαυίδ,
ἐν σπηλαίῳ καταλαβὼν ἀφύλακτον
τὸν Σαοὺλ ὑπνοῦντα,
ὅτε ὑπ' αὐτοῦ ἐδιώκετο

Ἔχω σε τὸν διώκτην ὁ δραπέτης ἐγώ, ἔχω σε τὸν εἰς
ἀναίρεσιν ἕτοιμον, εἰς τὸ παθεῖν ἑτοιμότερον. Ὦ τῆς ἐκ
Θεοῦ τῶν πραγμάτων ἐπιφορᾶς! Ἀντέστραπταί σου τὸ
βούλημα καί, ὃ δρᾶν ἠπείλεις, τοῦτο νῦν αὐτὸς πρόκεισαι
καί, ὃν λάκκον ὤρυξας, εἰς τοῦτον ἐμπέπτωκας. Διώκων
ἑάλως καὶ φεύγων κεκράτησαι. Ὕπνῳ βέβλησαι καὶ τὸ
σῶμα μετὰ καὶ τῆς φυλακῆς καταβέβλησαι. Κἂν εἰ βού-
λοιτό τις, ἄπονον τὸ θήραμα, εὐάλωτος ὁ πολέμιος. Κεῖται
μὲν ὁ φυγαδεύων, ἄφρακτος τὴν δεξιάν, ἀφύλακτος τὸ
σῶμα. Ὡς τά γε τῶν δορυφόρων ὕπνος ἐτρέψατο καὶ τὴν
πολλὴν φυλακὴν ἐκείνην διέλυσεν. Ἐφέστηκα δὲ ὁ φυγάς,
καὶ τὸ ξίφος ἐγγὺς καὶ ἡ χεὶρ οὐκ ἄνοπλος.

2 Τί φής, ὦ γενναῖε; Διώκεις, ὃν ἐν σπηλαίῳ καθεῖρξας.
Ζητεῖς, ὃν ἔχεις ξυνέστιον. Σὺ μὲν ἠπείλεις, ἐγὼ δ' ἐπυνθανόμην τῆς ἀπειλῆς· σὺ μὲν ἐσκαιώρεις τὴν ἐπιβουλήν,
ἐμὲ δ' οὐκ ἐλάνθανε τὸ μηχάνημα. Ἐμελέτας τὴν δίωξιν
καὶ ὁρῶν ἐφαντάζου τὰς κορυφὰς καὶ τοὺς ὑψηλοτέρους
περιεσκόπεις τῶν λόφων, ὁ δ' ἐγγύς που παρεδυόμην

5

What David would say when, being pursued by Saul, he catches him unguarded and asleep in a cave

I, the fugitive, have you, the pursuer. I have you, who are ready to kill, but more ready to suffer. Oh, the outcome of God's works! Your plan has been reversed, and you yourself are now exposed to what you threatened to do to me, and *you have fallen into the ditch that you dug.* Pursuing, you were caught, and fleeing, you were overcome. You have been overcome with sleep and overwhelmed physically, along with your guards. And if someone should wish it, you would be an effortless quarry, an enemy easily caught. The one who makes me flee lies there with his right hand unprotected, his body unguarded. Thus sleep defeated the defense of your bodyguards and destroyed their great protection. I, the fugitive, stand over you; my sword is close to you and my hand is not unarmed.

What do you say, sir? You are pursuing the one whom you 2 shut in a cave. You are seeking the one you invited to dinner. You threatened, and I learned of the threat. You devised a wicked plot, but the contrivance did not escape my notice. You planned the pursuit, and you scanned and imagined the mountain peaks and highest hills, but I, somewhere nearby,

αὐτός. Ὦ Θεὲ πάτριε! Εἰς χεῖρας ἔχων, ὃν ἔσπευδε, λαβεῖν οὐκ ἐγίνωσκεν. Ἀλλ᾽ ἦμεν ἐφ᾽ ἑνὸς τοῦ σπηλαίου καὶ μία πέτρα φυγάδα καὶ διώκτην ἐδέχετο. Εἶθ᾽ ὁ μὲν ὑπνώττει καὶ πέπτωκε, καὶ φροῦδοι μὲν οἱ φύλακες, φροῦδα δὲ τὰ τῆς ἐπιβουλῆς, καὶ μικροῦ δεῖν ὡς ἐκ πολιορκίας ἁλόντες τὸ παθεῖν οὐ δεδοίκαμεν.

3   Τίνες ἄρα σοι νῦν, ὦ βασιλεῦ, προσβάλλουσιν ὄνειροι; Ἆρα δοκεῖς ἔχειν, ἐχόμενος; Ἆρα νομίζεις ἁλίσκειν, αὐτὸς ἁλισκόμενος; Τάχα που διώκεις, καὶ κείμενος; Ἐπισπεύδεις ἴσως τὴν καταδρομήν, καὶ δεσμώτης ὕπνου γενόμενος; Ἀλλ᾽ ὦ κακοὶ φύλακες, ὦ δορυφόροι πρὸς ὕπνον διωκόμενοι, εἴ μοι παρῆν, ἡδέως ἂν ὑμᾶς ἐκόλασα. Τὸ γὰρ ἐφ᾽ ὑμῖν, ἀφύλακτος ὁ βασιλεὺς καὶ προδέδοται. Οὕτως ἐγὼ προδότας ὑμᾶς τίθεμαι.

4   Ἀλλ᾽ ἔγωγε καὶ ὡς βασιλέα φυλάξω καὶ ὡς μισοῦντα φυλάξομαι. Κἂν γὰρ ὡς ἐλαύνοντα νομίζω πολέμιον, ἀλλ᾽ ὡς χριστὸν Κυρίου σεβάζομαι, κἂν ὡς δυσμεναίνοντα μὴ στέργειν βιάζωμαι, ἀλλ᾽ ὡς κηδεστοῦ περιέχομαι. Φείδεσθέ μοι καὶ ὑμεῖς, ὦ συστρατιῶται, τοῦ βασιλέως, ὃν πολλάκις ἐδορυφορήσαμεν, μὴ νῦν τοῦτον ἀνέλωμεν. Οὐ βούλομαι τυραννίδα συναναμίξαι μου τοῖς ἀριστεύμασι. Μή μοι τὰ τρόπαια φόνῳ παρανόμῳ συγκρύψηται, μηδὲ μετὰ Γολιὰθ καὶ χριστὸς Κυρίου τὴν ἐμὴν δεξιὰν αἰτιάσθω.

5   Μωσῆν οἶδα νομοθέτην καὶ νομοδοτοῦντα Θεόν, ὑφ᾽ οὗ νῦν σεσώσμεθα καὶ ᾧ βασιλέα πολέμιον χαρισόμεθα.

slipped past you. O God of my fathers! Having in his hands the one whom he eagerly sought, he did not know how to catch him. But we were in the same cave, and a single rock received fugitive and pursuer alike. Then the pursuer goes to sleep and is defeated, and the guards are useless, and their plot is in vain, and although we were almost caught as if in a siege, we are not afraid of suffering.

What dreams assail you now, O king? Do you imagine 3 that you hold me, when you are held yourself? Do you suppose that you are catching me, when you are caught yourself? Perhaps you are pursuing me, even as you lie there? Perhaps you are urging on the attack, even when you have become a prisoner of sleep? O wicked guards, O bodyguards being pursued until you fell asleep, I would have gladly punished you if I could. For as far as you were concerned, the king was left unguarded and has been betrayed. Thus I reckon you as traitors.

But I will both guard you as king and guard against you 4 because you hate me. For even if I believe that you are my enemy because you drive me out, I still revere you as the Lord's anointed, and even if I am compelled to feel no affection for you because you hate me, I still embrace you as my kinsman. My fellow soldiers, show mercy to the king as I do, and let us not kill this man for whom we have often served as bodyguards. I do not wish to combine tyranny with my heroic deeds. Let my triumphs not be obscured by an illegal murder, and, after Goliath, let the anointed one of the Lord not find fault with my right hand.

I know Moses the lawgiver, and I know the lawgiving 5 God, by whom we have just now been saved and to whom we will now offer our enemy, the king. The whole of the

Φόνον ἅπας Νόμος ἀπείρηται, τὸ δὲ τῆς βασιλείας σεμνό-
τερον καὶ τὸν φόνον ποιεῖται δεινότερον. Ἀφαιρετέον
μικρὸν τῆς χλαμύδος, περιαιρετέον τι καὶ τοῦ δόρατος.
Ὡς ἐγὼ τῆς πέτρας ἐξιόντι ταυτησὶ τὰ σύμβολα ἐπιδείξομαι
καὶ κακίσω μὲν τοῦ ὕπνου τοὺς φύλακας, διηγήσομαι δὲ
καὶ ὡς ἡμῖν εἴληπται καὶ ὡς ἐφεισάμεθα δυσμεναίνοντος.

6

Τίνας ἂν εἴποι λόγους ὁ Δαυίδ, ὑπὸ τοῦ Ἀβεσσαλὼμ τοῦ παιδὸς αὐτοῦ διωκόμενος

Οὐκ ἐπιλείπω καὶ μετὰ βασιλείαν φυγαδευόμενος. Καὶ
πρὸ τῆς ἀρχῆς ἐδραπέτευον καὶ μετὰ τὴν ἀρχὴν αὖθις
ἐλαύνομαι. Ὦ χρῆμα φθόνου μεστόν, καὶ πρὶν ἥκειν
ὑποπτευόμενον, καὶ προσιὸν αὖθις ζηλοτυπούμενον! Ὦ
πάντα παθὼν ἐγὼ καὶ πρὸς τοῦ γένους βαλλόμενος! Οὐχ
ἵσταταί μοι τὰ τῆς ἐπιβουλῆς, ἀλλ᾽ οἴκοθεν ἔχω τὸν
πόλεμον, ἀφ᾽ ἑστίας βάλλομαι καὶ φθόνον Σαοὺλ ὕβρις
παιδὸς διαδέχεται. Ἔφυγον κηδεστὴν ἐπίβουλον καὶ πρὸς
παῖδα τύραννον αὖθις ἐμπέπτωκα.

2   Ἀλλὰ τίς οὗτος ὁ πόλεμος; Πόθεν τὰ τῆς καινῆς ταύτης
πείρας; Αἰσθάνομαι τοῦ κακοῦ, προβάλλει μοι τὸ δεινόν.

Law forbids murder, and the more sacred status of kingship makes this murder even more terrible. I must take away a bit of his mantle, and I must remove a part of his spear. And so I will show him these tokens as he leaves this rocky cavern, and I will reproach the guards for sleeping, and I will narrate both how we caught him and how we spared him, even though he is our enemy.

6

What David would say
when his son Absalom
is pursuing him

I am not a failure, even though I am in exile after reigning as king. I was a fugitive before my rule, and after my rule I am being driven out again. Alas, affair full of envy, which was both suspected before it happened and in turn envied when it arrived! Alas, I who have suffered everything and am under attack by my family! The plotting against me never ends, but I face a war originating from my own home; I am expelled from my hearth, and the violence of my son follows upon the envy of Saul. I fled a kinsman plotting against me and in turn have encountered a tyrannical son.

But what is this war? What is the source of this novel attempt against me? I perceive the evil; the horror is set be- 2

175

Εἰς νοῦν λαμβάνω, πόθεν μοι τὰ τῆς φυγῆς ἐπεψήφισται. Αὐτὸς ἐμαυτῷ τὸν παῖδα ἐφώπλισα. Δίκης ἔργα ταῦτα καὶ Θεόθεν ἐλαύνομαι.

3 Κατετρύφησα τῆς ἀρχῆς καὶ πρὸς ἡδονὴν ὑπήχθην παράλογον. Εἶδον ἀδίκοις ὀφθαλμοῖς, ἔπαθον εἰς ἔρωτα. Παρέβην γάμων θεσμούς, ὑφειλόμην εὐνὴν μὴ προσήκουσαν, ἐπέθηκα τούτοις καὶ φόνον. Ταῦτά με νῦν βάλλουσι, τοῖς ἐμοῖς ἁπλῶς ἁλίσκομαι. Ὦ δίκης βαρείας μέν, ἀλλ᾽ ἀπὸ τοῦ πεπονθότος ἐχούσης τὴν ἀρχήν! Γάμον ὕβρισα καὶ πρὸς γάμου κολάζομαι· ὅθεν ἠδίκουν, ἐκεῖθεν καὶ πέπληγμαι. Εἰς παιδὸς ἡμάρτανον γένεσιν καὶ παῖδα νῦν ἔχω τὸν δήμιον καί, πατὴρ εἰς παίδων γονὰς ἀδικῶν, ὑπὸ παιδὸς σωφρονίζομαι.

4 Παρέβην, ὦ παῖ, τὴν φύσιν ἐγὼ καὶ γίνῃ παρὰ τὴν φύσιν αὐτὸς ἀδικώτερος. Πότερον ἐμαυτὸν τῆς ἀτοπίας, ἢ τὸν παῖδα τῆς παρανομίας ἀποκλαύσομαι; Ἐμιμήσω τὸν τεκόντα, ὦ παῖ, τὰ μὴ προσήκοντα καί, πατέρα ἁμαρτόντα τιμωρῶν, ἁμαρτάνεις διπλάσια, καὶ μὴ προσήκουσαν ἀρχὴν ὑφαιρούμενος καὶ τὸν εἶναί σοι δόντα μηκέτ᾽ εἶναι βουλόμενος.

5 Ἆρ᾽ οὖν εἰς τὰ ὅπλα βλέψω; Καὶ πολέμῳ διακρινοῦμαι περὶ τῆς ἀρχῆς; Καὶ πῶς ἂν ὑπεξέλθω τοῖς ἐμοῖς σπλάγχνοις; Οὐκ ἔχω πῶς ἂν ἐπανατείνω τὸ ξίφος κατὰ τοῦ παιδός, αἰσχύνομαι πατὴρ καλεῖσθαι πολέμιος. Φεύγων οἰχήσομαι, τῆς ἐρημίας καὶ νῦν ἐπιλήψομαι. Οὕτως ἐγὼ περιεῖναι πειράσομαι, οὕτω τῷ παιδὶ πατροκτονίας διδοὺς ἀφορμὴν καὶ παιδοκτονίας αὐτὸς οὐ δεχόμενος τρόπαια. Εἰ δέ που δεήσει καὶ μάχεσθαι, ἔχω τὸν στρατηγήσοντα.

fore me. I understand why I have been condemned to flight.
I myself armed my own son against me. This is the work of
justice, and I am being driven out by the will of God.

I delighted in my rule and was seduced by unreasonable 3
pleasure. I gazed with unjust eyes; I experienced desire. I
violated the laws of marriage, I stole a marriage bed that did
not belong to me, and to these crimes I even added murder.
These actions now assail me; I am openly convicted by my
own actions. Alas, the grievous penalty, but one with its origin in the man who suffered it! I violated a marriage and am
being punished by a marriage; from where I did wrong, from
there I have also been struck. I sinned in producing a son,
and now I have a son as my executioner, and doing wrong as
a father in the procreation of sons, I am being chastised by a
son.

O my son, I transgressed against nature, and contrary to 4
nature, you yourself have become more unjust. Should I
mourn for myself because of my outrageous act, or for my
son because of his transgression? O son, you emulated your
father's inappropriate acts, and in punishing your father for
his sins, you sin doubly: you steal a kingship that does not
belong to you, and you want the man who gave you life to
live no more.

And so should I look to weapons? And should I decide 5
the kingship by war? How could I go out against my own
flesh and blood? I cannot raise my sword against my son. As
his father, I am ashamed to be called his enemy. I will depart
as a fugitive; I will reach the wilderness even now. Thus I
will attempt to survive; thus I will give my son an opportunity to kill his father, but I will not claim victory for killing
my son. If it becomes necessary to do battle, I have a man to

Τοῦτον ἐπαφήσω τοῖς ὅπλοις, πρότερον παρακελευσάμενος ὡς παῖδα ζωγρεῖν, μὴ κτείνειν ὡς τύραννον. Οὕτω καὶ Σαοὺλ ἐκεῖνον, ὑπνοῦντα λαβών, ἐφεισάμην, οὐχ ὡς ἐχθρὸν ἀναιρῶν, ἀλλ᾽ ὡς κηδεστὴν περιποιούμενος.

7

Τίνας ἂν εἴποι λόγους Ζαχαρίας, ὁ πατὴρ τοῦ Προδρόμου, μετὰ τὸ γεννηθῆναι τὸν Πρόδρομον καὶ αὐτὸν ἀπολυθῆναι τῆς ἀφωνίας

Ἐπανῆκέ μοι μετὰ τοῦ παιδὸς ἡ φωνὴ καὶ τὰ τῆς ἐπαγγελίας οὐ διέψευσται. Ἄγγελος μὲν ἐπηγγείλατο τὴν γονήν, ἐγὼ δ᾽ ἐνεδοίαζον· γῆρας ἐγὼ προὐβαλλόμην καὶ στείρωσιν γυναικός, ὁ δ᾽ αὖθις τὰ τῆς ἐπαγγελίας ἐπέτεινεν. "Ἀκούσῃ," φησί, "καὶ μετὰ γῆρας πατὴρ καὶ στεῖραν ὄψει μητέρα. Τὰ γὰρ τῆς στειρώσεως λέλυται, ὁ δέ σοι παῖς οὐκ ἐπιγνοίη τρυφήν· οὐ πίεται σίκερα, ἐξ αὐτῆς γονῆς Πνεύματος ἁγίου καὶ σοφίας πλησθήσεται." Ταῦτα ὁ μὲν ἔλεγεν, ἐγὼ δ᾽ ἠπίστουν, σημεῖον ᾔτουν, ὁ δ᾽ ἐπένευεν, οὐκ εἰς καιρὸν ἐχρησάμην τῇ φωνῇ, τοιγαροῦν εἰς τὴν

serve as my general. I will send him against my son's weapons, after ordering him to take Absalom alive as my son and not kill him as a tyrant. Thus also I spared Saul when I caught him asleep, not killing him as an enemy but protecting him as a kinsman.

7

What Zacharias, the father of the Forerunner, would say after the Forerunner is born and he is freed from his inability to speak

My voice has returned to me along with my child, and the proclamation has not proven false. An angel proclaimed the birth, but I doubted it. I brought up my old age and my wife's barrenness, but he again delivered the proclamation more forcefully. "You will be called father," he said, "even in your old age, and you will see your barren wife become a mother; for her barrenness has been cured. And your child will not know luxury: *he will not drink strong drink;* from his very birth *he will be filled with the Holy Spirit* and wisdom." These were his words, but I did not believe; I demanded a sign, and he granted it; I had not made appropriate use of my voice, and therefore I suffered the loss of my voice; and

φωνὴν ἐζημίωμαι καί, λέγειν οὐκ εἰδὼς καίρια, κατεκρινόμην σιγήν.

2   Τί γὰρ οὐκ ἐπειθόμην μητέρα καὶ στεῖραν ἰδεῖν, ἀπόγονος εἶναι καὶ ταῦτα τῆς Σάρρας αὐχῶν; Ταύτην δίδωμι τῆς ἀπειθείας δίκην, τοῦτο λαμβάνω τῆς ἐπαγγελίας ἐνέχυρον· καὶ τὸ ἐντεῦθεν ἐνεκυμονεῖτο μὲν ὁ παῖς ὑπὸ τῇ μητρί, ἐγὼ δ᾽ ἐσίγων. Ἀλλ᾽ ἅμα τε τὸ βρέφος ἀνῆκεν εἰς φῶς ἐκείνη καὶ παρ᾽ ἐμοὶ αὐτίκα ὁ λόγος ἐπέλαμπε· λέλυται τῇ μητρὶ τὰ τῆς ὠδῖνος κἀμοὶ τὰ τῆς ἀφωνίας λέλυται.

3   Ἀποδίδωμι τὸν εὐχαριστήριον, ὑπεραγάλλομαι τῷ παιδί, ἠσθόμην ἤδη καὶ Πνεύματος. Ἐμπνεῖ μοι τὰ μέλλοντα, συνίημι τῆς ἐπὶ τῷ βρέφει χάριτος, ὑπὲρ τὸν Σαμψὼν διαγωνιεῖται πρὸς τρυφήν, ὑπὲρ τὸν Σαμουὴλ ἡγήσεται τοῦ λαοῦ. Ὦ παῖ, προφήτης ὑψίστου κληθήσῃ καὶ σὺ καὶ λαὸν προσάξεις Θεῷ. Ἐπέρχεταί μοι τὸ μεῖζον εἰπεῖν. Ἑτοιμάσεις Κυρίῳ τὴν πρόοδον, κηρύξεις τὸν προσδοκώμενον.

4   Ἤδη ξυνῆκα καὶ τῆς σιωπῆς, ξυμβάλλομαι τὴν ἀφωνίαν ἐκείνην, μανθάνω τί βούλεται, δεσμῶν τὴν φωνήν, ἄγγελος· Φωνῆς ἔμελλον κληθῆναι πατήρ, τοιγαροῦν ἔδει με τὴν φωνὴν ἐγκυμονῆσαι πρότερον καὶ σιγᾶν μέχρι καὶ τόκου, ὡς ἔδει καὶ τοῦ Λόγου προδραμεῖν τὴν Φωνὴν καί, πρὶν ἢ παρθένον τεκεῖν, καὶ στεῖραν ἀκοῦσαι μητέρα. Τὸ δ᾽ ἀπὸ τοῦδε σὺ μὲν ὁ παῖς ἡ μεγάλη Φωνὴ τοῦ τῆς μήτρας νέφους περιρραγέντος ἐξέλαμπες, κἀμοὶ δὲ ἡ φωνὴ συνεξέλαμπε καὶ τὰ τῆς ἀφωνίας διέρρηκται. Ἥξει μετ᾽ οὐ μακρόν, εὖ οἶδα, καὶ ὁ Λόγος, καὶ σὺ μὲν ὑπηρετήσεις ἡ Φωνὴ καὶ κηρύξεις τὸν ἐλπιζόμενον, ὁ δ᾽ ἐκπληρώσει τοῦ

because I did not know how to speak as the situation demanded, I was condemned to silence.

For why did I not believe that I could see even a barren   2
woman become a mother, boasting that I was a descendant of Sarah, no less? I paid this penalty for my disbelief; I received this guarantee of the proclamation: thereafter the child was carried in his mother's womb, while I remained mute. But as soon as the infant came into the light, immediately speech shone upon me; his mother has been delivered from her birth pangs, and I from my speechlessness.

I give my thank-offering, I rejoice exceedingly in the   3
child, and I have already perceived the Spirit. It inspires in me knowledge of the things to come. I understand the grace that is shed upon the infant. He will surpass Samson in his struggle against luxury; he will surpass Samuel in his leadership of the people. O child, *you too will be called prophet of the most high,* and you will lead the people to God. I am inspired to say something even greater: you will prepare the way for the Lord; you will herald the awaited one.

Now I understand my silence; I comprehend my former   4
speechlessness; I know what the angel meant by binding my voice: I was about to be called father of the Voice, and so first I had to be pregnant with voice and remain silent right up until birth, just as the Voice also had to be the Forerunner of the Word, and just as a barren woman had to be called mother before a virgin could give birth. From that point on, you, my child, the great Voice, shone forth after the cloud of the womb was broken, and at the same time my voice shone forth too, and my speechlessness was broken. Very soon, I know well, the Word will come, and you will serve as his Voice and will proclaim the awaited one, and he will fulfill

Πατρὸς τὴν βουλὴν καὶ πρὸς τὸν Πατέρα νοῦν ὁ Λόγος
ἀναδραμεῖται καὶ τὸ ἐντεῦθεν ἔσται τὰ προσδοκώμενα.

8

Τίνας ἂν εἴποι λόγους ἡ Θεοτόκος, ὅτε μετέβαλεν ὁ Χριστὸς τῷ γάμῳ τὸ ὕδωρ εἰς οἶνον

ʿΩς παῖδά σε περιπτύξομαι ἢ ὡς Θεὸν σεβασθήσομαι;
Τὸ μὲν γάρ, οἷς ὑπήκουσας, πέφηνας, τὸ δ᾽, οἷς ἐκαινούργησας, δέδειξαι. Ὡς μήτηρ περιβαλεῖν σε γλίχομαι καὶ ὡς
ἄνθρωπος προσελθεῖν ὑποστέλλομαι καὶ ὡς Θεὸν πέφρικα
καὶ ὡς παῖδα θαρρῶ. Ὦ Θεὲ παῖ, μετέβαλες μὲν τὸ ὕδωρ
εἰς οἶνον, εἰς εὐφημίαν δὲ τὸν ὑμέναιον· ἐξέστησας λόγῳ
μὲν τὸ ὕδωρ, ἡμᾶς δὲ τῷ θαύματι.

2   Ἀκόλουθα ταῦτα τοῖς πρότερον· θεία μὲν ἡ γονή, θεῖος
δὲ ὁ τοκετός, καὶ μήτηρ ἐγὼ καὶ τὸ μέντοι τοῦ τόκου
φυλάξασα · τὸ δ᾽ ὑπερβᾶσα θειότερον. Οὔτε τὸ φυλαχθὲν
ἐστέρηται θαύματος καὶ τὸ διαλειφθὲν οὐκ ἀνέκπληκτον.
Ἔτικτόν σε, ὦ παῖ βασιλεῦ, σὺ δέ μοι, τὰς ὠδῖνας ἔνδοθεν
ἀφελόμενος, τὸν τοκετὸν ἐτήρησας· μήτηρ ἤκουσα καὶ

the will of his Father, and the Word will run back to the Father, that is, to the Intellect, and thereafter the awaited events will come to pass.

8

What the Theotokos would say when Christ transformed the water into wine for the wedding

Shall I embrace you as a son or revere you as God? For you revealed yourself as my son by obeying, but you showed yourself as God by doing something novel. As a mother I desire to embrace you, but as a human I hesitate to approach you; I tremble before you as God but have no fear of you as my son. O God-and-son, you changed the water into wine, and the bridal song into a song of praise; you confounded the water with a word, and us by your miracle.

This is consistent with earlier events. Divine was the conception, divine the delivery. I became a mother and experienced childbirth, yet I also transcended labor even more divinely. What I experienced was not devoid of a miracle, and what I did not experience was not without astonishment. I was giving birth to you, O son-and-king, and though you removed the birth pangs from within, you preserved for me the delivery; I was called mother and yet remained a virgin. 2

παρθένος πάλιν μεμένηκα. Οὐρανὸς τῷ τόκῳ ἐφύμνησε καὶ πρὸ τοῦ τόκου μὲν ἄγγελον παρεῖχέ μοι νυμφοστόλον, μετὰ δὲ τόκον ἀστέρα καινὸν ἄλλον ἀνέτελλε. Κήρυξ ἦν ἐκεῖνος τοῦ τόκου καὶ Περσίδος εἴχομεν δῶρα καὶ βασιλεὺς αὐτὸς ἤκουες.

3   Καὶ νῦν δὲ τοῖς περὶ τὴν γένεσιν τὰ τῆς ἀνατροφῆς ὡς ἀνάλογα! Γάμος ἦν καί, παρθένον ἔχων μητέρα, καὶ γυναῖκας μητέρας ἰδεῖν οὐκ ἀπώκνησας, ἀλλ᾽ ἐφείπου τῇ μητρί, τοῦτο μὲν ὡς παιδίων νόμους τηρῶν, τοῦτο δ᾽ ὡς καὶ γάμον νομοθετῶν καὶ συγχωρῶν τὸν ὑμέναιον. Ἐτίμησας μέν, ὦ παῖ, πολλοῖς τὴν παρθενίαν πρότερον θαύμασι, νῦν δὲ καὶ τὸν γάμον καὶ δι᾽ αὐτὸν τὴν μητέρα ἐμέ. Γάμος ἦν καὶ τὸ τῶν ἡδυσμάτων ἥδιστον οἶνος ἐλείπετο. Ἔπινον μὲν οἱ δαιτυμόνες, ἀλλ᾽ ὕδατος· ἐχόρευον μέν, ἀλλ᾽ ἀνήδυντα. Ἀλλ᾽ ᾔδειν ἐγώ σου τὴν ἰσχύν, οὐκ ἠγνόουν οἷον ἔτεκον, ᾔδειν καλῶς τὸν ἔνδον κρυπτόμενον.

4   Ἐντεῦθεν πρόσειμι τῷ παιδί, ἐπιλέγω τὸ τῆς γάμου τελετῆς ἀτέλεστον, παραθήγω θαυματουργίας ἅψασθαι, "᾽Επιδείξῃ," λέγουσα, "πάντως, ὦ παῖ, μετ᾽ οὐ πολὺ τὴν ἰσχύν. Εὖ οἶδα ὡς τῆς ἡλικίας ἀναμένεις τὸ τελεώτερον, χρόνον ἀποταμιεύεις τῇ διδασκαλίᾳ, καιρὸν ὁρίζεις τοῖς θαύμασιν. Ἀλλ᾽ ἄρξαι νῦν. Ἐπείγομαί σε τερατουργοῦντα θεάσασθαι, χάρισαι τὴν τῶν θαυμάτων ἀπαρχὴν τῇ μητρί." Ὁ δέ—ὦ νόμοι πατέρων ἐπὶ τέκνοις κείμενοι!—οὐκ ἀνένευσεν, οὐκ ἀπεῖπεν, οὐκ ἀπεδοκίμασε μητρὸς αἴτησιν, ἀλλ᾽ ὕδωρ ἤγετο, καὶ ὁ μὲν ἐπέταττε, τὸ δ᾽ εἰς οἶνον παρήγετο. Ὡς καλὸν καὶ τοῖς παισὶν εὐπειθείας δίδως ὑπόδειγμα! Εὐγνωμονεῖτε, ὦ παῖδες, περὶ τὰς τεκούσας,

Heaven hymned the birth and before the birth provided me an angel as a bridal escort, and after the birth it made a new star arise. That star heralded your birth, and we received gifts from Persia, and you yourself were called king.

And now, how the events of your upbringing match those surrounding your birth! There was a wedding, and although you have a virgin mother, you did not shy away from seeing married women as mothers; rather, you followed your mother, in part obeying the laws for children, in part sanctioning marriage and allowing the wedding. You honored virginity, my son, with many prior miracles, and now you honor both marriage and, through it, me your mother. There was a wedding, and the wine, the sweetest of sweets, ran out. The guests kept drinking, but it was water; they kept dancing, but without sweet enjoyment. But I knew your power; I was not unaware of what sort of child I had given birth to; I knew well the one who was hiding inside.

Therefore I approach my son; I mention that the wedding's finale is incomplete; I urge him to work a miracle, saying, "Certainly, my son, you will soon display your power. I know well that you are waiting until you are older; you are reserving time for teaching and setting a definite occasion for miracles. But begin now. I am eager to see you working wonders; offer the first miracle to your mother." And he—O laws of parents governing children!—did not decline, did not refuse, did not deny his mother's request; rather, water was drawn, he gave a command, and it was changed into wine. How fine a demonstration of obedience he gives also to sons! Be considerate of those who gave birth to you, O

ἀπὸ τῶν μητέρων τῆς χάριτος ἄρχεσθε, ὅτι καὶ Θεός, γενόμενος παῖς, μητέρα αὐτοῦ αἰτοῦσαν ἐτίμησε θαύματι. Ὢ Λόγος ἐκεῖνος ἐξ ἀφανῶν πηγῶν ἀναδιδοὺς οἴνου ῥεύματα! Ὅσην ἔχεις, ὦ παῖ βασιλεῦ, τὴν δύναμιν! Δίχα βοτρύων οἶνος ἀνέβλυζεν, ἄμπελος οὐκ ἦν καὶ οἶνος ἀνεδίδοτο. Τίς ληνὸς τοσοῦτον τὸν οἶνον ἐξέθλιψε; Τίς ἄμπελος τοῦτο τὸ πόμα ἐθρέψατο; Τρυφᾶτε νῦν, ὦ δαιτυμόνες, τὰ γαμικά, σπᾶτε οἴνου, σπᾶτε δὲ πλέον τοῦ θαύματος.

5   Οἱ πατέρες ἡμῶν ἐκ πέτρας ὕδωρ ἔπιον, ἀλλ᾽ ἡμεῖς οἶνον ἐξ ὕδατος. Ἐκεῖ ῥάβδος ἔπληττε καὶ χεὶρ ἀνετείνετο, ἐνταῦθα λόγος μόνος ἐπαρκεῖ τῷ θαύματι. Ἐκεῖ γογγυσμὸς ἐξηκούετο καὶ ὁ Δημιουργὸς ἀνεδοίαζεν, ἐνταῦθα μητρὸς μόνης παράκλησις καὶ τὸ θαῦμα ἐπακολουθεῖ ἀνενδοίαστον. Ὅσῳ τῶν πατέρων ἡμεῖς μακαριώτεροι! Θεοῦ θεράπων ἐκείνοις ἐτερατούργει, νῦν δ᾽ ἡμεῖς αὐτὸν ἐκεῖνον ἔχομεν τὸν τῶν σημείων δεσπότην καὶ τεράτων κύριον. Λόγῳ τὰ πρῶτα τὸ πᾶν συνεστήσατο, οὐρανὸν καὶ γῆν, θάλασσαν, ποταμούς, τἄλλα πάντα, λόγῳ καὶ νῦν τὴν ὕδατος φύσιν εἰς οἶνον μετεκίνησε. Πίετε τοῦ καινοῦ τούτου πόματος καὶ πρότερον τούτου τῆς πίστεως.

6   Ἤδη τι καὶ νεανιεύσομαι, ὡς μακαρία μήτηρ ἐγὼ Θεοῦ καὶ κληθεῖσα μήτηρ καὶ γενομένη! Ὢ γάμος οὗτος μακάριος, οὗ καὶ Θεὸς γέγονε δαιτυμὼν καὶ δαιτυμόνες οἶνον θαύματος ἔπιον!

sons; begin showing kindness to your mothers, because even God, having become a son, honored his mother with a miracle when she asked. Oh, that Word producing streams of wine from invisible springs! How much power you have, O son-and-king! Wine gushed forth without grapes; there was no grapevine, and yet wine was produced. What winepress ever extracted so much wine! What grapevine nurtured this drink? Revel now, O guests, in the wedding feast. Drink deeply of the wine; drink even more deeply of the miracle.

Our forefathers drank water that came from a rock, but 5 we drink wine that came from water. Of old a rod struck and a hand was extended; now a word alone is sufficient for the miracle. Of old the people grumbled and the Creator delayed; now a mother only makes a request and the miracle follows without delay. How much more blessed are we than our fathers! A servant of God worked wonders for those people, but now we have God himself, the master of signs and lord of wonders. In the beginning he created the whole world by means of the Word—heaven and earth, the sea, rivers, and everything else—and now too with a word he changed the nature of water into wine. Drink of this new wine, but before that, drink of faith.

Now I will make a bold proclamation: how blessed am I 6 as the mother of God, both in having been called and having become his mother! Oh, this blessed wedding, to which God came as a guest and where the guests drank miraculous wine!

9

Τίνας ἂν εἴποι λόγους ὁ ἐκ γενετῆς τυφλός, ἀναβλέψας

Ὕπαρ ἔστι μοι τὰ τῆς ὄψεως ἢ ὄναρ ηὐτύχησα καί, μὴ βλέπων, αὖθις ἠπάτημαι; Τὰ μὲν γὰρ ἔργα βεβαιοῖ τὸ φαινόμενον, τὸ δὲ τῆς θεραπείας καινὸν μικροῦ τὴν πίστιν παρείλετο. Ἡμέρα μὲν ἥδε καὶ φῶς ἐξ ἀκοῆς τὸ πρότερον γινωσκόμενον, ὀφθαλμοὶ δ᾽, οἱ πρὸ τοῦ μηδὲ ὄντες τὴν ἀρχήν, οὐκ οἶδ᾽ ὅπως, νῦν ἀνεῴγασι καὶ γεύομαι φωτός, ὃ πρὶν ὁρᾶν οὐκ εἶχον, γλιχόμενος.

2   Ὦ, οἷον εἶδες, ἥλιε! Ἅμα σε βλέπων, ἐξέστηκα καὶ συν-εξέστης αὐτὸς οὐδὲν ἧττον, βλεπόμενος, καί, μὴ βλέπων, τοὺς οὐχ ὁρῶντας ὑπερέβαλλον πάντας τῷ μεγέθει τῆς συμφορᾶς καὶ νῦν, ἐξαίφνης ἰδών, ὑπερβέβληκα τοὺς ὁρῶντας τῷ καινῷ τῆς ὄψεως. Οὔτε μοι τότε τὰ τῆς ἀβλεψίας ἀνέκπληκτα καὶ νῦν αὖθις τὰ τῆς ὄψεως οὐκ ἀθαύμαστα. Ἐλύετο μέν μοι τὰ τῆς ὠδῖνος, τὰ δὲ τῆς ὄψεως ἐπεπέδητο· καὶ παρηγόμην μὲν εἰς φῶς, φωτὸς δ᾽ οὐκ ἀπήλαυον· ἑώρων μὲν οἱ γονεῖς αὐτοὶ πρὸς τοῦ παιδὸς οὐχ ὁρώμενοι, βαθὺ δέ μοι σκότος ἐπῆν καὶ πρὸ τοῦ τόκου καὶ μετὰ γένεσιν. Ἐντεῦθεν σύντροφον τὸ κακόν. Νὺξ ἦν τὰ πάντα καὶ ζόφος ἄλυτος. Ἧκεν ἡμέρα, ἐγὼ δ᾽ ἤκουον· ἐπῆλθε νὺξ καὶ πάλιν ἐπυνθανόμην καί, ἃ μὴ βλέπειν εἶχον, ἀκούων ἐμάνθανον, ὅλως ἑώρων οἷς ἤκουον καὶ τὴν ἀκοὴν

9

What the man blind from birth would say upon gaining his sight

Do I really have sight, or is my good fortune only a dream and, still blind, have I been deceived again? For actual results confirm mere appearances, but the novelty of my healing has almost taken away my belief. This is day and light, which I previously knew only through hearing about them, and my eyes, which before this did not exist at all, have now opened—I do not know how—and I experience light, which previously I could not see, though I longed to.

O sun, what a marvel you have seen! I am astounded to see you, and at the same time you yourself are no less astounded at being seen. When I was unable to see, I surpassed all the sightless in the magnitude of my misfortune and now, suddenly seeing, I have surpassed the sighted in the novelty of my sight. My blindness was astonishing to me then, and now in turn my sight is miraculous. My mother's birth pangs were relieved, but my sight had been shackled; I was brought into the light but could not enjoy the light; my parents themselves could see but could not be seen by their child, and deep darkness was upon me both before and after my birth. From then on, this suffering was my companion. Everything was night and indissoluble gloom. Day arrived, but I only heard about it. Night came, and again I discovered it by hearsay, and I learned by hearing what I could not see; I saw entirely from what I heard, and I translated

εἰς ὅρασιν μετελάμβανον. Ἀπείρηκα πολλάκις ξυμποδιζό-
μενος, ἀπεῖπον τοὺς πόδας οἷς ἔτυχον συντριβόμενος.
Ἐπεχωρίαζον τῷ ναῷ καὶ τὸ κάλλος ὑφ' ἑτέρων ἐμάνθανον.
Οὕτω μοι ξύμφυτον ἦν τὸ δεινόν, οὕτω μοι τὰ τῆς συμφορᾶς ἀμετάβλητα!

3   Ἐπ' ἐμοὶ μόνῳ τῶν ἀπάντων ἀλαμπὲς ἐδόκει τὸ πᾶν καὶ
σκότος αὖθις ἀρχέγονον. Ἔφερον εἰκόνα τοῦ παντός, πρὶν
ἢ τὸ φῶς ἥκειν καὶ νύκτα μεταλαβεῖν, καὶ Μωσῆν ἐκεῖνον
ἐθαύμαζον. Ἐζήτουν τῷ πάθει παραβάλλειν ἕτερον, ἀλλ'
ἦν τὸ κακὸν ἀπαράβλητον. Παρῆσαν ἕτεροι ταὐτὰ δυστυ-
χοῦντες καί, τὴν συμφορὰν ἐρευνῶν ὑστέραν εὕρισκον
ὄψεως. Ἐγὼ δ' ἀλλά, πρὶν ἰδεῖν, τὸ βλέπειν ἀφήρημαι καί,
πρὶν ἐλθεῖν εἰς ἕξιν, ἐστέρημαι· ἐπὶ τοσοῦτον καινότητος
ἦλθέ μοι τὸ κακόν!

4   Ἀλλ' ὦ τῆς εἰσέπειτα μεταβολῆς! Ὡς οὐχ ἧττον ὁ τῆς
ὄψεως τρόπος ἐπ' ἐμοὶ κεκαινούργηται. Ἐφοίτων ἐν τῷ
ναῷ, προσῄτουν τὰ πρὸς τροφήν, ἤκουον τοῦ Ἰησοῦ διδάσκοντος, ἐπηκολούθει τῇ διδασκαλίᾳ καὶ θαύματα. Ἐπὶ
τούτοις ὑποφλέγομαι τὴν καρδίαν, ἀναζέω πρὸς πίστιν,
ζηλῶ τοὺς ἰαθέντας τῆς δωρεᾶς. Ἕρμαιον ἡγοῦμαι τὸ
πρᾶγμα, ἐντεῦθεν ἱκέτης πρόσειμι, Θεὸν ἐπιβοῶμαι, σωτῆρα καλῶ, τὸ πάθος εἰς οἶκτον προβάλλομαι, καὶ προ-
βαίνει μοι τὰ τῆς ἐλπίδος εἰς ἔργον. Καὶ τὰ τῆς θεραπείας,
ὡς ἄρρητα! Γῆν συνέφυρεν ὕδατι καὶ φέρων τοῖς ὀφθαλμοῖς
ἐπιτίθησι καὶ τὸ φῶς εὐθὺς ἀνεδίδοτο. Θεὸν ἐγώ σε,
θαρρῶν, ἀποφαίνομαι καὶ πρό γε ἐμοῦ τὰ τοῦ θαύματος.
Ὅλον ἐκ πηλοῦ τὰ πρῶτα συνεστήσω τὸν ἄνθρωπον καὶ
νῦν παρὰ μέρος οὐκ ὄντα πηλῷ μεταπλάττεις. Ταῦτά σε

my hearing into vision. I have often been discouraged as I stumbled around; I grew frustrated with stubbing my toes on whatever I encountered. I frequented the temple and learned of its beauty from others. So congenital was my suffering; so unchangeable was my misfortune!

To me alone of everyone the whole world seemed without light, and again darkness seemed primordial. I imagined the world as it was before the light came and replaced night, and I marveled at the great Moses. I sought another to whom to compare my suffering, but my misery was incomparable. There were others around me suffering from the same affliction, and by investigating I discovered that their loss of sight came later. I, on the other hand, was robbed of my sight before I could see, and before I came to possess vision I was deprived of it. So unique was my malady! 3

But oh, the subsequent transformation! A no less unique means of sight has been devised for me. I was visiting the temple; I was begging for my sustenance; I heard Jesus teaching, and miracles followed the teaching. In response to this I was inflamed in my heart, I was boiling with faith, and I envied those he healed for their bounty. I considered the event a godsend, and so I approached him as a suppliant, I cried out to God, I called him savior, and I demonstrated my suffering for his mercy. My hopes came to fruition, and the healing—how indescribable! He blended earth with water, and taking it he put it on my eyes, and the light was immediately imparted. I confidently declare that you are God, and the results of the miracle are right before me. In the beginning you made a whole man from clay, and now you refashion with clay a man who was not whole. These actions 4

κηρύττει Θεόν, ταῦτα Δημιουργὸν ἀνθρώπου, ταῦτα υἱὸν
Θεοῦ ἐν θνητῷ τῷ προσχήματι.

5 Ὦ φῶς, νῦν σε πρώτως καὶ βλέπω καὶ τέθηπα! Ὦ καλὸν
ἥλιε δημιούργημα, οἷος ὤν, ἡμῖν οὐκ ἐπέλαμπες! Τίνα
ταύτην ὁρῶ τὴν πολλὴν ὑπὲρ κεφαλῆς ἐπίχυσιν; Καὶ ὡς
κάτοπτρον διαφαίνει καὶ ὡς ὕδωρ κέχυται. Τίς καὶ ὁ καλὸς
καὶ μέγας οὗτος ὄροφος, δημιουργὲ βασιλεῦ; Ὅσος μὲν
ἐπῆρται, ἡλίκος δὲ ἀναπέταται! Θαρρεῖτε, ὦ πόδες, οὐκέτι
προσπταίοντες, συντριβήσεσθε. Ἀπήλλαχθε μὴ βλεπομέ-
νης ὁδοῦ καὶ βακτηρίας ὑμῖν οὐ δεήσει λοιπόν. Ὦ τεκόντες,
ὄψις γλυκεῖα, νῦν καὶ αὐτὸς ὑμᾶς ὄψομαι καὶ γονεῖς
ἐπικαλέσομαι βεβαιότερον, οὐδὲν ὑμῖν εἰς ἁμαρτίαν τοῦ
λοιποῦ διαγνώσομαι. Ἀλλ᾽ ἐφυλαττόμην τηλικούτῳ θαύματι, ἀπείληφα τὴν λειπομένην τῶν αἰσθήσεων καὶ τῆς
ἀκοῆς ὡς τά γε τῆς ὄψεως οὐ δεήσομαι.

6 Ὦ ναοῦ κάλλος ἄρρητον, οὐκέτι σε λοιπὸν ὑφ᾽ ἑτέρων
ὀφθαλμοῖς θεάσομαι, ἀλλ᾽ αὐτοψὶ τοῦ θαύματος ἐμπλήσο-
μαι. Κἂν εἰς τὴν συναγωγὴν δεήσῃ μοι παρελθεῖν, οὐ
καταπροήσομαι τὴν ἀλήθειαν, ἀλλ᾽ ἐρῶ πάντα πυνθανομένοις καὶ διηγήσομαι τὴν ἐξ αὐτῶν ὠδίνων πήρωσιν, τὴν ἐν
τῷ ναῷ προσαίτησιν, τὸν ἐπὶ τούτοις οἶκτον, τὸν ἐπιτεθέντα
πηλόν, τὴν ἐκεῖθεν ἀνάβλεψιν καὶ ἐπὶ πᾶσι τὸν ἰασάμενον.

proclaim you as God, Creator of humans, son of God in mortal guise.

O light, now for the first time I see you and I am amazed! 5 O beautiful creation, sun, such as you are, you did not shine upon us! What is this great outpouring I see over my head? It is transparent like a mirror, and it flows like water. What is this beautiful, huge roof, Creator-and-king? How high the roof rises, and how wide it extends! Have confidence, my feet: no longer will you stumble and be bruised. You have been freed from the road you could not see, and you will have no need of a walking stick from now on. O mother and father, sweet sight, now I will see you myself and will more confidently call you my parents; no longer will I be judged as your sin. Rather, I was reserved for such a great miracle; I have received the sense that I lacked, and I will not need my hearing, now that I have vision.

O ineffable beauty of the temple, I will no longer see you 6 hereafter through the eyes of others, but I will fill myself with the miracle by seeing you for myself. And if I must go into the synagogue, I will not abandon the truth, but I will tell everything to those who ask, and I will narrate how I was born blind, my begging in the temple, the pity that followed, the clay that was applied, the resulting ability to see, and above all the one who healed me.

10

Τίνας ἂν εἴποι λόγους ὁ Ἅιδης, τετραημέρου τοῦ Λαζάρου ἀνεγερθέντος

Ὦ πάντα πρότερον ἰδεῖν τε καὶ παθεῖν ἐλπίσας ἐγὼ ἢ νεκρὸν ἀφαιρεθῆναι! Καὶ μετὰ τὴν ἐκφορὰν ἔπαθον τὰ ἀνύποιστα, εἶδον τὰ ἀπροσδόκητα, περιήρημαι τοὺς ἐπὶ τοῖς οἰχομένοις θεσμούς. Ὦ μάτην ὑπὸ γῆν κρατοῦντες ἡμεῖς! Τίνα ταύτην ἀρχὴν ἄρξομεν, εἰ καὶ μετὰ τὸ λαβεῖν ἀφαιρούμεθα καί, κατασχόντες, εἰς τέλος οὐκ ἔχομεν; Ψυχὴν ἀπέσπασα σώματος καί, τὸ κρατεῖν ἤδη θαρρῶν, παρ᾽ αὐτὴν τὴν τοῦ κρατεῖν ἀκμὴν τὸ κράτος ἀποσεσύλημαι καί, νεκρῶν ἔχων τὴν ἀρχήν, τοῖς γε περιοῦσιν ἔτι περι- υβρίζομαι. Πόθεν ὁ καινὸς οὗτος ἡμῖν πόλεμος; Τίς, θνητὴν ἔχων φύσιν, καὶ θανάτου κατηλαζονεύσατο; Τίς, ἐς Ἅιδου μέλλων ἐλθεῖν, αὐτὸν Ἅιδην ἀπήλεγξεν; Ἀλλ᾽ οἶδα, πόθεν ὁ πόλεμος, ἤδη ξυνῆκα τοῦ βάλλοντος. Ἐξ Ἰουδαίων αὖθις βάλλομαι, ἐκεῖθεν αὖθις ἔχω τὸν πόλεμον.

2   Ἑλλήνων ἄρχω καὶ Ἀσσυρίων ἐκράτησα, ἐμοὶ καὶ Περ- σῶν ὀφρὺς καταβέβληται καὶ Μῆδος ἀλαζὼν οὐκ ἀντέ- τεινε. Τί μὴ λέγω τῶν ἐθνῶν, ὡς ἕκαστα πάντες οἴδασι τοὺς κατὰ γῆν νόμους καὶ δέχονται καὶ μετὰ τὸ θανεῖν οὐκ

10

What Hades would say when Lazarus is raised from the dead on the fourth day

Alas, I who expected to see and experience everything before I had a dead man snatched away from me! After this burial I experienced the intolerable, I saw the unexpected, and I have been deprived of my authority over the departed. Alas, we who rule the underworld in vain! What kind of kingdom will we rule, if after we receive the dead we are deprived of them, and if after holding them fast, we do not hold them forever? I tore a soul from a body and, although already confident of my mastery, I have been despoiled of my power at the very height of my power, and although ruling over the dead, I am insulted by those still living. From where has this strange, new war come to us? Who, although having a mortal nature, has boasted even against death? Who, although destined to go to Hades, has vanquished Hades himself? But I know the source of this war; I have already perceived my attacker. I am being attacked again by the Jews; I am embattled again from that quarter.

I rule the Greeks and have mastered the Assyrians; I have 2 struck down the arrogance of the Persians, and the boastful Mede offered no resistance. Why do I omit to mention how all the Gentiles individually know and accept the laws on earth and none of them commits a transgression after he

ἔστιν ὅστις ἐκείνων παρεβιάσατο, ἀλλ᾽, εἰς γένεσιν ἐλ-
θόντες, ὑποπτεύουσι τὴν ἀνάλυσιν καί, προσιούσης, οὐκ
ἀντιτείνουσι; Μόνοι τῶν ἁπάντων Ἰουδαῖοι βιοῦσι, καὶ
θνήσκοντες. Τοῦτο τὸ γένος ἔχω πολέμιον, ὑπὸ τούτων ὁ
μάτην ἐγὼ αὐχῶν τῶν ὑπὸ γῆν κρατεῖν ἀπελέγχομαι. Ἧκε
παρὰ τὸν βίον Ἐλισσαῖος προφήτης, Ἰουδαῖος ἄνθρωπος,
καὶ θνήσκοντας, ὡς εἰπεῖν, λόγῳ μόνῳ ἀφύπνιζε, τὸ δὲ δὴ
μεῖζον, καὶ παρ᾽ αὐτὴν τὴν τελευτὴν κατεγέλασε τελευτῆς.
Ἄπνους ἥψατο παρακειμένου νεκροῦ καί μου τῶν χειρῶν
μέσων ἀπέσπασεν, ὃν ἐγὼ τοῦ σώματος πρότερον. Οἶδα
καὶ τὸν ἐκείνου διδάσκαλον. Καὶ κατεγέλα μου τῆς ἀρχῆς
καί, τελευτῶν, ἔφυγε τελευτήν, ἣν ἅπας εἶδε γενόμενος.

3   Τούτων ἀπόγονος ὁ νῦν οὗτος πολέμιος· οὗτός μου τὴν
ἀρχὴν παρεσάλευσεν, οὗτος ὑπὲρ τοὺς ἄλλους ἀνέλυσε
τὴν ἀνάλυσιν καὶ κειμένους οὐκ ἐᾷ καὶ πεσεῖν μέλλοντας
οὐκ ἀφίησιν. Ἐπαφίημι πρὸς τελευτὴν τὸ βέλος ἐγὼ καὶ ὁ
τρωθεὶς ἀλγεῖ τὰ ἔσχατα· ὁ δ᾽, εὐθὺς ἐλθών, ἐπαπειλεῖται
τῇ νόσῳ καὶ παραχρῆμα οἴχεται, δραπετεύουσα. Εἰς βάθος
ἕτερον βέβληκα, ὁ δὲ πάλιν τῆς ὁρμῆς τὸ βέλος ἐξέκρουσεν.
Ἤδη τις ἐβλήθη καὶ πέπτωκεν, ὁ δ᾽ ἀντετάξατο καὶ
τελευτῆς ἔφυγε νόμους ὁ δεξάμενος τελευτὴν καὶ φῶς εἶδε
μετὰ φωτὸς ἀποβολὴν καὶ στέρησιν σώματος.

4   Οὗτός με καὶ νῦν βάλλει καὶ τέτρωμαι καὶ τῆς βολῆς ὁ
τρόπος ὡς ἄρρητος οὐκ ἐπὶ κλίνης κείμενον ἤγειρεν, οὐ
παραπαίοντα ἐσωφρόνισεν, οὐχ ἁπλῶς ἄνθρωπον τεθνη-
κότα ἐζώωσεν, ἀλλ᾽ ἄνθρωπον, οἴμοι, νεκρὸν καὶ ἐν Ἅιδου
χρονίσαντα. Ἔβαλλον τὰ καίρια καὶ πέπτωκεν, ἀπέσπασα

dies, but rather, as soon as they are born, they have an inkling of their demise, and when it comes to them, they put up no resistance? Of all people the Jews alone continue to live, even when dead. I consider this people as my enemy; it is by these people that I, who boast in vain that I rule over those in the underworld, am refuted. While he was alive, the prophet Elisha, a Jewish man, came and awakened the so-called dead from sleep with a word alone, and what is more, even after his own death, he mocked death. Though lifeless, he touched a dead man as he lay there and tore right out of my hands a man whom I had previously torn from his body. I also know his teacher Elijah. He too mocked my authority and in dying fled death, which every man ever born has seen.

This new enemy of mine is their descendant. This man 3 has undermined my rule; more than any other, this man has put an end to death, does not let the dead be, and does not let go those who are destined to die. I shoot my deadly arrow, and the wounded person suffers the utmost pains, but as soon as this man comes and threatens the disease, it immediately departs in flight. I shot another person deeply, but this man again repulsed the arrow of my attack. Already someone has been shot and has died, but this man confronted death and so the person who received death escaped the laws of death and saw the light after losing the light and being deprived of his body.

This man now shoots me, and I have been wounded, and 4 the ineffable nature of his shot has not raised one lying on a bed, not brought a madman to his senses, not simply restored a dead man to life, but rather has restored to life a man—alas!—a dead man who had already spent time in Hades. I inflicted mortal wounds and he died; I tore him from

τοῦ σώματος, ὁ δ᾽ οὐκ ἀντέτεινε. Ξύμμαχον ἥξειν ἔφασκε καὶ πληγάς μοι προσεπεμαντεύετο, ἐγὼ δ᾽ ἐποιούμην κατάγελων καὶ λήρους εἶναι πάντα ἐνόμιζον. Ἐπυθόμην καὶ τίς ὁ ξύμμαχος, ὁ δὲ τὸν Ἰησοῦν ἔλεγεν. Ἤκουσα καὶ μόνον τὴν κλῆσιν καὶ τὸ ἐντεῦθεν ὑπώπτευον τὴν ἀφαίρεσιν.

5   Παρῆλθεν ἡ πρώτη καὶ ὁ μὲν ἐθαύμαζε τὴν ἀναβολήν, ἐμοὶ δὲ πάλιν τὰ τῆς ὑποψίας οὐκ ἔληγεν. Ἦκεν ἡ μετ᾽ αὐτὴν καὶ ὁ μὲν εἰς ἐλπίδας ἦν τὸν φίλον ἥξειν ποτὲ καὶ βιώσειν. Τὸ δεύτερον ἰσχυρίζετο καὶ πάλιν ἐμὲ τὸ δέος ἐλάμβανε. Μικροῦ τέτταρας ἡλίους οὐκ εἶδεν, ὑπὸ γῆν καταδύς, καὶ προσεδόκει τὴν ἀναβίωσιν. Ἤδη τι καὶ τοῦ σώματος ὄδωδε καὶ τὰς τῶν μελῶν ἁρμονίας ὁ χρόνος διέσπασεν. Ὅλος φύσεως δεσμὸς διελύετο. Ἐντεῦθεν τὴν εἰς τὸ σῶμα δευτέραν μετοικίαν ἀπέγνων ἐγώ, καὶ τέλος τὴν ἐπαγγελίαν οὐκ ἤλπιζον δέξασθαι.

6   Ἀλλ᾽ ὦ τῆς ἀθρόας ἐπιβουλῆς! Ὦ τῆς ἐξαίφνης ἐπιθέσεως! Ἦκεν, ἐδάκρυσε· καί, δάκρυον ἰδών, τὸ πάθος ᾤμην ἀνθρώπινον καὶ τὸ μηδέν τι παθεῖν ὁ δείλαιος ἐντεῦθεν ἐθάρρησα. Ὁ τάφος ἀνέῳγει, ἐγὼ δ᾽ οὐκ εἰς νοῦν ἔτι τὴν μάχην ἐλάμβανον· τὸ γὰρ ἤδη λελύσθαι τὸ σῶμα κἀμὲ τοῦ δέους ἐξέλυε καὶ θαρρεῖν ἐποίει μηκέτι ψυχὴν καθέξειν δυνήσεσθαι. Ἐλογιζόμην τούς, ὅσοι καὶ μετὰ τελευτὴν βεβιώκασι, καὶ μετὰ πρώτην ἡμέραν εἰς τὸ παντελὲς κειμένους ἅπαντας εὕρισκον· ὁ δέ, ὦ γῆ καὶ Ἅιδου νόμοι καὶ θεσμοὶ φύσεως, ἐνεβριμήσατο, ἐπέταξεν, ἐπηπείλησε καὶ τὴν ἀπειλὴν οὐχ ὑπήνεγκα. Ὁ δέ μου τῶν χειρῶν ἀπέπτη καὶ τὸ σῶμα ἐνέδυ καὶ ὁ πολὺς ἐκεῖνος

his body, and he offered no resistance. He claimed that an ally would come and prophesied an attack against me, but I considered this absurd and believed that it was all nonsense. I asked him who the ally was, and he said "Jesus." I merely heard the name, and from that moment I suspected that the dead man would be taken away.

The first day passed, and he was surprised at the delay; 5 for me, however, the suspicions did not cease. The next day came, and he was hopeful that his friend would come at last and revive him. He made the same claim a second time, and again fear took hold of me. It was the beginning of his fourth day in the underworld, and he still expected his resurrection. His body had already begun to smell, and time had torn apart the joints of his limbs. The natural bond was completely breaking down. I therefore gave up anticipating his second migration back to his body, and in the end I was not expecting to receive the command.

But alas, the sudden scheme! Alas, the surprise attack! Je- 6 sus came, *he wept,* and seeing his tears I thought his suffering was human, and I, the wretch, became confident from this that I would suffer nothing at all. The grave opened up, but I still did not comprehend the battle; for the fact that his body had already been broken down was also breaking down my fear and making me confident that his body would no longer be able to possess a soul. I considered all those who have come back to life after death, and I found that they were all absolutely dead after the first day, but—O earth and laws of Hades and divine laws of nature!—Jesus rebuked, ordered, and threatened, and I did not endure the threat. But Lazarus flew out of my hands and put on his body, and that

χρόνος ἠλέγχετο καὶ τὸ τοῦ σώματος παρειμένον καινὸν αὖθις ἐδέχετο σύνδεσμον.

7   Ἆρα δέξομαί ποτε τὸν πολέμιον τοῦτον εἰς χεῖρας ἐγώ; Ἆρά ποτε κρατήσω τοῦ βάλλοντος; Μανθάνω τοὺς λοιποὺς Ἰουδαίους ὁπλίζεσθαι καὶ τάχα τοῦτο τὸ μέρος οὐκ ἀτυχήσομαι· πολλοὶ γὰρ τὴν ἀρχὴν ἐθρασύνοντο μὲν καθ᾽ ἡμῶν, ἀλλ᾽ ὕστερον ἥττηνται καὶ πεπτώκασιν. Ἀλλ᾽ οἴμοι πάλιν ὑποπτεύω τὸ μέλλον, δέδοικα μὴ καὶ Θεὸς ᾖ, κἂν θνητὸς τὸ φαινόμενον. Οὕτως ἐγὼ θαρρῶ τὸ φαινόμενον καὶ τρέμω τὸ κηρυττόμενον.

II

Τίνας ἂν εἴποι λόγους ὁ δοῦλος τοῦ ἀρχιερέως, ἀποκοπεὶς τὸ ὠτίον παρὰ τοῦ ἁγίου Πέτρου καὶ ἰαθεὶς παρὰ τοῦ Χριστοῦ

Τὸν μαθητὴν κατηγορήσω τοῦ θράσους ἢ τῆς ἐπιεικείας θαυμάσομαι τὸν διδάσκαλον; Ὁ μέν μοι τὸ ξίφος ἐπέσεισεν, ὁ δὲ τῆς τόλμης ἐπέπληξε καί, τὸ δὴ μεῖζον, εἰς ἐπιείκειαν, εἰς ὁλομέλειαν ἀποκαθιστᾷ τὸ τμηθὲν καὶ τὸ πεπληγὸς ἰᾶται τοῦ σώματος. Ἐπιτίθησι θαῦμα τῷ θαύματι,

great passage of time was refuted, and the slackness of his body again received a new unifying bond.

Will I ever receive this enemy into my hands? Will I ever master my attacker? I hear that the rest of the Jews are at arms, and perhaps thanks to this I will not be unlucky. For at first many have been emboldened against me, but ultimately they have been defeated and have died. But, alas, I again have a suspicion about the future; I fear that Jesus may even be God, even if he is mortal in appearance. Thus I take confidence in his appearance, but tremble at what is proclaimed.

7

II

What the slave of the high priest would say when his ear is cut off by Saint Peter and healed by Christ

Shall I blame the student for his rashness or admire the teacher for his forbearance? The former brandished his sword at me, but the latter rebuked him for his audacity and, what is more, as a sign of his forbearance, he restored the severed ear to wholeness and healed what was struck from my body. He added miracle to miracle, both healing me and

καὶ θεραπεύων καὶ φιλανθρωπευόμενος. Ἄγαμαι τὸ φιλάνθρωπον, ἀλλ᾽ ὑπεράγαμαι τὸ τεράστιον. Οὔτε τὰ τῆς
ἐπιεικείας ἀνθρώποις ἐγχώρια καὶ τῆς θεραπείας ὁ τρόπος
ὡς ἔνθεος! Τίς, ἐν μέσοις φόνοις ἑστώς, οὐκ ἐπτόηται; Ἢ
τίς ὑπεραλγεῖ βεβλημένου τοῦ βάλλοντος; Ἥψατο μόνον
καὶ συνέφυ τὸ διεστώς, ἐπέθηκε τὴν χεῖρα καὶ τοῦτο μόνον
πρὸς ἴασιν ἤρκεσεν.

2 Ὦ θεραπείας καινῆς, ἣ μὴ φαρμάκων ἐδέησεν! Ὦ χειρὸς
ἀρτιζούσης ἑτοίμως τὰ λειπόμενα πρὸς ὁλότητα! Εἶδον
ὑγείαν ἀνέλπιστον, εὗρον θεραπευτὴν ἀπροσδόκητον. Οὐ
χρόνος τὴν θεραπείαν ὡρίσατο, οὐ μῖσος δίκαιον τὸν
θεραπευτὴν διεκώλυσεν. Ἅμα πέπληγα καὶ τὸ πεπληγὸς
οὐ πεπόνηκα, σύνδρομος ἡ θεραπεία τῷ τραύματι. Οὐδ᾽
ἀκριβῶς ἥψατό μου τῆς ψυχῆς ἡ τομὴ καὶ ὁ θεραπεύσων
ἐφίσταται καί, τὸ καινότατον, ἀφῇ μετρεῖται τὴν ἴασιν. Ὦ
τίνα σε καὶ λογίσομαι; Ἡ μὲν ὄψις ἄνθρωπον λέγειν
δίδωσι, τὰ δ᾽ ἔργα τὴν κλῆσιν οὐ συγχωρεῖ. Ὅσον ἐπὶ
ψυχῆς ἔχω τοῦ θαύματος! Ἡλίκον ἐφ᾽ ἡμῖν τὸ θάμβος
ἐκίνησας! Σφαγεὺς ἐγὼ σός εἰμι. Οὐχ ὁρᾷς μου τὴν δεξιὰν
ὡς ὥπλισται; Εἶθ᾽ ὑπερμαχεῖς τοῦ σφαγέως, οὔκουν τοῦτό
γε ἀνθρώπινον.

3 Ὦ θρασὺς γέρων ἐκεῖνος, ὃς οὔτε τὸ πολὺ τῶν ἐπι-
βουλευόντων ἔδεισεν, οὔτε τὸ τοῦ διδασκάλου φιλάνθρωπον ἐμιμήσατο, ἀλλ᾽ ἀντέτεινε πρὸς οὕτω πολλοὺς καὶ πρό
γε τούτου πρὸς αὐτὴν τὴν τοῦ διδάσκοντος ἐπιείκειαν!
Τίνα δὴ καὶ ζηλῶν ταῦτα τολμᾷς τὸν συμφοιτητὴν ἢ τὸν
διδάσκαλον; Ὁ μὲν ὑπεραλγεῖ τοῦ πλήττοντος, εἰ πλη-
γήσεται, ὁ δ᾽ ἐξήρτυσε τῷ διδασκάλῳ τὴν ἐπιβουλήν.

behaving humanely. I admire his humane behavior, but I particularly admire his wondrous act. His forbearance is unusual for humans, and how divine is the nature of his healing! Who, standing in the midst of slaughter, is not terrified? Or who feels pain when his attacker has been struck? He merely touched me, and what had been separated grew back together; he applied his hand, and this alone was sufficient for healing.

Oh, the novel healing, for which he needed no medicine! 2 Oh, the hand that promptly restored to wholeness what was missing! I experienced unexpected healing. I found an unforeseen healer. No time intervened before the healing, nor did justifiable hatred hold back the healer. As soon as I was struck I did not suffer from the blow; the healing was concurrent with the wound. But the cut did not actually endanger my life, and the one who was to heal me stood over me and, strangest of all, measured out his healing with a touch. Oh, what should I consider you? Your appearance suggests that you are human, but your actions do not match that name. How much wonder do I have in my soul! What great amazement you have stirred in me! I am your killer. Do you not see how my right hand is armed? If you defend your killer, this is beyond human nature.

Alas, that rash old man, who neither feared the great 3 number of conspirators nor emulated the humane behavior of his teacher, but rather resisted so many people and, even before this, resisted the very forbearance of his teacher! Whom are you emulating when you dare to do this, your fellow disciple or your teacher? The latter felt pain for his attacker, worrying that he might be struck, but the former contrived the plot against his teacher. Neither did you

Οὔτε τοῦτον ἐμιμήσω τῆς ἐπιεικείας, οὔτ' ἐκεῖνον τῆς προδοσίας ἐζήλωσας. Ἀλλὰ γὰρ τί καὶ μέμφομαι τὸν ἐς τοσοῦτο δέον προκινδυνεύσαντα; Θρασὺς μὲν ὁ ἀνήρ. Ἀλλ' ὅσον τὸ θράσος παραλογώτατον, τοσοῦτον τὸ τοῦ διδασκάλου προκινδυνεύειν τολμᾶν εὐλογώτατον. Ὡς πολλὴν δέ γε τὴν εἰς τὸν διδάσκαλον ζέσιν ἐνέφηνας, ἄνθρωπε, οὕτω θρασυνόμενος ἄτοπα! Ἀλλ' ἔχεις ἱκανῶς τὴν ὑπὲρ τοῦ διδασκάλου τόλμαν μαθών, μάθε δή μοι καὶ τὴν τούτου λοιπὸν ἐπιείκειαν.

4   Ἀλλὰ γάρ, ὦ σὺ νόθε μαθητὰ καὶ φιλόχρυσε, ἐφ' οἷον ἡμᾶς ἄγεις τὸν διδάσκαλον, εἰς ἡλίκον ἡμᾶς ἐκίνησας τὸ κακόν; Ἀνελεῖν τὸν ἰώμενον, δεσμεῖν τὸν οὐκ ἀντιτείνοντα, ξυναρπάζειν τὸν οὐ μαχόμενον; Ὦ καὶ σὺ δέσποτα καὶ πάντες οἱ λοιποὶ τοῦ γράμματος ἔμπειροι, μή μοι φθόνος ὑμᾶς ἕλοι καὶ νόσημα βάσκανον. Ἀκριβῶς οἴδατε τὸν Νόμον, τὸν Μεσσίαν οὐκ ἠγνοήσατε. Ἐμβαθύνατε τῷ γράμματι τὸν νοῦν, ἐρευνήσατε τὴν ἐθνῶν προσδοκίαν, ἐξακριβώσασθε καὶ γνοίητ' ἂν τοῦτον εἶναι τὸν προσδοκώμενον. Μηδὲ πρὸς τὴν ἀλήθειαν μύσωμεν, μηδὲ φθόνος ἡμῶν στρατηγείτω. Ἔχομεν ὃν ἠλπίζομεν, ἔχομεν ὃν αἱ γραφαὶ κηρύττουσιν, ἧκεν ὁ προσδοκώμενος. Ἐπίστασθε τὴν γένεσιν, τὸν ἀστέρα, τὴν ἐξ οὐρανῶν ἐν Ἰορδάνῃ φωνήν, τἄλλα πάντα ὡς καινὰ καὶ Θεὸν ἥκειν τοῦτον ἡμῖν μαρτυροῦντα. Κἂν θνητὸς ᾖ τὸ φαινόμενον, ἀλλά γε Θεὸς τὸ νοούμενον. Μὴ δὴ τὸν νομοθέτην ἀνέλωμεν, ἵνα μὴ καὶ τὸν Νόμον αὐτὸν συνανέλωμεν. Οὐκ εἰς καλὸν ἡμῖν, εὖ οἶδα, τελευτήσει τὰ τῆς ἐπιβουλῆς· δώσομεν δίκας, εἰ καὶ μηδὲν ἄλλο, τόν γε πάντως οὐχ ὑπεύθυνον εὐθύνοντες. Ὁ

imitate the latter in his forbearance, nor did you emulate the former in his treachery. For indeed, why do I blame the man who was first to brave the danger in a time of such great need? The man is rash. But his rashness is just as unreasonable as his daring to risk danger for his teacher is reasonable. What great fervor you displayed toward your teacher, sir, showing such unusual boldness! But you already know well enough how to be daring on behalf of your teacher; please now learn his forbearance.

For indeed, O you false, gold-loving disciple, against what 4 sort of teacher are you leading us? To how great an evil have you roused us—to kill the one who heals, bind the one who puts up no resistance, seize and carry away the one who does not fight back? O you, my master and all the rest who are acquainted with scripture, please do not let envy and malicious disease destroy you. You know the Law in detail; you are not unaware of the Messiah. Plunge your minds deeply into scripture; search for the *expectation of nations;* study carefully and you will learn that this man is the awaited one. Let us not shut our eyes to the truth. Let us not be guided by envy. We have the one we have been expecting; we have the one whom the scriptures proclaim; the awaited one has come. You know about his birth, the star, the voice from heaven at the Jordan, and all the other novel signs that testify that this man has come to us as God. Even if he is mortal in appearance, he is to be understood as God. Let us not kill the lawgiver, so that we may not kill the Law itself along with him. Our plot, I know well, will not succeed; we will be punished, even if for nothing else, for calling to account a man who is by no means answerable to us. But he, I suspect,

δέ, οἶμαι, καινοτομήσει τὴν τελευτήν, ὡς καὶ τὴν γένεσιν πρότερον.

12

Τίνας ἂν εἴπῃ λόγους ἡ Θεοτόκος, περιπλακεῖσα κηδευομένῳ τῷ ταύτης υἱῷ τῷ Θεῷ καὶ Σωτῆρι Χριστῷ

Τοῦτο ἐκεῖνο, γλυκύτατε Ἰησοῦ, τὸ τοὺς ἐκ Περσίδος ἀφιγμένους εἰς Βηθλεὲμ οὐ μόνον χρυσὸν ὡς βασιλεῖ καὶ λίβανον ὡς Θεῷ, ἀλλὰ καὶ σμύρναν ὡς θνητῷ προσενεγκεῖν γεννηθέντι σοι. Τοῦτο ἐκεῖνο τὸ ρομφαίαν μέλλειν διελθεῖν τὴν καρδίαν μου, καθὼς ὁ Συμεὼν προηγόρευσεν. Τοῦτο ἐκεῖνο τὸ πῦρ, ὃ βαλεῖν ἦλθες ἐπὶ τὴν γῆν, ὥσπερ αὐτὸς προεδίδαξας· καυστικώτερον γὰρ καὶ πυρὸς μητρὶ φιλοτέκνῳ παιδὸς μονογενοῦς ἀπονέκρωσις. Μικροῦ πρὸς τοὐναντίον μοι περιΐσταται καὶ ὁ τοῦ Γαβριὴλ ἀσπασμός· οὐ γὰρ καὶ νῦν ὁ Κύριος μετ᾽ ἐμοῦ, καθὼς ἐκεῖνός μοι ἐπηγγείλατο.

2 Ἀλλὰ σὺ μὲν ἄπνους καὶ ἐν νεκροῖς εἰς Ἅιδου ταμεῖα περιφοιτᾷς τὰ ἐνδότερα, ἐγὼ δὲ τὸν ἀέρα πνέω καὶ μετὰ τῶν ζώντων περίειμι. Καίτοι οὐ συνορῶ διὰ ποῖον ἄτοπον

will do something novel in his death, just as he previously did in his birth.

12

What the Theotokos would say when she embraces her son, God and the Savior Christ, when he is being prepared for burial

This, sweetest Jesus, is what it meant when the men who came from Persia to Bethlehem brought you at your birth not only gold, as befits a king, and frankincense, as befits God, but also myrrh, as befits a mortal liable to death. This is what was meant by the sword destined to pierce my heart, as Symeon foretold. This is what was meant by *the fire* that *you came to cast upon the earth,* as you yourself foretold. For even more searing than fire for a mother who loves her child is the death of her only begotten son. The greeting of Gabriel has almost been reversed for me; for no longer, as he once proclaimed, is *the Lord with me.*

Rather, you wander lifeless among the dead in the inner 2 chambers of Hades, while I still breathe the air and survive among the living. And yet I cannot comprehend for what

ἔργον πεφόνευσαι. Ἐκάλυψε γὰρ οὐρανοὺς ἡ ἀρετή σου
κατὰ τὸν Ἀββακούμ, καὶ νῦν ἄμορφος κεῖσαι ὁ ὡραῖος
κάλλει παρὰ τοὺς υἱοὺς τῶν ἀνθρώπων, καὶ ἄδοξος κηδεύῃ
ἐν γῇ, οὗ τὴν δόξαν διηγοῦνται οἱ οὐρανοί. Καὶ μνῆμα φέρει
σε λελατομημένον, ὃν ἐξ ὄρους ἀλαξεύτου τμηθέντα λίθον
εἶδεν ὁ Δανιήλ. Ἀπαθής σου ἡ γέννησις ἐντεῦθεν
ἐδείκνυτο, ὡς καὶ ἐν τῇ βάτῳ ἡ θεϊκή σου πρὸς ἀνθρώπους
συνάφεια, καὶ ἐν τῷ Ἰωσὴφ ἡ τῶν Ἰουδαίων ἐπιβουλή, καὶ
ἐν τῷ Ἰσαὰκ τὸ τοῦ θανάτου ὁμοίωμα. Λείπεται οὖν τὸ ἐν
τῷ Ἰωνᾷ τῆς ἀναστάσεώς σου μυστήριον. Οἴμοι, ὅτι ἐν
λίθῳ κεῖσαι νεκρὸς ὁ ἐκ τῶν λίθων ἐγείρων τέκνα τῷ
Ἀβραάμ· ἢ γὰρ οὐ τῶν λίθων ῥαγέντων διὰ τὸ πάθος σου
τὸ σωτήριον πολλοί σου τῷ ὀνόματι πεπιστεύκασιν;

3   Οὐκ εἶχες ποῦ τὴν κεφαλὴν κλῖναι ζῶν, <ὡς> εἶπας Ἰου-
δαίοις αὐτός, οὓς καὶ ἀλώπεκας ᾐνίξω διὰ τοὺς δολεροὺς
αὐτῶν λογισμούς· ἀλλ᾽ ἔκλινας ταύτην τεθνηκὼς ἐπὶ τοῦ
σταυροῦ ὑπεστρωμένην ὡς κλίνην εὑρὼν εὐγνώμονος τὴν
πίστιν λῃστοῦ. "Παρέβλεψέ με ὁ ἥλιος," λεγέτω ἡ ᾀσμα-
τίζουσα· "Ἐπέδυ ὁ ἥλιος ἔτι μεσούσης ἡμέρας," Ἰερεμίας
φθεγγέσθω μοι. Ναὶ γὰρ καὶ ἥλιον αἰσθητὸν ὑπέδραμε
στύγνασις, τοῦ νοητοῦ ἡλίου τῆς δικαιοσύνης ἐκλείποντος,
καὶ πέτραι ῥῆξιν ὑπήνεγκαν, αἷς συρραγῆναι κινδυνεύει
καὶ ἡ καρδία μου.

4   Ὦ σὰρξ ἁγία, ἥτις ἐξ αἱμάτων ἐμῶν ἐτυρώθης ὑπερφυῶς!
Τὸ γὰρ ἀρχαῖον χρέος ἀπεδόμην πληρέστατον. Εἰς τοῦτο
μοι τοὺς οὐρανοὺς ὑπέκλινας, Δέσποτα, καὶ ὡς ὑετὸς ἐπὶ
πόκον κατέβης, ἵνα καὶ νέκρωσιν ὑποστῇς ἁγίων μὲν κεκοι-
μημένων ἐξεγείρουσαν σώματα, νεκροῦσαν δὲ τὴν τεκοῦσαν

kind of heinous act you have been slain. For *your virtue covered the heavens,* in the words of the prophet Habakkuk, and now you, who were *more beautiful than the sons of men,* lie dead and unsightly, and you, whose *glory the heavens describe,* are being ingloriously buried on earth. A hewn tomb holds you, whom Daniel saw as *a stone cut* from an unhewn *mountain.* Your birth therefore proved to be without suffering, just as in the bush your divine relationship to humans was revealed, and in Joseph the plot of the Jews, and in Isaac the image of death. Missing, then, is the mystery of your resurrection as foretold in Jonah, alas, because you, the one who *could raise up children for Abraham from the stones,* lie there dead on a stone slab. For surely, when stones had been broken, did not many people believe in your name because of your suffering that brings salvation?

You did not have a place to lay your head when you were   3 alive, as you yourself said to the Jews, whom you suggestively called *foxes* because of their treacherous schemes. But after you died on the cross, you laid down your head, having found the faith of a right-believing thief spread beneath you like a bed. *"The sun has looked upon me,"* let the one who sings her song of rejoicing say. *"The sun set while it was still midday,"* let Jeremiah utter to me. For yes, darkness even stole over the visible sun when the intelligible *sun of righteousness* was in eclipse, and stones were broken, and my heart is close to breaking with them.

O holy flesh, you who were supernaturally curdled like   4 cheese from my blood! For I have repaid the ancient debt in full. For this *you made the heavens bow* to me, Master, and *you descended like rain on a fleece,* that you might endure a death that *would raise up the bodies of saints laid to rest,* but bring

σε. Τί ταῦτα, παῖ ποθεινότατε; Ἀβλαβῶς μὲν ἐμίχθη πάλαι τὰ ἄμικτα καὶ πῦρ θεότητος ἄϋλον σπλάγχνον ἐμὸν οὐ κατέφλεξεν. Ἄρτι δ' ἕτερον πῦρ τὰ ἐντός μου βόσκεται πάντα καὶ μέσην λυμαίνεται τὴν καρδίαν μου. Χαρᾶς ἐγγύας δι' ἀγγέλου παρέλαβον καὶ ἀφειλόμην δάκρυον πᾶν ἀπὸ προσώπου τῆς γῆς, νῦν δ' ἀλλὰ τοῦτο μόνοις τοῖς ἐμοῖς πιαίνεται δάκρυσιν. Εἰς Ἅιδου καταβαίνεις, οἶδ' ὅτι, τὰς ἐγκεκλεισμένας ἀπολύσων ψυχάς, ἀλλὰ καὶ τὴν ἐμὴν καρδίαν ἐκεῖσε συγκατασπᾷς, ἔμπνουν νεκρὰν παρατρέχων με.

5   Ὦ γυμνὲ νεκρὲ καὶ ζῶντος Λόγε Θεοῦ, ἑκουσίως ὑψωθῆναι κατακεκριμένε σταυρῷ, ἵνα πάντας ἑλκύσῃς εἰς ἑαυτόν, ποῖον σου τῶν μελῶν τοῦ σώματος διέμεινεν ἀπαθές; Ὦ θεία μοι κορυφὴ ἀκάνθας δεδεγμένη καὶ ταύτας μετεμπήξασα τῇ καρδίᾳ μου! Ὦ κοσμία καὶ ἱερὰ κεφαλή, ἥτις πάλαι μὲν οὐκ εἶχες ποῦ κλιθῆναι καὶ ἀναπαύσασθαι, νῦν δὲ πρὸς τάφον μόνον ἐκλίθης καὶ ἀναπέπαυσαι καὶ κατὰ τὸν Ἰακὼβ ὡς λέων κεκοίμησαι! Ὦ ποθεινὴ καὶ ἐρασμία μοι κεφαλή, καλάμῳ τετυμμένη ὡς ἀνορθώσῃς τὸν ὡς εὐρίπιστον τῷ πονηρῷ κατεαγότα πνεύματι κάλαμον καὶ μακρὰν τοῦ παραδείσου γενόμενον!

6   Ὦ σιαγόνες δεδεγμέναι ῥαπίσματα! Ὦ στόμα σίμβλον ἕτερον μέλιτος, εἰ καὶ χολῆς ἐδέξω πικρότητα καὶ ὄξους ἐποτίσθης δριμύτητα! Ὦ στόμα καὶ λόγῳ μόνῳ νεκρὸν ἐξαναστῆσαν τὸν τετραήμερον! Ὦ στόμα, οὕπερ οὐχ εὑρέθη δόλος ἐντός, εἰ καί σε δολερὸν εἰς θάνατον προὔδωκε φίλημα! Ὦ χεῖρες αἱ τὸν ἄνθρωπον πλαστουργήσασαι καὶ νῦν προσηλωμέναι μὲν τῷ σταυρῷ, ἐν Ἅιδου δὲ

death to the woman who gave birth to you. Why has this happened, my most longed-for son? Of old, formerly irreconcilable things were combined without harm, and the immaterial fire of divinity did not burn up my inner organs, but now a different fire consumes all my insides and ravages the core of my heart. I received pledges of joy from an angel and *wiped away every tear from the face* of the earth, which is now enriched by my tears alone. You descend into Hades, I know, to release the imprisoned souls, but you also drag my heart down there with you, leaving me behind, a breathing corpse.

O naked corpse and Word of the living God, willingly 5 condemned to be raised up high on a cross so that you might draw everyone to yourself, which limbs of your body remained without suffering? O divine head, bound with thorns with which you pricked my heart! O decorous and holy *head*, once *you did not have a place where you could lie and* rest, but now you have been laid down alone to rest in a grave, and *you sleep*, in the words of Jacob, *like a lion!* O head desired and beloved by me, you were beaten by a reed so that you might restore the reed of your body, the flimsiest of reeds, which has been broken by the evil spirit and removed far from paradise!

O cheeks that received blows! O mouth that is another 6 beehive of honey, even if you were given bitter gall and drank sour vinegar! O mouth that also by a word alone raised a man dead for four days! O mouth, within which no deceit was found, even if a treacherous kiss betrayed you to death! O hands that fashioned humankind and have now been nailed to the cross, but stretching forth into Hades, grasped

προτεινόμεναι καὶ χειρὸς ἁπτόμεναι τῆς ἁψαμένης τοῦ ξύλου πάλαι καὶ τοῦ πτώματος ὅλον τὸν Ἀδὰμ ἐξεγείρουσαι! Ὦ πλευρὰ λογχευθεῖσα διὰ τὴν ἐκ πλευρᾶς πλασθεῖσαν προμήτορα! Ὦ πόδες ἐφ᾽ ὑδάτων πεζεύσαντες καὶ τὴν ῥοώδη φύσιν εἰλικρινῶς ἁγιάσαντες!

7 Ὦ μοι υἱὲ μητρὸς παλαιότερε, ποίους θρήνους ἐπιτυμβίους καὶ τίνας ὕμνους ἐπικηδείους σοι ᾄσαιμι; Οὐκέτι στάμνος μανναδόχος ἐγώ· τὸ μάννα γὰρ τὸ ψυχοτρόφον ἀμφὶ τὸν τάφον ἐκκέχυσαι. Οὐκέτι βάτος ἀκατάφλεκτος ἔγωγε· ὅλη γὰρ τῷ νοητῷ πυρί σου τῆς ταφῆς καταπέφλεγμαι. Οὐκέτι χρυσῆ λυχνία ἐγώ· τὸ γὰρ φῶς ὑπὸ τὸν μόδιον τέθεισαι.

8 Ὡς πολλὰ τὰ μεγαλεῖα ὁ δυνατὸς ἐνεδείξω μοι. Ἐκ πασῶν τῶν γενεῶν ἐξελέξω με, γλώσσας προφητῶν ἐτράνωσας δι᾽ ἐμέ. Μέλλων οὐρανόθεν καταφοιτᾶν, ὡς οἶδας αὐτός, τὴν ἐμὴν εἰς τὸν κόσμον ἀνέμενες πρόοδον, μὴ ἔχων σκεῦος ὑποδοχῆς θεότητος ἄξιον. Σοὶ μόνῳ κατηγγυήσαντό με καὶ πρὸ τῆς συλλήψεως οἱ γεννήτορες· οὕτω γὰρ προεπαγγείλασθαί σοι τὸ τῆς ἀτεκνίας τούτους κατηνάγκασεν ὄνειδος. Εἰς φῶς ἐξήχθην τοῦτο τοῦ βίου, καὶ βραχύ τι τοῖς γονεῦσι παρέμεινα. Ὁμοῦ γὰρ μαστοῖς ἀπεταξάμην καὶ γάλακτι, καὶ συναπεταξάμην καὶ τοῖς γεννήτορσι, καὶ ὅλη ὅλῳ προσαπεδόθην σοι, καὶ ναῷ ἀνετέθην ναὸς γενησομένη σοι καθαρώτατος. Ὁ πατήρ μου καὶ ἡ μήτηρ μου ἐγκατέλιπόν με, σὺ δὲ προσελάβου με καὶ δι᾽ ἀγγέλου ἐξέθρεψας καί, ὅ φησιν ὁ Δαβίδ, "Ἄρτον ἀγγέλων ἔφαγεν ἄνθρωπος."

9 Προσέτι ῥάβδον ξηρὰν καὶ γεγηρακυῖαν δι᾽ ἐμὲ

the hand that once touched the tree, and raised Adam whole from his fall! O side pierced with a spear because the first mother was fashioned from a rib! O feet that walked on water and in their purity sanctified its flowing nature!

O my son, older than your mother, what kind of lamentations at your tomb and what funeral dirges should I sing for you? No longer am I the jar that holds manna; for you have poured out the soul-nourishing manna around the grave. No longer am I the unconsumed bush; for I have been consumed entirely by the intelligible fire of your burial. No longer am I the golden lampstand; for you have *placed* your light *under the bushel.* 7

So many magnificent works have you, the mighty one, shown me. You selected me from all the generations and instructed the tongues of prophets on account of me. Intending to descend from heaven, as you yourself know, you awaited my entrance into the world, since you did not have a receptacle worthy of your divinity. To you alone my ancestors betrothed me even before I was conceived; for the disgrace of childlessness so compelled them to promise me to you. I was brought forth into the light of life, and I remained with my parents for only a short time. For as soon as I renounced breasts and milk, I also renounced my parents, and I was wholly devoted to you and dedicated to your temple, to become a most pure temple for you. My father and my mother left me behind, but you took me in and raised me through an angel, and, as David says, "*A human ate the bread of angels.*" 8

Moreover, you have made an old, dry staff sprout and 9

213

ἀναθηλῆσαι καὶ ἀνηβῆσαι πεποίηκας ὁ καὶ τὴν μητρικήν μου πρὶν διαλυσάμενος στείρωσιν. Ἄγγελον εἶδον πρωτοστάτην ὡς δεσποίνῃ προσομιλοῦντα μοι, ὃν Ζαχαρίας πρὶν ἰδὼν ἐκωφεύσατο καὶ γλωττοπέδην ὑπέμεινεν. <...> ἠγαλλιάσατο καὶ βρέφος ἔνδον γαστρὸς καὶ τὸν ἀσπασμὸν ἠμείψατο τῷ σκιρτήματι σὲ προσκυνοῦν τὸν ἐν γαστρί μου κυοφορούμενον. Νόμους ἐν ἐμοὶ κατέλυσας φύσεως, ἀσπόρως συνελήφθης, ὡς οἶδας, καὶ μετὰ τόκον με παρθένον ἐφύλαξας. Τέθεικάς με "μητέρα ἐπὶ τέκνῳ εὐφραινομένην" κατὰ τὸν δι᾽ ἐμὲ θεοπάτορα, καὶ πασῶν ὑπερκειμένην θυγατέρων, ἃς ὁ Σολομὼν προηνίξατο. Βασιλεῖς καὶ πτωχευούσῃ μοι προσῆλθον καὶ δουλοπρεπῆ παρέσχον προσκύνησιν. Οὐρανῶν με πλατυτέραν ἀνέδειξας, ἐξ ἧς ὁ τῆς δόξης ἔλαμψας ἥλιος· καὶ ἵνα τὰ λοιπὰ τῶν περὶ ἐμὲ τεραστίων παραδραμοῦμαι, μακαριστὴν ἐν πάσαις γενεαῖς με πεποίηκας καὶ δι᾽ ἐμοῦ τὸν ἄνω κόσμον πληρωθῆναι διῳκονόμησας.

10   Νῦν ἀλλ᾽ οὐκ οἶδ᾽ ὅπως συγκέχυται ταῦτα καὶ ἀψινθίῳ μοι τὸ μέλι συμπέφυρται· καὶ γὰρ συννεκροῦσθαι προάγομαι νῦν καὶ συνθάπτεσθαι καὶ μέχρις Ἅιδου συγκαταβαίνειν σοι. Νεφέλην με φωτὸς ὁ προφήτης ὠνόμασεν ἀντὶ νιφετῶν, ὡς ἔοικε, τὰ δάκρυα στάζουσαν. Μήποτε ἄρα περὶ ἐμοῦ καὶ τοῦτο προείρηται, "Ἐγκαταλειφθήσεται ἡ θυγάτηρ Σιὼν ὡς σκηνὴ ἐν ἀμπελῶνι," καὶ τὸ ἑξῆς. Ἰδοὺ γὰρ ἀποτετρυγημένος μοι πρόκειται ὁ βότρυς τῆς ζωῆς ὁ ἀκήρατος, ὁ τὸ ζωηφόρον αἷμα κενώσας ὡς οἶνον πιστῶν καρδίας εὐφραίνοντα. Βαβαὶ πῶς ὁ κατάψυχρος οὗτος λίθος ὡς σιδήρῳ πληττόμενος τῷ κραταιῷ σου βραχίονι

grow again because of me, you who earlier had abolished my mother's barrenness. I saw an archangel conversing with me as his mistress; when Zacharias saw him earlier, he became deaf and remained mute. <. . .> the baby inside his wife's womb exulted and responded to my greeting with a leap, worshipping you as you were carried in my womb. You abolished the laws of nature in me: you were conceived without seed, as you know, and after your birth you kept me a virgin. You have made me "*a mother rejoicing in a child,*" in the words of the one who became the ancestor of God because of me, and surpassing all daughters, to whom Solomon alluded. Kings came to me although I was impoverished and paid worship as befits slaves. You proclaimed me wider than the heavens, from whom you, the sun of glory, shone forth, and—so that I may pass over the rest of the wonders about me—you have made me most blessed among all generations, and you arranged for heaven above to be filled through me.

But now, I do not know how these things have been con- 10 founded and how honey has been mixed for me with wormwood; for now I am induced to die and be buried along with you, and to descend with you to Hades. The prophet called me a cloud of light rather than one of rain, as it seems, dripping tears. Perhaps this too was once foretold about me: "*The daughter of Zion will be deserted like a tent in a vineyard,*" and so on. For behold, you lie before me as the plucked grapes of life, you the undefiled one, who poured out his life-bringing blood like wine that cheers the hearts of the faithful. Alas, how this icy cold stone being struck by your

σπινθῆρας ἐπιπέμπει νοητοὺς τῇ καρδίᾳ μου! Τί μὴ καὶ διαρρήγνυμι τὸ στέρνον καὶ μυστικώτερον τάφον ἀντιλαξεύω, ὡς ἐν σπλάγχνοις μου καὶ πάλιν εἰσδέξομαι καὶ ἐν καρδίᾳ κηδεύσω σε; Λεπὰς ἐγὼ μυστικὴ τῆς πέτρας οὐκ ἀπορρηγνυμένη τῆς τὸν μαργαρίτην φερούσης μου τὸν ἐξ ἀστραπῆς τῆς θεαυγοῦς ἐμφυέντα μοι.

11 Ὦ οἶα ἀνθ᾽ οἵων ὁρῶ! Ἀστὴρ ἡμεροφαὴς τῷ τοκετῷ σου παρὰ τῆς σῆς ἐκαινουργήθη μεγαλειότητος καί σε λεληθότως τεχθέντα οὐρανὸς ἀνεκήρυττεν. Ἀλλὰ σήμερον καὶ αὐτὸν τὸν αἰσθητὸν ἀπέκρυψας ἥλιον καὶ νύκτα ἐν ἡμέρᾳ μέσῃ παρήνεγκας τοὺς ἀσεβεῖς ἀπελέγχουσαν. Καὶ γὰρ νὺξ ἀβλεψίας τοὺς νοεροὺς ἐκείνων ὀφθαλμοὺς ἀπετύφλωσε. Πέρσας ἐκεῖ γονυπετοῦντας ὁ ἀστὴρ μετεστείλατο, ὧδε καὶ γνωστούς τε καὶ φίλους ὁ τῶν θεοκτόνων φόβος ἀπεμακρύνατο. Ἐκεῖσε δώρων προσαγωγὴ καὶ προσκύνησις, ἐνταῦθα χιτώνων μερισμὸς καὶ χλευασμὸς καὶ στέφανος ὕβρεως.

12 Νῦν Ἰουδαῖοι, ὡς πρὶν ἐζήτουν ἐξ οὐρανοῦ σημεῖον, βλεπέτωσαν ἥλιον σκοτιζόμενον καὶ τὸ φῶς ἐκ τῶν ἀξίων σκότους συγκρύπτοντα. Νῦν καὶ ὁ ἄψυχος οὗτος ναὸς κατὰ τὴν Ἰουδαϊκὴν πενθεῖ σε συνήθειαν· ὡς γὰρ Ἰουδαῖοι βλασφημοῦντος τινὸς εἰς Θεὸν τοὺς ἑαυτῶν χιτῶνας ῥηγνύουσιν, οὕτω δὴ καὶ οὗτος ὡς χιτῶνα περισχίζει τὸ καταπέτασμα, παρὰ τῶν θεομάχων ἐμπαροινούμενον βλέπων σε. Συντρίβεται καὶ γῆ σειομένη παθαινομένη τῷ πάθει σου.

13 Ἀλλὰ ποῦ τὸ πλῆθος τῶν πεντακισχιλίων ἀνδρῶν, οὓς θαυματουργήσας ἐξέθρεψας; Ὅτι μόνος Ἰωσὴφ πρὸς

mighty arm as if by iron sends intelligible sparks into my heart! Why do I not break open my breast and hew a more mystical grave instead, so that I may again receive you in my bosom and bury you in my heart? I am a mystical oyster not dislodged from the rock that supports my pearl, which was implanted in me by the divinely radiant lightning.

Alas, what sort of exchange am I witnessing? A new star 11 shining by day at your birth was created by your magnificence, and heaven proclaimed that you had been secretly born. But today you hid the visible sun itself, and in the midst of the day you brought on a night that convicted the impious. For indeed, the night of their sightlessness blinded their spiritual eyes. Then, the star summoned Persians to bow down on their knees; now, the fear of the god killers has removed far away your friends and acquaintances. Then, an offering of gifts and worship; now, a division of your garments and mockery and a crown of insults.

Now, since the Jews of old *were seeking a sign from heaven,* 12 let them look at the darkened sun, hiding the light from those who are worthy of darkness. Now even this lifeless temple mourns you in keeping with the Jewish custom; for just as the Jews tear their garments when someone blasphemes against God, so also this temple rips its curtain like a garment, beholding you violently abused by the enemies of God. The earth too quakes and is shattered, distraught by your suffering.

But where is the crowd of five thousand men, whom you 13 fed by a miracle? Joseph of Arimathea alone courageously

Πιλᾶτον τολμηρῶς ἐπαρρησιάσατο καὶ τὸ σὸν ἠτήσατο σῶμα, ὡς ἂν μὴ διαμείνῃ καὶ ἄταφον. Ποῦ τῶν ἀσθενῶν αἱ χορεῖαι, οὓς ἐκ ποικίλων ἐρύσω νοσημάτων ἤπου καὶ ἀπὸ Ἅιδου ἐξήγειρας; Ὅτι μόνος Νικόδημος τοὺς ἥλους τῶν χειρῶν καὶ τῶν ποδῶν σου διΐστησι καὶ ὅλον ἐκ τοῦ ξύλου σε καθελὼν ἐμαῖς ἀγκάλαις ἐπωδύνως ἐντίθησιν, αἵ σε καὶ πρώην ὄντα βρέφος χαρμοσύνως ἐβάστασαν· καὶ γὰρ χεῖρες ἐμαὶ καὶ πρὶν βρεφουργηθέντι ἐξυπηρέτησαν καὶ νῦν κηδευομένῳ δουλεύουσιν.

14   Ὦ πικρῶν ἐνταφίων! Ὁ τοῖς νεκροῖς τὸ ζῆν χαρισάμενος πρὸ ὀφθαλμῶν μου νενέκρωσαι, καὶ ἡ πάλαι σοι ἀμφὶ τὰ βρεφικὰ διακονήσασα σπάργανα νῦν περὶ τὰ νεκρικά σου τυρβάζομαι. Χλιαροῖς κατελουσάμην σε νάμασι καὶ θερμοτέροις ἄρτι καταντλῶ σε τοῖς δάκρυσιν. Ὠλέναις μητρικαῖς ἀνεκούφιζον, ἀλλὰ σκιρτῶντα καὶ κατὰ νηπίους ἁλλόμενον· ἀνακουφίζω σε καὶ νῦν ταῖς αὐταῖς, ἀλλ᾽ ἄπνουν καὶ κατὰ νεκροὺς ἀνακείμενον. Ἐνέβαπτόν μου τότε τὰ χείλη τοῖς μελιχροῖς σου καὶ δροσώδεσι χείλεσιν, ἐμβάπτω καὶ νῦν, ἀλλ᾽ αὐαλέοις καὶ μεμυκόσι τοῖς χείλεσι. Μακαρίζεσθαί μοι τὸ τηνικαῦτα παρῆν, ὅτι παραδόξως ὡράθην τοῦ πλαστουργοῦ μου λοχεύτρια· νῦν δὲ ταλανίζεσθαί μοι ἀντεπεγένετο, ὅτιπερ εὑρέθην τοῦ υἱοῦ μοῦ κηδεύτρια. Ἐκεῖ ὠδῖνας ἐν τῷ τίκτειν ἐξέφυγον, ἔνθεν ὀδύνας ἐν τῷ θάπτειν εἰσδέχομαι. Βρεφοπρεπῶς μοι πολλάκις ἐν τοῖς στέρνοις ἀφύπνωσας καὶ νῦν νεκροπρεπῶς ἐν τούτοις κεκοίμησαι. Μακαρίζω τὸν Συμεὼν τὸν ἐξ ἐμῶν χειρῶν ἐν τῷ ναῷ σε δεξάμενον· προφῆται γὰρ τὰ χαροπὰ

addressed *Pilate and asked for your body,* so that it might not remain unburied. Where are the crowds of the sick, whom I understand you rescued from various illnesses and raised from Hades? Nicodemus alone removed the nails from your hands and feet and, after lowering you unbroken from the wooden cross, sorrowfully placed you in my embrace, which once joyfully held you as an infant; for indeed my hands once tended to you in your infancy, and now they serve you in your burial.

Alas, the bitter winding sheet! You who bestowed life on 14 the dead have been killed before my eyes, and I who once attended you as an infant in swaddling clothes now busy myself with your grave clothes. I once washed you in warm spring water, and now I bathe you with even warmer tears. I once lifted you up with a mother's arms, but you were wriggling and jumping about as children do; I now lift you up with the same arms, but lifeless and laid out like the dead. Then I wetted my lips with your honey-sweet, moist lips, and now I wet them too, but with your dry and silent lips. At that time I could count myself blessed, because I was paradoxically seen as the mother of my creator, but now it has befallen me instead to deem myself miserable, because I have ended up preparing my son for burial. Then I escaped pain in giving birth; now I receive pain in burying you. You often slept at my breast as befits a baby, but now you lie on it as befits a dead man. I consider Symeon blessed, the man who received you from my hands in the temple; for

καὶ τὰ τῆς δόξης μοι προεφήτευσαν, αὐτὸς δὲ μόνος τὰ σκυθρωπὰ καὶ τὰ τῆς λύπης προείπατο.

15 Ὤ πῶς ἐμπτυσθεὶς κατεδέξω, ὃς διὰ πτύσματός σου ὀφθαλμοὺς ἐκαινούργησας! Πῶς ῥαπισμάτων ἠνέσχου, ὃς διὰ φραγελλίου τοὺς θεοκαπήλους ἐμάστιξας καὶ τῶν ἱερῶν θριγγίων ἐξήλασας! Πῶς ὑπομένεις θάνατον ἐπονείδιστον, υἱὲ ἀναμάρτητε! Ἐτρήθης χεῖρας καὶ πόδας, ἀλλὰ τοὺς ἥλους ἔγνων εἰς μέσην μου τὴν ψυχὴν τὰς ὀδύνας ἐκπέμποντας· τὴν πλευρὰν ἐκεντήθης, ἀλλὰ καὶ ἡ ἐμὴ καρδία τηνικαῦτα συνεκεντεῖτό σοι. Ἐσταύρωμαί σου τοῖς πόνοις, νενέκρωμαί σου τῷ πάθει καὶ θαπτομένῳ συνθάπτομαι.

16 Τί ἐμοὶ καὶ τῷ βίῳ, σου μὴ παρόντος, ὦ πλαστουργέ μου καὶ υἱὲ ποθεινότατε; Ἀλλὰ ποῦ τῶν μαθητῶν ὁ χορός, ἵνα μοι παθαινομένῃ συγκλαύσαιτο; Ἐπατάχθης ὁ ποιμαίνων καὶ τὰ πρόβατα σκύλλονται. Ὑπνώττεις ἡ κεφαλή, καὶ χεῖρες ὁμοῦ καὶ πόδες ἄπρακτοι μένουσιν. Κλίνουσι τὰς κεφαλὰς καὶ ἄλλοι νεκρούμενοι, ἀλλὰ προεκλελοιπότος τοῦ πνεύματος· σὺ δ᾽ ἐναλλὰξ προέκλινας κεφαλήν, εἶτα καὶ τοῦ θανάτου κελευσθέντος ἐλθεῖν τὸ πνεῦμα παρέδωκας. Διὸ οὐδὲ κατεαγότα σου τὰ σκέλη γεγόνασιν, ὅτι μηδὲ τοῦ πάλαι θυομένου ἀμνοῦ ὀστοῦν ὁποιονοῦν κατεθραύετο. Ὡς προσκυνῶ σου τὰ πάθη καὶ τὸ ὑπομεῖναν σῶμα προσπτύσσομαι. Αἴρω τὸ ὕδωρ τὸ ἐκ πλευρᾶς σου ῥυέν, δι᾽ οὗ μοι τὸ λουτρὸν τῆς παλιγγενεσίας χαρακτηρίζεται. Ἐξαίρω καὶ τὸ αἷμα τὸ συρρυέν, δι᾽ οὗ τὸ διὰ μαρτυρίου εἰκονίζεται βάπτισμα, ὃ καὶ τὸν εὐγνώμονα περιρραντίσαν

the prophets foretold the bright times and my glory, but he alone foretold the gloomy times and my grief.

Alas, how you consented to be spat upon, you who with 15 your spittle created new eyes! How you endured the lashings, you who with a whip flogged the traffickers in the divine and drove them outside the temple walls! How you endure a disgraceful death, O son without sin! You were pierced in your hands and feet, but I felt the nails sending pains to the core of my soul; you were stabbed in the side, but my heart was stabbed at the same time along with you. I was crucified by your pain, I was killed by your suffering, and as you are being buried, I am being buried along with you.

What is left for me and my life when you are not here, O 16 my creator and most longed-for son? But where is the band of your disciples, so that they might mourn along with me as I grieve? You, their shepherd, were struck, and your sheep are being harassed. You, the head, are sleeping, while your hands and feet together remain idle. Other dead men bow their heads, but only when their breath has already left them; but you, in inverted order, first *bowed* your *head,* and then, after death had been ordered to come, *you gave up your spirit.* Therefore, your legs have not been broken, because no bone whatsoever of the ancient sacrificial lamb was shattered. As I venerate your suffering and embrace the body that endured it, I exalt the water that flowed from your side, by which *the washing of my rebirth* is symbolized. I also exalt the blood that flowed out with it, representing the baptism through martyrdom, which, by sprinkling the

ληστὴν καθηγίασε βαπτισθέντα καὶ αὐτὸν τῷ ἐπὶ σοὶ
συμβάντι βαπτίσματι.

17 Ὦ πικρᾶς ἐκείνης τοῦ ξύλου γεύσεως, ἥτις τοὺς ἀπὸ
γῆς εἰς γῆν παλινοστεῖν παρεσκεύασεν! Σὺ δὲ οὐκ ἐκ γῆς
ἐπλάσθης, οὐκ ἀπὸ χοὸς ἐδημιουργήθης, οὐ παρακοὴν
ἐπλημμέλησας· καὶ γὰρ αὐτὸς εἶ ὁ πλάστης, αὐτὸς ὁ Δημι-
ουργός, αὐτὸς ὁ τὴν ἐντολὴν νομοθετήσας τῷ πλάσματι.
Καὶ τί σοι καὶ τῷ θανάτῳ κοινόν; Τίς ἕνωσις ταφῇ καὶ
αὐτοζωῇ; Τίς μετουσία θρόνῳ ἐν οὐρανοῖς καὶ τάφῳ ἐπὶ
τῆς γῆς; Ἐκεῖ συνεδριάζεις μετὰ τοῦ πατρός, ὧδε συνθάπτῃ
τῷ πλαστουργήματι. Ἀπέδωκέ σοι πονηρὰ ἀντὶ ἀγαθῶν ἡ
μοιχαλὶς γενεά· νῦν ὁ μαργαρίτης ἐρρίφης ἔμπροσθεν τῶν
χοίρων, νῦν προτίθεται τοῖς κυναρίοις τὰ ἅγια, νῦν ξύλον εἰς
τὸν θεῖον ἄρτον ἐμβάλλεται. Ὦ λύττα φιλαργυρίας, ἣν
Ἰούδας ἐνόσησεν· οὐκ ἀργύρια γάρ, ἀλλὰ μισανθρωπίαν
ἐκέρδησε. Καὶ γάρ, φιλάργυρος ὤν, ἵνα τί προσεφοίτα τῷ
τοὺς πτωχοὺς μακαρίζοντι καὶ τὰ ἄμικτα μιγνύων ἐφαίνετο;

18 Ὦ τῆς ἀρρήτου οἰκονομίας σου, Δέσποτα· τίς ὡς Θεὸν
ἀξίως ὑμνήσει σε; Τίς ὡς νεκρὸν πρεπόντως θρηνήσει σε;
Ἀλλ᾽ οἰκοδόμησον τὸν ναὸν διὰ τριῶν ἡμερῶν, ὡς εἶπας, ὃν
καταλέλυκας, ἐπεὶ μὴ ὕμνους ἀξίους μηδὲ προσήκοντας
θρήνους ἔχω προσφέρειν σοι, μεγαλύνω τὰ ἔργα ὡς ἐν
σοφίᾳ τὰ πάντα ποιοῦντος σου.

right-believing thief, also sanctified him as he was baptized
by the baptism that occurred in you.

Alas, that bitter taste of the tree, which made those who   17
came from earth return to earth! But you were not created
from earth; you were not fashioned from soil; you did not
err through disobedience. For indeed, you yourself are the
molder, the very Creator, the very one who ordained rules
for his creation. And what do you and death have in common? What unity is there between burial and life itself?
What partnership is there between a throne in heaven and a
grave on earth? There you sit with your Father; here you
are buried along with your creation. The *adulterous generation*
gave you evil in return for good: now you are thrown as *the
pearl before the swine;* now *what is holy* is set before *the dogs;*
now *wood is being put into the* divine *bread.* O madness of ava-
rice, which afflicted Judas! For he gained not silver coins,
but the hatred of humanity. For indeed, being greedy, why
did he associate with the one who *blessed the poor* and who
manifestly combined the irreconcilable?

Oh, your ineffable dispensation, Master! Who will wor-   18
thily hymn you as God? Who will fittingly lament you as a
dead man? But *the temple* which *you have destroyed, build again
within three days,* as you said you would. Since I do not have
worthy hymns or fitting dirges to offer you, *I magnify your
works, because you do them all with wisdom.*

13

Τίνας ἂν εἴποι λόγους ὁ ἅγιος Πέτρος,
καταβαλὼν τὸν Σίμωνα
ἀρθέντα εἰς τὸν ἀέρα καὶ
μέλλων κύμβαχος σταυρωθῆναι
ὑπὸ Νέρωνος

Ἤδη μοι πέρας ἔχει τὰ τοῦ κηρύγματος καὶ γέμει
πάντα Χριστοῦ καὶ ὁ Πονηρὸς ἀπελήλεγκται. Εἷς ἆθλος
ἐλείπετο καὶ τοῦτον ἐκράτησα. Κεῖται μὲν ὁ κατάρατος
Σίμων, ὁ πρὶν ὑπερνέφελος, ἐπὶ γῆς· πεφόβηται δὲ τὰ
δαιμόνια, ὑφ᾽ ὧν ἦν ἐκεῖνος μετέωρος. Καὶ τὰ τῆς γοητείας
εἰς κακὸν ἀπετελεύτησε τῷ δειλαίῳ· πέπτωκεν ἀπ᾽ οὐρανοῦ, βληθείς, ὁ τοῦ Χριστοῦ καὶ τῆς ἀληθείας πολέμιος.

2 Οὐκ ὀλίγην ἐπῆλθον γῆν· Ἰουδαίων φθόνον ὑπήνεγκα·
Ἑλλήνων μανίαν ἐθάρρησα· βαρβάρων χεῖρας οὐκ ὤκνησα.
Ἀλλ᾽ ἦν ἐκεῖνα πάντα μοι φορητὰ καὶ κρατεῖν ἐποίει τὸ
πάντα θαρρεῖν, ὅτι καὶ Θεὸς ἦν τὸ κήρυγμα. Ταῦτα ὁ
Πονηρός, ὁ τῆς ἀπιστίας πατὴρ οὐκ ἤνεγκε καὶ τρόπον
ἄλλον ὁπλίζεται· οὐδὲν ἡγήσατο διψῶσαν φόνου χεῖρα
βάρβαρον· μικρὸν ἐνόμισε καὶ δεισιδαιμονίαν Ἑλλήνων
καὶ τυράννων δεσμούς, οὓς ἡμῖν τοῖς Χριστοῦ μαθηταῖς
πολλοὺς πολλάκις ἐχάλκευσεν. Ἀλλ᾽ εἰς μόνον ὁρᾷ τὸν

13

What Saint Peter would say when, after striking down Simon who was raised up into the air, he is about to be crucified upside down by Nero

My preaching career has now come to an end, and everything is filled with Christ, and the Evil One has been thoroughly refuted. One struggle remained, and I overcame it. The accursed Simon, who once was above the clouds, now lies dead on the ground; the demons that raised him up in the air have fled in fear. The practice of magic has ended badly for the wretch; he has fallen from the sky, struck down, the enemy of Christ and the truth.

I traveled over no small portion of the earth; I endured 2 the hostility of the Jews; I was courageous in the face of the madness of the Greeks; I did not shrink from the hands of barbarians. Rather, I endured all those things, and facing them all with courage made me overcome them, because God is what I preached. The Evil One, the father of unbelief, could not tolerate this and armed himself in another way; he gave no regard to the barbarian hand thirsting for murder; he thought little, as well, of both the superstition of the Greeks and the chains of tyrants, the many chains that he often forged for us, the disciples of Christ. Instead, he

Σίμωνα καὶ τὴν ἐκείνου τέχνην τὴν μάγον καὶ τὰ ἐκ ταύτης φαντάσματα. Κατ᾽ αὐτῆς ἐπεγείρει πόλεμον τῆς αἰσθήσεως, ἵν᾽, ὑποκλέψας, λάθῃ τὸν νοῦν, οἷς ἀπατήσει τὴν αἴσθησιν, καί, πολλοῖς πρότερον ἐπασκήσας τοῖς φάσμασι, θέατρον συγκροτεῖ. Πᾶν γένος συγκαλεῖται πρὸς θέαν καὶ κριτὴν ἐφιστᾷ τῆς μάχης ταύτης ἄλλον αὐτοῦ δορυφόρον τύραννον. Καὶ δὴ πρῶτα μὲν ἠκροβολιζόμεθα λόγοις καὶ πολὺς ἦν ἀπὸ γλώττης ὁ ἀγών, ὡς δὲ ἤδη τὸ ψεῦδος ἡλίσκετο.

3 Ὢ οἷον ἐκεῖνος ἠλαζονεύσατο, ἐπὶ τὰ φάσματα ἔβλεψεν, ἐπὶ τὴν ἀρρητουργίαν ἔδραμε! Θεὸς εἶναι διετείνετο καὶ πρὸς αὐτοὺς οὐρανοὺς ἀνιέναι δυνήσεσθαι καὶ καθίσαι μετὰ τοῦ Πατρὸς ἐκομψεύετο. Ὡς τοῦτό γε τὸ μέρος οὐκ ἐψεύσατο τὸν διδάσκαλον, θεῖναι τὸν θρόνον ἐπὶ τῶν νεφελῶν ἀλαζονευόμενον! Τοιγαροῦν κἀκεῖνος ἐξέπιπτε καὶ νῦν οὗτος ὡς ἀπ᾽ οὐρανοῦ καταβέβληται καὶ κεῖται τὰ ἔσχατα ταῦτα. Ὁ μὲν ἐκόμπαζε καὶ τὸ θέατρον ἐπηλάλαξεν· ἐγὼ δὲ Φαραὼ μὲν ἐπεκάλουν τὸν τύραννον, τῶν δ᾽ ἐπ᾽ Αἰγύπτου μάγων ἐκείνων πολλῷ τὸν Σίμωνα χαλεπώτερον. Μωσῇ δὲ παρεβεβλήμην αὐτὸς καὶ Παῦλον Ἀαρὼν εἶχον ἕτερον καί, Θεοῦ θεράπων εἶναι λαχών, Θεὸν ἐπεκαλούμην, ὃν ἐκήρυττον, ὑπὲρ οὗ ταῦτα ἔφερον. Ῥάβδον ᾔτουν ἐπαφεῖναι τῷ γόητι· ὁ δ᾽ οὐκ ἠμέλησεν, ἀλλ᾽ ἐπέδωκε καὶ ῥάβδος ἦν Λόγος καὶ κλῆσις Χριστοῦ. Ταύτην ἐπαφῆκα τὴν ῥάβδον ἐγὼ καὶ τὰ ξυνεφαπτόμενα τῶν δαιμονίων ἐπλήττετο καὶ πᾶσα τοῦ μάγου ῥάβδος, ἰσχὺς δηλαδὴ πονηρά, πρὸς τῆς ἐμῆς ῥάβδου ταύτης ἐκπέποται καὶ ὁ πρὸ τοῦ κομψὸς γέλως νῦν καὶ πτῶμα καὶ δάκρυα. Ἡμῖν

looks to Simon alone and his skill in magic and the illusions that come from it. He stirred up a war against the very senses, so that he might secretly steal the mind by deceiving the senses, and by toiling beforehand over many delusions, he cobbled together an audience. Every nation was called together to watch, and he set up as judge of this battle another man, his bodyguard, a tyrant. At first we skirmished with words, and the contest of our tongues was great; already his falsehood was defeated!

Oh, how Satan boasted, how he looked to his delusions, how he ran to his abominable acts! He maintained that he was God and bragged that he could ascend to the very heavens and sit with the Father. How Simon did not belie his teacher Satan in this respect, by boasting that he could set his throne upon the clouds! Therefore just as his teacher fell, now Simon too has been cast down as if from heaven and lies dead. He began boasting, and the audience gave a rowdy cheer, but I called the tyrant "Pharaoh" and called Simon much more dangerous than those magicians in Egypt. I myself paralleled Moses, and I had Paul as a second Aaron, and, since my lot was to be a servant of God, I called upon God, whom I proclaimed in my preaching and on whose behalf I was suffering this attack. I asked God to hurl a staff at the sorcerer, and he did not ignore my request, but granted it, and this staff was the Word and the name of Christ. I hurled this staff at him, and it struck the demons joining him in the attack, and the magician's whole staff—namely, an evil force—flew away in the face of this staff of mine, and his previous witty laughter now gave way to both a fallen

3

δὲ τὸ θέατρον εἰς μαρτυρίαν ἀντιπεριΐσταται καὶ τῷ Πονηρῷ τὰ τῆς βουλῆς ἀντέστραπται. Πάντες γεγόνασι θήρα τοῦ θαύματος καὶ προσίενται τὴν ἀλήθειαν, τῶν δ᾽ ἐκείνου φασμάτων οὐ μικρὸς παρ᾽ αὐτοῖς ὁ κατάγελως. Ἀπόστολος ἐγὼ Χριστοῦ καὶ τὸν τοῦ πονηροῦ πνεύματος ἀπόστολον κατηγώνισμαι, μαθητὴς ἐκράτησα μαθητοῦ, καὶ διδάσκαλος ἀληθείας καθεῖλε ψεύδους διδάσκαλον.

4   Ἅλις οὖν ἔχω τῶν πόνων καὶ τοῦ κηρύγματος, ἱκανῶς διεπύκτευσα τὸν πολέμιον. Δεῖ δή με λοιπὸν καὶ πρὸς τὸν στρατηγὸν ἀνελθεῖν καὶ τοὺς τῆς ἀριστείας στεφάνους κομίσασθαι. Ἀλλ᾽ ἤδη καὶ τὴν ἄνοδον ὁρῶ καὶ πολλῆς ὅσης γέμω τῆς ἡδονῆς. Ἀριστεύς εἰμι Χριστοῦ, ἔτι νεάζει μοι τὸ ἀρίστευμα, οὐκοῦν δεῖ με πεφοινίχθαι καὶ τὸ σῶμα, τὴν τῆς ψυχῆς ἐσθῆτα, τῷ αἵματι. Τοῦτό τις ἐπ᾽ οὐρανοῦ τὸ σύμβολον ἰδών, τὸν ἀριστέα ἐπιγνώσεται καὶ θαυμάσεται μὲν τὴν ἀριστείαν, προσαποθαυμάσεται δὲ καὶ τὸ λάφυρον, ὃ νῦν εἰς Χριστὸν ἐφειλκυσάμην, ὅλον θέατρον. Οὕτως ἐκεῖνος πρὸς τὸν Πατέρα ἀνέδραμεν, οὕτως ἐγὼ βαδιοῦμαι πρὸς τὸν διδάσκαλον. Ἀλλ᾽ ἦν ἐκεῖνος ἀπ᾽ οὐρανοῦ καὶ πρὸς οὐρανὸν ἐτείνετο, ἐγὼ δ᾽ ἁπλῶς καὶ θνητὸς καὶ κάτωθεν ἀπὸ γῆς. Τοιγαροῦν δεῖ με καὶ τέλος ἀλλάττειν, ἐπεὶ καὶ τὴν γένεσιν. Τοῦτο, καὶ τελευτῶν, χαριοῦμαι τῷ διδασκάλῳ.

body and tears. The audience has come over to our side in witness, and the plans of the Evil One have been reversed. Everyone has become captivated by the miracle, and they accept the truth, and their mockery of Satan's delusions is not insignificant. I am an apostle of Christ, and I have prevailed against the apostle of the evil spirit; I, a disciple, overcame a disciple, and the teacher of truth destroyed the teacher of falsehood.

And so I have had enough of my labors and my preaching; 4 I have sparred enough with the enemy. I must now ascend to the general and receive the crowns for my valor. Already I see the upward path and am filled with immense pleasure. I am a hero for Christ; my act of heroism is still a novelty; therefore, I must also dye my body, the clothing of the soul, crimson with my blood. Anyone in heaven upon seeing this token will recognize the hero and admire his heroism, and will also admire the spoils, namely the whole audience, which I have now drawn toward Christ. In this way he ran up to his Father; in this way I shall walk to my teacher. But he was from heaven and was pulled back toward heaven, while I am plainly mortal and from the earth below. Therefore I must invert the ending, since I also inverted the beginning. In this way, even as I die, I will gratify my teacher.

14

Τίνας ἂν εἴποι λόγους Ἀταλάντη,
εἰς τάχος Ἱππομένους ἀπολειφθεῖσα
χρυσῶν μήλων ἀπάτῃ καὶ πρὸς
γάμον ἀπαγομένη

Δέχομαι τὴν ἧτταν μεθ᾽ ἡδονῆς, οὐ δυσχεραίνω τὸν γάμον, Ἱππόμενες. Μετ᾽ Ἀφροδίτης τοὺς πόδας πεπέδημαι, οὐ ῥόδῳ μὲν ἐμπαγεῖσα, μήλων δὲ χρυσῶν ἡττηθεῖσα. Μετὰ Δανάης ὑπὸ χρυσοῦ τὸ παρθενεύειν ἀφήρημαι. Χρυσὸς εἷλεν ἐκείνην, διὰ τοῦ ὀρόφου ῥυείς, χρυσὸς εἷλε κἀμέ, διὰ τοῦ σταδίου ἐπαφεθείς. Αὐτοῦ Διὸς τοῦτο τὸ σόφισμα, οὐ σόν, Ἱππόμενες, τὸ μηχάνημα. Ζεύς με πρῶτον εἷλεν, εἶτα χρυσός, σὺ δὲ τρίτος μετὰ Δία, μετὰ χρυσόν. Ἀπὸ Διὸς ἔχω τὸ γένος, τοιγαροῦν ἀπὸ Διὸς καὶ νενίκημαι, Ζεύς με πρόγονος εἰς γάμον ἄγει καὶ κομίζει μοι τὰ ἕδνα χρυσόν· δεῖ με λοιπὸν πείθεσθαι.

2   Ἅλις ἔχω τῆς παρθενίας, ἐφ᾽ ἱκανὸν Ἀρτέμιδι ξυνεθήρευσα, μετατάξομαι καὶ πρὸς Ἀφροδίτην καὶ ξυνθαλαμεύσομαι. Ἐπεθώυξα τὰ κυνηγετικά, ᾄσομαι καὶ τὰ ἐπιθαλάμια. Ὑπὸ πλάτανον ἢ πίτυν ἀνεκείμην, ὀριτροφουμένη, ὑπὸ παστάδα νῦν ἀνακείσομαι, σκηνὴν Ἀφροδίτης, Ἔρωτος ὄροφον. Οὐχ ὑμνήσω τόξον Ἀρτέμιδος, ἀλλ᾽ ἔχω τόξον Ἔρωτος ἕτερον, οὐ παντελῶς τὴν τοξικὴν

14

What Atalanta would say when she is being led away into marriage after falling short of Hippomenes in swiftness through the trick of the golden apples

I accept my defeat with pleasure, Hippomenes, and I bear no grudge against our marriage. Like Aphrodite, my feet have been held fast, though I was not pricked by a rose but conquered by golden apples. Like Danaë, I am robbed of my virginity by gold: gold that flowed through the ceiling captured her, while gold thrown onto the racetrack caught me. This trick belongs to Zeus himself; it is not your device, Hippomenes. Zeus caught me first, then the gold, and then you third, after Zeus, after the gold. I am of Zeus's lineage, and so Zeus also has defeated me; Zeus my ancestor is marrying me off and providing gold as my dowry. It is necessary, then, for me to obey.

I have had my fill of being a virgin; I have hunted with   2 Artemis long enough. I will align myself with Aphrodite and share her wedding chamber. I have urged on the hunt with a shout; I will also sing the wedding hymns. I have lain under the plane tree and the pine, finding my food in the mountains; now I will lie in the bridal chamber, the tent of Aphrodite and the shelter of Love. I will not praise the bow of Artemis, but I have a different bow, of Love; I have not

περιήρημαι, ἔχω καὶ πάλιν τοξότην θεόν· τούτου τὰ βέλη τιμήσω, τούτῳ καὶ συστρατεύσομαι. Ἤσκημαι τοὺς πόδας εἰς δρόμον, οὐκοῦν πτερωτὸν ἔχω καθηγητὴν τὸν μέγαν τὸν δυνάστην τὸν Ἔρωτα. Πεπείραμαι τῶν τούτου βελῶν, εἶδον τὸ τάχος, οὐκ ἀγνοῶ τὸ πτερόν. Ταχεῖα μὲν ἐγὼ καὶ τοὺς πόδας τούτους δὴ τοὺς ἐμοὺς οὐ λαγωὸς ὑπερεβάλλετο, οὐ παρέδραμεν ἔλαφος. Ἄνδρας δὲ πολλοὺς μὲν ἐκάλει πρὸς ἀγῶνα τὸ κάλλος, ἀλλ᾽ ἀπράκτους αὖθις ἠφίει τὸ τάχος. Παριππεύειν ἁπλῶς ἐδόκουν τοὺς παραθέοντας, ἀλλ᾽ ἧκεν Ἔρως Ἱππομένει συστράτηγος καὶ παραυτίκα κατεστρατήγημαι. Αἰσθάνομαι τῆς ξυμμαχίας, ξυνῆκα τῶν βελῶν, χρυσῆς Ἀφροδίτης παῖς ὁ Ἔρως καὶ χρυσοῖς ἔβαλλεν μήλοις—ταῦτα γὰρ Ἔρωτος βέλη—τάχα που καὶ τοῖς πτεροῖς Ἱππομένει συνανεκούφιζεν.

3   Ὦ σόφισμα σύνθετον καὶ πάντοθεν ἀφροδίσιον! Μῆλον ὡς ὀπώρα Ἔρωτος, χρυσὸς ὡς θεοῦ χρυσῆς ἀνάθημα. Πόθεν οὕτω καλὸν ἔδρεψας μῆλον, Ἱππόμενες; Ποῖόν σοι φυτὸν τὴν χρυσῆν ὀπώραν ταύτην ἐθρέψατο; Μή πού σοι, τὸ τῆς μητρὸς ἐκεῖνο μῆλον ὑφελόμενος, ὁ παῖς Ἔρως λάθρα ἐκόμισε. Γνώσομαι, εἰ "τῇ καλῇ" τὸ μῆλον ἐπιγέγραπται. Ἀλλὰ τί δεῖ μοι σκιᾶς καὶ γραμμάτων; Αὐτόθεν ἐγὼ καὶ καλή σοι δοκῶ καὶ τὸ ἆθλον ἔχω τοῦ κάλλους, ὡς Ἀφροδίτη πάλαι πρὸς Ἀλεξάνδρου. Τοιγαροῦν ἦκέ μοι δεῦρο πρὸς θάλαμον, ὡς ἐκεῖνος εἰς Λακεδαίμονα, καὶ λάμβανε παρ᾽ ἐμοῦ τὴν εὐνήν, ὡς πρὸς Ἀφροδίτης τὴν Ἑλένην Ἀλέξανδρος.

completely lost the art of shooting, but again I follow an archer god. I will honor this god's arrows, and I will march alongside him. I have exercised my feet in racing, and so I possess a winged guide: the great, the mighty Love. I have experience of his arrows, have seen his swiftness, and am not ignorant of his wings. I myself am fast: indeed, no hare has surpassed these feet of mine, nor has any deer outrun them. My beauty has invited many men to compete, but my speed has sent them away empty-handed. I thought that I would easily outstrip my fellow runners, but Love arrived to assist Hippomenes, and immediately I was outmaneuvered. I perceived the alliance, noticed the arrows: Love, the child of golden Aphrodite, shot me with golden apples—for these are Love's arrows—and perhaps even lifted Hippomenes up with his wings.

Alas, clever device, contrived and altogether seductive! 3 An apple, as the fruit of Love; gold, as an offering for the golden goddess. Where did you pick such a fine apple, Hippomenes? What sort of tree produced for you this golden fruit? Perhaps the boy, Love, stole that apple from his mother and secretly brought it to you. I will know for certain, if "to the beautiful woman" is inscribed on the apple. But what need have I of shade and letters? I know for myself that I appear beautiful to you and that I possess the prize of beauty, just as Aphrodite long ago received it from Alexander. And so, Hippomenes, come here into my bedroom, just as Alexander came to Sparta, and take possession of my bed from me, just as Alexander took possession of Helen from Aphrodite.

15

Τίνας ἂν εἴποι λόγους ὁ Ἡρακλῆς,
χρησμὸν λαβὼν ἐκ Διὸς ὡς ὑπὸ
νεκροῦ μέλλει ἀναιρεθῆναι

Τί φῄς, ὦ πάτερ πρόμαντι Ζεῦ; Νεκρός με δείξει νεκρόν;
Πρὸς ἀνδρὸς ἤδη κειμένου βαλλόμενος, κείσομαι; Περιὼν
ἔτι καὶ χεῖρας ἔχων, ἐγὼ τὸν μηκέτ᾽ ὄντα φοβηθήσομαι;
Ἀξύνετον τὸ μέλλον, ἀπίθανος ὁ χρησμός! Πρὶν ἢ πυθέσθαι
Διός, ἠγνόουν τὴν τελευτήν, νυνὶ δέ, μαθών, ἀγνώστερος
γέγονα καὶ δεῖ μοι πάλιν ἑτέρου χρησμοῦ. Λοξὰ γάρ μοι
πάντα καὶ μαντείας δεῖται δευτέρας. Μή που πεπλάνημαι
καὶ πρὸς Ἀπόλλωνος ἥκων ἐκ Διὸς ἥκειν δοκῶ. Ἀπόλλωνος
ἐγὼ ταύτην λοξίου τίθεμαι· οὕτω πολλὴ νὺξ ἐπικέχυται τῷ
χρησμῷ, τοσοῦτον ἐπιφέρεται γνόφον ἡ πρόρρησις.

2   Τίς μοι τὴν νύκτα ταύτην περιαυγάσει; Τίς ὑπαναπτύ-
ξει τὸ αἴνιγμα; Πόθεν ἡ καινὴ παράταξις αὕτη; Τίς ὁ
παράδοξος οὗτος πόλεμος; Ἀγνοῶ τὸν τρόπον τῆς μάχης,
οὐ ξυμβάλλομαι τὸν πολέμιον. Κατασυστάδην μαχεῖται
νεκρός, ἐπιόντα δέξεται δόρατι, ἀλλ᾽ ἀπὸ τόξου ποιήσεται
τὴν παράτασιν; Ἀναφανδὸν ἐπιθήσεται, ἀλλ᾽ ἐξ ἐνέδρας
ἐπεισπεσεῖται, καὶ δόλῳ περιέσται καὶ τὴν νίκην σοφίσεται;

15

What Heracles would say when he receives the oracle from Zeus that he will be killed by a dead man

What are you saying, Zeus, my father and prophet? Will a corpse make me a corpse? Struck down by a man who already lies dead, will I lie dead? Though I still exist and possess hands, am I to fear one who no longer exists? This future is inscrutable, the oracle unbelievable! Before I inquired of Zeus, I was ignorant of the mode of my death, but now that I have learned about it, I have become even more ignorant and must ask again for another oracle. The whole oracle is ambiguous to me, and a second prophecy is needed. Perhaps I am confused, and think that I have come from Zeus's oracle when actually I have come from Apollo's. For I consider this prophecy to be from Apollo Loxias: so deep is the darkness that covers the oracle, so gloomy is the prediction that it brings.

Who will illuminate this night for me? Who will solve the 2 riddle? What is the source of this new opposition arrayed against me? What is this strange war? I am ignorant of the manner of battle; I do not understand the enemy. Will a dead man fight at close quarters? Will he meet an attacker with a spear or keep himself out of bowshot? Will he attack openly or from an ambush, and will he win through deceit and be victorious through cunning? By what stratagems, by

Ποίοις ταῦτα λογισμοῖς, ποίαις χερσί; Ὦ Ζεῦ καὶ χρησμὲ καὶ δρὺς μαντική, εἰ χεῖρας εἶχεν, οὐκ ἂν ἠπίστησα τὴν παράταξιν· εἰ πόδας, ἐδεξάμην ἂν καὶ τὴν ἔφοδον· εἰ δὲ καὶ μὴ φρενῶν αὐτῶν ἀπεστέρητο, δόλον ἂν προσυπώπτευσα. Νῦν δ' ἀλλὰ ταῦτα πάντα μάχης μὲν ὄργανα καὶ νίκης ἐχέγγυα, τῷ δὲ νίκη μὲν ἔσται, τὰ δὲ τῆς νίκης ἐπιλελοίπασι καί, μὴ φέρων ὅπλα, κρατήσει καί, κείμενος, ἀντιτάξεται.

3 Τίς ποτε νεκρὸν ἐπτόηται; Τίς εἶδε πολέμιον ἄψυχον; Ἠγωνισάμην πρὸς Γίγαντας καὶ μετὰ τὸ πεσεῖν οὐδεὶς ἀντετάξατο. Ἀπέκτεινα λέοντα καί, πεσών, οὐκ ἐφόβησεν. Ἅπασαν ἐκάθηρα γῆν καί, μετὰ τὸ πεσεῖν τὸ πολέμιον, ὁ πόλεμος ἔπιπτε. Νῦν δ' ἀλλ' ἕτερος ἀγὼν οὗτος καινότερος καὶ τὸ τοῦ πολέμου τέλος ἐφ' ἅπασιν, νῦν ἔσται μοι μάχης ἑτέρας ἀρχὴ καὶ τοῦτό με διαθήσει νεκρός, ὃ μηδεὶς τῶν ἔτι περιόντων ἴσχυσεν. Ὦ χεῖρες καὶ τόξον καὶ βέλη! Ὦ πολέμιος οὗτος βάλλων καὶ κείμενος!

4 Ὦ νεκρὸς οὗτος ἀήττητος, ποῖ ποτε γῆς ἔτι περιὼν ἐλάνθανες, ὅτε τὴν γῆν ἐξεκάθαιρον; Εἰ δ' ἔφθης ὑπὸ γῆν οἰκεῖν παρὰ τῷ Πλούτωνι, τί μὴ περὶ τὴν ἐμὴν εἰς Ἅιδου κάθοδον τὴν ἰσχὺν ἐπεδείκνυσο καὶ νεκρὸς ἐχαρίζου τῷ κρατοῦντι νεκρῶν καὶ παρ' αὐτὴν βαλλομένῳ τὴν μάχην ἐπήμυνες; Οὐκ ᾤμην ἐγὼ ξίφους ἔτι καὶ δεξιᾶς ἔργον κείσεσθαι μετὰ τοὺς ἐν σπαργάνοις δράκοντας καὶ μετὰ τὸν ἐν Νεμέᾳ λέοντα, μετὰ τὴν Ὕδραν ἐκείνην, μετὰ τοὺς Κενταύρους, μετὰ τοὺς Γίγαντας, μετὰ τὴν τῆς ὅλης γῆς ἀνακάθαρσιν, ἀλλ' αὐτὸν οὐρανὸν ἀλλάξασθαι τῆς κάτω διατριβῆς καὶ τοῦ λοιποῦ ξύνοικος εἶναι θεοῖς. Ἀλλ' ὁ

what hands will these things come about? O Zeus, both oracle and prophetic oak, if he had hands, I would not have had doubts about the battle. If he had feet, I would also have awaited his attack. If he had not been deprived of his wits, I would also have suspected a trick. But now, despite all of these weapons of battle that promise victory, the victory will be his; though he lacks the tools to be victorious and carries no weapons, he will prevail; though lying dead, he will oppose me in battle.

Who was ever afraid of a dead man? Who has ever seen a 3 lifeless enemy? I have fought against Giants, and after they fell none opposed me again. I have killed a lion, and once he had fallen, he no longer threatened me. I purged the entire earth, and when my enemies fell, the war was over. But now this next conflict and the outcome of the war will be novel in every way. Now there will begin for me a new battle, and this situation, which a dead man will create for me, is something that no one who is still living has managed. Alas, hands, and bow, and arrows! Alas, that enemy, who shoots even though he lies dead!

Alas, invincible dead man, where on earth were you hid- 4 ing while you still lived, when I was purging the earth? If you had already gone underground to dwell with Pluto, why did you not make a show of strength during my descent to Hades, and as a dead man why did you not help the ruler of the dead and defend him against me as I brought on the battle? I did not think I would again fall victim to a sword or someone's right hand after the serpents in my crib and the Nemean lion, after that Hydra, after the Centaurs, after the Giants, after purging the entire earth, but I thought I would exchange my sojourn below for heaven itself and for the rest

χρησμὸς μετὰ καὶ τοῦ Διὸς ἀπονεκροῖ μοι τὰς ἐλπίδας, οἷον νεκρὸν ὑπεγείρει πολέμιον.

5 Ὑπὸ γῆν ἦλθον, αὐτὸν Ἅιδην ἐχειρωσάμην, εἷλον τὸν Κέρβερον, γῆς συνέμιξα πέρασιν, ὅλα θαλάττης ἐξέκοψα δείματα, μάχην τοῖς ἄνω ξυνῆψα θεοῖς. Οἶδε ταυτηνὶ τὴν δεξιὰν Ἄρης, ὁπόσα περὶ τὴν μάχην δεδύνηται. Ἐγεύσατο καὶ Ἥρα τούτων δὴ τῶν βελῶν καὶ σὺ δέ, ὦ πάτερ, ἀπεπειράσω μου τῶν χειρῶν καὶ τῆς ἀλκῆς τὸν παῖδα οὐκ ἐμέμψω. Ἔπειτα καθελεῖ τὸν σὸν Ἡρακλέα νεκρὸς καὶ τεθνεὼς ἀπελέγξει τὸν καὶ θεῶν ἀθανάτων κρατήσαντα, τὸν ἐκ Διὸς τριέσπερον ὁ τὸ πᾶν ἐξ Ἅιδου καὶ τῶν ἐκεῖθεν νόμων ἑσπέριος, ὁ τὴν τύχην ἀλαμπὴς καὶ τὸν γνόφον οἰκεῖν λαχὼν μὴ παυόμενον τὸν ἐξ οὐρανοῦ καὶ τῆς ἐκεῖθεν αἴγλης τὴν τῆς γονῆς ἀπορροὴν εἰσδεξάμενον. Οὐ δέχομαι ταῦτα, οὐ πείθομαι. Ἧπου, Ζεῦ πάτερ, εἰρωνεία ταῦτα καὶ γέλως πλατὺς καὶ πατρὸς εἰς παῖδα σωφρονισμός, ἵνα μικρόν μοι τῆς ὀφρύος ὑφέλῃς καὶ μὴ δόξω πάντα κρατεῖν, οἷς μέχρι καὶ θεῶν τὴν μάχην ἐθάρρησα.

6 Ἀλλ' οὐχ οὕτω κοῦφος ἐγὼ καὶ φρονῶ τὰ ὑπέραυχα· σοί, πάτερ, ἐπεγραφόμην τὰ τρόπαια, μετὰ τῆς ἀδελφῆς Ἀθηνᾶς ἐπετέλουν τοὺς ἄθλους· πατρόθεν ἔχω τὸ καλλίνικον, Διόθεν μοι καὶ τὸ ἀλεξίκακον, οὐδὲν ἐπῆρέ μοι τὴν ὀφρῦν. Μᾶλλον μὲν οὖν καὶ τοῦ γένους πάντα τίθεμαι δεύτερα, ἢ τί σοι καὶ βούλεται τὸ χρησμώδημα; Νεκρὸς ἄψυχος, νεκρὸς ἀληθῶς μένει με πολέμιος, ἢ νεκρὸς ἐκεῖνος ἔσται, καὶ περιών, ἅτε τὰς χεῖρας ἀπόλεμος; Ἀμφοτέρωθεν ἀμήχανος ἡ τελευτή, ἄπορος ὁ χρησμός! Γένοιτο

of time live among the gods. But the oracle, along with Zeus, is killing my hopes, as it rouses a dead enemy.

I have ventured underground, taken on Hades himself, 5 stolen Cerberus, been to the ends of the earth, eradicated all the monsters of the sea, and joined battle with the gods above. Ares came to realize all this right hand could accomplish in battle. Even Hera has tasted my arrows, and you too, father, have tested my hands and have not found fault with your son's strength. Now a dead man will conquer your Heracles and though dead will defeat the one who overpowered immortal gods; a man of the night, subject entirely to Hades and his laws, will defeat the three-night son of Zeus; a man of obscure fortune, who is fated to live in unending gloom, will defeat one who has received his lineage from heaven and from its light. I do not accept this situation; I do not tolerate it. Perhaps, father Zeus, this situation is comical, an enormous joke, a wise lesson from a father to his son, so that you might temper my pride a little and I might not think that I am all-powerful, since I dared to wage war even against the gods.

But I am not so frivolous, and I am careful about exces- 6 sive boasting. To you, father, I have attributed my triumphs, and accompanied by my sister, Athena, I fulfilled my labors. My penchant for marvelous victory comes from my father; from Zeus also comes my skill at fending off trouble; nothing has made me haughty. So, am I to reckon everything related to my lineage as secondary, or what else does your oracle mean? Does a dead, lifeless man—a truly dead man—await me as my enemy, or will that man be considered dead, though still living, because he is not able to fight with his hands? The outcome is impossible either way; the oracle is

δέ μοι, ὦ Ζεῦ πάτερ καὶ ἀδελφὴ πρόμαχος Ἀθηνᾶ, εἰς
καλὸν ἐκβῆναι τῆς τύχης καὶ δεξαίμην καὶ τελευτὴν ἀξίαν
μὲν τοῦ γένους, ἀξίαν δὲ τῶν τροπαίων.

16

Τίνας ἂν εἴποι λόγους ὁ Αἴας, ἰδὼν ἐν Ἅιδῃ τὸν Ὀδυσσέα μετὰ σώματος

Ὀδυσσεὺς οὗτος ἐνταυθοῖ μετὰ σώματος ἢ διέστραπταί
μοι τὰ τῆς ὄψεως αὖθις καὶ μαίνομαι; Καὶ μὴν οὐκ ἔστι
νοσεῖν, ὅτε μὴ τὸ σῶμα περίεστιν. Ἐγὼ δέ, καὶ περιὼν ἔτι,
τοὺς λογισμοὺς ἀπέβαλον καί, πρὸς καιρὸν τῷ ξίφει χρησάμενος, τῆς αἰσχύνης ἐμαυτὸν αὐτῷ τῷ σώματι προσ-
απέλυσα. Οὐκ ἔστι ταῦτα, οὐκ ἔστι μανία καὶ φρενῶν
παραφορά, οὐκ ὀφθαλμῶν διαστροφαί, οὐ πολέμιος
Ἀθηνᾶ. Ὀδυσσεὺς οὗτος ἀληθῶς, Ὀδυσσεὺς ὁ θεοῖς
ἐχθρός, ὁ πανοῦργος, ὃν ἐγώ ποτε μέσων ξιφῶν ἀφήρπασα
Τρωϊκῶν. Τοιγαροῦν αὐτὸς εἰς ξίφος ἐνέπεσον, τοιαῦτά
μοι τὰ λύτρα ἀπέδωκεν. Ἀλλὰ πῶς; Ἐν Ἅιδου μετὰ σώματος παράδοξος ἡ κάθοδος. Ἦπου δόλῳ παρῆλθε τὸν
Κέρβερον, ἤπου καὶ τὸν Ἑρμῆν παρεκρούσατο, ὃν τοῖς
δόλοις αὐτὸς ἐπεγράφετο.

inexplicable! O father Zeus and sister Athena, the protector, may it come to pass that I meet with a good fortune, and that I receive a death worthy of my lineage, and worthy also of my triumphs.

16

What Ajax would say when he sees Odysseus in the flesh in Hades

Is that Odysseus here in the flesh, or has my vision been distorted again and have I gone mad? But it is not possible to be ill when one's body no longer survives. While I was still alive I lost my mind, and having made good use of the sword, I freed myself from shame, and from the body itself. These things no longer exist: there is no madness and mental confusion, no distorted vision, no hostile Athena. That man is truly Odysseus—Odysseus, enemy to the gods, the schemer, whom I myself once snatched away from the midst of Trojan swords. And so I fell upon a sword myself; that is how he repaid me. But how can this be? A descent to the realm of Hades in the flesh is strange. Perhaps he eluded Cerberus by some trick; perhaps he also deceived Hermes, to whom he ascribed his deceptions.

2 Ὦ τῆς ἀπάτης καθηγητὰ καὶ δόλων πάτερ Ἑρμῆ, ὁ σὸς παρῆλθέ σε μύστης, ὅλον σου τὸ δόλιον ἀπεσύλησεν. Ἀμή- χανον κακὸν Ὀδυσσεὺς μικρὸν εἰς ἀπάτην ἑλεῖν ἄνδρας ἐνόμισεν· οὐκοῦν ἐπ' αὐτόν σε τὸν διδάσκαλον μεταφέρει τὸ σόφισμα. Παρῆλθέ σου τὴν ῥάβδον, παρῆλθε τὸν Κέρ- βερον, οὐχ ὑπώπτευσε τὸν Αἰακὸν καὶ νῦν ἐν Ἅιδου διάγει καὶ πολυπραγμονεῖ τὰ ὑπὸ γῆν. Ὦ πάντα δόλῳ πράττων ἄνθρωπε, κινδυνεύω μηκέτι δυσχεραίνειν τὴν κρίσιν, μηκέτι μέμφεσθαι τοὺς Ἀτρείδας. Ἔργον σου τῆς ἀπάτης κἀκεῖνοι γεγόνασι καί, πρὶν ἢ τῶν ὅπλων ἐμέ, τῆς δίκης ἐκείνους ἐκβέβληκας.

3 Ἀλλ' οἴμοι καὶ τὰ ὅπλα ἐπενδέδυται καὶ φέρει ξίφος ἐν χερσίν, ἐφ' ᾧ κατὰ τῆς πλευρᾶς ξίφος ἕτερον ὤθησα. Τί μοι τὸ ξίφος ἐνταῦθα ἐπισείεις; Τί τὰ τῆς ἀνδρείας ἐν νεκροῖς ἐπιδείκνυσαι; Εἰ χεῖρας ἱκανὰς εἶχες ἀποχρῆσθαι τῷ ξίφει, τί μὴ μετὰ τὴν ἄδικον ψῆφον ἐκείνην καὶ ἔτι μου περιόντος τὴν ὄψιν ἐθάρρεις καὶ τὸ ξίφος ἐπέσειες; Τάχα που καθ' ἡμῶν καὶ τοῦτό σοι μεμηχάνηται, ἵνα καὶ σώματος λυπήσῃς γυμνόν, ὃν ἔτι λυπεῖν οὐκ εἶχες ἐν σώματι, καὶ θεάσωμαί σε τοῖς ἐμοῖς ὅπλοις ἐν Ἅιδου κοσμούμενον, ὅν, ἔτι περιών, ἄνω βλέπειν οὐκ ἔφερον.

4 Παλάμηδες, Ὀδυσσεὺς ἐνταῦθα, ὁ κοινὸς ἐχθρός, νό- θος ἐν νεκροῖς ὑποδύεται. Λάμβανε δίκας τῶν λίθων, οὕς σοι δι' αὐτὸν πολλοὺς ἐπαφῆκε τὸ στράτευμα. Πάρελθε, διαμήνυσον Αἰακῷ τὴν ἐπιβουλήν, προσκάλεσαι Μίνω, Ῥαδάμανθυν καὶ τάχα καὶ λίθον ὡς ἄλλος Τάνταλος λήψεται τῶν πολλῶν λίθων ἐκείνων ἀντίποινον. Συγχέει

O Hermes, guide in deceit and father of deceptions, your 2
initiate has eluded you, and he has despoiled you of all your
guile. Odysseus thought it was a small, though irresistible,
evil to entrap men by deceit, and therefore he has applied
his trickery to you yourself, his teacher. He eluded your staff,
he eluded Cerberus, he was unconcerned about Aeacus, and
now he wanders in the realm of Hades and meddles in the
affairs of the underworld. O man who attempts everything
through trickery, I am at risk of no longer despising the
judgment, of no longer blaming the sons of Atreus. They too
were instruments of your deception, and you robbed them
of justice before you robbed me of the armor.

But alas, he wears the armor and in his hands carries the 3
sword which made me thrust another sword into my side.
Why do you threaten me here with the sword? Why do you
make a show of your courage among the dead? If you have
hands capable of wielding the sword properly, why did you
not face me with courage while I still lived, after that unjust
judgment, and why did you not brandish the sword then?
Perhaps you have contrived this deed against me so that you
might cause me grief when I am stripped of a body, though
you were not able to cause me grief while I still had a body,
and so that I might see you in the realm of Hades arrayed in
my armor, though I could not bear to look at you in the
world above while still alive.

Look, Palamedes: our common enemy, Odysseus, slips in 4
here illicitly among the dead. Take revenge for the numerous stones that the army launched against you because of
him. Go on, disclose the plot to Aeacus, summon Minos and
Rhadamanthys, and perhaps, like another Tantalus, he will
receive a stone as recompense for those many stones

καὶ ταράττει τοὺς κάτω θεσμούς, ἤδη πρὸς φῶς ἄξει πάντα
τὰ ὑπὸ γῆν, κοινώσεται τὰ ἀπόρρητα καὶ τοῦτο γενήσεται
τοῖς κάτω θεοῖς ὃ τοῖς ἐν οὐρανῷ Τάνταλος. Δέδοικα μὴ
προσαποσυλήσῃ τὸν Κέρβερον· τὰ τοῦ Ταντάλου τετόλ-
μηκε, τοιγαροῦν ἐπὶ κεφαλῆς ἐχέτω καὶ ἄχθος Ταντάλειον.
Τὰ Σισύφου πεπανούργευκεν, οὐκοῦν παρὰ τῷ Σισύφῳ
δεδέσθω, γινέσθω τὴν δίκην ὡς καὶ τὸν δόλον ἕτερος
Σίσυφος.

5   Ἀλλ᾽ εὖγε ξυνῆκα τῆς τόλμης, ξυνορῶ τὸ μηχάνημα.
Σισύφου παῖς ἐστιν Ὀδυσσεύς, Σισύφου παῖς ἀληθῶς,
πρὸς ἐκεῖνον ἄγει τὸν ζῆλον. Αἰσχύνεται τοῦ πατρὸς ἐπὶ
δόλοις φέρειν τὰ δευτερεῖα καὶ δεύτερα εἰς ἀπάτην τῶν
κάτω θεῶν. Ὥρμησε μετὰ τὸν πατέρα ὁ παῖς, μετὰ τὸν
Σίσυφον Ὀδυσσεύς. Πρὸς πατρὸς καὶ παιδός, ἀμφοτέρωθεν
Ἅιδης ἠδίκηται, πατρὸς ψυχὴν ἐκ μέσου κευθμῶνος
ἀποβαλὼν καὶ παῖδα μήπω τὸ σῶμα ἐκδύντα δεξάμενος. Ὁ
μὲν περὶ τὴν ἄνοδον ἐκακούργησεν, ὁ δὲ περὶ τὴν κάθοδον
αὖθις ἠσέβησεν. Ἡράκλεις, ὑβρίζει σου τὸ τρόπαιον! Μεθ᾽
Ἡρακλέα τὸν Διὸς παῖδα, ὁ Σισύφου παῖς Ὀδυσσεὺς παρῆλθε τὸν Κέρβερον. Προσεπιφέρεται καὶ ξίφος ὡς αὐτὸς
τότε τὸ ρόπαλον, ὡς τάχα καὶ πλήξων, εἰ δεήσει, τὸν
Πλούτωνα.

6   Ὢ πάντα δυστυχὴς ἐγώ! Ὅτε τὸ ξίφος ἐλάμβανον,
ἔχαιρον—προσέτι φέρεται—ὡς μηκέτι Ὀδυσσέα ὀψόμενος,
ἀλλ᾽ οὔτε μὴν τῆς μανίας, οὔτε τῶν ὅπλων ᾤμην εἰσέτι
μεμνήσεσθαι. Τὸ γὰρ τῆς Λήθης πόμα ταῦτα πάντα
προσαφελέσθαι παρασκευάζει. Νῦν δ᾽ ἀλλὰ καὶ πάλιν τῇ
μνήμῃ τῶν προτέρων ἀλγῶ καὶ γίνομαι καὶ νεκρὸς

launched at you. He confounds and unsettles the laws here below; now he will bring to the light everything in the underworld, and share all its secrets, and what Tantalus did to the gods above will happen to those below. I fear that he will even carry off Cerberus. He has dared the deeds of Tantalus; therefore let him also bear the burden of Tantalus upon his head. He has committed the crimes of Sisyphus, and so let him be bound alongside Sisyphus; let him become a second Sisyphus in his punishment, just as he has in his deception.

But bravo, I have discerned his daring and understand his 5 scheme. Odysseus is a son of Sisyphus, a true son of Sisyphus, and he emulates him. He is ashamed to take second place to his father in trickery or to be second in deceiving the gods below. The son made his move after his father, Odysseus after Sisyphus. Hades has been wronged by both father and son: he released the father's soul from the depths of the pit, and he received the son before he had discarded his body. The one abused the ascent, while the other, in turn, profaned the descent. O Heracles, he insults your triumph! Following Heracles, the son of Zeus, Odysseus, the son of Sisyphus, eluded Cerberus. And he wields a sword just as Heracles once wielded a club, perhaps to strike Pluto, if necessary.

Alas, how completely ill-fated am I! When I took up the 6 sword, I was rejoicing—and the story is still told—because I would look upon Odysseus no more, but I thought I would no longer remember either my madness or the armor. For the cup of Lethe makes one forget all these things. But now I am pained again by the memory of the past, and though

δυστυχής. Οὐ φέρω τὸν ἐμὸν αὐτόχειρα βλέπειν, δι᾽ ὃν τὸ ξίφος ὤθησα κατὰ τῆς πλευρᾶς. Οὐ φέρω τὴν ἐμὴν πανοπλίαν ὁρᾶν, ἧς πεσόντα τὸν ὁπλίτην ὕβρεως ἐξήρπασα Τρωϊκῆς, καί, τελευτῶν, αὐτὸς εἰς ὕβριν ἐξέπεσον.

7   Πορεύσομαι περί που τοὺς Ἅιδου μυχούς. Γένοιτο δή μοι, ὦ Πλούτων καὶ Αἰακὲ καὶ πάντες ὑπὸ γῆν θεοί, μήτε τὰ ὅπλα καὶ τὴν ἐπ᾽ ἐκείνοις μανίαν εἰς νοῦν αὖθις λαβεῖν, μήτ᾽ αὐτὸν ἰδεῖν Ὀδυσσέα. Ἢ δεήσει μοι καὶ τὸν Ἅιδην ἀπολιπεῖν, ὡς πάλαι τὴν γῆν, καὶ καταδῦναι πάλιν ἐνθένδε εἰς Τάρταρον.

17

Τίνας ἂν εἴποι λόγους ἡ Δανάη, ὑπὸ Διὸς εἰς χρυσὸν μεταβληθέντος διαπαρθενευθεῖσα

Ὦ πάτερ Ἀκρίσιε καὶ χάλκεος παρθενὼν καὶ σωφρο- σύνης προμήθεια, οὐδὲν ἡμῖν εἰς φυλακὴν ἐπηρκέσατε. Χρυσός με τυραννεῖ, χρυσός μου τὴν παρθενίαν ἀποσυλᾷ, χρυσός με βιάζεται. Ὦ χρυσὸς κάλλους ἐπίβουλος! Ὦ χρυσὸς φιλοπάρθενος! Μηκέτι κόσμου χάριν, ὦ παρθένοι, χρυσῷ τὸ σῶμα πιστεύετε, ὡς χρυσὸς ἐπυραύγησεν, ὅτε τὴν ἀρχὴν ἐξ ὀρόφου ἐρρύη, καὶ νῦν ὡς ἐραστὴς ἐκ κόλπου

dead I have become ill-fated. I cannot bear to look upon my own killer; because of him I thrust the sword into my side. I cannot bear to see my own suit of armor, whose original wearer, having fallen dead, I snatched away from Trojan insult and which, dying myself, I lost through insult.

I will go somewhere into the depths of Hades. O Pluto, 7 Aeacus, and all you gods of the underworld, may I never again recall the armor and the madness caused by it, and may I never again see Odysseus. Otherwise I will have to abandon Hades, as I once abandoned the earth, and descend again from here into Tartarus.

17

What Danaë would say after she lost her virginity to Zeus, who had transformed himself into gold

O father Acrisius, and virgin's chamber of bronze, and precautions for my chastity, you were not sufficient protection for me at all. Gold holds sway over me; gold strips away my virginity; gold violates me. Alas, gold is treacherous to beauty; alas, gold is fond of virgins! O virgins, no longer entrust your bodies to gold for adornment, because gold shone brightly when it first flowed down from my ceiling, and now like an ardent lover it envelops my bosom. Already I even

θερμὸς περικέχυται. Ἤδη καὶ χρυσῆς Ἀφροδίτης γεύομαι, ἀλλὰ πόθεν ἐκείνη τὸν χρυσὸν τοῦτον ἐμεταλλεύσατο; Ἐκ Μυκήνης ταύτης τῆς ἐκ γειτόνων τῆς πολυχρύσου; Ἀλλ᾽ ἐκ ποταμοῦ Πακτωλοῦ χρυσοδίνου τὸν χρυσὸν ἡμῖν ἐπωχέτευσεν; Ἀλλ᾽ οὐκ ἔστιν ἀπὸ γῆς, ἀλλ᾽ οὐκ ἔστι θνητός, ἀλλ᾽ οὐρανόθεν τὸν χρυσὸν ἡμῖν ἐπεψέκασεν. Ἀλλ᾽ οὐκ Ἀθηνᾶς ταῦτα, γοναὶ καὶ βωμὸς ἄπυρος καὶ Ῥόδος ὅλη πόλις ἐπ᾽ Ἀθηνᾷ χαίροντες.

2   Χρυσοῦν καὶ τὸ τῶν θεῶν δάπεδον, ἀλλ᾽ ὁ χρυσὸς οὗτος κἀκείνου στιλπνότερος. Τίς χρυσογνώμων οὕτω τὸν χρυσὸν ἐξεπύρωσε; Δία τὸν χρυσὸν εἶναι μαντεύομαι καὶ πολὺς ὁ Ἔρως ἐξέκαυσε. Μάτην ἄρα, ὦ πάτερ, τὴν παῖδα ἐφρούρεις! Μάτην <ὡς> ἐν κόχλῳ πορφύραν τῷ χαλκῷ τὴν ὥραν ἐκάλυπτες! Μάτην ὡς αἱμασιὰν τὸν χαλκὸν τῆς ἐμῆς ῥοδωνιᾶς προὐβέβλησο! Οὐκ ἦν ἀτειρὴς ὁ χαλκός, ὑπεῖξεν, ἐμαλθακίσθη, προὔδωκε κλέπτοντι χρυσῷ τὴν εἴσοδον, οὐκ ἀντέτεινεν. Ὅτε σὺ τὸν χαλκὸν εἰς παστάδα ἐφιλοτέχνεις, Ἔρως εἰς χρυσὸν ἐμεταλλούργει τὸν Δία. Οἷον νέφος σελήνην, τὴν σὴν παῖδα ἐπεσκίαζε χαλκός, ἀλλ᾽ ὁ Ζεὺς ἐμελέτα πάλαι τὴν ξύνοδον. Ἥλιος καὶ τὸ ἐπιπροσθοῦν ἀναρρήγνυται, Ἔρως ἐπήθετο τῷ Διΐ, ὅλας καμίνους ὑφῆψεν ἱμέρου. Τὸ δέ γε πῦρ τῶν ἐμῶν ἐξ-επυρήνιζε παρειῶν καὶ παρθένου θνητῆς ἐρυθήματι τὸν θεῶν ὕπατον ἔκαυσεν, ὅλον ἀφροδισίῳ πυρὶ κατηνθράκωσε τὸν ἀστέκτῳ πυρὶ καὶ Τιτᾶνας κοιμήσαντα. Ὁ δὲ καὶ ὡς δαλὸς ἐκπυροῦται καὶ χρυσὸς ἀστερωπὸς γίνεται, ὡς ἐν νυκτὶ τὸν χαλκὸν πῦρ αἰθόμενον περιηύγασε καὶ ὡς ἕσπε-ρος ἐν οὐρανῷ κυανῷ τῷ χαλκῷ περιήστραψεν.

taste golden Aphrodite, but from where has she mined this gold? From Mycenae, rich in gold among the neighboring cities? Or did she draw the gold for me from the river Pactolus with its golden eddies? But it cannot be from the earth, cannot be mortal; rather, she showered the gold upon me from heaven. But this is not the story of Athena, her birth, the fireless altar, and the whole city of Rhodes rejoicing in her.

Even the gods' floor is golden, but this gold is brighter than that. What goldsmith ever melted gold in this way? I divine that the gold is Zeus, and a great love has inflamed him. In vain, then, father, did you guard your daughter! In vain did you conceal her beauty in bronze like purple in a murex shell! In vain did you enclose my rose garden with bronze as with a wall! The bronze was not indestructible: it yielded, was softened, betrayed its entrance to a golden intruder, and did not put up any resistance. When you crafted the bronze as a chamber, Love forged Zeus into gold. As a cloud casts a shadow over the moon, the bronze shadowed your daughter, but Zeus had been contemplating the liaison for a long time. As the sun breaks through what stands in front of it, Love set Zeus aflame and kindled whole furnaces of desire. He even drew fire out of my cheeks and burned the highest of the gods with the blushing of a mortal virgin, completely reducing to ashes with a lustful fire the god who had put even the Titans to rest with an unbearable fire. And Zeus caught fire like a torch and became shining gold, as when in the night gleaming fire reflects off of bronze and when the evening star in a blue sky flashes off of bronze.

3   Ὦ Ζεῦ, ὕπατε θεῶν καὶ παίγνιον Ἔρωτος, ὦ πάντων
ἀνδρῶν κρατῶν καὶ παρθένου νικώμενος, πάλαι σε ὡς
ὄρνιν Ἔρως ἐπτέρωσε καὶ ὡς κύκνον ᾄδειν ἔπεισε, πάλαι
σε ὡς βοῦν ὁπλαῖς τοὺς πόδας ὥπλισε καὶ ὡς ταῦρον
μυκᾶσθαι παρεβιάσατο, καὶ νῦν ὡς χρυσὸν ἐπέχρωσε καὶ
ὡς ἕδνον ἐπέδωκεν. Ὡς Δία προσκυνῶ, ὡς χρυσὸν φιλῶ
καὶ ὡς ἐραστὴν περιπτύσσομαι. Εἴη δέ μοι καὶ λαμπρᾶς
ἀπόνασθαι τῆς γονῆς καὶ κρατοίη τῶν ἄλλων ὁ παῖς, ὡς
τῶν θεῶν Ζεύς, ὡς τῶν μετάλλων χρυσός.

18

Τίνας ἂν εἴποι λόγους ὁ Ζεύς,
ἰδὼν τὴν Ἰοῦν μεταβληθεῖσαν εἰς βοῦν

Ἀφροδίτης καὶ τῶν Ἀφροδίτης κατηγορήσω βελῶν ἢ
τὴν Ἥραν καὶ τὸ τῆς Ἥρας ζηλότυπον μέμψομαι; Βάλλει
μέν με παῖς Ἀφροδίτη, Ἥρα δὲ ξύνοικος ἐπέχει τὸ φάρμακον. Ἡ μὲν τῷ τῶν Ἐρώτων ὑπεκκαίει πυρί, ἡ δὲ διψῶντι
φθονεῖ τῆς πηγῆς. Ἡ μὲν ὡς λειμῶνα τὸ κάλλος ἀνα-
πετάννυσιν, ἡ δ᾽ οὐ ξυγχωρεῖ τῆς ὥρας ὡς ὀπώρας δρέ-
πεσθαι. Ὡς ἐκ καλύκων ῥόδον τῶν χειλέων ἀπαστράπτει
τὸ χαρίεν, ἡ δ᾽ ὡς κέντρον ἐπανατείνεται τὸ βαρύζηλον.

O Zeus, highest of the gods and plaything of Love, you 3
who hold power over all men but are defeated by a virgin,
long ago Love made you winged like a bird and convinced
you to sing like a swan; long ago he fitted your feet with
hooves like an ox and compelled you to bellow like a bull;
and now he has colored your skin like gold and presented
you as a gift. I venerate you as Zeus, I adore you as gold, and
I embrace you as a lover. May I enjoy brilliant offspring, and
may my child rule over other men, as Zeus rules over the
gods, as gold rules over the metals.

18

What Zeus would say after seeing
Io turned into a cow

Shall I condemn Aphrodite and Aphrodite's arrows, or
shall I blame Hera and Hera's jealousy? My child Aphrodite
shoots at me, while Hera, my wife, withholds the remedy.
The former inflames me with the fire of love, while the latter begrudges me the spring when I am thirsty. The former
spreads forth beauty like a meadow, while the latter will not
allow me to pluck the ripe beauty as I would pluck fruit.
The grace of Aphrodite's lips flashes forth like a rose among
buds, while Hera brandishes her tremendous jealousy like
an ox-goad.

2   Ὦ δυστυχὴς ἐραστὴς ἐγὼ καὶ δύσερως! Ὦ καὶ πρὸς τῆς παιδὸς βαλλόμενος καὶ πρὸς τῆς ξυνοίκου φθονούμενος! Ἐπαθύρει μὲν Ἔρως ὁ παῖς καὶ δέχομαι τὴν παιδιὰν ὁ πατήρ. Ἐπιτείνει τὸ τόξον καὶ βάλλειν καθ᾽ ἡμῶν ἀπειλεῖ καὶ χαίρω ταῖς βολαῖς, οὐκ οἶδ᾽ ὅπως· ἐγὼ ὑποκύπτω μειδιῶντι τοξότῃ· ἂν ὡς τοξότης ἀλγύνει με, ὡς μειδιῶν περισαίνει με. Ὅσα μοι κατὰ τῶν ὀφθαλμῶν ἐπαφῆκε τὰ βέλη! Καὶ πάντα βάπτει πρῶτον ἱμέρῳ. Οὐδὲν ἐτόξευσεν ὃ μὴ πρότερον ὑπεφάρμαξεν, οὐδὲν ἠπείλησεν, ὃ μάτην ἐκόμπασε. Παίζων, ἐγώ ποτε τῶν πτερῶν ἐδραξάμην, ὁ δ᾽, ἐπαθύρας, μικρὸν ἐμειδίασε καὶ πτερωτὸς ὁ πατὴρ ἄφνω γίνομαι καὶ τὰ κύκνων μουσουργεῖν οὐκ αἰσχύνομαι. Ἀλλ᾽ οὐ πρότερον Ἔρως ἀνῆκε, πρὶν ἂν θέλξαι μὲν τὴν ἐρωμένην ἐπὶ ζεφυρίοις ᾠδαῖς, ᾆσαι δὲ ὕμνους εἰς Ἔρωτα. Ἐμυκησάμην ποτὲ καὶ ὡς βοῦς διὰ τὸ παιδίον τὸν Ἔρωτα, ὁ δ᾽ ἐπεκερτόμει καὶ βουπλῆγας τὰ βέλη ὠνόμαζεν. Ἠπείλει καὶ θύειν μικροῦ καὶ ὡς ἐπιβώμιον πῦρ ἐφῆπτέ μοι τὸ λαμπάδιον.

3   Κατὰ παντὸς γένους Ἔρως ἐκόμπασε καὶ θνητοῖς ἐφυβρίζει καὶ θεῶν κατεπαίρεται καὶ ἰχθύας ἐφ᾽ οὕτω πολλῇ τῇ θαλάττῃ φλέγει καὶ πτηνῶν ἀγέλας εἰς ἀέρα φθάνει. Οὐκ ἔστιν ὃ μὴ γέγονεν Ἔρωτος ἄθυρμα. Ἄμπελον οὐ φυτεύει καὶ μέθην σοφίζεται, βότρυν οὐ γεωργεῖ καὶ βαρὺν τὸν κῶμον τεχνάζεται. Μικρὸν ὡς βότρυν τὴν καρδίαν Ἔρως ἔθλιψε, μικρὸν κατὰ σπλάγχνων ἐληνοβάτησε καί, σπᾷ τις τοῦ κρατῆρος καὶ μέμηνε, μικρὰ μεθύσκειν οἶνος ἐδίδαξε, μικρὰ βακχεύειν οἶδε Διόνυσος.

Alas, I am an ill-fated, lovesick lover! Alas, I am both at- 2
tacked by my daughter and envied by my wife! The child
Love is playing, and I, the father, am part of his game. He
stretches his bow and threatens to shoot at me; I rejoice in
the arrows — I know not how — and submit to the smiling archer. If he causes me pain as an archer, he wins me over with
his smile. So many are the arrows he has shot into my eyes!
First, he dips them all in desire. He does not shoot any arrow that he has not already treated with his drug; he does
not threaten anything that he has boasted in vain. Once, I
myself playfully grabbed his wings, and he, playing too, gave
a little smile, and I, the father, suddenly grew wings and was
not ashamed to sing the song of the swan. Love did not let
me go until I beguiled my beloved with songs of the west
wind and sang hymns to Love. I bellowed once like a bull,
thanks to Love, the little boy, and he mocked me and called
the arrows ox-goads. He even threatened (almost) to sacrifice me and touched me with a small torch, like fire on an altar.

Love can boast over every race: he abuses mortals; he 3
riles gods; he inflames the fish in the sea, which is so immense; he outpaces *flocks of birds* in the air. There is nothing that is not the plaything of Love. He does not plant a
grapevine, yet he devises drunkenness. He does not culti-
vate grapes, yet he designs the grievous revel. Love squeezes
the heart little by little, like a bunch of grapes; little by little
he presses the guts, like pressing wine; and whoever draws
from the mixing bowl and becomes mad with wine, little by
little the wine instructs him in drunkenness, and little by
little Dionysus knows how to make him revel.

4 Ἀδελφὸς μὲν Διόνυσος Ἔρωτος, ἀλλ' ἥττων, ἀλλ' ὑποστράτηγος, ὅλους κρατῆρας ἐπισπένδει πυρὸς καὶ προσ-
αναρριπίζει πῦρ φιλοτήσιον καί πού τις ἀπανθρακοῦται
διπλῷ τῷ πυρί, καὶ μέγαν ὑμνεῖ δυνάστην τὸν Ἔρωτα.
Προσκυνεῖ καὶ Διόνυσον, ἀλλ' ὡς Ἀφροδίτης ξύμμαχον,
ἀλλ' ὡς Χαρίτων ὑπασπιστήν, ἀλλ' ὡς θεράποντα Ἔρωτος.
Στρατεύουσιν ἄμφω καὶ χοροὶ γυναικῶν τὰ στρατόπεδα.
Ἀλλ' ὁ μὲν Ἰνδοὺς αἱρεῖ καὶ Θήβας ἀναβακχεύει καὶ
Τυρρηνοῖς ἐπιτίθεται· Ἔρως δὲ κατὰ θεῶν ὁπλίζεται, κατὰ
θνητῶν παρατάττεται, εἰς οὐρανὸν ἵπταται, καὶ χωρεῖν
οὐρανὸς οὐκ ἔχει τὰ τρόπαια. Κατὰ γῆς πεζεύει καὶ πάντα
ξυνδήσας ἄγει καὶ φέρει τῷ βλέμματι Ἔρως οὐκ ὀλίγα καὶ
τὸν ἀδελφὸν Διόνυσον ἐδουλώσατο. Ἱμέρῳ τὰς Ἀριάδνης
ἔχρισέ ποτε παρειὰς καὶ προσίεται τὸ βέλος ὁ Βάκχος καὶ
προσκυνεῖ τὸν ἀδελφὸν Ἔρωτα καὶ κόρης αἰχμάλωτος
γίνεται.

5 Καὶ κατ' αὐτῆς Ἀφροδίτης ὁ παῖς Ἔρως νεανιεύεται καὶ
τὸν ἀδελφὸν οὐκ ᾤκτειρε καὶ τοῦ πατρὸς οὐκ ἐφείσατο.
Ἀργόθεν μοι τὸ τῆς Ἰοῦς ἐπήστραψε κάλλος καὶ τἄνδον
εὐθὺς ἀποσμύχομαι. Ἀλλὰ τίς κόχλῳ τὴν πορφύραν
ἐπέκρυψε; Τίς ἐλύτρῳ τὸν μάργαρον ἐπεκάλυψεν; Οἴμοι!
Καὶ πάλιν Ἥρα ζηλοτυπεῖ καὶ πάλιν ὡς ἐραστὴν
ὑποβλέπεται, τὴν ἐρωμένην εἰς βοῦν ἐμορφώσατο, καὶ
πάλιν ὅσην προβάλλεται τὴν εἰδέχθειαν.

6 Ἀλλ' ὦ καὶ βοῦς εὐπρεπὴς καὶ παρθένος οὐκ ἄμορφος,
κοινωνεῖς τῷ Διῒ τῆς τύχης καὶ τῆς μορφῆς καὶ καρτέρει,
μετὰ Διὸς μυκωμένη. Εὐφραίνεις μᾶλλον τὸν ἐραστήν, οἷς
τὴν μορφὴν εἰς ταῦρον ἠλλάξατο, ἵνα ζυγὸν ἄμφω τὸν

Dionysus is the brother of Love, but inferior, a subor- 4
dinate. He pours whole mixing bowls of fire as offerings
and, moreover, rekindles the fire of Love; if ever anyone is
reduced to ashes in the double fire, he honors the great
leader Love in song. Love also venerates Dionysus, but as an
ally of Aphrodite, as the shield-bearer of the Graces, as the
servant of Love. The two campaign together, and choruses
of women are their armies. But Dionysus seizes Indians,
rouses Thebes to Bacchic frenzy, and attacks the Tyrrhe-
nians, while Love arms himself against the gods, arrays himself against mortals, and flies up to heaven, and heaven cannot contain his triumphs. Love marches against the earth,
and after binding everything together, pillages and plunders
it all with his glance, and has enslaved his brother Dionysus.
He once anointed Ariadne's cheeks with desire, and Bacchus submitted to his arrow, venerated his brother, Love,
and became the prisoner of a girl.

This boy, Love, even acts insolently against Aphrodite 5
herself; he did not show pity for his brother, and did not
spare his father. The beauty of Io flashed forth to me from
Argos, and immediately my insides were being consumed as
though by fire. But who hid this purple in a murex shell?
Who concealed this pearl in an oyster? Alas! Once again
Hera is jealous and once again she eyes me suspiciously as a
lover. She has transformed my beloved into a cow. What an
ugly creature she presents to me!

But, O fair cow and virgin not misshapen, you share with 6
Zeus his fortune and his form, and you endure, bellowing
along with Zeus. You give greater joy to your lover, because
he changed his form into a bull so that we might pull the

Ἔρωτος ἕλκωμεν. Οἶστρος τὴν ἐμὴν ἔπληξε βοῦν καὶ πολλὴν μὲν ὅσην ἐπῆλθες ἤπειρον, οὐκ ὀλίγα δὲ διεμετρήσω κύματα! Οἶστρος κἀμὲ τὸν θεῶν ὕπατον ἔτρωσε καὶ γέγονα ταῦρος μυκώμενος. Κατέπτην ἐξ οὐρανοῦ, διέδραμον γῆν, κατέδυν εἰς θάλατταν, κἂν τοῖς Διὸς νώτοις κόρη θνητὴ καθιππάσατο. Ἐγώ σε καὶ ὡς βοῶπιν ἀποθαυμάζω καὶ ὡς σελήνην φιλῶ. Ἡλίκον εἰς κύκλον τὸ κέρας ἑλίσσεται! Κἂν ὡς νέφος τὸ τῆς μορφῆς εὐπρόσωπον ὑπεζόφωσεν, ἀλλ᾽, ὡς φῶς ἥλιος, ἐγώ σοι τὸ κάλλος ἀποχαρίσομαι. Βοῦς εἶ τὴν μορφὴν καὶ τὸ χρῆμα πανταχόθεν ὅσιον εἰς θεοὺς ἀφωσίωται, εἰς βωμὸν ἀφιέρωται. Σὲ δὲ τὴν ἐμὴν φίλην βοῦν στέψουσι μὲν Ἔρωτες, κανηφορήσουσι δὲ Χάριτες, ἱερεύσει δὲ Ἀφροδίτη καὶ Ζεὺς εὐωχήσεται καὶ προσεποπτεύσει τὸ καλλιέρημα.

7   Δεινὸς ὁ βουκόλος καὶ πολλοῖς φρουρεῖ σε τοῖς ὀφθαλμοῖς, ἀλλὰ δεινὸς ὑποκλέπτειν Ἑρμῆς καὶ κρεῖττον αὐχεῖ πολλῶν ὀμμάτων τὸ δόλιον. Ἔχει ῥάβδον οὐκ ἀνδρῶν μόνον ὀφθαλμοὺς θέλγουσαν, ἀλλὰ καὶ βουκόλον πανόπτην κοιμίζουσαν. Ὡς ἐγὼ καὶ τὴν Ἥραν ἀμυνοῦμαι τῆς ὕβρεως, βουκόλον ἐπιστήσω κριτὴν καὶ παρ᾽ Ἀλεξάνδρῳ κάλλους εὐτυχήσει τὰ δεύτερα. Τί γάρ σοι βουκόλον πανόπτην ἐπέστησε; Τί δ᾽ οὕτω καλὴν μορφὴν ἀπηγλάϊσεν; Οὕτως ἐπιτεχνάσομαί σοι τὸ βουλητόν, οὕτω, πεσούσης μου τῆς βοός, καὶ σίμβλον ἀναφανήσεται μέλιτος. Δεῖ γάρ σε εἰς ἄνθρωπον αὖθις ἐπανελθεῖν, ἐμὲ δ᾽ ὀψέ ποτε καὶ τῶν Ἀφροδίτης χαρίτων γεύσασθαι καὶ γλυκὺν ἐπιγνῶναι τὸν Ἔρωτα.

yoke of Love together. A gadfly has stung my cow, and when you arrived at such a wide mainland, you had crossed not a few waves! Once, a gadfly also wounded me, the highest of the gods, and I became a bellowing bull. I flew down from heaven, ran across the earth, dove into the sea, and a mortal girl rode on the back of Zeus. I marvel at you for being ox-eyed and adore you like the moon. Into how great a circle do your horns twist! And if a cloud were obscuring the fair appearance of your beauty, I would restore your beauty to you, as the sun restores the light. You are a cow in form, and everywhere this beast has been consecrated to the gods as holy and has been dedicated upon the altar. You, my dear cow, the Erotes will crown, and the Graces will carry the baskets; Aphrodite will perform the sacrifice, and Zeus will hold the feast and also witness the auspices.

The cowherd Argus is clever and guards you with his 7 many eyes, but Hermes is clever at theft and boasts that his trickery is mightier than many eyes. He has a wand that not only charms the eyes of men, but also puts to sleep the all-seeing cowherd. In this way I will also take revenge on Hera for her insult: I will appoint a cowherd as a judge, and Hera will take second prize for beauty from Alexander. For why did she set the all-seeing cowherd over you? Why did she diminish the splendor of such a beautiful form? Thus I will contrive for you what you wish for; thus, after my cow has passed away, there will appear a hive full of honey. For you must return again to human form, and I must finally taste the pleasures of Aphrodite and know sweet Love.

19

Τίνας ἂν εἴποι λόγους ὁ Ἡρακλῆς, δουλεύων Ὀμφάλῃ

Μετ᾽ Εὐρυσθέως δουλείαν γυναικὶ δουλεύω βαρβάρῳ καὶ φθόνον Ἥρας Ἀφροδίτης ἐπιβουλὴ διαδέχεται· δοῦλος Μοιρῶν ἐφ᾽ Ἑλλάδος ἤκουσα καὶ νῦν εἰς Λυδοὺς Ἔρως ἀπεμπολεῖ με. Ὢ θεοί! Τίνα τοῦτον ἆθλον αὖθις ἀθλῶ; Τίς ὁ καινὸς οὗτος πόλεμος; Δράκοντας εἷλον ἔτι βρέφος εὐθὺς μετὰ γένεσιν, ἐλάφου ταχύτερος ἐγενόμην, ὤφθην καὶ λέοντος ἀλκιμώτερος. Ἀλλὰ νῦν ἐπέλιπέ μοι τὰ τῆς ἀλκῆς, ἐπεσχέθην τοῦ τάχους καὶ μόνον οὐ πέπηγα, πρὸς Ἀφροδίτης βαλλόμενος. Ἥρας φθονούσης, τῶν ἄθλων Ἀθηνᾶ συνεφήπτετο, Ἰόλεως τῆς πρὸς Ὕδραν μάχης ξυνήρατο, Θησεὺς τὸν πρὸς Ἀμαζόνας ἀγῶνα συνήθλευσε. Νῦν δὲ τίνα μὲν ἡρώων, τίνα δὲ θεῶν ἐπικαλέσομαι ξύμμαχον; Ἀκατάβλητος Ἔρως ἀνίκητος ὁ πολέμιος.

2   Εἰς ξυμμαχίαν δεήσομαι τοῦ πατρὸς καὶ τὸν κεραυνὸν Ἔρως πεφρίξεται. Ἀλλ᾽ ἀναρριπίζει ἕτερον καὶ κατὰ Διὸς πολλάκις ἐξεπυρήνισεν. Οἶδε Ζεὺς καί, κτῆμα γενόμενος Δήμητρος καὶ οἴστρῳ πληγεὶς καὶ ζυγὸν ἕλκων Ἔρωτος τοῦ παιδός, ἐμυκήσατο ὁ πατήρ. Ἀλλ᾽ εἰς ἀρωγὴν χρησιμεύσει τὸ τόξον Ἀπόλλωνος, ἀλλὰ μείζων Ἔρως τοξότης καὶ κατὰ τῶν Ἀπόλλωνος ὀφθαλμῶν πολλάκις ἐτόξευσεν.

19

What Heracles would say
while serving as a slave to Omphale

After being in servitude to Eurystheus, I am a slave to a barbarian woman, and Aphrodite's scheme succeeds Hera's envy. In Greece I was called a slave to the Fates, and now Love is selling me to the Lydians. O gods! What is this contest in which I now contend? What is this strange, new war? I killed serpents while still a newborn infant; I became swifter than a deer; I proved to be braver than even a lion. But now my strength has failed me; I have been denied my swiftness and am all but paralyzed, now that I am under attack from Aphrodite. When Hera was jealous, Athena joined me in my struggles; Iolaus took part in the battle against the Hydra; Theseus struggled with me in the contest against the Amazons. But now, whom among the heroes, whom among the gods will I summon as my ally? My invincible enemy is the unassailable Love.

I will beg my father to form an alliance, and Love will 2 shudder at his thunderbolt. But no, he ignites a different weapon and has often launched it against Zeus. Zeus has experienced Love: one time, when my father became the property of Demeter, he was stung by a gadfly, dragged the yoke of his son Love, and bellowed. Apollo's bow will be useful for bringing help; but no, Love is a better archer and has often shot his arrows into Apollo's eyes. Brazen Ares will

Ἄρης ἐπαρήξει μοι χάλκεος, ἀλλὰ καὶ τοῦτον Ἔρως τῷ πυρὶ κατεμάλθαξεν. Ὅλας πηγὰς ἐπαντλήσει μοι Ποσειδῶν καὶ τοὺς Ἔρωτος ἄνθρακας ἀποσβέσει, ἀλλ᾽ οἶδεν αὐτὸς Ποσειδῶν, ἐπὶ μέσης θαλάττης φλεγόμενος καί, ὡς εὐρύστερνος, μείζω καὶ τὴν ἀνθρακιὰν κατὰ στέρνων ἐδέχετο. Ποῖ τράπωμαι; Ποῖ φεύξομαι; Ἂν εἰς οὐρανὸν ἀναπτήσομαι, μετὰ θεῶν πάντως βεβλήσομαι. Ἂν εἰς θάλατταν καταδύσομαι, ξυναναζέσει πάντως καὶ θάλαττα. Ἀλλ᾽ ἀντιπαρατάξομαι κατὰ γῆν, θαρρήσω τῷ τόξῳ, πιστεύσω τοῖς βέλεσιν. Ἀλλ᾽ ὡς βολίδας τὰς τοῦ κάλλους ἀκτῖνας αὐχεῖ καὶ φάρμακον ἄλλο φέρει τὸν ἵμερον. Ὡς πυρφόρος κεραυνοβολεῖ καὶ ὡς τοξότης βάλλει καὶ ὡς πτερωτὸς φθάνει ἀπανταχόθεν Ἔρως ἄτρεπτος, ἀπανταχόθεν ἀχείρωτος. Παρακαλέσω τὴν φίλην Ἀθηνᾶν καὶ τὴν Ἄϊδος κυνῆν περιθήσομαι καὶ φύγω τοὺς δεινοὺς Ἔρωτος ὀφθαλμούς. Ἀλλ᾽ οὐδ᾽ αὐτὸς Ἅιδης, ὑπὸ γῆν ὢν καὶ σκότον οἰκῶν, ἔλαθε. Νικᾷ τὴν ἀετῶν ὀξυδέρκειαν—οὐδὲν ὁ πανόπτης, μικρὸν ὁ Λυγγεύς—μεθ᾽ ἡμέραν ὀφθαλμοῖς ἀκοιμήτοις ὁρᾷ καὶ νυκτὸς λαμπαδίῳ θηρᾶται τοὺς φεύγοντας.

3   Τέτρωμαι τὸ στέρνον, ὑποσμύχομαι τὴν καρδίαν, οὐ φέρω τὴν πληγήν, ἀλγῶ τὴν βολήν. Τίς λαθικηδὲς ἐπισκευάσεται φάρμακον; Τὸν ἀδελφὸν αἰτήσομαι Βάκχον καί, κρατῆρα παυσίλυπον κερασάμενος, κοιμίσει μοι τὴν ὀδύνην. Ἀλλὰ πῦρ ἐπὶ πυρὶ καθ᾽ ἡμῶν ἀνασείσει καὶ ξυνεπικωμάσει Διόνυσος Ἔρωτι καὶ μεθύσω μέθην διπλῆν, καὶ πρὸς Διονύσου βακχευόμενος καὶ πρὸς Ἔρωτος ἐκμαινόμενος. Μάτην ἐκ Διὸς ἐγώ, μάτην καλλίνικος.

come to my aid; but no, Love has softened even this god with his fire. Poseidon will gush forth whole springs for me and will extinguish Love's coals; but no, Poseidon himself has experienced Love and, inflamed in the midst of the sea, as the broad-chested one has received an even greater fire within his chest. Where am I to turn? Where will I flee? If I fly up to heaven, I will certainly be attacked among the gods. If I descend into the sea, even the sea will certainly boil with me. But I will make my stand upon the earth; I will take courage in my bow; I will trust in my arrows. But Love exults in the rays of his beauty as though they were missiles, and he brings desire as another drug. As a fire-bearer he hurls the thunderbolt, as an archer he shoots, and as a winged god Love has the advantage, unyielding from all sides, from all sides invincible. I will summon dear Athena, put on Hades's helmet, and flee Love's terrible eyes. But not even Hades himself escapes notice, though he lives below the earth and dwells in darkness. Love possesses keener eyesight than eagles—the all-seeing one does not, though Lynceus does by a little—and in the day Love watches with unsleeping eyes and at night hunts down fugitives by torchlight.

I am wounded in my chest; I smolder in my heart; I cannot bear the blow; I am pained by the wound. Who will prepare the drug to make me forget my cares? I will ask my brother Bacchus, and he will mix a jar of grief-ending wine and lull my sorrows to sleep. But Dionysus will brandish fire upon fire against me and join Love in the reveling, and I will be drunk with a double drunkenness, driven to a Bacchic frenzy by Dionysus and driven mad by Love. In vain am I

Ζωστῆρα κομίζειν μιᾶς γυναικὸς ἐπέταττεν Εὐρυσθεὺς καὶ Θησεὺς εἰς ἀρωγὴν ἐφείπετο, καὶ νῦν Ὀμφάλη μόνη, γυνὴ Λυδή, τὸν Διὸς ἀθλητὴν τῷ κάλλει κατήστραψε, κατέαξε τὸ ῥόπαλον, τὸ τόξον ἐξέλυσε, τὴν λεοντὴν περιείλετο. Ὡς ἄρα γυναῖκες ἀνδρῶν ἄφυκτα θήρατρα. Κἂν ᾖ τις κόρη καλὴ τὴν μορφήν, ἀκραιφνὴς ὑποστράτηγος Ἔρωτος, καὶ Ζεὺς ὑποκύπτει καὶ κόρης ἄγεται δέσμιος. Πρὸς Ὕδραν ἠγωνιζόμην καὶ πυρὶ καὶ ξίφει τὸν ἆθλον ἐκαινοτόμουν. Ταύτην ἐπ᾽ ἐμοὶ τὴν μάχην Ἔρως ἐζήλωσε. Κατ᾽ αὐτῆς ἐπέθετό μοι τῆς κεφαλῆς καὶ τοὺς ἐκεῖθεν σώφρονας λογισμούς, ὡς ἑτέρας ἀνατρέχοντας κεφαλάς, ἐξαιρεῖ, θερίζει, πορθεῖ, φλέγει τῷ λαμπαδίῳ, τέμνει τοῖς βέλεσιν. Ἀλλ᾽ ὦ Ζεῦ πάτερ καὶ ἀδελφὴ πρόμαχος Ἀθηνᾶ, ἐγὼ μὲν ὅλην ἐξεκάθηρα γῆν, ὑμεῖς δέ μοι τὴν ψυχὴν ἐκκαθαίροιτε καὶ διδοίητε σωφρονεῖν, καὶ τάχα καὶ τοῦτον κρατήσω τὸν ἆθλον καὶ νικήσω τὸν Ἔρωτα καὶ πάλιν ἀκούσω καλλίνικος.

the son of Zeus; in vain am I a glorious champion. Eurystheus ordered me to fetch one woman's girdle and Theseus
came along to help, but now Omphale alone, a Lydian
woman, has dazzled Zeus's champion with her beauty, has
broken my club, has unstrung my bow, has stripped off my
lion skin. Thus are women inescapable snares for men. If
there is some maiden who is beautiful in appearance, an innocent deputy of Love, even Zeus bows down to her and is
led away as the girl's prisoner. I contended with the Hydra,
and with fire and sword waged an ingenious fight. Love envied me for that battle. He invaded my very head, and he
strips away, mows down, ravages, burns with his torch, and
cuts with his arrows the thoughts of self-control found there
as though they were other heads spurting up. But O father
Zeus and sister Athena, the protector, since I purged the entire earth, may you purge my soul and grant me to be sober-
minded: then perhaps I will also be victorious in this contest, will defeat Love, and will once again be called glorious
champion.

20

Τίνας ἂν εἴποι λόγους ναυτίλος,
ἰδὼν τὸν μὲν Ἴκαρον εἰς ὕψος ἱπτάμενον,
τὸν δὲ Δαίδαλον ἄκροις πτεροῖς τῆς
θαλάττης ἐπιψαύοντα

Ὦ Ζεῦ καὶ Πόσειδον, τίνα ταύτην φύσιν αὖθις ὁρῶ;
Τίνος ἔλαχε κλῆρον; Τῆς Διὸς ἀρχῆς ἐρῶ τοῦτο τὸ τέρας
ἢ Ποσειδῶνος καὶ θαλάττης τὸ θέαμα; Ὡς αἰθέριον ἵπταται καὶ ὡς θαλάττιον ἐπινήχεται· οὔτε τῶν κυμάτων
ἀφίσταται καὶ πρὸς ἀέρα μετεωρίζεται. Εἶδον ἐγὼ καὶ
ἰχθύας ἀνιπταμένους καὶ τὸ θαῦμα δαίμοσι θαλαττίοις
ἐπεγραφόμην· τὸ δὲ νῦν τοῦτο ἄπορον εἰπεῖν τὴν θέαν
ἀμήχανον. Ἦν ἂν ἰχθὺς τὸ φαινόμενον, εἰ μὴ καὶ πόδας
τοῖς πτεροῖς ἐπεσύρετο· εἶπον ἂν ὄρνιν ὁρᾶν, εἰ μὴ καὶ
μορφή τις ἀνδρὸς ὑπεφαίνετο· ἐκάλεσα ἂν ἄνθρωπον, εἰ
μὴ καὶ πτερὰ προύβέβλητο. Ἀνδρὸς ἔχει τὴν ὄψιν, ἰχθύος
τὴν νῆξιν, ὀρνίθων τὴν πτῆσιν. Τίς οὗτος ἔρανος φύσεων;
Πόθεν οὕτω κρᾶμα πολύμορφον; Ἀκούω Κενταύρους
φύσιν ἱππάνθρωπον καὶ μέχρις ἀκοῆς ἐθαύμασα. Πρὸς
γὰρ αὐτὴν ὄψιν οὐκ ἦλθέ μοι τὰ τοῦ θαύματος, νῦν δὲ
βλέπων ἐκπέπληγμαι καὶ πρὸς ἀμηχανίαν ἐπιλείπω
θεώμενος. Πῶς ἄρα καὶ δέξεται τὸ καινὸν ἀκοή, πρὸς ὃ
καὶ ὄψις ἠπίστησεν;

20

What a sailor would say after seeing Icarus flying high, but Daedalus skimming the sea with the tips of his wings

O Zeus and Poseidon, what is this creature that I now observe? From which god's territory does it come? Shall I call it a marvel from the realm of Zeus, or a spectacle from Poseidon and the sea? Like an ethereal creature it flies, and like a sea creature it skims the water; it does not retreat from the waves, and it lifts itself up in the air. I myself have seen fish flying upward, and I attributed the miracle to the spirits of the sea, but now I am at a loss to explain the impossible sight. The marvel might be a fish, except that it trails feet behind its wings; I might say that I am looking at a bird, except that it appears to have something of the form of a man; I might call it human, except that it also possesses wings. It has the appearance of a man, the swimming ability of a fish, the flight of birds. What is this collection of natures? What is the source of these many forms, thus mixed together? I have heard about Centaurs, horse-men in form, and I marveled at them, but that was only hearsay. For as regards the sight of them, the actual marvel never reached me, but now I see and am amazed, and as I look I am at a loss in my perplexity. How will the ears receive the novelty, which even the eyes have disbelieved?

2   Ἔρως οὗτος, οἶμαι, καὶ κατ' αὐτοῦ Ποσειδῶνος ἐπιστρατεύει, ἀλλ' οὐκ ἐξήρτηται τὸ τόξον, οὐχ ὁρῶ τὸ
λαμπάδιον. Ἑρμῆν ἄν εἴποι τις τὸν πτηνὸν ἄγγελον, τὸν
Διὸς κήρυκα· καὶ ποῦ μοι τὰ λαμπρὰ πέδιλα; Ποῦ δὲ ἡ
χρυσῆ ῥάβδος, τὸ καινὸν ἐκεῖνο κηρύκειον; Ἀλλὰ Ζεὺς
οὗτος καὶ τὴν τῆς Εὐρώπης ἁρπαγὴν μελετᾷ καί, πολλῷ
τῷ τοῦ παιδὸς Ἔρωτος λαμπαδίῳ φλεγόμενος, ἀπ'
οὐρανοῦ κάτεισι καὶ πρὸς ὕδωρ πτερύσσεται· καὶ μὴν ὡς
ταῦρον ἐξ οὐρανοῦ τὸν θεῶν ὕπατον Ἔρως ἀπεβουκό-
λησεν. Εἰ Περσεὺς ἦν, καὶ τὴν ἅρπην ἄν ἐχειρίζετο. Εἰ
Βελεροφόντης, ἵππον ἄν εἶχε πτηνόν, ἀλλ' οὐκ αὐτὸς
πτεροῖς, ὡς εἰπεῖν, ἐναυτίλλετο. Εἰ Μήδεια, ὡς ἐφ' ἅρματος
ἄν δρακόντων ἐφέρετο.

3   Ἀλλὰ τίς οὗτος ἕτερος πολλῷ τὴν πτῆσιν μετέωρος; Ἡ
μορφὴ μὲν ἴση, τὰ δὲ τῆς πτήσεως οὐκ ἰσόδρομα. Ὁ μὲν
ἄκροις πτίλοις ἐφάπτεται τῶν κυμάτων—ἱέρακα ἄν τις
ἰδὼν εἴποι θαλάττιον—ὁ δ' ὑπερνεφὴς καὶ ὑπὲρ τὰς
τευθίδας πέταται. Τίς οὗτος τάχους ἀγών; Τί τοῦτο πτήσεως στάδιον; Καὶ θεατὴς ἐγώ, τοῖς ὀφθαλμοῖς ἀπιστῶν,
οὕτω τὸν Ἑρμῆν ἐν γραφαῖς εἶδον ἐγὼ διαμιλλώμενον
Ἔρωτι, καὶ Ζεὺς ἐπεμειδία τοῖς παισὶν ἀθύρουσιν. Ἁρπυίας
ὁ μῦθος κατὰ Φινέως ἐπλάσατο καὶ Βορεάδας αὖθις εἰς
ξυμμαχίαν ἐπτέρωσε, νῦν δὲ παρὰ τοσοῦτον Βορεάδας
οὐκ εἶναι μαντεύομαι, παρόσον μὴ καὶ Ἁρπυίας ὁρᾶν ἡ
τύχη προσεχαρίσατο. Μή που καὶ πάλιν ἕτερον φῦλον
ἀνθρώπων ὁ Διὸς δεσμώτης ἐτόλμησε Προμηθεύς;

4   Ὦ Ζεῦ καὶ θεοί, ὡς ἀκρόπολιν ὑμᾶς φρουρεῖν δεήσει
τὸν οὐρανὸν ἢ τάχα καὶ ὑπ' ἀνθρώπων ἁλώσεσθε· ὑπὲρ

This is Love, I suppose, and he is marching even against 2
Poseidon himself, but he is not armed with a bow, and I do
not see his torch. Someone might say that it is Hermes, the
winged messenger, herald of Zeus. But where, I ask, are his
shining sandals? Where is the golden staff, that special herald's wand? But this is Zeus, intent on abducting Europa. Inflamed by the great torch of his child, Love, he descends
from heaven and is winging his way along the water. But it
was in the form of a bull that the highest of the gods was seduced out of heaven by Love. If it were Perseus, he would be
wielding his curved sword. If it were Bellerophon, he would
have a flying horse, but even he did not, so to speak, sail with
wings. If it were Medea, she would be carried upon a chariot
pulled by dragons.

But who is this other person, lifted high into the air in 3
flight? His form is identical, but his flight follows a different
course. While the first one skims the waves with the tips of
his wings (one who saw him would call him a sea hawk), this
one flies above the clouds and higher than the squids. What
is this contest of speed? What is this competition in flight?
I, the spectator who disbelieves his own eyes, have seen
paintings of Hermes contending vehemently like this with
Love, and Zeus smiling at his children as they frolic. Myth
told the story of the Harpies against Phineus and also gave
wings to the sons of Boreas, to be his allies. But I divine that
these are not the sons of Boreas, since fortune has not
graced me with the sight of Harpies. Can it be that Prometheus, Zeus's prisoner, has dared to make yet another
race of humans?

O Zeus and gods, you will have to guard heaven as an 4
acropolis, or perhaps you will be captured by humans, an act

τοὺς Ἀλωάδας τὸ τόλμημα· οὐ δεῖται λόφων τοῦτο τὸ
γένος, αὐτοῖς πτεροῖς καθ᾽ ὑμῶν ἀποχρήσεται, κἂν εἰς
πλῆθος εὐτυχήσῃ τὴν γένεσιν, εἰς οὐρανὸν ἀναπτήσεται
καὶ Ζεὺς πολιορκηθήσεται. Ὦ χρόνος οὗτος, τεραστίων
πατήρ! Πρὸ μικροῦ Δαίδαλον ἐπὶ Κρήτης ἤκουσα χαλκῷ
κεραννύντα τὴν τέχνην καὶ βοῦν ἀπὸ χαλκοῦ μυκώμενον
ἐμάνθανον· καὶ ταῦρος, ἀπὸ τέχνης οἴστρῳ πληγεὶς Ἔρωτος, ὡς εἰς ἀληθῆ βοῦν ἐπεβάκχευε καὶ παστὰς ὁ χαλκὸς
τῇ Πασιφάῃ γίνεται. Τοῦ μύσους ἀσφάλιε Πόσειδον καὶ
δαίμονες ἀλεξίκακοι!

5   Ἀλλ᾽ εἰς καιρὸν ἐπὶ νοῦν ἧκέ μοι Δαίδαλος, οὗτος
ἐκεῖνος ὁ Δαίδαλος ὁ δεινὸς σφυρηλατῆσαι χαλκόν, ὡς καὶ
ταῦρον οἰστρηλατῆσαι πρὸς Ἔρωτα. Διὰ τοῦτον πάλαι
χαλκὸς ἐμυκήσατο, διὰ τοῦτον καὶ νῦν ἵπτανται ἄνθρωποι.
Φεύγει τὸν Μίνω καὶ τὴν ἐκείνου δίκην, οἷς τὸν Πασιφάης
γάμον ἄθεσμον ἐσοφίσατο. Δαίδαλος οὗτος ὁ χθαμαλὸς
τὴν φύσιν ὁ θαλάττης αὐτῆς ἐπιψαύων, Ἴκαρος ἐκεῖνος ὁ
Δαιδάλου παῖς, ὁ μικροῦ τοῖς πτίλοις ἐπεντρυφῶν, ὁ καὶ
πρὸς τοὺς τῶν ὀρνίθων ἀντερίζων ὑπερνεφεῖς.

6   Ἀλλ᾽ ὦ σοφιστὰ τῶν ἀμηχάνων Δαίδαλε, Μίνω μὲν καὶ
τὴν ἐκεῖθεν ποινὴν ἐκπέφευγας, ὁρᾷ δέ σε Ἥλιος ὁ πάντα
ἐφορῶν· κἂν τὴν Μίνωος ὑπερέπτης ἀρχήν, ἀλλ᾽ οὔτι καὶ
πᾶσαν τὴν γῆν ὁπόσην οὗτος ὁ μέγας ἐποπτεύει θεός·
εἶδεν ὑπὸ χαλκῷ κρυπτομένην τὴν παῖδα, μέμνηται τοῦ
ταύρου, τὸν τοῦ μύσους σοφιστὴν οὐκ ἠγνόησεν. Εἰς
παῖδα ἐλύπει τὸν Ἥλιον Δαίδαλος καὶ Δαίδαλον εἰς παῖδα
τιμωρήσεται Ἥλιος, ὡς νόθον ἀετιδῆ ἐλέγξει ταῖς ἀκτῖσιν

of daring surpassing that of the Aloadae. This race has no need of hills—it will make full use of its very wings against you—and if it succeeds in reproducing and becomes plentiful, it will fly up to heaven and Zeus will be besieged. Alas, this era, progenitor of monsters! Only recently I heard that Daedalus in Crete was alloying his art with bronze, and I learned about the bellowing cow made of bronze. And the bull, stung by this goad of Love through art, went mad as if for a real cow, and the bronze became a wedding chamber for Pasiphaë. O Poseidon, protector from defilement, and you spirits who ward off evil!

But Daedalus has entered my mind at just the right moment! This is that Daedalus, clever at hammering bronze, and so also clever at driving the bull mad with love. Because of him did the bronze once bellow; because of him now do humans also fly. He is fleeing from Minos and that man's revenge, because he devised an illicit marriage for Pasiphaë. This one is Daedalus, lowly in his nature and flying low over the very sea, while the other is Icarus, Daedalus's son, who all but treats his wings with insolence, who even contends with the birds that fly high above the clouds. 5

But O Daedalus, deviser of impossible things, you may have escaped Minos and his punishment, but *the Sun, who looks down on everything,* sees you; even if you flew over Minos's kingdom, still you did not fly over the entire earth, all of which this great god observes. He saw his daughter hidden in the bronze; he remembers the bull; he was not ignorant of the one who devised the defilement. Daedalus made the Sun grieve for his child, and the Sun will punish Daedalus through his child: he will expose Icarus as an illegitimate eaglet as he looks upon the Sun's rays. Icarus, 6

ἐπεντρανίζοντα. Οὐ γνήσιος ἄρα Δαιδάλου παῖς Ἴκαρος τὴν ξύνεσιν τοῦ πατρὸς ἔψευσται, ἀκτῖσι πιστεύει κηρὸν καὶ πτερορρυήσει πάντως, ὑφ᾽ Ἡλίῳ βαλλόμενος. Ἀλλὰ τί καὶ δράσεις ὑπὸ γῆν ὁ πάντα κατὰ γῆν μηχανώμενος; Εὑρήσεις καὶ πάλιν ἐν Ἅιδου τὸν Μίνω, ὄψει θεσμοθετοῦντα τοῖς κάτω. Γνωριεῖ σε τὸν τοῦ ταύρου νυμφοστόλον καὶ τὴν ἀξίαν ἐπιψηφιεῖται. Οὕτω σε καὶ περιόντα Ἥλιος ἀμυνεῖται καὶ Μίνως αὖθις μετὰ τελευτὴν διαδέξεται.

21

Τίνας ἂν εἴποι λόγους ὁ τοῦ Ξέρξου κυβερνήτης, στεφανούμενος ἅμα καὶ ἀναιρούμενος

Ὦ ναυτίλος ἐγὼ καὶ μετὰ θάλατταν δυστυχής! Ὦ τύχης ἀλλοκότου παίγνιον! Ἀπωθεῖται καὶ προσεφέλκεται· παίει καὶ περιπτύσσεται· ἁρπάζει θαλάττης καὶ πρὸς δημίου χεῖρας μεταρριπτεῖ· τιάραν φιλοτιμεῖται καὶ προσαφαιρεῖται τὴν κεφαλήν. Ἀναιρεῖ τὴν ἐκ τῶν λίθων μαρμαρυγὴν ἡ τοῦ ξίφους αὐγή· ἡδονὴν ὁ στέφανος μειδιᾷ, τὸ δὲ ξίφος φόνον γεννᾷ· βασιλέως ἐπαγλαΐζει με χείρ, καὶ δημίου χεὶρ ἀπειλεῖ. Ποῖος Τελχὶν ταῦτα καθ᾽ ἡμῶν

not a rightful child of Daedalus, has belied his father's wisdom: he entrusts the wax to the rays and, under attack from the Sun, will certainly shed his feathers. But what will you do below the earth, you who contrive everything upon the earth? You will meet Minos once again in the house of Hades; you will see him making laws for those in the underworld. He will recognize you as the matchmaker for the bull, and he will vote to approve the proper penalty. Thus the Sun will take his vengeance on you while you are living, and Minos in turn will succeed him after your death.

21

What Xerxes's pilot would say while being crowned and at the same time executed

Alas, I am a sailor and unfortunate at sea! Alas, I am the plaything of a strange fortune! Xerxes pushes me away and in turn draws me close; he hits me and embraces me; he snatches me from the sea and throws me into the hands of the executioner; he honors me with a tiara and cuts off my head. The gleam of the sword destroys the sparkling of the stones; the crown smiles and brings pleasure, but the sword begets murder; the king's hand honors me, while the executioner's threatens. What sort of Telchis insults me in this

εἰρωνεύεται; Ποῖος δαίμων τηλικαύτην τραγῳδίαν ἐπέχρισε γέλωτι; Τίς μοι τοιαύτην ἐκεράσατο κύλικα, ὀλίγον
μὲν ἐπιστάξας τοῦ μέλιτος, ὅλην δὲ ἀψινθίαν θανάτου
ἐπεγχεάμενος; Τίς μοι τοιοῦτον ἐπλέξατο στέφανον, ὡς ἐκ
ῥόδων μὲν στίλβοντα καὶ ὡς ἐξ ἀκανθῶν αἱμάσσοντα;
Ὅσην προβέβληται τὴν αἱμασιάν! Ἡλίκα περιφρίσσει τὰ
κέντρα! Λειμών τις οὗτος ἄτης καὶ πλέγμα Κηρῶν καὶ
Τελχίνων ἀπαρχὴ καὶ Πλούτωνος στέφανος. Βοῦν τις
οὕτω στέψας παρὰ βωμὸν ἐστήσατο καὶ θεοῖς σωτῆρσιν
ἐκαλλιέρησεν. Ἱερεῖον ἄρα Ἐριννύων ἐγὼ καὶ δαιμόνων
ἀλαστόρων ἱερεὺς ὁ δήμιος;

2   Ἀθλοθέτην ἀπόπληκτον δυστυχῶ, τύχης καινὸν
ἀεθλεύω παγκράτιον. Ὦ Ξέρξη τὰ πάντα παλίμβολε, ὦ καὶ
θάλατταν ἀπογαιώσας καὶ ἤπειρον ἐκπελαγώσας καὶ νῦν
σοφοῦ κυβερνήτου τύχην μετασκευάσας καὶ καινοτομήσας
τὰ ἀπροσδόκητα, τί τὸν ἀριστέα θαυμάζεις, εἰ τὰς χεῖρας
ἀφελεῖν ἐμελέτησας; Τί τὸν σταδιοδρόμον ἀνακηρύττεις,
εἰ τοῖς ποσὶν ἐπεβούλευσας; Γλῶτταν τίς τέθηπε ῥήτορος
καὶ τὴν πληγὴν μελετᾷ; Σοφὸν τίς κυβερνήτην ἀποκαλεῖ
καὶ πρὸς ξίφος δήμιον ἀπερράπισεν; Ὦ βασιλεὺς οὗτος
καὶ θαλάττης αὐτῆς ἀγριώτερος! Ἐκείνη μου τὴν τέχνην
ᾐδέσθη καὶ τὸ περὶ τὴν εὔπλοιαν σοφὸν οὐκ ἀπήλεγξεν.
Ὦ θάλαττα καὶ Πόσειδον ἀσφάλιε καὶ Νηρηΐδων χοροὶ
καὶ θεοὶ πάντες ἐνάλιοι, ὑμετέραν ἐγὼ τοῦτο τίθεμαι
νέμεσιν. Ὑμεῖς με τῷ τοῦ βασιλέως ἐτηρήσατε ξίφει, ὑμεῖς
με πρὸς τὴν παροῦσαν συμφορὰν ἀπεταμιεύσασθε. Τί γὰρ
τὸν ἡμέτερον ἐχθρὸν ἔσῳζον; Τί δὲ καθ᾽ ἡμῶν τὰ τῆς
ἡμῶν τέχνης ἐπεδεικνύμην; Ἐμάστιζε θάλατταν καὶ πικρὸν

way? What sort of spirit has stained such a great tragedy with mockery? Who has mixed such a cup of wine for me, first dripping in a bit of honey, then pouring in a full bitter potion of death? Who wove for me such a crown, which gleams as though made from roses, but draws blood as though made from thorns? How great a hedge of thorns it projects! How great are its bristling spikes! This is a meadow of ruin, a wreath of the goddesses of death, the first fruits of the Telchines, the crown of Pluto. After thus placing a wreath on an ox, someone has made it stand before the altar and performed a propitious sacrifice to the salvific gods. Am I then the sacrificial victim to the Erinyes, and is the executioner the priest of avenging spirits?

I am competing in a strange *pancratium* of fortune, and I 2 am unfortunate because the one awarding the prize is out of his mind. O Xerxes, you who reverse all things, you who have turned sea into land and turned land into sea, and now have transformed the fortune of your wise pilot and inaugurated unforeseen events, why do you marvel at your hero if you have set your mind on removing his hands? Why exalt your sprinter if you have plotted against his feet? Who admires the tongue of an orator and then contemplates cutting it out? Who proclaims his pilot wise and then drives him away to the executioner's sword? Alas, this king, more savage than the sea itself! The sea respected my skill and did not refute that I have the wisdom to make a safe voyage. O sea, and Poseidon the protector, and chorus of Nereids, and all you gods of the sea, I consider this to be your vengeance. You preserved me for the king's sword; you safeguarded me for my present hardship. For why did I save my own enemy? Why did I display my skills to my own detriment? Xerxes

ἀπεκάλει καὶ ἁλμυρὸν ποταμόν, οὐκοῦν εὐλόγως ἠγρίαινεν. Ἠδίκει τὸν Ποσειδῶνα καί, θαλάττης ἄρχειν ἐθέλων, οὐκοῦν εἰκότως ἐπεβρυχᾶτο τοῖς κύμασι. Νηρηΐδας εἰς Ἄθω μετῴκισεν, οὐκοῦν δικαίως τὸν σάλον ἡμῖν ἐπωρύοντο. Ἔφθασε καὶ θεοὺς Ἑλληνίους ἐκπολεμῶσαι καὶ τῆς φίλης θεοῖς Ἑλλάδος κακῶς ἀπηλλάττετο. Συντέτριπτο μὲν ὁ μυριόστολος ἐκεῖνος, ἡ δὲ τῶν Περσῶν ὀφρὺς ξυνεθραύετο καὶ τὸ φρόνημα ἔπιπτεν. Φυγὰς δὲ ὁ βασιλεύς, καὶ φυγὰς ἐφ᾽ ἑνὸς πλοίου κλέπτων τὴν διαπεραίωσιν καὶ τοὺς Ἕλληνας ὑφορώμενος βασιλεὺς ὁ πάντα κινῶν, ὁ μέγας, ὁ μυριάνθρωπος.

3   Ἑλλήνιε Ζεῦ καὶ θεοὶ ἐλευθέριοι καὶ Δίκη καὶ Νέμεσις! Ἡ μὲν θάλαττα ὤδινεν ἴσα καὶ ὄρεσι κύματα, ἐπηύλει δὲ ὁ Βορρᾶς ὄρθιον—εἶπεν ἄν τις περισαλπίζειν τὸ ἐνυάλιον— οἱ κάλως ἐτετρίγεσαν, ἡ ναῦς διεταλαντεύετο. Θεοὶ τότε πάντες ἡμῖν ἐπεστράτευσαν· κάτωθεν ἐκύκα τὸ πέλαγος Ποσειδῶν, ἄνωθεν συνῆγε τὰς νεφέλας ὁ Ζεύς· ὁ μὲν ὥσπερ πόλιν τὸ σκάφος ὑπώρυττεν, ὁ δ᾽ ὡς ἐκ μετεώρων ἠκροβολίζετο. Πολιορκία τίς ἦν τὸ πρᾶγμα καὶ πόλεμος ἄφυκτος; Θεοί τε ἐστρατήγουν καὶ ὁ μεγάλαυχος Ξέρξης πανταχόθεν ἐβάλλετο· ἐπὶ θαλάττης ἠτύχησεν, οὐκ ἐθάρρει τὴν ἤπειρον, φεύγειν ἐξ Ἑλλάδος ὥρμητο. Καὶ τὰ δεινὰ πάλιν ὑφείπετο· στρόμβος πνευμάτων, ῥόχθος κυμάτων, σατραπῶν ἀποβολή, βασιλέως φυγή, πάντα Περσῶν ἀτυχήματα. Ὁρᾷ τὸν κίνδυνον, πυνθάνεται τὴν τῶν κακῶν λύσιν, μανθάνει τὴν σωτηρίαν, ἡ δὲ ἦν ἄχθους ἀποβολὴ καὶ νεὼς κουφισμός. Φόρτος δὲ τῆς Περσικῆς μοίρας

whipped the sea and called it a *bitter* and *salty river,* and so the sea reasonably became angry. He wronged Poseidon by wishing also to rule the sea, and so Poseidon naturally roared at him with his waves. He transferred the Nereids to Athos, and so they justly howled at us with the swell of the sea. He managed to make the Greek gods hostile too, and he barely escaped Greece which is dear to the gods. That massive fleet was shattered; the Persians' pride was broken; their ambition was ruined. The king was a fugitive, and a fugitive with a single ship, making his crossing in secret and fearful of the Greeks—the king, who sets everything in motion, the great one, who rules countless men.

Zeus of the Greeks, and gods who grant freedom, both 3 Justice and Nemesis! The sea was in travail with waves as high as mountains, the North Wind provided accompaniment with its high-pitched wail (one would say that it was sounding the call to war), the ropes creaked, and the ship rocked back and forth. Then all the gods made war against us: from below Poseidon stirred up the sea, while from above Zeus gathered the clouds, the one undermining the vessel as if it were a city, the other firing from afar as though from the heights. What siege was this event, and what inescapable war? The gods were waging war, and vainglorious Xerxes was beset on all sides. Unsuccessful upon the sea and without confidence on land, he hastened to flee from Greece. And again his troubles followed him: the swirl of winds, the roaring of waves, the loss of the satraps, the flight of the king, and all the misfortunes of the Persians. He sees the danger, inquires about a solution to our troubles, and learns the method of our salvation: the jettisoning of our load and the lightening of the ship. The cargo was all the

ὅσον ἀπόλεκτον. Ἐντεῦθεν οἱ μὲν εἰς θάλατταν ἀπεσφεν-
δονῶντο πάντες αὐτόβουλοι, ἐγὼ δὲ διεκυβερνώμην τῷ
μὲν δοκεῖν τὴν ναῦν εἰς ἤπειρον, τὸ δ' ἀληθὲς ἐμαυτὸν εἰς
Ἀχέροντα.

4   Ἔξεισι τῆς νεὼς ὁ βασιλεύς, ἐπιβαίνει τῆς γῆς, θαρρεῖ
τὸ ἀπὸ τοῦδε καὶ σοφῷ κυβερνήτῃ τῆς προμηθείας
μνησικακεῖ. "Τί γάρ," φησι, "μὴ καὶ τοὺς σατράπας περι-
εσώσω; Οἷς μὲν οὖν βασιλέως ἐγεγόνεις σωτήρ, στέφου
τὰ βασιλέως καὶ γέρας ἔχε βασίλειον. Οἷς δὲ σατραπῶν
ὅλην ἐζημίωσας φάλαγγα, προσαποζημιοῦ καὶ σὺ τὸ ζῆν
παρ' ἡμῶν. Ἐγώ σοι καὶ κρᾶμα τύχης ἐπιτεχνάσομαι, οἷς
τὸ καλὸν οὐκ ἐφύλαξας ἄκρατον." Τί φής, ὦ βασιλεῦ;
Χάριτας ὀφείλων, ἐπισείεις τὸ ξίφος, φοβεῖς τὸν φόβους
θαλαττίους λύσαντα. Τοιαῦτά σοι πρὸς ἐμὲ τὰ σῶστρα τὸν
σοφόν, τὸν σωτῆρα, τὸν κυβερνήτην; Οὐ ταῦτα ἐκάλεις
πρὸ μικροῦ, κύματα ὁρῶν ἐπαφρίζοντα καὶ θάλατταν
ζέουσαν; Ἦπου καὶ στήλην ἐπεγείρεις καὶ σπείσεις
φιλοτιμότερον. Ἀλλὰ τί καὶ προσεπιγράψεις τῷ σήματι;
"Ἐνταῦθα κεῖται βασιλέως σωτὴρ καὶ πεσόντα Ξέρξης
τιμᾷ." Πρόσθες, ὦ βασιλεῦ, παρ' ὅτου καὶ πέπτωκε· "πρὸς
αὐτοῦ Ξέρξου τῆς δωρεᾶς" (Ἄπολλον ἀποτρόπαιε καὶ θεοὶ
ἀλεξίκακοι!), τοῦ δι' ἐκεῖνον περισωθέντος, τοῦ περιόντος
ἔτι, τοῦ μὴ πεσόντος, τοῦ μὴ ναυαγήσαντος.

5   "Τί γὰρ μὴ καὶ τοὺς σατράπας τῷ βασιλεῖ συνετήρησας;"
Βίαν μοι λέγεις θαλάττης, καιροῦ μοι λέγεις ἀνάγκην,
κυμάτων ἀπειλήν, πνευμάτων ἐπίθεσιν, δαιμόνων ἐπιβουλήν, τύχης ἐπήρειαν. Σύ μοι δοκεῖς μηδ' ἂν φυτηκόμον

elite members of the Persian contingent. And so all the men hurled themselves into the sea of their own will, and I imagined I was steering the ship toward land, but really I was steering myself to the Acheron.

The king disembarks from the ship, steps upon the land, takes courage immediately, and rebukes his wise pilot for his foresight. "Why did you not preserve the satraps as well?" he asks. "Because you were the savior of the king, be crowned in a regal fashion, and receive a royal gift of honor. But since you caused the loss of an entire phalanx of satraps, you should also forfeit your own life by my hand. I will in turn devise a mixed fortune for you, because you did not preserve my good fortune unmixed." What are you saying, O king? You owe thanks, but you brandish your sword, and you strike fear into the one who freed you from fear at sea. Is this the sort of reward for saving your life that you give to me, your wise man, your savior, your pilot? Did you not call me by these epithets a short time ago, when you saw the waves foaming and the sea boiling? Perhaps you will erect a column and pour a very generous libation. But what will you add as an inscription on my gravestone? "Here lies the savior of the king, and Xerxes honors the one who has died." Add also, O king, at whose hand he died: "by the gift of Xerxes himself" (O Apollo, averter of evil, and gods, defenders against troubles!), Xerxes, who was saved because of him, who still lives, who has not died, who did not suffer a shipwreck.

"For why did you not preserve the satraps for the king?" You acknowledge to me the violence of the sea; you acknowledge to me the pressure of the moment, the threat of the waves, the assault of the winds, the conspiracy of the evil spirits, the abuse of fortune. I suppose that you would

αἰνεῖν, ὅς ἐστιν οὗ καὶ τῶν κλάδων ἐνίους μαραινομένους ἀπέτεμε, συνθνήσκειν οὐκ ἐῶν τὰ λειπόμενα, οὐδ' ἂν ἀριστέα θαυμάσεις, εἴ τί που τοῦ σώματος τέτρωται. Μαρδόνιε, δίχα τραυμάτων καὶ φόνου Περσῶν σπεῦδε νικᾶν Ἕλληνας, οὐ γὰρ ἂν φθάνοις ὑπὸ Ξέρξου κτεινόμενος. Καὶ τῶν Ἀσκληπιαδῶν οἱ σοφώτεροι, μικρὰ τὰ πρῶτα λυπήσαντες, μειζόνως ἐσύστερον θέλγουσιν. Ἐκεῖνοι καὶ ἄρθρα ποδῶν ὑπεκκαίουσιν, ἵνα τὴν κεφαλὴν περισώσαιντο, πόδας καὶ νῦν παρ' ἐμοῦ τὰ Περσῶν ἐζημίωται καὶ τὴν κεφαλὴν ἀπεκέρδανε. Σατράπας προὔδωκα καὶ βασιλέα κλύδωνος καὶ ναυαγίου ἀφήρπασα.

6   Μηκέτι θαρρεῖτε, ὦ ναυτίλοι, τὴν γῆν, μηκέτι πτοεῖσθε τὰ κύματα. Θαλάττης οὐ γεγόναμεν ἔργον καὶ κακοπραγοῦμεν περὶ τὴν ἤπειρον. Τίς ἡμῶν κακοδαιμονέστερος, παρ' οἷς ὕποπτα καὶ τὰ εὐτυχήματα; Νῦν μὲν ἔχω τῆς ἀριστείας τὴν ἀμοιβήν—τοὺς λίθους, τὴν τιάραν, τὸν στέφανον—ἐπικρέμαται δέ μοι τὸ ξίφος ἑτέρωθι, μικρὸν ἤδη καὶ τὰ ἐπιθανάτια ἐπορχήσομαι καὶ σκηνοβατήσω τὰ ὕστατα. Τίς οὕτω ταχὺ κύβος μετακεκύβευται; Τίς οὕτω σφαῖρα θᾶττον μετακεκύλισται; Ἧπου καὶ διήγημα τοῖς πολλοῖς ἀπιστούμενον ἔσομαι. Τάχα μοι καὶ οἱ ἐν Ἅιδου θαυμάσονται καὶ πυνθανομένοις ἐρῶ πάντα καὶ διηγήσομαι τὴν τῶν Περσῶν ἧτταν, τὴν τῶν Ἑλλήνων τόλμαν, τὸν ἐξ Ἑλλάδος δρασμόν, τὸν ἐκ θαλάττης φόβον, τὴν ἐμὴν ἐπὶ τούτοις προμήθειαν, τὴν τῶν σατραπῶν ἀποβολήν, τὴν τοῦ βασιλέως ἀπόνοιαν, τὴν ἐντεῦθεν σφαγὴν καὶ ἐπὶ πᾶσι τὸν στέφανον.

not even praise the vinedresser who here and there cuts away some of the withering branches and prevents the remaining ones from dying along with them, nor would you admire a hero, if he bears a wound somewhere on his body. Mardonius, hasten to conquer the Greeks without suffering wounds or the murder of Persians, for you will not escape death by Xerxes. Even the very wise sons of Asclepius, though they cause a little pain at first, later charm us to a greater extent. Those men cauterize the joints of the legs so as to preserve the head, and so now the Persian side has lost its legs but has preserved its head, thanks to me. I surrendered the satraps and snatched the king from rough seas and shipwreck.

No longer take courage in the land, O sailors, and no 6 longer fear the waves. We were not victims of the sea, but we fare badly on dry land. Who is more ill-fated than us, for whom even good fortune is suspect? Now I possess the reward for my heroism—the precious stones, the tiara, the crown—but on the other side the sword hangs over me, and soon I will perform the dance of death and act my final scene. What die so quickly changes its toss? What ball so swiftly rolls the other way? Perhaps I will become a tale disbelieved by most. Perhaps even those in Hades will marvel at my story, and I will tell them everything when they inquire, narrating the defeat of the Persians, the daring of the Greeks, our flight from Greece, our fear of the sea, my foresight in these matters, the casting overboard of the satraps, the senselessness of the king, the slaughter that followed, and, above all, the crown.

RHETORICAL EXERCISES OF NIKEPHOROS BASILAKES

22

Τίνας ἂν εἴποι λόγους Ἔρως,
ἰδὼν δρυτόμον ἐπιχειροῦντα
τέμνειν τὴν Μύρραν
ἔτι ἐγκυμονοῦσαν τὸν Ἄδωνιν

Ἐπίσχες, ὦ δρυτόμε, τὴν ἀξίνην, ἐπίσχες, μὴ θῆγε κατὰ
Μύρρας τὸν σίδηρον. Οὐ δρῦς ἐστι Πανὸς ὀρείου φυτόν,
ἵν' ἢ καὶ δρυτόμοις ἐγκείμενον εἰς τομήν· οὐ μελία φίλον
Ἄρεϊ δένδρον, ἵν' ὑπὸ σιδήρου τέμνοιτο καὶ εἰς αἰχμὴν
αὖθις ὁπλίζοιτο· ἀλλ' Ἔρωτος δρᾶμα καὶ Ἀφροδίτης
σκηνὴ καὶ κόρη καλὴ προσωπεῖον ὑποδῦσα φυτοῦ. Δέδιε
πατρὸς ἀπειλὴν καὶ φύσιν ἀναίσθητον σχηματίζεται. Τί
γίνῃ καὶ Θείαντος χαλεπώτερος; Τί κατὰ κόρης ἁπαλῆς
οὕτω τραχὺν ἀνατείνεις τὸν σίδηρον; Φείδου τῶν ὁσίων
Ἔρωτος, τίμα τὸν Ὑάκινθον, μὴ τέμνε τὸν Νάρκισσον,
οὓς φύσις ἠγλάϊσεν, οὓς Ἔρως ἐφυτηκόμησε. Σέβου τὴν
Δάφνην τὴν καλήν, τὴν μαντικήν, τὴν Ἀπόλλωνος, τὴν ἐξ
Ἔρωτος.

2   Ἂν ὄψει *μηλέαν ἀγλαόκαρπον,* μετ' Ἀφροδίτης τοῦ
χρυσοῦ μήλου μέμνησο καὶ τῆς ὥρας θαύμαζε τὴν ὀπώραν
καὶ προσκύνει τὸν Ἔρωτα. Ἂν ὄψει τὸν Ἀσσύριον φοίνικα,
μάνθανε καὶ φυτὸν πρὸς Ἀφροδίτην οὐκ ἀναίσθητον. Ἂν
δὲ καὶ Μύρραν ἴδῃς, ἐντεῦθεν παρείσθω καὶ χείρ, ἀφείσθω

280

22

What Love would say when he sees a woodcutter attempting to chop down Myrrha while she was still pregnant with Adonis

Hold your ax, O woodcutter! Hold on! Do not whet the blade against Myrrha! It is not an oak, a tree of Pan who lives in the mountains, to be chopped down by woodcutters, nor is it an ash, a tree dear to Ares, to be cut down with the blade and then furnished, in turn, with a point. But it is a drama of Love, a stage for Aphrodite, a beautiful girl who put on the mask of a tree. She fears her father's threat and has assumed a nature that feels nothing. Why should you become even harsher than Theias? Why do you apply such a harsh blade to a tender girl? Spare those who are pious toward Love: honor Hyacinthus and do not cut Narcissus, both of whom nature has glorified and Love has cultivated. Respect Daphne, the beautiful, the oracular, the tree of Apollo, transformed by Love.

If you see *an apple tree with its beautiful fruit,* recall Aphro- 2 dite and the golden apple, marvel at the beauty of the fruit, and venerate Love. If you see the Assyrian date palm, note that it too is a tree not without feeling for Aphrodite. And if you should see Myrrha, let your hand relax, let the blade

καὶ σίδηρος· μικρὸν ἑρκίον ἐκτὸς ὁ φλοιός, ἀλλ᾽ ἔνδον
μέγας κάλλους λειμὼν ὑπανθεῖ. Ἔρως ὁ σοφὸς ἐγὼ καὶ
δρᾶμα μελετῶ φιλοτήσιον, Ἔρως ὁ δεινὸς ἐγὼ καὶ καλός,
ὁ νέος ἅμα καὶ παλαιός, ὁ τοξεύων ἅμα καὶ μειδιῶν, ἵν᾽ ᾖ
καὶ τὸ λυποῦν οὐκ ἀνέραστον καὶ τὸ σαῖνον οὐκ ἄλυπον.
Οἴνῳ τουτὶ τὸ φυτὸν ἐμόσχευσα καὶ καρπὸν οἴσει πυρὸς
Ἀφροδισίου λόχευμα. Ἡ μήτηρ Ἀφροδίτη τὸν κρατῆρα
τοῦτον πίεται καὶ τῶν Ἄρεος παιδικῶν ἐπιλήσεται. Οὕτω
τῆς μητρὸς ἐγὼ κατορχήσομαι, οὕτω καταπολεμήσω τὸν
Ἄρεα.

3   Καλὴ μὲν οὖν ἡ Μύρρα· καλὸς δὲ ὁ πατὴρ καὶ τῆς
παιδὸς οὐκ ἐλείπετο, ἀλλ᾽ ἐτήρει τοὺς τῆς φύσεως θεσμοὺς
καὶ τοὺς ἐμοὺς οὐ προσίετο. Ἠγνόει δέ, ὡς καὶ φύσιν
Ἔρως παράγει καὶ γένος ἅπαν ἐξ Ἔρωτος. Ζεὺς μὲν πατὴρ
ἀνδρῶν τε θεῶν τε, ἐγὼ δὲ καὶ αὐτοῦ Διὸς προπάτωρ καὶ
Κρόνου ἀρχαιότερος καὶ Οὐρανοῦ ἀρχαιογονώτερος.
Κλῆρος μὲν Διὸς οὐρανός, Ποσειδῶνος δὲ θάλαττα καὶ
Ἅιδης ἄρχει τῶν ὑπὸ γῆν. Ξυνάμα δὲ πάντων ἐγὼ καὶ θεὸς
πανδαμάτωρ γνωρίζομαι, ὡς πτερωτὸς ἄφυκτος, ὡς τοξότης ἀνίκητος, ὡς λαμπαδοῦχος ἀλάθητος. Δίειμι πάντα τῷ
πτερῷ, βάλλω τοῖς βέλεσι, κἄν τις ὑπὸ σκότον πειρῷτο
κρύπτεσθαι, ἀκάματόν μοι τὸ πῦρ καὶ θηρῶμαι τὸν φεύ-
γοντα.

4   Ἠγνόει ταῦτα ἐκεῖνος, θεοὺς ὁμογνίους ἠδεῖτο, Δία
προὔτίθει πατρῷον, ὑπὸ παρθενῶνι τὴν παῖδα ἐφρούρει
καὶ τὸ καλὸν ἐφ᾽ ἑστίας ἔχων ἠμέλει. Οὐχ ὡς κόρην
ἐραστὴς προσέβλεπεν, ἀλλ᾽ ὡς παῖδα πατὴρ ἐθαλάμευε.
Σύμμαχον ἐπὶ τούτοις δίδωμι τῇ κόρῃ τὸν Βάκχον καὶ

spare her. Her bark is a thin covering on the outside, but inside there blooms a great meadow of beauty. I, the wise Love, rehearse a drama of love, I, the clever and beautiful Love, who am both young and old, who both shoots the bow and smiles, so that what causes pain is not without love and what brings gladness is not without pain. I planted this very tree with wine and it will bear as fruit a child of Aphrodite's fire. My mother, Aphrodite, will drink from this mixing bowl and will forget her lover, Ares. So will I dance in triumph over my mother; so will I make war upon Ares.

Myrrha, then, was beautiful, and her father was no less 3 beautiful than his daughter, but he obeyed the laws of nature and did not comply with mine. He was ignorant of how Love brings forth nature and how all creation comes from Love. Zeus is the father of both men and gods, but I am the forefather of Zeus himself, more ancient than Cronus, more primal than Uranus. Zeus received the sky as his lot, Poseidon the sea, and Hades rules the underworld. But I rule all these places together and am known as the god who dominates everyone, as the inescapable winged one, the invincible archer, the all-seeing torchbearer. I go everywhere with my wings and shoot my arrows, and if anyone should attempt to hide himself in darkness, my fire never grows weary, and I hunt down the fugitive.

But that man, Theias, was ignorant of this: he showed 4 reverence for the gods who protect the family, putting ancestral Zeus before all, shielding his daughter in the maidens' apartment, and neglecting the beauty that he had in his house. He did not look upon the girl as a lover would, but as a father he kept his daughter locked away. In response, I made Bacchus an ally of the girl and divided the war with a

διπλῷ πυρὶ μερίζω τὸν πόλεμον, ἵνα καὶ παῖς ἱμέρῳ πατρὸς τὴν ψυχὴν ὑπεκκάοιτο καὶ πατὴρ σωφρονῶν οἴνῳ πρὸς τῆς παιδὸς ἐκβακχεύοιτο. Ἐπεὶ δέ μοι καὶ πέρας εἶχεν ὁ πόλεμος, αὐτὴν τὴν κόρην ἵστημι τρόπαιον καί τις, φυτὸν τὴν Μύρραν ταύτην ἰδών, τῆς μάχης ταύτης μεμνήσεται καὶ θαυμάσει τὸν στρατηγήσαντα.

5   Εἶτ᾿ οὐ δέδιας, ἀγρότα, θεοῦ μεγάλου τρόπαιον ἀνασπῶν; Εἶτ᾿ οὐχ ὑφορᾷ τὸ τόξον θεοῦ φιλομύθου καὶ τοξότου μῦθον οὕτω καλὸν πειρώμενος ἐκτεμεῖν; Ἀδικεῖς, Ἄρες, καὶ πρὸ τῆς ὠδῖνος τὸ βρέφος ζηλοτυπῶν, ἀδικεῖς αὐτῇ τῇ μητρὶ καὶ πρὸ βλάστης τὸν παῖδα ῥιζοτομῶν. Τί χεῖρα δενδροτόμον εἰς μιαιφονίαν ὁπλίζεις; Ἀνελεῖς, εὖ οἶδα, τὸν Ἄδωνιν, ἀνελεῖς, ἀλλὰ μετὰ γένεσιν, ἀλλ᾿ ὑπ᾿ Ἀφροδίτης ἐρώμενον καὶ τὴν ἡλικίαν μειρακιούμενον. Τότε δή σε περικνίσει καὶ τὸ ζηλότυπον, ἵνα καὶ τὴν Ἀφροδίτην ἄκανθα καὶ τὸ ῥυὲν αἷμα εἰς πορφύραν βάψῃ τὸ ῥόδον. Δεῖ γὰρ ἐκ θεῶν καὶ θεορρύτου αἵματος τὰ πάντα φῦναι κάλλιστα, ἐν θεοῖς μὲν Ἀφροδίτην, ἐν ζῴοις δὲ ἄνθρωπον, τὸ δὲ ῥόδον ἐν ἄνθεσι. Τότε καὶ ἀποκτενεῖς τὸν ἀντεραστὴν καὶ ἀμυνῇ τὴν ἐρωμένην καὶ γενήσῃ βροτολοιγὸς οὐκ ἀμφίβολος. Ὡς νῦν γέ σοι καὶ τὸ ἀνδροφόνον εἰς δενδροτομίαν μεταπεσεῖται, καὶ ζημιώσεις σεαυτὸν μὲν ἀρχαῖον ὄνομα καὶ φίλον, ἐμὲ δὲ τὸ πάγκαλον τοῦτο δρᾶμα καὶ μέγα, τὰς Χάριτας δὲ τὸ βρέφος, τὴν Ἀφροδίτην δὲ τὸν πόθον, τὴν ὥραν δὲ τὸ ῥόδον, τὰς Μούσας δὲ τὴν ᾠδήν. Ἀλλ᾿ οὔ σοι καὶ Μοιρῶν ἐφεῖται κρατεῖν καὶ τροποῦσθαι τὸν Ἔρωτα· δεῖ γάρ με καὶ τῇ μητρὶ τῶν βελῶν ἐπαφεῖναι, ἵν᾿ εἴσηται, οἷον ἔτεκε. Διὰ

double fire, so that the child would burn in her soul with desire for her father, and her father, though chaste, would be
driven by wine to a frenzy for his daughter. And when the
war devised by me had reached its conclusion, I set up the
girl herself as a trophy, and so anyone who sees this Myrrha
in the form of a tree will recall this battle and marvel at its
general.

So then, rustic woodsman, do you have no fear as you pull ₅
down the trophy of a great god? Are you not wary of the bow
of Love, the myth-loving god, as you attempt to cut down so
fine a myth of the archer? You, Ares, are acting unjustly, if
you are jealous of the infant even before it is born; you are
acting unjustly by uprooting the child along with his mother
even before he sprouts. Why do you arm his tree-cutting
hand for murder? You will kill Adonis—I know it well—you
will kill him, but not until after his birth, after he reaches
adolescence, when he becomes the beloved of Aphrodite.
Then jealousy will gnaw at you, so that the thorn will prick
Aphrodite and her flowing blood will dye the rose bright
red. For everything that comes from the gods and their divinely flowing blood must grow to be most beautiful: among
the gods, Aphrodite; among living beings, the human; and
among flowers, the rose. Then you will kill your rival in love,
you will defend your beloved, and you will become an un-
mistakable misery for humans. But if you act now, your man-
slaughter will transform into tree-cutting, and you will cause
yourself to lose your ancient and dear reputation, me to lose
this splendid and great drama, the Graces to lose the infant,
Aphrodite to lose her passion, springtime to lose its rose,
the Muses to lose their song. But you are not permitted to
conquer the Fates and to rout Love. For I must shoot my
mother with my arrows, so that she may know what sort of

ταῦτα καὶ φυτὸν ἐξ ἀνθρώπου παρήγαγον καὶ αὖθις ἀπὸ φυτοῦ μαιεύσομαι ἄνθρωπον.

23

Τίνας ἂν εἴποι λόγους ὁ Ἄδραστος, νικησάντων Θηβαίων καὶ μὴ ἐώντων ταφῆναι τοὺς πεσόντας Ἀργείους

Ὦ δυστυχοῦς στρατείας! Ὦ πονηρῶν νυμφευμάτων! Ἀργεῖοι Θηβαίων ἡττήμεθα, Θηβαίων, ὦ θεοί, τῶν οὐκ ἀκριβῶς Ἑλλήνων, τῶν ἐπηλύδων τῶν ἐκ Φοινίκης. Κεῖται μὲν ὁ τῆς Ἥρας γίγας ἐκεῖνος ὁ Καπανεύς, κεῖται ὁ τῆς Ἀθηνᾶς φίλος Τυδεύς, οἴχεται δὲ ὁ λοιπὸς τῶν ὁπλιτῶν κατάλογος καὶ μετροῦμεν τὰς ἐναντίων πύλας ἀριστέων πτώμασι. Παρ' ἑκάστην Ἀργεῖος ἐφήδρευε λοχαγός, παρ' ἑκάστην καὶ πέπτωκε. Νεκροῖς ἅπαν τὸ πεδίον ἀνθεῖ, γέμει λαφύρων ἡ πόλις. Τρυφῶσιν ἐφ' ἡμῖν, ὦ Ζεῦ, καὶ κειμένοις Θηβαῖοι καί, τὰς ψυχὰς ἀφελόμενοι, φθονοῦσι τοῖς σώμασι καὶ ταφῆς. Μεθ' ἡμᾶς ἐπὶ τὴν φύσιν χωροῦσι, μεθ' ἡμᾶς ἐπὶ τοὺς κοινοὺς τῶν Ἑλλήνων νόμους στρα- τεύονται, οὐδὲ πεσοῦσι τοῖς πολεμίοις σπένδονται. Ἐν θνητοῖς σώμασι καὶ κατὰ θνητῶν ἀθάνατον ἔτι περιφέρουσι

child she bore. Therefore I have made a tree from a human, and in turn I will bring forth a human from a tree.

23

What Adrastus would say after the Thebans were victorious but did not allow the fallen Argives to be buried

Alas, what a disastrous campaign! What evil marriages! We Argives have been defeated by the Thebans, the Thebans—O gods!—who are not really Greeks but outsiders from Phoenicia. Capaneus lies dead, that giant of Hera; Tydeus lies dead, dear to Athena; the remaining host of soldiers is lost, and we count the gates of our enemy by the corpses of our champions. At each gate, an Argive commander lay in wait, and at each gate one also fell. The whole plain blooms with corpses; the city brims with spoils. The Thebans exult over us even as we lie dead, O Zeus, and after taking away our souls, they also begrudge our bodies a tomb. After us, they move against nature; after us, they take the field against the common laws of the Greeks, and they do not make a truce even when their enemies have fallen. In their mortal bodies they still bear their immortal anger

τὸν θυμόν, καὶ ὁ μὲν πόλεμος πέπαυται, Θηβαῖοι δὲ κατ᾽ Ἀργείων ἔτι μεμήνασιν· οὐκ εὐλαβοῦνται τοὺς ὑπὸ γῆν θεούς, οὐκ αἰδοῦνται τοὺς Ἕλληνας, τοὺς οὐκ ἀντιτείνοντας βάλλουσι, τοὺς οὐκ αἰσθανομένους κολάζουσιν, ἐπιπηδῶσι καὶ κειμένοις θηριωδέστερον.

2   Βάρβαρος ὁ τρόπος, ὁ θυμὸς οὐχ Ἑλλήνιος· οὐκ ἦν ἄρα λόγος ἄλλως, ἀπὸ δράκοντος φῦναι Θηβαίους, ἐκείνου τοῦ σπέρματος οὗτος ὁ στάχυς. Ἔτι τῆς θηριωδίας ἀπόζουσι, τηροῦσιν ἔτι τὸν ἰὸν ἐγκαθήμενον ταῖς ψυχαῖς, ζηλοῦσι καὶ μετὰ τὸν ἄνθρωπον τὸν πρόγονον δράκοντα καὶ τοῖς ἀδελφοῖς θηρίοις τὰ τῶν ἀνθρώπων ἐπιρρίπτουσι σώματα. Ἥρα πολιοῦχε καὶ Ἄργους ἔφορε δαῖμον, ἡ σὴ πόλις ἐπ᾽ Ἰσμηνοῦ κεῖται καὶ τὸ Κάδμου χωρίον κατὰ τοῦ τῆς Ἥρας τεμένους χορεύει. Ὁ Ζεὺς ἡμῖν ὁ σὸς πεπολέμηκε, τῆς περὶ τὴν Σεμέλην ἀπάτης ἐμέμνητο καί, τὴν σὴν πόλιν ἐπὶ Θήβης ἑλών, ἄλλο πῦρ ἀντανῆψε κεραύνιον καὶ στρατόπεδον ὅλον ἀνάλωσε. Πυρὶ καὶ σιδήρῳ καὶ λίθοις ἡμᾶς ἐπενείματο καὶ νῦν ἔχουσι τὰς μὲν ψυχὰς οἱ κάτω θεοί, τὰ δ᾽ ὅπλα Θηβαῖοι, θῆρες δὲ τὰ σώματα. Ἐν Θήβαις ἠτυχήσαμεν, ἐπὶ Κιθαιρῶνος πεπτώκαμεν. Ὢ πόλις εὐρεῖα σκηνὴ καὶ πλουτοῦσα ταῖς συμφοραῖς! Ὢ Κιθαιρὼν Ἐριννύων ἄλσος, ὅλα φύων δράματα! Σὺ τὴν ὑπόθεσιν ἡμῖν ἐχορήγησας, ἐπί σοι καὶ τὸ δρᾶμα ὁ δαίμων ἐσκεύασεν.

3   Ἧκεν ἐς Ἄργος, ὡς μὴ ὤφελεν, ὁ σὸς Πολυνείκης ὁ καὶ τὴν γονὴν ἀπαίσιος καὶ τὴν τελευτὴν ἀποτρόπαιος· ἧκε φυγὰς ἀλήτης ἀνέστιος. Ἠιδέσθην ἐπὶ τούτοις τὸν ξένιον· καί, τῆς ὥρας θαυμάσας καὶ τῆς τύχης οἰκτείρας, συνάπτω

against mortal men. And even though the war has ended, the Thebans still rage against the Argives. They do not revere the gods of the underworld; they do not respect the Greeks; they attack those who do not resist them; they punish those who are no longer conscious; they trample even more brutally upon men who lie dead.

Their manner is barbarous, their anger not Greek. The 2 story, then, was not unfounded, that the Thebans were born from a serpent: this is the progeny of that seed. They still reek of brutality; they still preserve the poison that is implanted in their souls; after man they imitate their ancestor-serpent, and they hurl the bodies of humans to their brethren, the wild beasts. O Hera, protector of our city and guardian spirit of Argos, your city lies dead along the river Ismenus, while Cadmus's town dances in the precinct of your temple. Zeus, your Zeus, has made war against us: he remembered how you tricked him with Semele, and, after destroying your people in Thebes, he ignited another fiery lightning bolt and destroyed our entire camp. He attacked us with fire and iron and stones, and now the gods below possess our souls, the Thebans our weapons, the beasts our bodies. We met disaster in Thebes; we fell at Mount Cithaeron. O city, a broad stage, rich in misfortunes! O Cithaeron, grove of the Erinyes, source of all dramas! You produced our play; upon you also the spirit staged our drama.

He came to Argos—would that he had not!—your Poly- 3 nices, ominous in his birth and ill-omened in his death. He came as a refugee, a wanderer, a homeless man. In response, I respected the god of hospitality and, because I marveled at his vigor and took pity on his fortune, I arranged his

πρὸς γάμον τῇ θυγατρί. Ἧκεν ἐξ Αἰτωλίας καὶ Τυδεύς, ἄλλος οὗτος τοῦ τραγικοῦ κόμματος ἄνθρωπος· καί, τυχὼν τῶν αὐτῶν, ἱκέτης ἐπὶ τοῖς αὐτοῖς γίνεται. Ἐπινεύω τοίνυν ἀμφοτέροιν τὴν ξυμμαχίαν καὶ τὴν ἐς τὴν σφῶν αὐτῶν κάθοδον παρεγγυῶμαι θαρρεῖν. Ἀλλ', ὦ Πυθία πρόμαντι, ἀληθῶς ἄρα ἦσθα μαντικοῦ δαίμονος ἔμπνους, θεοῦ μεγάλου πρόσπολος, ἀληθὴς ἔφεδρος τοῦ τῆς Θέμιδος τρίποδος· οἷς γὰρ θηρίων κηδεστὴν γενέσθαι με προὔλεγες, τοῦ μὲν τὴν μιαιφόνον προὔφαινες τύχην, τοῦ δὲ καὶ τὴν ἐκ γένους θηριωδίαν ἀπεμαντεύου καὶ τὴν ἐκ μάχης ἀδελφοκτονίαν τὴν πικράν. Ἐπάρατον τὸ ἀπόπτυστον ἐκεῖνο καὶ ἀμφήριστον τρόπαιον, ὃ καὶ πεσὼν παραλογώτερον ἔστησε, καὶ παρὰ μέρος ἡττηθεὶς ἐτροπώσατο. Κρεῖσσον ἦν μοι θηρίοις ἐκδοῦναι τὰς παῖδας· εἰς ἐμὲ γὰρ ἂν μόνον τὰ τῆς ζημίας ἐνέσκηψε. Νῦν δέ μοι καὶ τὰ κατ' οἶκον λυπρὰ καὶ τὰ τῆς πόλεως οὐκ ἀδάκρυτα. Ἀκούω πατὴρ παίδων, ἀλλὰ δυσγάμων· ἀκούω καὶ κηδεστὴς ἀλλ' οὐκ εὐτυχής, καὶ στρατηγὸς ἀλλ' οὐκ ἀσφαλής. Καίτοι δίκαια μὲν ἐβουλόμην, ἐπὶ δικαίοις δὲ τὰ ὅπλα ἐκίνουν, εἶξαι καὶ Πολυνείκει τὸν ἀδελφὸν τῆς ἀρχῆς καὶ μὴ γένους μὲν κοινωνεῖν, κλήρου δὲ πατρῴου καὶ κοινῆς ἑστίας φθονεῖν. Ταῦτα Θηβαίοις ἐπρεσβευόμην, οὕτως Ἑλληνικῶς ἔστελλον τὸ κηρύκιον· ἐπεὶ δ' ἐκεῖνοι καὶ πρὸς αὐτὴν ἀπεδυσπέτουν τὴν ἀκοήν, ἐνταῦθα καὶ αὐτός, τοὺς λόγους ἀφείς, ἐπὶ τὰ ἔργα ἔβλεψα καί, Δίκῃ καὶ θεοῖς τὸ πᾶν ἐπιτρέψας, κριτὴν καθίζω τὸ ξίφος. Ζεὺς δὲ ἄρα, ὡς ἔοικεν,

betrothal to my daughter. There also came Tydeus from Ae-
tolia, and this man was another of the tragic ilk. Having experienced the same misfortunes, he became a suppliant on
the same terms. I agreed, therefore, to an alliance with both
of them and bid them to have confidence that they would
return to their own lands. But, O prophetic Pythia! Truly
you knew, inspired by an oracular spirit, attendant of a great
god, true occupant of the tripod of Themis, for in foretell-
ing that I would become a father-in-law to beasts, you revealed in advance Tydeus's murderous fortune, and you
prophesied Polynices's innate brutality and the bitter fratri-
cide in battle. Accursed is that despised and contested trophy, which he very strangely erected even though he had
fallen, and which in turn he destroyed by his own defeat. It
would have been better for me to have surrendered my
daughters to actual beasts, for then the penalty would have
fallen on me alone. But as it is, my situation at home is dis-
tressing, and the city's condition is a cause for tears. I am
called a father of children, but badly married children; I am
also called a father-in-law, but not a fortunate one, and a
general, but not one who is in a secure position. However,
my desires were just, and I took up arms for just causes: for
Polynices's brother to yield the throne to him, and not,
while sharing a lineage, at the same time to begrudge him
his father's inheritance and their common hearth. I was in-
terceding with the Thebans about these matters, and thus in
Greek fashion I was sending embassies, but when they lost
patience and declined to listen, then I myself, after giving up
on words, looked to deeds: having entrusted everything to
Justice and the gods, I made the sword sit in judgment of the
matter. But Zeus, so it seems, did not decree precisely and,

οὐκ ἀκριβῶς ἐθεμίστευε καὶ Θηβαίοις οὐ πρὸς δίκην τὰ τῆς Δίκης ἐπρυτάνευσε τάλαντα.

4   Τοῦτο ἦν καὶ ὁ τῆς Δίκης πεττὸς πρὸς τοὺς ἠδικηκότας μετεπεττεύετο, ἔσειε μὲν τὴν αἰγίδα ὁ Ζεύς, ὑπερρήγνυε δὲ τὰς βροντάς. Ἐστόμου τὸ μέγα βέλος, τὸν κεραυνόν, περιεστρόβει τὸ πῦρ καὶ πρηστῆρας ὅλους κατὰ τῶν ἡμετέρων κεφαλῶν ἀπεδίσκευεν. Ἐκάλει δὲ πρὸς ἐπικου-ρίαν τὸν παῖδα τὸν Ἄρεα, φιλαίματον δαίμονα, θεὸν ἀλλο-πρόσαλλον. Τηλικοῦτον ἡμῖν κακὸν ἐπηρτύετο! Ἐμυκᾶτο μὲν ἐρίγδουπον Οὐρανὸς καὶ πρὸ τῶν τοῦ Διὸς ἀκρο-βολισμῶν τὸ ἐνυάλιον ἐπηλάλαξεν. Ἔπνει δὲ θυμοῦ πῦρ ὁ τῶν θεῶν ὕπατος καὶ πᾶν ὅσον ἔμπυρον οὐρανόθεν ἐξ-ηκοντίζετο καὶ ὁ τῆς Ἥρας ἀριστεὺς ὁ μέγας ὁ Καπανεὺς ἀντὶ Σεμέλης, ὡς ἄλλος Τυφώς, ὑπὸ Διὸς ἐβάλλετο. Ἄρης δὲ τὸ ἔγχος ἐνώμα καὶ τὰς τῆς μητρὸς ἐστυφέλιζε φάλαγγας καὶ ὁ τῆς Ἀθηνᾶς ὁπλίτης Τυδεύς, ἀντὶ δράκοντος λίθῳ κατεαγὼς τὴν κεφαλήν, ἐπὶ γῆς ὑπέστρωτο ὕπτιος, ἐξ Ἄρεος ἔκειτο. Πυρὶ πῦρ ἀνθυπεξέκαυσε Ζεὺς καὶ λίθῳ λίθον Ἄρης ἀντεταλάντευσεν, ὁ μὲν τὴν σύνοικον εἰς ἀγαθὸν λοχαγὸν ἀντὶ τῆς ἐρωμένης ἐλύπησεν, ὁ δὲ τὴν ἀδελφὴν ἀντὶ φιλίου θηρὸς οὐκ ἀγεννῆ στρατηγὸν ἐζη-μίωσεν. Οὐδὲ Ποσειδῶν τῆς μάχης ταύτης ἐλείπετο, ἀλλὰ συνεστρατεύετο καὶ αὐτὸς τἀδελφῷ καὶ καθ' ἡμῶν ἐκίνει τὴν τρίαιναν καὶ τῶν ἐπ' Ἀμυμώνῃ παιδικῶν τῶν αὐτοῦ τοὺς ἐπὶ Σεμέλῃ Διὸς προὔθηκεν ἔρωτας· ὅλην πόλεως φίλης ἧτταν καταψηφίζεται, ἵν' ἀδελφὸν εὐφράνῃ βαρύμη-νιν. Γῆ δὲ τὸ στόμα περιεβόθρευε καὶ πλατὺν ὑπέχαινε φάρυγγα, οὐχ ἵνα πολυδιψίῳ πόλει πηγή τις ἀναρροιβδήσῃ

to the Thebans' benefit, did not manage the scales of Justice justly.

So it happened, and Justice's game piece was moved in favor of those who had acted unjustly. Zeus shook his goatskin shield and rent the sky with his thunder. He steeled his great missile, the lightning bolt, set fire spinning, and hurled entire storms against our heads. He summoned as reinforcement his son Ares, a bloodthirsty spirit, a fickle god. Such a great evil he prepared for us! Uranus bellowed with thunder and raised the war cry before Zeus began his skirmishing. The highest of the gods breathed forth angry fire, and all that burns was hurled down from heaven. Hera's champion, the great Capaneus, in retribution for Semele, was attacked by Zeus as another Typhoeus. *Ares was wielding the spear* and assaulting his mother's phalanxes. Athena's soldier, Tydeus, his head broken by a stone in repayment for the killing of the serpent, was stretched out on his back on the ground, lying dead by the hand of Ares. Zeus ignited fire upon fire, and Ares weighed stone against stone: Zeus made his wife Hera grieve for the death of a good commander in retribution for the death of his beloved Semele, and Ares deprived his sister Athena of a noble general in retribution for the killing of his cherished beast, the serpent. Nor was Poseidon absent from this battle, but he himself took the field alongside his brother Zeus. He wielded his trident against us and put Zeus's love for Semele ahead of his own affection for Amymone: he condemned his own city to utter defeat in order to please his deeply enraged brother. And the earth carved out a trench like a mouth and gaped underneath with a broad throat, not so that some stream of water, issuing

πολύκρουνος καὶ διειδής, γλυκέος Ἔρωτος ξύμβολον, ἀλλ᾽
ἵνα στρατιώτης Ἀργεῖος αὐτοῖς ὅπλοις καταποθήσεται. Ὦ
πονηρᾶς ταύτης αὔλακος! Ἣν οὐ γηπόνος ἐπήσκησεν,
οὐκ ἐπόλευε βοῦς, οὐ περιελάκισεν ἄροτρον, τῇ τριαίνῃ δὲ
διέστησε Ποσειδῶν καὶ μάντιν σοφὸν ἀντὶ σπέρματος
ἐγκατέχωσεν.

5   Ὦ γῆς καὶ φυούσης ὁπλίτας παράδοξα καὶ αὖθις ἀπο-
κρυπτούσης ἀνέλπιστα! Ὦ γῆς, ἐφ᾽ ἧς οὐδὲ θεοὶ κακῶν
ἀκήρατοι! Θηβαῖος ἦν Διόνυσος καὶ θεὸς προσγενής, ἀλλ᾽
οὐκ ἦν αἵματος ὁμογνίου καθαρός, οἷς μητέρα κατὰ παιδὸς
ἐβάκχευσε. Θηβαῖος ἦν Ἡρακλῆς, ἀλλ᾽ εἰς τὸ γένος ἐλύτ-
τησε καί, τοῖς παισὶ τὰς χεῖρας ἐπιβαλών, τὸ Θηβαῖος εἶναι
τοῖς κακοῖς ἐβεβαίωσε. Τοῦτον, οἴμοι, καὶ Πολυνείκης
ἐπλήρωσε τὸν κατάλογον καί, τοῦ γένους ἡμῖν κοινωνήσας,
καὶ τῆς τύχης μετέδωκεν. Οἴους θεοὺς ἐφ᾽ ἡμᾶς αὐτοὺς
ἐκινήσαμεν! Ἡλίκους ἐκπεπολεμώκαμεν δαίμονας! Ζεὺς
τὸν καταιβάτην μετεχειρίζετο, Ἄρης ἔθηγε σίδηρον,
Ποσειδῶν τὴν γῆν ἀνεμόχλευε, πάντα ἦν ἡμῖν ἄπορα καὶ
μαχομένοις καὶ δραπετεύουσιν. Ἠνδρίζετό τις Ἀργεῖος καὶ
τὰ μεγάλα παρεκινδύνευεν, ἀλλ᾽ Οὐρανὸς αὐτῷ τῆς ψυχῆς
τὸ σιδήρεον εἰς φυγὴν τῷ πυρὶ κατεμάλθαξεν. Ἀπεδραπέ-
τευέ τις οὐ θαρρῶν διὰ πολέμιον, ἀλλ᾽ ἡ γῆ τοῦτον αὖθις
ἐπέδησε καὶ λόχος βαθὺς ἦν ὁ βόθρος καὶ πάγη τις
ἄφυκτος. Οὐκ οἶδεν ὁ μάντις τὰ ἐν ποσί· Ζεὺς γὰρ αὐτῷ
συνεθόλου τὸ μαντικόν. Ἧπου καὶ νῦν τῆς Ἥρας κατ-
ειρωνεύεται· οὐκ ἦν μόνος ὁ Ζεύς, οὐκ εἰδὼς ἐν Θήβαις ὅ
τι καὶ πείσεται, ἀλλὰ καὶ φίλος Ἥρας μάντις, ἐξ ἀγνοίας

clear from many springs, would gush forth for a parched city, a symbol of sweet Love, but so that an Argive soldier would be swallowed up, weapons and all. Alas, this evil furrow! No farmhand worked it, no ox turned it, no plow dug it, but Poseidon opened it with his trident and buried within it a wise prophet instead of a seed.

Alas, the land, which strangely caused soldiers to spring 5 up and in turn hid them away unexpectedly! Alas, the land, in which not even gods are untouched by evils! Dionysus was a Theban and born a god, but he was not untainted by his family's blood, for he caused a mother to rage against her son. Heracles was a Theban, but he raged insanely against his family and, by attacking his children with his own hands, confirmed by his evil actions that he was a Theban. Even Polynices—alas!—filled out this roster, and when he joined our family, he also gave us a share of his fortune. Such gods we brought upon ourselves! Such great spirits we have made hostile to ourselves! Zeus wielded the thunderbolt; Ares whetted his blade; Poseidon forced open the earth; and we were at a complete loss regardless of whether we fought or fled. One Argive took courage and dared great deeds, but Uranus softened the iron of his soul with fire and turned him to flight. Another Argive, Amphiaraus, lost heart in the face of the enemy and began to flee, but the earth in turn held him fast: its pit was a deep ambush, an inescapable snare. Our seer Amphiaraus did not know what was right in front of him, for Zeus was clouding his prophetic vision. Perhaps even now Zeus is mocking Hera. For Zeus was not alone in not knowing what would happen in Thebes, but even Hera's beloved seer did not know, and so he died in accordance with his ignorance. He did not know that he was

πίπτων. Ὡς τοῦτό γε τὸ μέρος ἐκεῖνος ηὐτύχησεν, αὐτῷ σώματι τὴν γῆν ὑποδὺς καὶ φυγὼν τὴν Θηβαίων ὠμότητα. Ὡς, εἴθε, καὶ πᾶσι τοῖς πεσοῦσιν Ἀργείων ταύτην ἐκύρωσε τὴν μοῖραν ὁ Ζεύς, νῦν δὲ στρατόπεδον ὅλον κατὰ πεδιάδος ἐφήπλωται καὶ βλέπει τὰ ἀθέατα ἥλιος.

6   Τί δράσω; Τί χρήσομαι τοῖς παροῦσιν; Οὔτε γὰρ περιορᾶν τοὺς οἰκείους οὕτω κειμένους καλὸν καὶ στρατὸν αὖθις ἐγείρειν ἐξ Ἄργους ἄπορον, Θηβαίους τὸ πείθειν ἄλλως ἀμήχανον. Ἐπὶ τὴν τῆς Ἀθηνᾶς πόλιν πορεύσομαι, ἐπὶ τὸν Ἐλέου βαδιοῦμαι βωμόν, ἐπισπείσω καὶ δάκρυα καὶ πείσω δῆμον φιλάνθρωπον. Οἱ δέ μοι τοὺς πολεμίους καταγωνιοῦνται, τοὺς θυμῷ βαρβάρῳ θύοντας, οἱ θεὸν εἰδότες τὸν Ἔλεον, οἱ αὐτόχθονες τοὺς Σπαρτούς, οἱ ἐξ Ἀθηνᾶς τοὺς ἐκ δράκοντος. Ταύτῃ τό γε νῦν ἰτέον, οὕτω τοῖς ἐμοῖς ἐπικουρητέον. Τὰ δ᾽ εἰσέπειτα, Ἥρα τε Ἀργεία καὶ θεοὶ ἐγχώριοι, ἡβήσαιεν οἱ τῶν πεπτωκότων παῖδες, ἴδοιμι τοῖς ὅπλοις ἀνθοῦντας καὶ στρατὸν αὖθις οἰκεῖον ἐπὶ Θήβας ἐλάσαιμι. Ἐκεῖνοι τὴν τελεωτέραν ἡμῖν ἐπικουρίαν δοῖεν καὶ ταχὺ τὴν τοῖς θεοῖς ἐχθρὰν γῆν, τὴν τῶν σπαρτῶν τῶν τοῦ δράκοντος, οἰκείου τε κορέσομεν αἵματος καὶ δείξομεν ἄσπαρτον ἐπὶ μακρόν.

in this respect fortunate in descending below the earth, body and all, and escaping the Thebans' savagery; nor did he know that Zeus, perhaps, decreed this fate for all the fallen Argives, and now he has spread out the whole camp along the plain, and the sun looks down upon what should not be seen.

What am I to do? How will I manage my present circum- 6 stances? For neither is it right to neglect one's own people thus lying dead, nor is it possible to raise an army once again out of Argos, or viable to persuade the Thebans in another way. I will go to the city of Athena; I will proceed to the altar of Mercy; I will make a libation even of tears and persuade a benevolent people. And they, who know Mercy as a god, will contend with me against my enemies, who sacrifice with barbarian anger: they who are autochthonous against the Sown Ones; they who were born from Athena against the ones who grew from a serpent. To this city I must now go. Thus must they come to the aid of my people. As for the sequel, O Argive Hera and you gods of my land, may the sons of the fallen reach manhood, may I see them abounding in weapons, and may I march an army of my people back against Thebes. May the Athenians grant us their complete support, and we will swiftly saturate with the blood of its own people the land hateful to the gods, the land of those sown from the serpent, and we will cause it to be unsown for a long time.

24

Τίνας ἂν εἴποι λόγους Ἰσμηνίας ὁ αὐλητής, βιαζόμενος παρ' Ἀλεξάνδρου ἐπαυλῆσαι τῇ τῶν Θηβαίων καταστροφῇ

Ὦ παῖ Φιλίππου, τίνα ταύτην προὔβαλες τὴν ὑπόθεσιν; Τίνι θεῶν ἀπάρξομαι τῆς ᾠδῆς; Ποῖον ᾄσω μέλος προνόμιον; Θήβας ἐπαινέσομαι καὶ κροτήσω Κάδμον τοῖς μέλεσιν; Ἀλλ' ἡ Κάδμου κεῖται καὶ πέπαυται τὰ Θηβαίων σεμνά. Βάκχον ἐπικαλέσομαι κωμαστὴν θεὸν εὐγενῆ; Ἀλλ' ὁ κῶμος οὗτος ἄγριος καὶ Μακεδόνες ἐπεβάκχευσαν. Ἡρακλέα παιανίσω καλλίνικον τὸν ἡμέτερον ἥρωα, τὸν ἐκ Διός, τὸν τῆς Ἀλκμήνης, τὸν Θήβηθεν; Ἀλλ' οὐκ ἔσθ' ὅτε καὶ Θήβαις ὁ μέγας οὗτος ἥρως ἐπήμυνεν.

2   Ὦ πάλαι μὲν πόλεως εὐτυχοῦς, νῦν δὲ οἰκοπέδου λυπροῦ καὶ δυστυχοῦς! Ὦ πάλαι μὲν εὐδαίμονος πολίτου, νῦν δὲ ἀπόλιδος αὐλητοῦ! Κεῖται μὲν ἡ θρεψαμένη τὸν αὐλητήν, ὁ δ' ἐπαυλεῖν ἐκβιάζεται καλλιεροῦσι τοῖς πολεμίοις καὶ στεφανοῦν τοὺς ἀλάστορας· ὡς ἐν μεταιχμίῳ καθέστηκα, ὡς ἐν ἀπόρῳ κατείλημμαι! Δυσερωτῶ περὶ τὴν ἐνεγκοῦσαν καὶ τὰ ἐκείνης πάθη θρηνῶ, ἀλλ' ἑτέρωθεν ἐπισείει μοι τὸ ξίφος ὁ Μακεδὼν καὶ πείθει παιανίζειν οὐχ

24

What Ismenias the *aulos* player would say when he is forced by Alexander to provide musical accompaniment for the destruction of Thebes

O son of Philip, what is this theme you have proposed? With which of the gods shall I begin my song? What sort of prelude am I to sing? Shall I praise Thebes and applaud Cadmus with my melodies? But no, the city of Cadmus lies dead, and majestic Thebes has come to an end. Shall I invoke Bacchus, the noble, reveling god? But no, this revelry is savage, and the Macedonians have raged like Bacchants. Shall I sing a paean to Heracles, the glorious victor, our own hero, son of Zeus, son of Alcmene, scion of Thebes? But no, not once did this great hero ever come to the aid of Thebes.

Alas, the once prosperous city, now a wretched and unfortunate plot of land! Alas, its once blessed citizen, now an *aulos* player without a city! The city that raised this *aulos* player lies dead, but he is forced to play musical accompaniment to his enemies as they sacrifice with good omens, and to crown avenging spirits. In what a no-man's-land I find myself! In what dire straits I am caught! I am disastrously in love with the city that bore me and I sing dirges for its calamities, but from the other side the Macedonian threatens me with his sword and persuades me to sing unholy praises.

2

ὅσια. Ἔρημον ὁρῶ τὸ σύνηθες ἐκεῖνο καὶ φίλον θέατρον καὶ τραγῳδίαν ὅλην ἐπισκευάζω τοῖς μέλεσιν, ἀλλ᾽ ἀντινομοθετεῖ μοι τρόπον βάρβαρον ἄλλον ὁ Μακεδὼν καὶ τυραννεῖ μετὰ τῆς πόλεως τοὺς αὐλούς. Μέσος εὐτυχοῦντος βαρβάρου καὶ πόλεως ἀτυχούσης γίνομαι· ἕλκει πρὸς ὀδυρμὸν ἡ πατρίς, πείθει τὰ πρὸς ἡδονὴν αὐλεῖν ὁ πολέμιος.

3   Τίς ποτε σταδιοδρόμος ἐπιπεσόντι σταδίῳ τὰ τῶν ποδῶν ἐπεδείξατο; Ποῖος ῥήτωρ ἐποιχομένῳ τῷ βήματι τὴν γλῶτταν οὐ πρὸς θρῆνον ἐκίνησεν; Αὐλητὴς ἐγὼ καί με Θῆβαι φίλη πόλις Ἑλλὰς τοὺς αὐλοὺς ἐξεπαίδευσε. Πολλάκις ἐν Πανελληνίῳ ταύτην ἐξύμνησα, πολλάκις ὀφθαλμὸν Ἑλλάδος ἐκάλεσα· ἀλλὰ νῦν ὁ καλὸς οὗτος τῆς Ἑλλάδος ὀφθαλμὸς ὀρώρυκται καὶ δεῖ με θωπεύειν βαρβάρους τοὺς τὴν φίλην θεοῖς ἀναρπάσαντας πόλιν, τοὺς κοινοὺς τῶν Ἑλλήνων ἐχθρούς, τοὺς ἐκ Πέλλης, τοὺς Μακεδόνας. Ὦ θεοί, τίνα ταύτην ᾄσω παλινῳδίαν; Πῶς βαρβάροις ἐπαυλήσω θύμασι; Πῶς ἐπισπείσω Διΐ τροπαίῳ τὸ μέλος; Οὐκ ἐπ᾽ Ἀργείοις ἐπὶ τῆς Κάδμου πεδιάδος πεσοῦσιν, οὐκ ἐπὶ Λάκωσι παρὰ Θηβαίων κομψοῖς ἐλεγχθεῖσιν, ἀλλ᾽ ἐπὶ παιδὶ Φιλίππου, νεανίᾳ Μακεδόνι Θήβας ὅλας καταβαλόντι.

4   Οὐκ ἄρα Τερψιχόρη νῦν προστήσεται τῶν αὐλῶν, φίλαυλος μοῦσα καὶ θεὰ παῖς Ἑλληνίου Διὸς καὶ φιλοῦσα τοὺς Ἕλληνας, ἀλλ᾽ Ἐρινύες τοῖς αὐλοῖς ἐπορχήσονται καὶ Μακεδονικοί τινες ἀλάστορες δαίμονες. Ἀποβδελύξεται καὶ Ἀθηνᾶ τὴν ᾠδὴν καί, τοὺς αὐλοὺς κατὰ γῆς ἀφιεῖσα, τὴν ἀρχὴν <τῆς> ᾠδῆς οὐ μεταμελήσεται. Ἐπιστενάξει καὶ

I see that dear, familiar theater deserted and compose an entire tragedy in my songs, but the Macedonian orders instead a different, barbarian style of music and tyrannizes the *auloi* along with the city. I am caught between a barbarian who prospers and a city that has met with misfortune. My homeland draws me toward lamentation, but my enemy persuades me to play songs that give him pleasure.

What sprinter ever demonstrated the prowess of his feet 3 before a hostile crowd? What orator moved his tongue except in lamentation before a hostile tribunal? I am an *aulos* player, and Thebes, my dear Greek city, taught me to play. Oftentimes in the Panhellenion I sang of my city; oftentimes I called it the eye of Greece. But now this beautiful eye of Greece has been plucked out, and I must flatter barbarians, the ravagers of this city that is dear to the gods, the common enemy of the Greeks, the men from Pella, the Macedonians. O gods, what is this palinode that I am to sing? How am I to accompany barbarian sacrifices? How am I to pour out a song as an offering to Zeus who grants victory? I do not pour it for the Argives who fell in Cadmus's field, nor for the noble Spartans who were repudiated by the Thebans, but I pour it for the son of Philip, a Macedonian youth who has destroyed Thebes entirely.

And so Terpsichore will no longer be the patron deity of 4 these *auloi,* although she is the muse who loves the *aulos,* the divine daughter of Hellenic Zeus and one who loves the Greeks, but the Erinyes and some avenging gods of the Macedonians will dance to the *auloi.* Athena will loathe my song and, leaving the *auloi* on the ground, will not regret it at

Ἄρης τοῖς ἐμοῖς αὐλήμασιν, ἦπου κἀκεῖνος ὑπὸ Μοιρῶν τὴν Θηβαίων ἅλωσιν ἐκβεβίασται, ὡς ὑφ' ὑμῶν, ὦ Μακεδόνες, ἐγώ. Τὰ αὐλήματα οἰμώξεται καὶ Ἀφροδίτη, μήτηρ Ἁρμονίας θεός, καὶ ἀναρμοστίαν πᾶσαν ἐνθείη τοῖς ᾄσμασιν. Οὕτως ἀναφρόδιτον ᾄσομαι, οὕτως ἀκαλλιέρητον θύσετε. Πεπτώκασι Θηβαῖοι παῖδες Ἁρμονίας, ἀπόγονοι Ἄρεος, πεπτώκασιν οἱ γηγενεῖς, οἱ ἐκ δράκοντος φίλου θεράποντος Ἄρεϊ. Ξίφος Μακεδονικὸν τοὺς Σπαρτοὺς ἐξεθέρισε, στάχυν χρυσεοπήληκα, γένος Ἄρεϊ κάτοχον, αὐτομαθὲς τὰ πολέμια, οὐχ ὑστέραν γενέσεως ἔχον τὴν ὅπλισιν. Τάχα καὶ πάλιν Ἄρης οὐχ ἑνὸς παιδὸς τελευτὴν ἀποκλαύσεται παρὰ τῷ Διῒ τῷ πατρί, ἀλλὰ τῶν ἐξ Ἁρμονίας ἁπάντων, ἀλλ' ὅλην τὴν τῶν Σπαρτῶν ἐπανάστασιν.

5   Ἤδη καὶ Κιθαιρὼν σιγηθήσεται, χωρίον ὡς ἐπὶ συμφοραῖς πάμφορον, καὶ ἡ Κάδμου πόλις ἀκούσεται, οὐ κατ' Ἀργείων καλλίνικος, ἀλλ' ὑπὸ Μακεδόνων ἀνάστατος· Ἐρινύων ἄλσος, λειμὼν ἄτης, κοινὸν πολέμου πολυάνδριον, πολέμου ναυάγιον πάνδεινον, ἡ ταῖς Ἀμφίονος χορδαῖς περισώζουσα τὸν ἀριθμόν, ἡ ἑπτάπυλος, ὦ Ζεῦ καὶ θεοί, κατέστραπται, ἀντέστραπται τὰ Θηβαίων σεμνολογήματα. Ἤροσε Μακεδὼν νεανίας τὴν τοῦ Διονύσου, τὴν τῆς Σεμέλης, οὐχ ἵνα πάλιν ἀναδοίη Σπαρτούς, ἀλλ' ἵνα μηδ' ἴχνος ὑπολείποιτο πόλεως. Ἄλλος οὗτος τῆς Μακεδόνων ὠμότητος ἄροτος, εἰς ἀγρὸν τὴν πόλιν μετασκευάζων, ἤρδευσεν ὁμογνίῳ λύθρῳ τὴν γῆν. Ἄλλος οὗτος ποταμός, ὃν ὁπλιτῶν Μακεδόνων νέφος ἐπλήμυρεν, ἵν' ᾖ καὶ Κάδμῳ

all. Ares will groan over my playing: I suspect he was compelled by the Fates to accomplish the fall of Thebes, just as
I am compelled by you, O Macedonians. Even Aphrodite,
mother goddess of Harmony, will lament at my playing and
will inject complete disharmony into my songs. Thus I will
sing in an unlovely fashion; thus you will make your sacrifice
with ill omens. The Thebans have fallen, children of Harmony, descendants of Ares; those sprung from the earth,
from the serpent, the dear attendant to Ares, have fallen. A
Macedonian blade has reaped the Sown Ones, the golden-
helmeted wheat, the race beholden to Ares, self-taught in
warfare, clad in its armor as soon as it was born. Perhaps
Ares will in turn mourn the death not of a single child, as his
father Zeus did, but the death of all who are descended from
Harmony, and the sprouting of all the Sown Ones.

And now Cithaeron will fall silent, a place very fruitful 5
for misfortunes, and the city of Cadmus will be celebrated,
not as the glorious victor over the Argives but for being
laid waste by the Macedonians. The grove of the Erinyes,
the meadow of destruction, war's common burial ground,
its dreadful shipwreck, the seven-gated city preserving its
number in the strings of Amphion has been razed, O Zeus
and you gods; the pride of Thebes has been reversed. The
Macedonian youth plowed the land of Dionysus, the land of
Semele, not so that it might once again produce the Sown
Ones, but so that no trace of the city might be left behind.
This is a different plowing, which arose from the Macedonians' savagery, and it watered the land with kindred blood
as it transformed *the city* into *a field*. This is a different river,
which the cloud of Macedonian hoplites caused to rise in
flood, so that Alexander might reverse Cadmus's plowing

νεώσας ἀντίθετα καὶ Ἰσμηνοῦ προχοαῖς ἀντερίζειν ἔχοι τοῖς αἵμασιν. Ἐπιτάττει καὶ Ἰσμηνίᾳ πεσούσῃ τῇ πόλει προσεπορχεῖσθαι τοῖς αὐλοῖς, ἵν᾿ ὑπ᾿ αὐλοῖς ᾖ καὶ πίπτουσα καὶ ταῖς τῶν πολισαμένων ᾠδαῖς ἀντηχήσῃ μέλος ἀντίμουσον.

6   Ὦ βάρβαρε Μακεδών, οὐκ εἶ σὺ τὸ γένος ἕλκων ἀφ᾿ Ἡρακλέους, μάτην τὸ πρὸς τὸν ἥρωα κομπάζεις ὁμόγνιον, οὐ γὰρ ἂν τὴν Ἡρακλέους ἠθάλωσας. Ἢ τάχα καὶ λυττῶντα τὸν Ἡρακλέα ζηλοῖς καὶ κτείνεις, ὡς ἐκεῖνος, τοὺς ἐξ αἵματος; Οὐκ ἦν ἐκεῖνος τότε καλλίνικος, οὐκ ἦν ἐκεῖνος ἀλεξίκακος, ἀλλ᾿ ἐνόσει τὴν γνώμην καί, λυσσῶν, οὐκ ᾔδει τὰ φίλτατα. Παῦσαι καὶ κειμέναις ἐπεμβαίνων ταῖς Θήβαις, ἀπέκειρας τοῦ τείχους τὸν βόστρυχον, καθεῖλες τὰς οἰκίας, ἀνέσπασας τοὺς βωμούς, ἀνέτρεψας τὰ τεμένη, ἐψίλωσας τῶν ἀναθημάτων τὰ ἀγάλματα, μῦθον ὅλως εἶναι τὴν πόλιν ἠγώνισαι. Τί καὶ αὐλητὴν δυστυχῆ τῆς θρεψαμένης ἐκβιάζῃ κατειρωνεύεσθαι; Ἰσμηνίας ἐγὼ ἀπ᾿ Ἰσμηνοῦ καλοῦμαι, Θήβης εἰμὶ πολίτης, ἐκεῖθεν ἔχω καὶ τοὔνομα. Μή μου καὶ τὴν κλῆσιν ἀποσυλήσῃς, μὴ πρὸς θεῶν, μὴ πρὸς Ἡρακλέους, ὃν τοῦ γένους αὐχεῖς ἀρχηγόν. Χάρισαι μεγάλῳ ἥρωϊ μικρὰν ταύτην χάριν, μὴ καὶ τὴν κλῆσιν τοῖς ἔργοις τὸν αὐλητὴν ἐξομόσασθαι. Ἐπεχαρίσω μουσοποιῷ καὶ Μούσαις οἰκίαν, καὶ ταῦτα τὴν λοιπὴν ἅπασαν πόλιν καταπιμπρῶν. Χάρισαι δή τι καὶ Ἀπόλλωνι μουσηγέτῃ καὶ αὐλητὴν οὐκ ἄμουσον ἔα μὴ πρὸς τὴν θρεψαμένην παρανομῆσαι. Ὦ θεοῖς φίλον ἔδαφος, ὦ πάλαι Χαρίτων χωρίον, ὦ πάλαι Μουσῶν τέμενος, ὦ μέχρι νῦν πόλις, ὦ μέχρι νῦν καλλίνικος, ὦ *μᾶτερ ἐμὰ χρύσασπι Θήβα, τὸ τεὸν καὶ*

and might be able to counter with blood the flowing waters of the Ismenus. He also commands me, Ismenias, to dance to the music of *auloi* for a fallen city, so that it might be subject to *auloi* also as it falls, and its responsive song might echo the songs of its founders.

O barbarian from Macedon, you are not descended from   6
Heracles; in vain do you boast of your kinship with that hero, for you would not have burned to ashes the city of Heracles. Or are you perhaps emulating Heracles in his madness, killing, as he did, your own blood relatives? For he was not then the glorious victor, nor the averter of evil, but he was sick in his mind and, as he raged in madness, did not recognize what was dearest to him. Stop trampling upon Thebes as it lies dead: you have leveled the walls, demolished the houses, pulled down the altars, destroyed the temple precincts, stripped the statues bare of their offerings, and fought to make the city nothing but a myth. Why do you compel a miserable *aulos* player to treat his mother city insincerely? I am called Ismenias from the river Ismenus; I am a citizen of Thebes, and from it I possess my name. Do not despoil me of this title; no, by the gods; no, by Heracles, of whom you boast as the first ancestor of your family. Grant this small favor to the great hero; do not deny the *aulos* player his name by these deeds. You granted a house to the singer and to the Muses, and you did that as you were burning all the rest of the city. Grant a favor also to Apollo, leader of the Muses: allow his gifted *aulos* player to commit no transgression against his mother city. O ground, dear to the gods; O former abode of the Graces; O former precinct of the Muses; O you, until now a city, until now a glorious victor; O *my mother, Thebe of the golden shield, I will put your inter-*

ἀσχολίας ὑπέρτερον θήσομαι καὶ Μακεδόνων ὠμότητος,
οὕτω ζηλώσω καὶ Πίνδαρον καὶ ταῖς νῦν τύχαις προσῆκον
ἐπαυλήσω καὶ γοερόν.

25

Τίνας ἂν εἴποι λόγους ἡ Πασιφάη,
ταύρου ἐρασθεῖσα

Οἷον εἶδον, ὦ θεοί, ἡλίκον ἔπαθον τὴν ψυχήν! Περι-
ήστραψέ μοι τὰς ὄψεις πάγκαλόν τι χρῆμα βοός, ταῦρος
καὶ ἀγαλματίας, ὅλος ἐπαφρόδιτος, ὅλος ἐπέραστος, εἴποι
τις ἄν, ὡς Πλοῦτος καὶ τὸ φιλομειδὲς Ἀφροδίτης καὶ τὸ
χαροπὸν Ἔρωτος· οὕτω πολὺν ἀποστάζει τῶν ὀφθαλμῶν
ἀφροδίσιον ἵμερον. Οὐχ ὡς θὴρ ἀγριαίνει, οὐχ ὡς ταῦρος
ὑποκαθήμενον βλέπει, ἀλλ᾽ ὡς νεανίας Χάρισι καὶ Ἀφροδίτῃ τελούμενος καὶ τοῦ προσώπου τὸ χάριεν ἀπαστράπτει
καὶ τοῦ βλέμματος τὸ μειλίχιον. Ὁ δὲ καὶ τοῦ κάλλους
αἰσθάνεται καὶ καλὸς ὢν οὐκ ἠγνόησε· καὶ δή, τὸν αὐχένα
ὑπογυρώσας, ἀγέρωχόν τι σοβεῖ καὶ πυκνὰ τὴν ὕλην
περισκιρτᾷ, καὶ βαίνων εὔρυθμα καὶ χορεύων τῷ σχήματι.
Τοιοῦτον ἄρα τὴν ἀρχὴν ὁ Ζεὺς τὸν ταῦρον ἔπλασεν,
ἡνίκα καὶ ὁ Προμηθεὺς τὸν ἄνθρωπον, ἢ καὶ Ζεὺς αὐτὸς
τοιοῦτος ἂν ἐγεγόνει ταῦρος, ὅτε τὴν Εὐρώπην ἥρπασεν·
οὕτω θεσπεσία τις αἴγλη τὸν βοῦν τουτονὶ περικέχυται.

ests above my occupation and the Macedonians' savagery. Thus I will emulate Pindar and accompany your present fortunes both fittingly and mournfully.

25

What Pasiphaë would say after falling in love with a bull

What a thing I saw, O gods, and how much did I suffer in my soul! An all-beautiful wonder of a bull dazzled my eyes, a bull as beautiful as a statue, entirely charming, entirely lovely, like Plutus, someone might say; his love of laughter is that of Aphrodite, his flashing eyes are those of Love — such great love-inducing desire does he drip from his eyes. He is not ferocious like a wild beast; he does not gaze insidiously like a bull; but like a young man being perfected by the Graces and Aphrodite he gleams with the gracefulness of his appearance and the gentleness of his gaze. He perceives his own beauty, and is not unaware that he is handsome. Indeed, arching his neck, he struts somewhat haughtily, and leaps about in the thick woods, walking rhythmically and moving like a dancer. Such was the bull Zeus created in the beginning, when Prometheus created humans, or Zeus himself might have become such a bull, when he abducted Europa. Such a divine radiance surrounds this bull of mine.

2   Ἂν ἴδω τὸ τῆς μορφῆς ἡλιῶδες, ἕνα τῶν Ἡλίου βοῶν
εἶναι νομίζω τοῦτον καὶ τέθηπα· ἂν ὄψομαι τὸ τῆς ὄψεως
ἀστερωπόν, ἐκεῖνον εἶναι πείθομαι τὸν ἐν οὐρανῷ τὸν
κατάστερον. Ὁρῶ καὶ τὸ κέρας ὡς ἀκριβῶς ἄκυκλον, ὡς
ἀκριβῶς κυρτουμένης Σελήνης εἰκόνισμα, καὶ Σελήνης
ὑποδίφριον εἶναι τοῦτον μαντεύομαι· καὶ τάχα τῶν ἄλλων
ὁμοζύγων μόνος ἀφηνιάσας τὸν κάτω καὶ ἡμέτερον χῶρον
τοῦτον περιπολεῖ καὶ θεατρίζει τὸ κάλλος καὶ τὴν ἀλκὴν
ἐπιδείκνυται καὶ νῦν τῇ θεῷ χωλεύει τὸ τέτρωρον, καὶ
παρὰ τοῦτο καὶ φαίνει βραδίων καὶ δύει σχολαιότερον.
Ἐνδυμίων δὲ καὶ τὰ Σελήνης παιδικά; Λόγος ἄλλος καὶ
μῦθος ἐξ ἀγνοίας πλαττόμενος. Θεός ἐστιν ὡς ἐν βουσὶν
οὗτος ὁ ταῦρος καί, οἶμαι, τοῦτον Ἆπιν καλοῦσι καὶ
τιμῶσιν Αἰγύπτιοι· καὶ νῦν ἡμῖν ἐπεφοίτησεν, ἵνα καὶ τὴν
ἡμετέραν ὡς τὴν ἐκείνων ἄκαρπον δείξει.

3   Ἀλλ᾽ ἡκέ μοι ταύρων ἀπάντων ὁ κάλλιστος, ἡκέ μοι· καὶ
τῆς ἐρώσης ἔφαψαι καὶ γενοῦ καὶ φιλάνθρωπος. Ἀνθέξομαι
μυκηθμὸν ἐρωτικόν, ἀντίδος τοῦ φθέγματος· ἂν δακρύσω,
ψυχαγώγησον ἁπαλῷ τῷ σκιρτήματι· ἂν δὲ καὶ θελήσω
περιπτύξασθαι, ὑπόκλινε τὴν κεφαλὴν ἠρέμα καὶ τοῦτό
σοι φιλήματος ἔστω σύνθημα. Σίμβλον ἔχεις τὸ στόμα καὶ
ζῶν καὶ τοῦτό σοι παρὰ πάντα ταῦρον ὑπερφερές, ᾧ μετὰ
τὴν τελευτὴν τὸ σμῆνος ἐναποτίκτεται. Ἐγώ σοι καὶ ὅλα
φιλοτιμήσομαι λήϊα καὶ σκιρτήσεις ἄνετα καὶ τρυφήσεις
ἐλεύθερα. Ἐγώ σοι καὶ ὅλα χαριοῦμαι βουκόλια καὶ βασι-
λεύσεις τῶν ἐν τῇ νήσῳ ταύρων ἀπάντων, ὥσπερ τῶν
ἀνδρῶν ὁ Μίνως. Ἅπας ὁ χρόνος ἔσται σοι βουλυτός, εἰ
μόνον τὸν Ἔρωτος ζυγὸν ἑλκύσομεν ἄμφω.

When I observe the sun-like radiance of his beauty, I ₂
consider him to be one of the cattle of the Sun, and am
amazed. When I see the star-like brilliance of his countenance, I am convinced that he is that constellation in the
sky. I see how his horn is precisely curved like a circle, how it
precisely reproduces the curvature of Selene, and I divine
that he is yoked to Selene's chariot. And perhaps of all his
yoke-mates he alone rebelled against the reins, roaming
about on our land here below as he shows off his beauty and
exhibits his strength, and hobbling the goddess's team, so
that she rises more slowly and sets more tardily. And Endymion, the darling of Selene? That is another story, a myth
contrived out of ignorance. This bull is a god among cattle,
and, I think, the Egyptians call him Apis and honor him.
And now he has come among us, to demonstrate that our
land is barren, as is theirs.

But this finest of all the bulls has come to me; he has come ₃
to me. Touch your lover, and become a lover of humans. I
will endure erotic bellowing; just respond to my voice. If I
cry, console me with a tender leap. If I wish to embrace you,
lower your head gently and let this be a sign of your kiss. You
hold a beehive in your mouth: while you live, you excel every
other bull in this, and after your death it will give rise to a
swarm of bees. I will lavish upon you whole crops of food,
and you will cavort without restraint and live sumptuously
in freedom. I will grant to you all the herds of cattle, and you
will rule over all the bulls on the island, just as Minos rules
over all the men. Every hour of the day will be the time to be
free of the yoke, if only we will drag Love's yoke together.

4   Οὐκ αἰσχύνομαι τὸν πόθον ὡς ἔκφυλον· καὶ γὰρ Εὐ-
ρώπη βοὸς ἤρα καὶ ἵππου αὖθις ἑτέρα, καὶ ἦν ἐπίσης, ἐπ᾽
ἀμφοῖς ἀλλογενὲς τὸ φιλούμενον, κἂν βοῦς ὑπέκρυπτε
τὸν ὕπατον τῶν θεῶν, κἂν ἵππος τὸν Ποσειδῶνα τὸν
ἵππιον. Ἀλλ᾽ οἱ θεοὶ τὸ προσωπεῖον παρὰ τὴν εὐνὴν
ἀπεδύοντο· καὶ τότε καὶ Ζεὺς ταῖς κόραις καὶ Ποσειδῶν
ἐγνωρίζετο ἴσως, καὶ νῦν θεῶν τις ὡς ἐν ταύρῳ δρᾶμα
μελετᾷ φιλοτήσιον καὶ ἡ παστὰς ἐλέγξει τὴν σκηνὴν καὶ
γνωριεῖ τὸν ἐρώμενον. Ἀλλὰ τί ταῦτα τηνάλλως φθέγγομαι;
Τί καὶ πεπλάνημαι; Οὐκ ἐθέλει ταῦρος γυναικὶ συζεύγνυ-
σθαι, κἂν Ἔρως βιάσαιτο· ζυγομαχήσει πάντως καὶ ἀποπη-
δήσει καὶ φεύξεται. Αἰτιῶμαι τὸν Ἔρωτα. Τί γὰρ τοιαύτην
καθ᾽ ἡμῶν ἐβουκόλησε; Προσαιτιῶμαι τὴν Ἀφροδίτην. Τί
γὰρ ὁμόζυγον ἡμῖν ἐμελέτησε θέσθαι βοῦν ἑτερόζυγον;
Διαλοιδοροῦμαι καὶ ταῖς Χάρισιν, ὅτι πρὸς ἄλογον φύσιν
γεγόνασιν οὕτω φιλότιμοι.

5   Μέμφομαι καὶ τὸν λόγον, ὅτι μὴ καὶ βοὸς οἶδεν εἶναι
θελκτήριος. Τί μὴν καὶ χρυσοφορεῖν, εἰ χρυσῆν Ἀφροδίτην
ταῦρος οὐκ ἐπίσταται; Τί μὴν καὶ φρονεῖν ἐπὶ κάλλει καὶ
στολὴν ἀμπίσχεσθαι περιπόρφυρον, εἰ τιμᾶν οὐκ οἶδε τὴν
ἀλουργίδα ταῦρος καὶ γυναικείας ὥρας οὐ γλίχεται; Ζηλο-
τυπῶ τὴν θήλειαν βοῦν, ὅτι καὶ γυμνὴ κάλλους ἐπιθέτου
καὶ ποικίλης ἀναβολῆς οὕτω καλὸν τὸν ἐραστὴν ηὐτύχησεν. Ἡ δὲ καὶ περισκαίροντος χαίρει καὶ προσιόντος
ἀκκίζεται. Εἴθε βοῦς ἦν καὶ τῷ ταύρῳ τούτῳ σύζυγος ἅμα
καὶ σύννομος! Νῦν δὲ μέσον Ἀφροδίτης καὶ φύσεως

I am not ashamed of this unnatural desire for another 4
species. For Europa loved a bull, and another woman in turn
loved a horse. This was the same situation: the beloved of
both women was of a different species, even if the bull concealed the highest of the gods and the horse concealed
Poseidon, patron deity of horses. But the gods discarded
their disguises in bed, and then Zeus was recognized by his
lover, and Poseidon likewise. And now one of the gods re-
hearses a drama of love in the form of a bull, and the bridal
chamber will reveal the act and make the lover known. But
why do I speak these words in vain? Why have I gone astray?
A bull will refuse to be yoked with a woman, even if Love
should compel him. He will always resist the yoke, turn
away, and flee. I find fault with Love. For why did he beguile
such a woman as me with a bull? I find fault with Aphrodite
too. For why did she take pains to make a bull, an incompat-
ible yoke-mate, my partner in the yoke? I am also furious
with the Graces, because they have been so generous to a
dumb animal.

And I also blame my speech, because it cannot seduce 5
even a bull. Why should I wear gold, when a bull does not
understand golden Aphrodite? Why should I fret over my
appearance and wrap myself in purple clothing, when a bull
cannot recognize the sea-dyed robe and does not desire
feminine beauty? I am jealous of the female cow, because
even while lacking artificial beauty and stylish clothing she
nonetheless gains such a handsome lover. She even rejoices
as he frolics about and shows indifference when he ap-
proaches. I wish I were a cow, yoked to this bull and grazing
in his herd! But as it is I find myself caught between Aphro-

ἕστηκα. Ἡ μὲν συμπνέειν ταύρῳ βιάζεται, ἡ δ᾽ οὐκ ἐφίησιν. Ἡ μὲν εἰς ἀλλότριον ἵμερον ἕλκει καὶ τυραννεῖ, ἡ δ᾽ ἀφέλκει καὶ προσαποσπᾷ βιαιότερον ὃ δίδωσιν Ἔρως. Ἡ φύσις οὐ βούλεται καὶ νικᾶν τὴν φύσιν Ἔρως αὖθις οὐκ ἀνέχεται.

6 Ἀλλὰ τίς ἄν μοι προσωπεῖα περιθείη βοός, ἵνα τὸν ταῦρον ὑπέλθω τῷ σχήματι; Ἢ πῶς ἂν τὴν μορφὴν εἰς βοῦν ἀλλαξαίμην; Ἥρα τοῦτό μοι χαριεῖται, ὡς ἐκεῖνο Δαίδαλος. Ἐκείνη τὴν Ἰνάχου κόρην εἰς βοῦν μετέπλασε, οὗτος οὐκ ὀλίγα τῷ χαλκῷ εἰς ὀφθαλμῶν ἀπάτην ἐσφυρηλάτησε. Ναὶ δή, φιλτάτη θεῶν, ὃ πάλαι, τὴν Ἰοῦν ζηλοτυποῦσα, ἔδρασας, τοῦτο νῦν ἡμῖν χάρισαι, τοῦ πάθους οἰκτείρασα. Οὕτω σε ζυγὸν καὶ γάμων ἔφορον καὶ ὡς ἐν βουσὶ τιμήσουσιν ἄνθρωποι. Εἰ δ᾽ οὖν—ἀλλὰ σύ μοι δεῦρο, Δαίδαλε! Νῦν εἴπερ ποτέ, τῆς τέχνης ἐπίδειξαι τὸ πολύτροπον, γενοῦ καὶ ταύρῳ σοφιστὴς ὡς ἐν χαλκῷ πολυμήχανος, γενοῦ σύμμαχος Ἀφροδίτης, ἐπίκουρος Ἔρωτος, θήλειαν ὑπογλυψάμενος βοῦν. Περίθες αὐτῷ πανταχόθεν ἀκριβῆ τὴν ἐμφέρειαν καὶ τάχα θέλξεις· οὕτω καὶ θηράσαις τὸν ταῦρον τὸν ὡς ἐφ᾽ ἡμῖν ἀθήρατον, τὸν ἀφρόδιτον τὸν ἀνέραστον. Τὸ δ᾽ ἀπὸ τοῦδε ἡμῖν μελήσει καὶ Ἔρωτι.

dite and my nature. The one compels me to unite with the bull, but the other restrains me. The one draws me into an unnatural passion and tyrannizes me, while the other draws me back and violently tears away what Love gives. My nature is unwilling, but Love in turn does not allow my nature to win out.

But who might put on me a cow's mask, so that I might 6 stealthily approach the bull in disguise? Or how might my shape be transformed into that of a cow? Hera will grant the latter favor to me, as Daedalus will grant the former. She transformed Io, the daughter of Inachus, into a cow, and Daedalus has hammered bronze not a few times into objects that deceive the eyes. Yes, most beloved goddess, what you once did when you were jealous of Io, grant to me now, taking pity on my suffering. Thus humans will honor you as the yoke and the overseer of weddings among cattle, as well. And so if this happens, then come here, Daedalus! Now if ever, demonstrate the versatility of your art, be a clever inventor in bronze for a bull, and be an ally to Aphrodite, a supporter of Love, by sculpting a female cow. Surround it on all sides with an exact likeness, and perhaps you will beguile the bull. Thus may you also catch the bull that has remained uncaught by me, the lovely bull that does not reciprocate my love. The consequences will be a concern for me and for Love.

26

Τίνας ἂν εἴπῃ λόγους κηπωρός,
κήπου ἐπιμελούμενος καὶ
μεταφυτευσάμενος καὶ κυπάριττον ἐπ᾽
ἐλπίδι καρπῶν καὶ τῶν
ἐλπίδων ἀστοχήσας

Ὦ κενῶν ἐκείνων πολλῶν ἐλπίδων, αἷς ἠνδραπόδισμαι!
Ὦ πόνων πολλῶν ἐκείνων ἀκαίρων, οὓς ἐκπεπόνηκα! Τὸν
Ἀλκινόου κῆπον ἐκηπευσάμην αὐτὸν καὶ ἦν μοι παρὰ τῷ
κήπῳ καὶ φυτὰ καὶ δένδρα καὶ ἄνθεα. Καὶ Χάριτες ἠρέμα
πως ὑπέτρεχον τὰ φυτὰ καὶ τοῖς ἄνθεσιν ὑπεχόρευον καὶ
ἐπὶ πᾶσι κερδῷος Ἑρμῆς, πόνους ἀμειβόμενος φυτουργοῦ.
Ἦν ἐκεῖ παρὰ τῷ λειμῶνι μηλέα πολύκαρπος—εἶπεν ἂν
Ὅμηρος, ταύτην ἰδών, "ἀγλαόκαρπον"—καὶ ἥρπαζέ μου
τοὺς ὀφθαλμούς, ὅτι καλὸν τὸ μῆλον, εὐπρόσωπον τὸ
μῆλον, ἡδὺ τὸ μῆλον ἰδεῖν, ἡδὺ τὸ μῆλον φαγεῖν, ἡδὺ τὸ
μῆλον ὀσφρήσασθαι. Πάντα καλὸν τὸ μῆλον καὶ ἰδεῖν καὶ
φαγεῖν καὶ ὀσφρήσασθαι· χαρίεν ὑποπνέει καὶ ὅλον ἐρωτικόν, τὸν φυτουργὸν ὀλβιοῖ, πολλοῦ ζητηθὲν καὶ πριά-
μενον. Εἴποις ἄν, ἰδών, ἐν εἰκόνι γεγραμμένην μηλέαν
ὁρᾶν καὶ παρὰ τοῖς κλάδοις γεγράφθαι τοὺς Ἔρωτας μῆλα
τρυγῶντας καὶ παίζοντας. Οὕτω καλὸν τὸ μῆλον, ὡς καὶ
τρυγητὰς ἔχειν Ἔρωτας. Ἐκείνην μηλέαν ἰδών, εἶδες ἂν

26

What a gardener would say when, after tending his garden and transplanting a cypress tree in the hope that it would bear fruit, he was disappointed in his hopes

Alas, that multitude of empty hopes to which I have been enslaved! Alas, those many, ill-timed toils in which I have labored! I cultivated the very garden of Alcinous and had plants and trees and flowers there. And the Graces in their gentle way darted through the plants and danced among the flowers, while Hermes made everything prosper, granting a return for the gardener's labors. There in the meadow was a heavily-fruited apple tree—if Homer saw it he would say "*shining-fruited*"—which caught my eye because the apple was beautiful, lovely, sweet to behold, sweet to eat, and sweet to smell. The apple was beautiful in every way: to see, to eat, and to smell. It swayed gracefully and very seductively in the breeze; it made the gardener prosperous because it was sought out and purchased for a high price. If you saw it, you would say that you were looking at an apple tree rendered in a painting, and that Erotes were depicted picking apples and frolicking among the branches; so beautiful were the tree's apples, that Erotes came to pick them. If you had seen this apple tree, you would have recalled Paris

καὶ Πάριν κριτὴν καὶ θεὰς περὶ κάλλους φιλονεικούσας καὶ μῆλον Ἀφροδίτῃ διδόμενον καὶ τῷ δικαστῇ τὰς ἀμοιβὰς φιλοτίμως ἀντιμετρούμενον.

2   Συκαῖ περὶ τὸν κῆπον ἦσαν γλυκύκαρποι καὶ τοὺς καρποὺς μελισσῶνας εἶχον. Τὸ γάρ τοι σῦκον κεχηνὸς ἀπέρρει τοῦ μέλιτος καὶ μονονοῦ προσεμειδία τὸν θεατήν· ὁ δέ τις ὠνούμενος τὰς ὀπώρας εἶδε τὸ σῦκον, ὠνήσατο, τῆς εὐτυχίας μακαρίσας τὸν φυτουργόν. Καὶ μῆλον Περσικὸν ἐκηπευσάμην παρὰ τῷ κήπῳ μου καὶ ἦν τὸ μῆλον ὑπόχνοον καὶ ὅλην τὴν παρειὰν κατὰ παρθένον ἐρυθραινόμενον καὶ παρὰ μέρη τὸ μῆλον ὑπόκιρρον. Κἂν τὸν καιρὸν προδράμοι καὶ προφοιτήσοι τῶν ὀπωρῶν, ζητητέον τὸ μῆλον, οὐκ ὀλίγου τὸν φυτουργὸν ἀμειβόμενον. Κἂν μετὰ τὴν ὀπώραν βραδυπορήσῃ, ἀργυρίων ἐπριάμην τὸ μῆλον καὶ τῶν πόνων ἀπωνάμην τὰς ἀμοιβὰς πολυχεύμονας. Ἤνθει τὸ ῥόδον καὶ σὺν αὐτῷ δὴ τῷ χρηματισμῷ καθηδυνόμην καὶ ὄψιν καὶ ὄσφρησιν. Οὐ διὰ κενῆς μοι τὰ τῶν ἱδρώτων, κἂν περὶ κρίνα τούτους κεκένωκα, κἂν περὶ δὴ τὴν ἰωνιάν, κἂν περὶ τὴν ἀναδενδράδα, κἂν περὶ νάρκισσον. Εἰ καὶ μαλάχην ἐφυτηκόμησα, ἣν ἀσφόδελον ἐκηπευσάμην, κἂν θριδακίνην καὶ εἴ τι τούτων ἐλάχιστον, ἀπωνάμην τῶν ἱδρώτων, ἀργυρολογούμενος. Δίκελλαν εἶχον καὶ τὴν ἀμάραν ἀνώρυττον καί, ὕδατος μεταδιδοὺς τοῖς φυτοῖς, χρυσᾶς ἀντεφιλοτιμούμην τὰς ἀμοιβὰς καὶ Πακτωλὸν ἐδόκουν μετοχετεύειν τῷ κήπῳ μου, ὅτι μοι τὰ τῶν πόνων ἐπικερδέστατα.

3   Ἐπεὶ δὲ τὰ τῶν ὀφθαλμῶν περιλιχνεύεται τὰ πολλὰ καὶ φιλοκερδεστέρα προαίρεσις τὰ μὴ παρόντα ζητεῖ καὶ τῶν

as judge, the goddesses quarreling about their beauty, and an apple being awarded to Aphrodite and bringing the judge abundant returns.

The fig trees in my garden were sweet-fruited and bore   2
beehives for their fruit, for the gaping fig flowed with honey and all but smiled at onlookers, and whoever was shopping for fruit and saw the fig would buy it, after pronouncing the farmer blessed in his good fortune. I also cultivated in my garden the Persian apple, which has a light down and red blushes on its surface like a maiden's cheek, but in some places is yellowish. Even if it ripened early and was ready to pick before harvest time, this apple was still in demand and brought the gardener no small return; and even if it ripened late, I still sold it for money and reaped the benefit of my labors in overflowing returns. The rose also bloomed and, in addition to the financial gain itself, I was gratified by both its appearance and its fragrance. My sweat has not been in vain whether I poured it out for the lilies, for the bed of violets, for the vine, or for the narcissus. If I tended the mallow, if I cultivated the asphodel, wild lettuce, or even the lowliest of plants, I benefitted from my sweat by earning income. I took up a mattock and dug out a trench, and by providing my plants with water, I vied jealously for my golden earnings and appeared to be diverting a Pactolus into my garden, since the return on my labors was so great.

And when my eyes greedily desired more and more, when   3
my profit-loving character sought what I did not possess,

ὄντων ἡγεῖται κρείττω τὰ προσδοκώμενα, εἶδον καὶ κυπάριττον εὐθαλῆ καὶ μετεκηπευσάμην ταύτην τῷ κήπῳ μου καί, περὶ μίαν ἀμάραν τὸ ὕδωρ συναγαγών, μετήγαγον παρὰ τὴν κυπάριττον. Μεταφυτευσάμενος τὸ φυτὸν παρὰ τῇ διεξόδῳ τοῦ ὕδατος, καὶ χοῦν ἐπέβαλον τῷ φυτῷ καὶ πασσάλοις περιεκύκλωσα καὶ λύγοις τοὺς πασσάλους ἐστεφάνωσα, ἐπιμελούμενος τοῦ φυτοῦ καὶ φυλακῇ καὶ ὕδατι καὶ χοΐ, ὅλους ὀφθαλμούς, ὅλην καρδίαν, ὅλην αὐτήν μου ψυχὴν περὶ μόνην ταύτην μεταγαγὼν τὴν κυπάριττον, κενάς τινας ἐλπίδας τῶν ἐν χερσὶ προτιμώμενος.

4 Ζέφυρος ἡδὺς ἠρέμα πως ὑποπνέει τῷ ἔαρι καὶ ἡ κυπάριττος ἐδόκει βλακεύεσθαι, κατά τινα παρθένον σεσοβημένην ἐξ Ἔρωτος. Ὥρων τοῦ φυτοῦ τὴν ἀναβολήν, κεχηνὼς εἱστήκειν, ὁρῶν ἀτενῶς, καὶ ἤμην ἐραστὴς ὁ γηπόνος καὶ ὁ φυτουργὸς αἰχμάλωτος τοῦ φυτοῦ. Ἔαρος καιρὸς καὶ διηρεθίζετο τὰ φυτὰ καὶ κατηνθίζετο καὶ κυπάριττος. Παρῆλθεν ἔαρ καὶ εἰς καρποὺς ἐτράφη τὰ ἄνθεα καὶ τὸ ἄλλο μὲν ἐκαρποφόρησε τῶν φυτῶν, ἡ δὲ καλὴ κυπάριττος ἀπηνθίσατο. Χειμῶνος καιρὸς καὶ φυλλορροεῖ τὰ φυτά, καὶ τὸν κόσμον ὅλον παντελῶς ἀποβάλλεται καὶ κατὰ κόμην τὸν ἐκ τῶν φύλλων ἀποκείρεται βόστρυχον, ἀλλ᾽ ἡ κυπάριττος βοστρυχοῦσα καὶ μέσῳ δὴ λειμῶνι τέθηλεν ἀμετάβλητα. Κἂν ἔαρ, ἡ κυπάριττος εὐθαλής· κἂν θέρος, ἡ κυπάριττος τέθηλε. Χειμὼν καὶ φθίνουσι τὰ φυτὰ καὶ οἷον νεκροῦται, τῷ ψύχει βαλλόμενα, ἡ δὲ κυπάριττος πά- λιν κυπάριττος καὶ ὅλον ἔαρ ἐνζωγραφεῖ καὶ φύλλοις καὶ τοῖς ἄλλοις ἀναβλαστήμασιν.

when I believed what I anticipated was better than what I had, I spied a flourishing cypress tree. I transplanted this tree into my garden and, after conducting the water into a single trench, I conveyed it to the cypress tree. When I had transplanted the tree near the outflow of water, I packed earth around it, encircled it with stakes, and then wove twigs into the stakes. I tended the tree with protection, water, and earth; I devoted my full gaze, my whole heart, the entirety of my very soul to this cypress tree alone, preferring some empty hopes to what I already possessed.

The Zephyr blew quite sweetly and gently in the spring-time, and this cypress tree appeared to run riot, like some maiden excited by Love. I was observing the tree's upward growth; I stood gaping, watching intently. I, the cultivator, was a lover, I, the gardener, a captive of the tree. It was the season of spring: the plants flourished, and the cypress bloomed as well. Spring passed, and blooms were transformed into fruit. But while the other trees bore fruit, the lovely cypress lost its flowers. The winter season arrived; the trees dropped their leaves, cast off completely all their adornment and, as with hair, were shorn of their locks of leaves. But the cypress kept its locks, and in the midst of the meadow it thrived without change. In spring, the cypress flourished; in summer, the cypress thrived; in winter, when plants wither and are as though dead, stricken by the cold, the cypress was still a cypress, fully displaying spring in its leaves and the rest of its growth.

4

5 Ἔχαιρον, ὁρῶν τὸ φυτόν, ὥρων ὑψίκομον τὸ φυτόν, ὥρων ἀνατρέχον εἰς οὐρανὸν καὶ τὸν καρπὸν ἐκαραδόκουν τὸν οὕτω πολλῶν χαρίτων ἐπάξιον. Τὰ δ᾽ ἦσαν ἐλπίδες κεναὶ καὶ ἀντικρὺς ὄνειροι καὶ νῦν κατὰ τὴν παροιμίαν ἄνθρακας εὑρίσκω τοὺς θησαυρούς. Καὶ τῶν περὶ τὴν κυπάριττον μόχθων καρποὺς καρποῦμαι τὰ δάκρυα καί, τῷ Προμηθεῖ μὴ σπεισάμενος, νῦν ὅλῳ συνανακέκραμαι τῷ Ἐπιμηθεῖ. Ὅλον τὸ ὕδωρ διεποτίζετο τὴν κυπάριττον, τὰ δ᾽ ἄλλα τῶν φυτῶν ἀπεψύγη τῷ δίψει καὶ τέτηκε μονονουχὶ καὶ ἀδικίας ἐπεγκαλοῦντα τὸν φυτουργόν, ὅτι μὴ φυτουργεῖται κατὰ τὴν ἄκαρπον ταύτην κυπάριττον.

6 Ἐγὼ δὲ ἄρα τῷ εὐθαλεῖ πεπλάνημαι τοῦ φυτοῦ, τῷ εὐσταλεῖ τὴν ὄψιν σεσύλημαι, τῷ οὕτως ἰθυτενεῖ κενὰς ἐλπίδας ἀπεθησαύρισα καὶ νῦν ἐκτέτηκα, τοῖς ὀφθαλμοῖς χαρισάμενος. Εἰ γοῦν κατὰ τοὺς εὐηθεστέρους τῶν ἁλιέων καὶ φυτουργὸς νοῦν οἴσει, πληγείς, μετοχετεύσω τὸ ὕδωρ ἐπὶ τὰ λάχανα, ἐπιμελήσομαι τῶν φυτῶν, ἀνακαθάρω τοὺς ὀχετούς, δενδροκομήσω τὰ νοσήσαντα τῶν φυτῶν, χαίρειν εἰπὼν τῇ κυπαρίττῳ καὶ ταῖς ταύτης ἀναβολαῖς. Κἂν τὸ ἰθυτενὲς προβάλληται, κἂν τὸ εὐσταλές, ἀντιπαραθήσω ταύτης τὸ ἄκαρπον, γνωμολογούμενος προσφορώτατα ὡς "Οὐδενὸς λόγου πριαίμην βροτόν, ὅστις κεναῖς ἐλπίσι θερμαίνεται."

I rejoiced as I looked upon the tree; I watched it, with its 5
lofty foliage; I watched it ascending skyward, and I awaited
the fruit that would be worthy of so many charms. But these
were empty hopes, contrary dreams, and now, as in the proverb, I discover my *treasures* to be *ashes*. As the fruit of my labors on behalf of the cypress I harvest my tears, and since I
did not pour a libation to Prometheus, I am now intimately
joined with Epimetheus. All of my water went to irrigate the
cypress, while the rest of the trees are faint from thirst, have
all but wasted away, and accuse their gardener of injustice,
because they were not tended like this barren cypress.

I, therefore, have been led astray by the flourishing of the 6
tree; I have been stripped of my vision by its orderly form;
I stored away empty hopes because it was so upright, and
now, after gratifying my eyes, I have wasted away. If, then, a
gardener too, just like the rather simpleminded *fishermen,*
will come to his senses after being struck, I will divert the water
to the vegetables, care for the plants, clean out the channels,
and tend to the trees that have suffered affliction, having
bid farewell to the cypress and its upward growth. Even if it
shoots straight upright, even if it is elegant, I will set against
this its barrenness and most fittingly utter the maxim, "*I*
would not buy at any price a man who is inspired by empty hopes."

27

Τίνας ἂν εἴποι λόγους ἡ ἐξ Ἐδέσσης παρὰ τοῦ Γότθου ἀπατηθεῖσα κόρη

Ὡς ἄρα πιθανώτατόν τι χρῆμα γλῶσσα ψευδὴς καὶ βάρβαρος γνώμη τυραννικώτατον! Ταῦτά μου τὴν παρθενίαν ἐσύλησε, ταῦτά μου τὴν παρθενίαν ἐσκύλευσεν. Εἶχε μὲν γάρ μοι τὰ τῆς πατρίδος οὐκ ἀγαθῶς καὶ κίνδυνος ἐπέκειτο κατὰ κεφαλῆς καὶ ὅλον ἔθνος κατεπεκύκλου τὴν Ἔδεσσαν, δουλαγωγῆσαι ταύτην βαρβαρικῶς φρυαττόμενον, ἔργον θέσθαι μαχαίρας καὶ ἀφελέσθαι τὸ ἐλευθέριον. Ἀλλ᾽ ἥκει συμμαχικὸν ἀξιόχρεων, ἀντιπαραταξάμενον πρὸς τὴν ἔφοδον. Εἰ μὲν οὖν ὅλον ἐπίορκον, εἰ μὲν οὖν ὅλον βάρβαρον ἐρωτόληπτον, οὐκ οἶδα, νὴ τὴν δουλείαν ταύτην, ἣν κατακέκριμαι, νὴ τὴν ἐλευθερίαν, ἣν ἀπολώλεκα. Ὁ δέ γε Γότθος ὁ περὶ τὴν ἐμὴν οὐκ ἀγαθῷ ποδὶ φοιτήσας οἰκίαν, βάρβαρος τὴν γνώμην, τὴν γλῶσσαν ἐπίορκος καὶ τὰ πολλὰ τοῖς ἔρωσι χαριζόμενος, εἶδέ με παρθένον οἰκουρουμένην παρθενικῶς καὶ ὅλην οὖσαν παρθένον αἰδοῖ καὶ συνέσει καὶ τῷ σοβήματι. Ὁ δέ—ἀλλ᾽ εἶδεν—ἀλλ᾽ ἐξετάκη τοὺς ὀφθαλμοὺς καὶ ὅλην αὐτὴν καρδίαν ὑπερεκάη τῷ ἔρωτι. Ἐγὼ δὲ ἄρα οὐκ ᾔδειν ἐπ᾽ αὐτοῦ δὴ τοῦ προσώπου φέρουσα τὰ δεινὰ καὶ τῷ κάλλει μέσῳ κατορωρυγμένα τὰ δυστυχήματα.

27

What the girl from Edessa would say after being deceived by the Goth

Surely a lying tongue is a most persuasive thing, and a barbarous mind most tyrannical! These two stripped from me my maidenhood; they despoiled me of my maidenhood. For my homeland was in distress, danger was upon our heads, and an entire nation surrounded Edessa, prancing barbarously to enslave it, put it to the sword, and take away its freedom. But there arrived a considerable force allied with us, which arrayed itself against the attackers. Whether this entire force swore falsely, whether every barbarian is captivated by desire, I declare by this slavery, to which I have been condemned, and by my freedom, which I have lost, that I do not know. But the Goth who came with sinister step to my own house, barbarous in mind, forsworn in his speech, given over almost entirely to sexual desires, saw me, a maiden keeping house as a maiden does, and being completely maidenly in my sober demeanor, my judgment, and my comportment. And he, when he saw me, his eyes were melted and his whole heart was inflamed with burning desire. But I did not know that I was facing the dangers that lurked in his very countenance or the misfortunes that were buried in the midst of his handsomeness.

2   Τὰ μὲν οὖν δὴ πρῶτα, Ἔρωτι συμμάχῳ χρησάμενος καὶ
τὴν γλῶτταν ἔχων ἐλέπολιν, κατ' αὐτῆς δὴ σωφροσύνης
κατεπεστράτευσε, πολιορκῆσαι θέλων τῆς παρθενίας μου
τὴν ἀκρόπολιν καὶ καταστρατηγῆσαι τῆς σωφροσύνης
αὐτῆς. Ἐπεὶ δὲ πείρᾳ φθάνει μαθὼν ὡς οὐχ ἱκανὰ ταῦτα
κατασεῖσαι τὰ τῆς σωφροσύνης πυργώματα, μέτεισι τὴν
μητέρα, τὴν ἀλωπεκῆν ἐνδυσάμενος, τὴν γλῶσσαν ὅλην
πρὸς ἄλλο σχῆμα μεταμειψάμενος. Ἐπαινεῖ τὸν γάμον καὶ
τὸν νυμφίον καθυποκρίνεται καὶ δοῦλος ὅλος γίνεται τῇ
μητρί, καὶ γλώσσῃ καὶ σχήματι· καὶ ζητεῖ με τὴν θυγατέρα
πρὸς γάμον, ἀλλ' ἔννομον, νόμου μεμνημένος ὁ τὰ πάντα
παράνομος. Ἐπεὶ δ' οὐκ ἔχει πείθειν μητέρα φιλόπαιδα,
τούτῳ δὴ τῷ πρὸς γάμον ἑτοίμῳ θορυβουμένην τὰ μά-
λιστα, μὴ καὶ προτέραν ἠγάγετο λέγουσαν, ὁ τοῖς ἔρωσιν
οὕτω πειθόμενος καὶ πᾶσιν ἀνέμοις ἐρωτικοῖς ῥιπιζόμενος,
μαρτύρεται Θεόν, μαρτύρεται Δίκην, μαρτύρεται μάρτυρας αὐτοὺς ἐκείνους, τοὺς ἐν Ἐδέσσῃ παθόντας ἕνεκα
Χριστοῦ καὶ τῆς καλῆς ὁμολογίας ἀναδησαμένους τὸν
στέφανον. Ἡ δέ γε μήτηρ—τί δ' ἄλλο πάντως ἢ μήτηρ καὶ
κηδομένη τῆς θυγατρός;—τοῖς ὅρκοις πιστεύει τοῦ μηδὲν
εὐορκήσαντος, πείθεται τοῖς λόγοις τοῦ καὶ Θεὸν αὐτὸν
παρ' οὐδὲν τιθεμένου παραλογώτερον καὶ τῷ παρανομω-
τάτῳ Γότθῳ νόμῳ γάμου με παραδίδωσιν.

3   Ἕως μὲν οὖν ἡ πατρὶς ἐκυμαίνετο, τὰ περὶ τὴν ἐμὴν
οἰκίαν ἦσαν ἀκύμαντα. Ἕως τὰ περὶ τὴν Ἔδεσσαν ἐκλο-
νεῖτο, ἀπερικλόνητά μοι τὰ περὶ τὸν ἄνδρα διατετήρηται.
Ἕως τὸ συμμαχικὸν ἐτήρει τὴν πόλιν, ἀνόθευτά μοι τὰ τῆς
στοργῆς ἐφυλάττετο. Καὶ ἦν ὁ Γότθος ἀνὴρ τὰ πάντα

At first, then, employing Love as his ally and possessing a   2
siege engine for a tongue, he led an assault against chastity
itself, wishing to besiege the acropolis of my maidenhood
and lead a campaign against my very chastity. But when his
many attempts taught him that these siege towers were not
sufficient to topple my chastity, he clothed himself in fox-
skin and transformed his speech entirely, and then turned to
my mother. He spoke highly of marriage, pretended to be an
eligible son-in-law, and became my mother's slave completely, both in speech and in appearance. And he sought
me, her daughter, in marriage, but a lawful one—the man
who acts illegally in everything, invoking the law! But when
he could not persuade a mother who loved her child, who
was especially disturbed by this man's eagerness for marriage, and who wondered whether he was already married,
the one who was so obedient to his sexual urges and fanned
by all the winds of desire, this man called upon God as a witness, he called upon Justice, he called upon those very martyrs who suffered in Edessa for the sake of Christ and bound
upon themselves the crown of their noble confession. And
my mother—what else was she, at any rate, but a mother
who cared for her daughter?—trusted in the oaths of the
man who had never sworn honestly; she was persuaded by
the words of the man who irrationally had no respect for
God himself; and she handed me over in lawful marriage to
the most lawless Goth.

As long as my homeland was tossed by rough seas, my sit-   3
uation at home was calm. As long as the war in Edessa was
raging, life with my husband remained tranquil. As long as
the allied force protected our city, his affection for me remained genuine. The Goth was a loving husband in every

φιλόστοργος καί μοι τὰ πάντα γενόμενος, ὅσα καὶ πρὸς γυναῖκα γένοιτ᾽ ἂν ἀνὴρ ἀγαθός. Ἐπεὶ δ᾽ ὁ κλύδων τῆς πόλεως νηνεμίαν ἔσχε καὶ κατεκοιμήθη τὰ κύματα, κατ᾽ ἐμῆς αὐτῆς ὅλον μετεγείρεται τὸ κλυδώνιον καὶ ἀγριοῦται τῶν δυστυχημάτων ἡ θάλασσα καὶ κύματα τῶν πειρασμῶν ἀλλεπάλληλα. Καὶ τῆς ἐλευθερίας δουλείαν ἀλλάσσομαι καὶ θεραπαινὶς ἀνθ᾽ ὁμοζύγου καὶ ἀντὶ δεσποίνης αἰχμάλωτος γίνομαι.

4   Ὦ πικρᾶς ταύτης μεταβολῆς, ἣν κενῶς μεταβέβλημαι! Ὦ πικρῶν ἐκείνων γάμων! Ὦ συναλλαγμάτων οὐκ εὐτυχῶν! Ἔλαθες, ὦ μῆτερ, ἀντὶ γαμηλίων συμβολαιογραφοῦσα πράτορα. Ἔλαθες ἀργυρολογησαμένη τὴν θυγατέρα, ἀνθ᾽ ὧν ἐδόκεις νυμφοστολήσασθαι. Ἔλαθες, τὸν ὑμέναιον ᾄδουσα, τὸν ἐξιτήριον τραγῳδήσασα. Οὐκ ἀνὴρ ὁ Γότθος, ἀλλὰ δεσπότης καὶ σὺν δεσποίνῃ λαμπρῶς ἀνακέκλιται. Ἐγὼ δὲ δούλη παρίσταμαι καὶ θεραπαινὶς ἡ πρὶν ἐλευθέρα καὶ δέσποινα. Ὦ τῆς ἐμῆς δυστυχίας! Ὦ τῆς σῆς ἀβουλίας! Ὦ τῆς ἐμῆς ταύτης πλάνης περὶ τὸν ἄνδρα! Ὦ τῆς σῆς ἐκείνης ἀπάτης, ἣν ἐξηπάτησαι! Ὄγκωταί μοι τὰ τῆς γαστρὸς καὶ συνογκοῦταί μοι τὸ τῆς δεσποίνης ζηλότυπον. Ἐπανθεῖ μου τῷ προσώπῳ τὸ κάλλος, εἴ που μὴ τὸ πᾶν κατεμαράνθη τοῖς δυστυχήμασι, καὶ τὸν θυμὸν ἡ δεσπότις ἐμφαίνει τῷ βλέμματι. Ἐρύθημά τι ταῖς παρειαῖς ὀλίγον ἐναπολέλειπται καὶ ὅλη κάμινος φθόνου περὶ μέσην αὐτὴν ἐκείνης ἐξῆπται ψυχήν. Καιρὸς ὠδίνων καὶ τοκετοῦ καὶ τίκτει σοι, μῆτερ, ἡ παῖς.

5   Ὦ πικρᾶς ταύτης φωνῆς! Κατὰ δούλην αἰχμάλωτον καὶ τὸ ζηλότυπον, ἐγκυμονούμενον τῇ δεσποίνῃ, γεννᾶται.

respect, and for me he became everything that a good husband might be for a wife. But when the city's rough waters were stilled and the waves calmed, the full storm rose up against my very home, the sea of my misfortunes raged, and waves of trials crashed one upon the other. I exchanged freedom for slavery, became a servant instead of a spouse, and a captive instead of a mistress.

Alas, this bitter transformation, which I have undergone   4
for no purpose! Alas, that bitter wedding! Alas, the disastrous marriage transaction! Unawares, O mother, you made a contract with a slave dealer and not for a wedding. Unawares you put a price on your daughter instead of arranging her marriage as you thought. Unawares you performed a tragic last farewell, while singing the wedding hymn. The Goth was not a husband, but a master, and has reclined splendidly with his mistress. And I am now a slave and a servant, who formerly was a free woman and a lady. Alas, my misfortune! Alas, your ill-advised action! Alas, this mistake of mine about my husband! Alas, that deception, by which you were deceived! My belly has swollen, and so has the jealousy of my mistress. Beauty blooms on my face, unless somehow it has all been withered by my misfortunes, and my mistress reveals her anger in her glare. A small trace of redness remains upon my cheeks, and a full furnace of envy has been kindled in the very interior of her soul. It is time for labor pains and childbirth, and your child, O mother, delivers a child.

Alas, what a bitter utterance! Jealousy toward an enslaved   5
prisoner, nurtured as though in a womb by my mistress, is

Πρὸς ὅλην ἀντιπαράταξιν καὶ κατὰ τοῦ παιδὸς ὁπλίζεται γενναιότατα, συμμάχῳ τῷ δόλῳ χρησάμενον. Ἡ δεσπότις ὑποκλέπτει τὴν δούλην καὶ θανατοῖ τὸν παῖδα μηδὲν ἀδικήσαντα, τοῖς χείλεσι τοῦ βρέφους—ὢ τῶν ἐμῶν ἐκείνων κενῶν ὠδίνων!—ἐγχύσασα δηλητήριον. Ὢ βρέφος μηδὲν ἀδικῆσαν καὶ θανὸν ἀδικώτατα! Ὢ νήπιον μηδὲν κακουργῆσαν καὶ κακουργηθὲν δολιώτατα! Καὶ μέχρι τοῦ σοῦ θανάτου, τέκνον, παρανομούμεθα. Ὢ τῶν ἐμῶν δυστυχῶν τούτων σπλάγχνων, ἅ σε πρὸς φῶς ἀθλίως ἐξήνεγκαν! Ὢ τῶν ἐμῶν ἐλεεινῶν τούτων χειρῶν, αἵ σε ἐξέφερον νεκρὸν ἀδικούμενον! Ἐκτέτηκα τοῖς δάκρυσι καὶ τοῖς ὀδυρμοῖς, τοῖς στεναγμοῖς ἀπεῖπα καὶ τοῖς ἀλγήμασι, καὶ ἐν ῥισὶν ἡ πνοή μοι ἐστί. Δέδοικα μὴ καὶ αὐτὴν φυσήσω ψυχήν.

6   Μὴ φύγοις, Γότθε, δίκην αὐτήν, μὴ παραδράμοις ὀργὴν παραθεωρουμένου Θεοῦ. Ἀντιπαράθου με τῷ σηκῷ τῶν μαρτύρων, ὅθεν παρέλαχες. Εἰ δ᾽ οὖν, ἐγὼ θαρρήσω τοῖς μάρτυσι, καὶ τὴν δίκην ἐνδυσαμένη καὶ θωρακισαμένη τοῖς ὅρκοις, οἷς πολλοῖς ἐκείνοις τῆς ἀνοχῆς σου, Χριστὲ βασιλεῦ, ἡμᾶς ἐξηπάτησας, ἀνδρίσομαι πρὸς τὴν ἄμυναν. Ὧι βέβλημαι βέλει, τούτῳ τὸν ἐχθρὸν ἀνταμύνομαι, κἂν χρήσωμαι βοηθῷ τῷ νηπίῳ πρὸ τῆς ὥρας κειμένῳ. Οὐχὶ καὶ βέλη νηπίων λογισθήσονταί μοι τὰ μηχανήματα, ὅτι συνερίθους ἔχω τοὺς μάρτυρας, οἷς βέλη νηπίων ἐλογίσθησαν αἱ πληγαί, ὅσας πολλὰς ἐκείνας ἕνεκα τῆς εὐσεβείας ἐπλήγησαν καθ᾽ ὅλου τοῦ σώματος.

also being born. It arms itself most valiantly against all opposition and against the child, with deceit as its ally. The
mistress tricks her servant, and kills the child who has done
her no wrong, pouring poison into the infant's lips; alas,
those birth pangs I endured to no purpose! Alas, my baby,
you who committed no wrong but have died most unjustly!
Alas, infant, you who have done no evil but have been
treated evilly with great treachery! Injustice has been inflicted upon me, child, to the point that they have killed
you. Alas, my ill-starred womb, which brought you to the
light wretchedly! Alas, my merciful hands, which carried out
your dead body, a victim of injustice! I am wasted away with
tears and lamentations; I give in to my groaning and pain;
and my breath is in my nostrils. I fear that I am about to
breathe out my very soul.

May you not escape justice itself, O Goth; may you not   6
circumvent the anger of a God who keeps accounts. Restore
me to the precinct of the martyrs from where you obtained
me. Otherwise, I will take courage from the martyrs, and
having clothed myself in justice and armed myself with the
oaths—those many oaths for your support, Christ king, by
which you, Goth, deceived us—I will strengthen myself for
revenge. I will fire back at my enemy with the arrow that
struck me, even if I enlist as my helper a child who lies dead
before his time. But my devices will not be reckoned as *children's darts* because I have the martyrs as allies, for whom *the
blows* were reckoned as *children's darts,* the many blows that
they received all over their bodies on account of their piety.

Abbreviations

AASS = *Acta Sanctorum* (Paris and Brussels, 1863–1940)

BHG = François Halkin, ed., *Bibliotheca Hagiographica Graeca,* 3rd ed. (Brussels, 1957)

CPG = Ernst L. von Leutsch and Friedrich G. Schneidewin, eds., *Corpus Paroemiographorum Graecorum,* 2 vols. (Göttingen, 1839–1851)

DOP = *Dumbarton Oaks Papers*

ODB = Alexander P. Kazhdan et al., eds., *Oxford Dictionary of Byzantium,* 3 vols. (New York, 1991)

Perry 1952 = Ben Edwin Perry, *Aesopica: A Series of Texts Relating to Aesop or Ascribed to Him or Closely Connected with the Literary Tradition That Bears His Name. Volume I: Greek and Latin Texts* (Urbana, 1952)

PG = Jacques-Paul Migne, ed., *Patrologiae cursus completus, series Graeca,* 161 vols. (Paris, 1857–1866)

Note on the Text

The Greek text presented in this volume is not a full critical edition. With the exception of Ethopoeia 12, for which we used Wolfram Hörandner's edition of 1981, our text is based on the 1983 edition of Adriana Pignani, who consulted sixteen manuscripts. One of these dates to the fifteenth or sixteenth century; all the others date to the thirteenth and fourteenth centuries. Pignani provides further information on these manuscripts on pages 51–57 and 69–70 of *Niceforo Basilace.*

We have made a number of changes to both the Hörandner and the Pignani editions, some of them tacitly. In formatting the text, we have corrected typographical errors, made changes to capitalization, divided paragraphs differently, and added section numbers. We have also occasionally changed punctuation to correct errors and to clarify the interpretation of the Greek, but we have not attempted to repunctuate the entire text.

In our Notes to the Text we have listed corrections and emendations suggested in published reviews of Pignani's edition by Albert Failler, Wolfram Hörandner, and Diether Roderich Reinsch (see Bibliography); many of the corrections are based on inspection of the manuscripts by these reviewers. Also included are emendations that we have pro-

posed ourselves and changes to the text where we have adopted a more plausible or attractive variant listed in Pignani's *apparatus criticus* or printed in Christian Walz's edition of 1832. We have not personally inspected the manuscripts.

We differ from Pignani with regard to orthography in two cases. We spell forms of Ἅιδης with the iota adscript, following Reinsch, and forms of Ἀλωεύς with a smooth breathing, following Walz. Pignani prefers Ἅδης and Ἁλωεύς.

References to our Greek text are by exercise number within each category and by section number. Readings in our text are listed first, followed by Pignani's readings, cited by her overall exercise number and by line number, in parentheses. Since for Ethopoeia 12 we have adopted the text of Hörandner with minor changes, we have not indicated differences between our version and Pignani's.

Sɪɢʟᴀ

Ba = Barb. gr. 240 (olim II 61 et 392)

L = Laur. XXXII 33

O = Ox. Barocc. 131

P = Par. gr. 2918

S = Escorial gr. 265 (Y II 10)

W = Vind. phil. gr. 321

W^{PC} = Manuscript W as corrected by a scribe

MSS = All manuscripts

< > = editorial insertion

<...> = lacuna suggested by editor

Notes to the Text

καταπυρσεύοντα Beneker-Gibson: καταπυρσεύουσαν Pignani (24.28)

2.1 μετὰ μοιχείαν Αἴγισθος Ba: μετὰ μοιχείας Αἴγισθος Pignani (25.11)

2.10 ἀρτίτοκον οὐκ ἀποδίδωσιν Beneker-Gibson: οὐκ ἀρτίτοκον ἀποδίδωσιν Pignani (25.86)

REFUTATION

1 φαίης Beneker-Gibson: φαίην Pignani (27.8)
3 καὶ τῶν μήλων Failler, Hörandner: καὶ <ἓν> τῶν μήλων Pignani (27.30)
4 ἔχουσι L: ἔχουσαι Pignani (27.46)
7 ἀλλά γε Hörandner: ἄλλα γε Pignani (27.73)
9 ἔπαθε, τί μὴ Hörandner: ἔπαθε, <τί ἐς> ἔρωτ' ἔσπευδε; <...> τί μὴ Pignani (27.95–96)

CONFIRMATION

4 τοὺς ἄρρενας Hörandner: τοῦ ἄρρενας Pignani (28.33)
5 καὶ τὸ θῆλύ Hörandner: καὶ <τί> τὸ θῆλύ Pignani (28.37–38)
θαύμασαι Hörandner: θαυμάσειν Pignani (28.38)
8 ἀλλ' ὡς μὲν Hörandner: ἀλλ' ὡς μὲν Pignani (28.63)
ὡς δὲ Hörandner: ὡς δὲ Pignani (28.64)
18 τούτους Beneker-Gibson: τούτοις Pignani (28.153)
20 ξυνέλεγε τὸ Hörandner: ξυνελέγετο Pignani (28.174)

ENCOMIUM

Title *Only Manuscript S provides a title for this exercise, which reads,* "τοῦ βασιλάκη κυροῦ νικηφόρου ἐγκώμιον κυνός"
2 ἀ<γέ>λαις Hörandner: <εἴ>λαις Pignani (29.29)
3 ὁ θηρευτὴς ἱππαζόμενος Hörandner: ὁ θερευτὴς ἱππαζόμενος Pignani (29.35)
8 ἐπανήκοντα Beneker-Gibson: ἐπανηκότα Pignani (29.127)
9 τὸ φυλάττον Beneker-Gibson: τὸ φυλαττόμενον Pignani (29.138)
τοῦ φύσαντος Beneker-Gibson: τοῦ φυλάσσοντος Pignani (29.139)

ETHOPOEIAE

2.1   με τὰ Hörandner: μετὰ Pignani (31.3)
3.1   ὑμῖν πέρας OW^PC: ἡμῖν πέρας Pignani (32.1)
       ὑμᾶς διεδέξατο PW^PC: ἡμᾶς διεδέξατο Pignani (32.2)
       ὦ γυναικῶν Beneker-Gibson: ὦ γυναικῶν Pignani (32.8)
3.5   πρὸ τοῦ Beneker-Gibson: προτοῦ Pignani (32.39)
3.7   ἐπὶ μᾶλλον MSS: ἔτι μᾶλλον Pignani (32.61)
4.3   τάχα Walz: ταῦτα Pignani (33.21)
5.1   τά γε Hörandner: τᾷδε Pignani (34.10)
6.5   κτείνειν Hörandner: κτένειν Pignani (35.39)
7.2   ἐπειθόμην Beneker-Gibson: ἐπιθόμην Pignani (36.13)
8.4   καιρὸν W: καὶ ὃ Pignani (37.33)
       ὦ νόμοι Beneker-Gibson: ὧ νόμοι Pignani (37.35–36)
9.2   ἀκούων Hörandner: εὐκόλως Pignani (38.20)
9.4   τοῖς ὀφθαλμοῖς Hörandner: ἐν τοῖς ὀφθαλμοῖς Pignani (38.43–
       44)
10.3   τις Beneker-Gibson: τίς Pignani (39.37)
10.4   ἥξειν Beneker-Gibson: ἥκειν Pignani (39.46)
       πάντα MSS: πάντας Pignani (39.47)
10.5   ἀπέγνων Beneker-Gibson: ἐπέγνων Pignani (39.58)
10.6   ἐνεβριμήσατο Hörandner: ἐνεβρίσατο Pignani (39.68)
10.7   ἀτυχήσομαι Walz: εὐτυχήσομεν Pignani (39.76)
       φαινόμενον Hörandner: φαινόμενον, τοῦτον εἶναι Λόγον
       ἐλπιζόμενον Pignani (39.79–80)
11.2   οὔκουν Hörandner: οὐκοῦν Pignani (40.24)
11.3   θρασὺς Hörandner: θερμὸς Pignani (40.26)
       ἐξήρτυσε Beneker-Gibson: ἐξήρτησε Pignani (40.32)
       λοιπὸν Reinsch: λοιπὴν Pignani (40.40)
11.4   μύσωμεν Hörandner: μύσομεν Pignani (40.50)
       ἡμῶν Hörandner: ἡμᾶς Pignani (40.50)
       κηρύττουσιν Hörandner, Walz: κερύττουσιν Pignani (40.51–52)
13.2   ὅτι Hörandner: ὅ τι Pignani (42.10)
14.3   πού Beneker-Gibson: που Pignani (43.36)
15.4   ὦ νεκρὸς . . . ἐλάνθανες Reinsch: ὁ νεκρὸς . . . ἐλάνθανεν Pig-
       nani (44.33–34)
       ξίφους Reinsch: ξίφος Pignani (44.38)

κείσεσθαι Reinsch: κήδεσθαι Pignani (44.39)
16.6 μεμνήσεσθαι Reinsch: με μνήσεσθαι Pignani (45.62)
17.3 ἐπέδωκεν Hörandner, Walz: ἐπέθωκεν Pignani (46.40)
18.2 ζεφυρίοις Failler: ζεφυρίαις Pignani (47.21)
19.2 γενόμενος Reinsch: γινόμενος Pignani (48.16)
  Λυγγεύς Reinsch: Λιγγεύς Pignani (48.38)
19.3 Βάκχον Reinsch: Βάκχιον Pignani (48.43)
20.1 πολύμορφον Hörandner, Reinsch: πολύμορφοι Pignani (49.13)
  ἄρα Reinsch: ἆρα Pignani (49.16)
20.6 ὑπερέπτης Hörandner: ὑπερέπτης Pignani (49.66)
21.1 ἐπέχρισε Reinsch: ἐπέχρωσε Pignani (50.9)
21.2 εἰς Ἄθω Beneker-Gibson: ἐξ Ἄθω Pignani (50.38)
  τῆς φίλης Reinsch: τοῖς φίλοις Pignani (50.40)
  μυριόστολος Reinsch: μυρίος στόλος Pignani (50.41–42)
  φυγὰς Reinsch: φυγὴν Pignani (50.43)
21.4 σήματι Hörandner, Reinsch: σώματι Pignani (50.78)
  ἐκεῖνον Beneker-Gibson: ἐκείνων Pignani (50.81)
22.5 ἀγρότα Reinsch, Hörandner: ἀγρώτηρα Pignani (51.51)
  ἐρώμενον Reinsch: ἐρωμένης Pignani (51.58)
  ἀνθρώπου Reinsch: οὐρανοῦ Pignani (51.73)
23.1 ἀθάνατον ἔτι MSS: ἀθάνατόν ἐστι Pignani (52.14)
23.3 ὡς μὴ ὤφελεν Reinsch: ὡς μὴ ὤφελλεν᾽ Pignani (52.38)
  ὡς ἔοικεν Beneker-Gibson: ὡς <οὐκ> ἔοικεν Pignani (52.66–67)
23.5 ἧς Beneker-Gibson: ἥς Pignani (52.101)
  οὐκ ἦν μόνος ὁ Ζεύς Walz: ὡς οὐκ ἦν μόνος ὁ Ζεύς Pignani (52.118–19)
  ὡς τοῦτό γε Walz: ὣς τοῦτό γε Pignani (52.120)
  ὡς, εἴθε Walz: ὣς, εἴθε Pignani (52.122)
24.6 κτείνεις Hörandner: κτένεις Pignani (53.77)
25.1 περισκιρτᾷ Reinsch: περισκιρτεῖ Pignani (54.12)
25.2 ἀκριβῶς: ἀκρυβῶς Pignani
25.4 ἐπίσης Reinsch: ἐπ᾽ ἴσου Pignani (54.46)
27.2 τὰ τῆς σωφροσύνης πυργώματα Beneker-Gibson: τὸ τῆς σωφροσύνης πυργώματα Pignani (56.25–26)
27.3 κατεκοιμήθη Beneker-Gibson: κατεποιμήθη Pignani (56.50)
27.6 καὶ βέλη Walz: καὶ βήλη Pignani (56.96)

Notes to the Translation

Fables

1   *Fable 1:* = Perry 1952, 469.
2   *Fable 2:* Aristotle, *Rhetoric* 2.20 (1393b) gives an abbreviated version attributed to Stesichorus (= Perry 1952, 269a); see Perry 1952, 269, for a similar fable involving a horse and a boar.
2.4 *This fable is Aesopic . . . concerning Fable:* This final statement may be a marginal note that has been transferred into the text.
      Hermogenes's treatise on progymnasmata: See Pseudo-Hermogenes, *Progymnasmata* 1.5–7, in *Corpus rhetoricum,* ed. and trans. Michel Patillon, vol. 1 (Paris, 2008).
3   *Fable 3:* See Perry 1952, 140, for a similar fable.
4   *Fable 4:* = Perry 1952, 451.
5   *Fable 5:* This fable is not found in the extant corpus of Aesop's fables; see Perry 1952, 2, for the similar fable of the eagle, the jackdaw, and the shepherd, and Babrius 37 for a different fable of a jackdaw imitating an eagle.
6   *Fable 6:* This fable is not found in the extant corpus of Aesop's fables, nor in the fables of Babrius or Phaedrus.
7   *Fable 7:* See Perry 1952, 101, for a similar fable.

Narrations

1   *The Story of Thamyris:* Thamyris was a mythical musician, sometimes said to be the son of a Muse and the teacher of Homer. For the myth of his challenging the Muses to a contest, see Homer, *Iliad* 2.594–600; Apollodorus, *Library* 1.3.3.

2   *The Story of Heracles:* Hera once inflicted a temporary madness on Heracles, and in this state he murdered his own children. The oracle at Delphi ordered him to serve Eurystheus, king of Tiryns, in order to cleanse himself of the crime. Eurystheus imposed on Heracles the famous Twelve Labors, of which killing the Hydra of Lerna, the theme of this narration, was the second. For the myth, see Apollodorus, *Library* 2.5.2.

2.2   *his helper Iolaus:* Heracles's nephew, the son of his brother Iphicles.

3   *The Story of Phaëthon:* In the most common version of this myth, Phaëthon was the son of Helius, god of the sun. Raised by his mother, Clymene, one of the daughters of Ocean, he did not learn his father's identity until he was an adolescent. Then he begged his father to let him drive the chariot of the sun, with the disastrous results recounted by Basilakes in this narration. For the myth, see Ovid, *Metamorphoses* 1.747–2.400.

4   *A Story also told by Plutarch in the* Parallel Lives*:* This story does not appear in the extant texts of the *Parallel Lives* but is included in Plutarch's *Moralia*, in the treatise called *Bravery of Women* (262d–63a).

4.1   *there was once a king:* Unnamed here, but in Plutarch's version he is Pythes, king of Lydia.

    really was a "Midas": For the myth of Midas and his love of gold, see Ovid, *Metamorphoses* 11.90–193.

4.2   *the queen:* Unnamed here, as in Plutarch. In a version of the story by Polyaenus, she is identified as Pythopolis; see *Polyaeni Strategematon libri VIII*, ed. Johannes Melber, Eduard von Wölfflin (Stuttgart, 1887; repr. 1970), 8.42.

5   *The Story of Danaë:* For a summary of Danaë's story, see the introduction to Ethopoeia 17 in this collection.

5.2   *Danaë received Perseus:* That is, Danaë bore a son, Perseus, to Zeus.

6   *The Story of Platanos:* For the story of Aloeus and his children, see the introduction to Narration 7 in this collection. *Platanos* is the Greek word for plane tree.

6.1   *Xerxes:* The Persian king Xerxes led a massive expedition against Greece in 480 BCE. See Herodotus, *Histories* 7.27, and Ethopoeia 21 in this collection.

7   *The Story of the Sons of Aloeus:* Aloeus was married to Iphimedia, who fell in love with Poseidon. She bore two children to the god, Otus and Ephialtes, who are known as the Aloadae, that is, the sons of Aloeus. They were giants and sought to challenge the gods, first by piling up mountains to reach heaven (the subject of this narration) and then by filling the seas to make them dry land. Killed either by Zeus, as in Basilakes's version, or by Artemis, they were bound to a pillar in Hades by snakes and eternally tormented by the shrieks of an owl. Basilakes's version omits the snakes and the owl, but it depicts them being tormented by vultures, perhaps conflating their punishment with that of Tityus. For the myth, see Homer, *Odyssey* 11.305–20; Apollodorus, *Library* 1.7.4.

7.1   *more arrogant than their nature:* That is, their nature as mortals.

    setting entire mountains upon mountains: The brothers stacked up Mounts Pelion, Ossa, and Olympus in their attempt to climb up to the sky.

8   *The Story of Achilles:* Achilles was the son of the mortal Peleus and Thetis, one of the divine daughters of Nereus. When Achilles was still a youth, Thetis received a prophecy that he would die in the war at Troy, and so to keep him out of the fighting, she disguised him as a girl and sent him to live among the daughters of Lycomedes, on the island of Scyros. The trick was discovered by Odysseus, who brought Achilles to Troy, where he died fighting. For the myth, see Apollodorus, *Library* 3.13.8.

8.1   *Ilium:* Another name for Troy.

8.3   *Palamedes had earlier exposed Odysseus's pretended madness:* For the myth, see Apollodorus, *Epitome* 3.7; Ovid, *Metamorphoses* 13.34–45, 56–62, 308–12; see also Narration 15 in this collection.

    when he stole the Palladium: A sacred image of Pallas Athena. The city that possessed it could not be conquered, and so Troy withstood the siege of the Greeks for ten years, until Odysseus snuck into the city and stole it. See Apollodorus, *Library* 3.12.3, and *Epitome* 5.10–13; Ovid, *Metamorphoses* 13.337–51.

9   *The Story of Narcissus:* Narcissus was the beautiful youth who famously fell in love with his own image as reflected in a stream.

Some versions of the myth explain that he was made to fall in love with himself to his own destruction after being cursed by others who fell in love with him but were spurned. For the myth, see Ovid, *Metamorphoses* 3.402–510.

10 *The Story of Polydorus:* Polydorus was the son of Priam and Hecuba. When the Trojan War began, Priam, king of Troy, sent Polydorus to King Polymestor in Thrace with part of his fortune, to preserve a remnant of both his family and his wealth in case Troy was defeated. Polymestor betrayed Priam by killing his son and stealing his fortune. After Troy fell, some Greek ships stopped in Thrace on the voyage home. Among the passengers was Polydorus's mother, Hecuba, now a slave. She took the opportunity to kill Polymestor in revenge for his betrayal. Euripides, in *Hecuba*, elaborates the story of Hecuba's revenge; see also Ovid, *Metamorphoses* 13.429–575.

10.1 *the assemblage of his sons:* Priam had fifty sons, among whom were Hector, the Trojans' best warrior, and Paris, who started the Trojan War by abducting Helen from Sparta.

Ilium: Another name for Troy.

11 *The Story of Daedalus:* Narrations 11–13 retell the myths of Minos, Pasiphaë, Daedalus, and Icarus. For a summary of the story, see the introduction to Ethopoeia 20 in this collection.

11.1 *Daedalus's cleverness:* In Greek, the name Daedalus means "cunning worker" or "artist."

11.2 *Pasiphaë, the Sun's child:* Pasiphaë was the daughter of Helius, the Sun god.

12 *The Story of Pasiphaë:* For the myth, see the introduction to Ethopoeia 20 in this collection.

12.1 *to enjoy her laughter:* "Laughter-loving" is an epithet of Aphrodite, the goddess of erotic attraction.

13 *The Story of Icarus:* For the myth, see the introduction to Ethopoeia 20 in this collection.

14 *The Story of the Fall of Troy:* In this narration, Basilakes presents a concise account of the mobilization of the Greeks, the long siege of Troy, and finally the trick of the Trojan horse. For the myth, see Apollodorus, *Epitome* 3–5.

14.2 *in the Chersonese:* The Thracian Chersonese, which is the modern Gallipoli peninsula.

snort and whinny: Herodotus, *Histories* 3.87.

15 *The Story of Odysseus:* When Tyndareus selected Menelaus as husband for his daughter Helen, he made all of her other suitors swear that they would protect the marriage. When Helen was abducted by Paris and taken to Troy, Agamemnon, king of Mycenae and Menelaus's brother, organized a campaign to attack the city and retrieve his brother's wife. Odysseus, as a former suitor, was called upon to join the campaign, but he attempted to avoid his duty by feigning madness. As recounted in this narration, Palamedes tricked Odysseus into revealing that his madness was fake, thus forcing him to join the war. For the myth, see Apollodorus, *Epitome* 3.7–8; Ovid, *Metamorphoses* 13.34–62, 308–12.

15.2 *his treachery against Palamedes:* In revenge for Palamedes's exposing his trick and forcing him to come to Troy, Odysseus either falsely accused Palamedes of betraying the Greeks to the Trojans, for which he was put to death, or simply killed him himself by crushing him with stones. See Apollodorus, *Epitome* 3.8, 6.9.

16 *The Story of Myrrha:* For a summary of the story, see the introduction to Ethopoeia 22 in this collection. Myrrha is sometimes called Smyrna, both Greek words for myrrh.

16.1 *Theias:* Sometimes called Cinyras.

16.3 *Adonis:* The son born from the incestuous union of Myrrha and her father. Adonis grew up to become the lover of Aphrodite but died tragically. For the myth, see Apollodorus, *Library* 3.14.4; Ovid, *Metamorphoses* 10.503–59.

Maxims

1 *"In doing good, consider that you are imitating God":* One manuscript labels this exercise as a verbal *chreia*. Unlike a typical verbal *chreia*, this exercise does not name the speaker (here the fourth-century theologian Gregory of Nazianzus, also known

as Gregory Nazianzen and Gregory the Theologian) in the title; this is the only distinction between the verbal *chreia* and the maxim (or *gnome*). The quotation comes from his *Moral Poems* (*Carmina Moralia* 30.5, *PG* 37.909.4). Basilakes follows ancient rhetorical theory in organizing his essay as follows: brief praise of the speaker (1–2), paraphrase of the statement (3), rationale for the statement (4–6), argument from the opposite (7), argument from analogy (8), argument from example (9), testimony of the ancients (10), brief epilogue (11).

1.2   *the mystery . . . was hidden from eras and generations:* See Colossians 1:26.

1.3   *poetically:* Literally, "in iambic meter."

1.9   *Abraham and Joseph:* Abraham showed hospitality by feeding three strangers who visited him (Genesis 18:1–8). Joseph fed poor Egyptians during famines (Genesis 41:53–57, 47:13–26).

1.10   *Solomon and David:* The idea of the cheerful giver can be traced to Solomon and the Book of Proverbs, but it is unclear to which of the Psalms, traditionally ascribed to David, Basilakes is referring.

       cheerful giver: See Proverbs 22:8.

2   *"Kindness always gives birth to kindness":* One manuscript labels this exercise as a verbal *chreia*. Three other manuscripts identify it as a maxim (*gnome*). Unlike a typical verbal *chreia*, this exercise does not name the speaker (here Sophocles) in the title; this is the only distinction between the verbal *chreia* and the maxim. The quotation comes from Sophocles, *Ajax* 522. Basilakes follows ancient rhetorical theory in organizing his essay as follows: brief praise of the speaker (1–4), paraphrase of the statement (5), rationale for the statement (6–11), argument from the opposite (12–13), argument from analogy (14), argument from example (15–16), testimony of the ancients (17–18), brief epilogue (19).

2.1   *a consequence of adultery:* In Sophocles's *Electra*, Orestes, son of the slain king Agamemnon, returns home to kill the murderers (his mother Clytemnestra and her lover Aegisthus) with the help of his sister Electra.

2.2   *Sophocles's play:* In Sophocles's *Ajax*, after the arms of Achilles are

awarded to Odysseus, Ajax wants to kill the Greek leaders, but Athena tricks him into killing plundered livestock instead. Afterward, he commits suicide out of shame. See Ethopoeia 16 in this collection.

2.3 *the wanderer Oedipus:* In Sophocles's *Oedipus the King*, Oedipus blinds and then exiles himself after discovering that he killed his father and married his mother. In *Oedipus at Colonus*, the wanderer Oedipus comes to Colonus near Athens, the place in which he is appointed to die.

2.4 *And the Sopho- part of his name: Sophos* means "wise" in Greek.

2.12 *And you, child, if you do not first give much labor in exchange, you will never profit in the currency of words:* Hock and O'Neil, *The Chreia and Ancient Rhetoric,* 303, n. 640, suspect that this sentence was added by a later author.

2.15 *an alliance against the Persians:* This story of the Athenian alliance with King Amasis (mid-sixth century BCE) is also found in the scholia to Aristophanes, *Plutus* 178.

Plataeans: For their service against the Persians at the Battle of Marathon (490 BCE), the Plataeans received from Athens the rights of citizenship at Athens after the fall of Plataea (427 BCE).

2.16 *Ajax repaid Hector:* As night began to fall after a long and indecisive single combat, the Trojan Hector proposed a truce and an exchange of gifts with the Greek Ajax; see Homer, *Iliad* 7.299–305.

Diomedes, the son of Tydeus, repaid Glaucus: After discovering that they had an ancestral relationship of guest-friendship, the Greek Diomedes proposed to the Trojan Glaucus that they exchange armor; see Homer, *Iliad* 6.230–36. Homer remarks on Glaucus's foolishness in this, because he exchanged his gold armor for the much less valuable bronze.

Agamemnon admired Teucer: As Agamemnon watched Teucer kill many Trojans in short order, he praised him and promised him gifts after Troy was sacked; see Homer, *Iliad* 8.278–91.

honoring in turn: After the single combat of Hector and Ajax, Agamemnon dedicated an ox and had it butchered for a feast; see Homer, *Iliad* 7.313–22.

rewarded him with long slices from the back: That is, from the back of the roast ox; Homer, *Iliad* 7.321.

2.17 *whatever Hesiod declares:* Hesiod, *Theogony* 22–34, claims to have received his poetic inspiration directly from the Muses.

Who repaid the giver? . . . kindness in return: Paraphrased from Hesiod, *Works and Days* 354–55.

2.18 *Prodicus the sophist:* Pseudo-Plato, *Axiochus* 366C, says that Prodicus borrowed these two lines quoted by Basilakes from the poet Epicharmus.

3 *"This just penalty . . . so much wrongdoing":* The manuscripts label this exercise as a maxim (*gnome*). The quotation comes from Sophocles, *Electra* 1505–7, though Basilakes's text differs from that found in modern critical editions. In this play, Orestes, son of the slain king Agamemnon, returns home to kill the murderers (his mother Clytemnestra and her lover Aegisthus), with the help of his sister Electra. Basilakes follows ancient rhetorical theory in organizing his essay as follows: brief praise of the speaker (1–2), paraphrase of the statement (3), rationale for the statement (4–9), argument from the opposite (10–12), argument from analogy (13–14), argument from example (15–16), testimony of the ancients (17), brief epilogue (18).

3.6 *lays his hands on one of the gods:* That is, robs statues of their adornment as a temple robber.

3.7 *unscrupulous demagogue:* Literally, "the man who speaks to gratify an assembly."

3.8 *"wishes":* Basilakes is referring to the word "wishes" in the second line of the maxim statement: "that whoever wishes to act outside of the laws should be killed."

3.15 *Pausanias:* When the Spartan general Pausanias was plotting to hand Greece over to the Persian king and, after receiving a favorable response from the king, began to dress and act like a Persian, the Spartan ephors tried to arrest him in 470 BCE; he took refuge, however, in a temple of Athena, where he starved to death (Thucydides, *History of the Peloponnesian War* 1.128–34).

The generals disregarded the law: After the naval battle of Arginusae (406 BCE), a storm prevented the Athenians from rescuing

the survivors, and so they drowned. Six of the eight generals stood trial as a group and were executed (Xenophon, *Hellenica* 1.7; Diodorus Siculus, *Library of History* 13.101–2).

3.16   *Palamedes:* He was stoned to death on a false charge that he was planning to betray the Greek forces at Troy. See Narration 15 in this collection.

    Sisyphus ... Tantalus ... Ixion and Tityus: These four suffered terrible punishments in the underworld for their crimes. Sisyphus was condemned to roll an enormous boulder uphill repeatedly. Tantalus was tempted with fruit to eat and water to drink, only to have them repeatedly removed beyond his reach. Ixion was strapped to a burning wheel. Tityus was stretched out for two vultures to feed on his liver, which regrew every night.

3.17   *Euripides:* Basilakes could be thinking of several Euripidean plots, but it is uncertain to which specific passage he refers.

    Pythagoras: An influential philosopher and mathematician of the sixth century BCE. Basilakes's source for this statement is unknown.

    Lycurgus: An important Spartan lawgiver of the seventh century BCE. Basilakes may be thinking of Lycurgus's attempt to reform Spartan behavior as described in chapter 5 of Plutarch's *Life of Lycurgus*.

REFUTATION

1   *That the story of Atalanta is implausible:* In the version of the myth related here, Atalanta agrees to marry any suitor who could beat her in a footrace. Hippomenes tricks her by dropping golden apples along the racecourse. When Atalanta stops to pick them up, Hippomenes wins the race and then marries her. For the myth, see Apollodorus, *Library* 3.9.2; Ovid, *Metamorphoses* 10.560–707. See also the Confirmation in this collection.

1.6   *"My child, the deeds of war are not granted to you":* Aphrodite withdrew from fighting in the Trojan War after she was injured by the Greek hero Diomedes. The quotation is from Homer, *Iliad* 5.428.

1.7   *one beast:* The Calydonian boar, which Atalanta helped her
        brother Meleager and others hunt.

        Ethiopian race: In Greek thought, Ethiopia (from the Greek for
        "burned face") usually referred to all of Africa south of Egypt.

CONFIRMATION

1   *That the story of Atalanta is plausible:* For the version of the myth
        related here, see the note on the title of the Refutation, just
        above in this collection.

1.2   *a critic:* Basilakes takes up the objections of an imagined critic, a
        usual practice in such exercises.

1.6   *Penthesilaea:* She led the Amazons to fight against the Greeks in
        the Trojan War and was killed by Achilles, who had previously
        defeated the Trojan champion Hector.

1.7   *her father's child:* A proverb along these lines, about the resem-
        blance of a child to his or her father, is preserved in Makarios
        Chrysokephalos 8.43 (*CPG* 2:220.2).

        "My child, the deeds of war are not granted to you": Zeus spoke this
        line (Homer, *Iliad* 5.428) to Aphrodite after she was injured and
        withdrew from fighting in the Trojan War.

1.11   *Antilochus:* In Homer's *Iliad*, Antilochus is noted for his speed
        (15.569–70, 23.755–56).

        Locrian Ajax: In Homer's *Iliad*, Locrian Ajax is noted for his
        speed (23.791–92).

1.12   *the tortoise:* In this fable related only in Libanius, a tortoise, an-
        noyed by a horse's constant bragging, challenges him to a race.
        While the horse spends his days in laziness and luxury, the tor-
        toise trains continuously, not resting even at night. The tor-
        toise wins the race, proving that hard work often triumphs
        over natural talent. For the fable, see *Libanius's Progymnasmata:
        Model Exercises in Greek Prose Composition and Rhetoric,* trans.
        Craig A. Gibson (Atlanta, 2008), 2–5.

1.15   *Meleager:* Meleager killed the Calydonian boar after Atalanta

wounded it, and he sailed as one of the Argonauts with Jason in pursuit of the Golden Fleece.

1.17   *Achelous and Heracles:* When Heracles and the river god Achelous fought over their beloved Deianira, Heracles defeated Achelous by pulling off his horn. See Ethopoeia 15 in this collection.

1.18   *"godlike":* A common epithet of heroes in Homer.

1.22   *Aeëtes was unable to catch Medea:* When Jason and Medea were trying to outrun the ship of her father (Aeëtes), Medea cut up her brother Apsyrtus and threw the parts into the sea. Aeëtes stopped to collect them, which allowed Jason and Medea to escape.

1.23   *as a prize for beauty:* Angry at not being invited to the wedding of Peleus and Thetis, Eris, the goddess of discord, delivered a golden apple inscribed with the words "for the most beautiful." When Hera, Athena, and Aphrodite argued over it, Zeus assigned the Trojan prince Paris (also called Alexander) to choose the most beautiful goddess. He chose Aphrodite. See Apollodorus, *Epitome* 3.1–2.

Encomium

1   *Encomium:* Only Manuscript S provides a title for this exercise, which reads, "Encomium of the dog by Kyr Nikephoros Basilakes."

1.1   *the criticism of Momus:* The characters and scenario are taken from Lucian, *The Parliament of the Gods* 5. Momus was the god of sarcastic criticism.

   that famous sophist: Basilakes praises Lucian in much the same terms in one of his letters; see Garzya, *Nicephori Basilacae orationes et epistolae,* 113.10.

   "dog-leading": The compound noun "dog-leading" *(kynegesia)* is the regular Greek term for hunting, and the adjective *kynegetis* is an epithet of Artemis.

   after the human being: See the comparison to follow in section 5 below.

1.2	*tracking it down:* Sophocles, *Ajax* 997.

1.2   *tracking it down:* Sophocles, *Ajax* 997.

sniffing it out: Sophocles, *The Searchers* fr. 314.94.

flocks of birds: Sophocles, *Ajax* 168; Euripides, *Ion* 106.

for delight follows the hunt more than sweat: Oppian, *Halieutica* 1.28.

1.3   *heart forged of adamant:* See Pindar, fr. 123.5: "a black heart forged from adamant or steel."

the gray sea bore him: See Homer, *Iliad* 16.34.

1.4   *an Apelles or a Praxiteles:* Famous sculptors of the fourth century BCE.

always killing the hindmost: Homer, *Iliad* 8.342, 11.178.

1.5   "Who are you? Where did you come from?": Literally, "Who, whence are you?" Based on a common Homeric greeting, "Who, whence are you of men?"

1.6   *a very fine story:* See the story of Aesop and the philosopher Xanthus in Perry 1952, 50–52, 89–90.

1.7   *The experience of Nicias:* Related by Aelian, *On Animals* 1.8.

the charcoal pit: The coals into which Nicias fell were at the bottom of a pit used for making charcoal.

1.8   *that famous old Ithacan dog:* See Homer, *Odyssey* 17.290–327. In Homer, Argus did not stand up or lick Odysseus's feet.

Homer rather ironically calls them "lazy": This is a play on two similar Greek words, both spelled *argos*. One means "idle" or "lazy" and the other "shining" and (metaphorically) "swift." Argus is also the name of Odysseus's dog.

Telemachus also took dogs with him: Homer, *Odyssey* 2.9–12.

reasonably called them soldiers: Plato, *Republic* 2.375a–76c.

1.9   *Then does someone ... brains of that ancestor:* This section is difficult to understand as printed by Pignani, and we were unable to consult the manuscript; therefore our translation and two suggested emendations are provisional.

a descendant: The apparently uncomplimentary word *sparagmata* usually refers to torn or mangled shreds or fragments, but it can also mean "slips" from which to grow new plants, thus "scions" or "descendants."

Melitides ... Coroebus: Proverbial fools, frequently mentioned together; see, for example, Pseudo-Lucian, *Affairs of the Heart* 53, and Aelian, *Historical Miscellany* 13.15.

ETHOPOEIAE

1 *What Joseph would say:* After his Egyptian master Potiphar puts Joseph in charge of his house, Potiphar's wife tries to seduce him; Joseph repeatedly rebuffs her, until one day she more aggressively grabs him by his tunic. When Joseph runs away without it, she accuses him of attempting to seduce her, and her husband throws Joseph into prison (Genesis 39:6–20). In Byzantine narratives, this story is often alluded to as emblematic of manly resistance to female temptation.

1.2 *in my dreams:* For these two dreams and his family's reaction to them, see Genesis 37:3–11, 23–28.

 stripped of the freedom: Joseph's envious brothers sold him into slavery (Genesis 37:1–35).

1.5 *My brothers' envy:* Envious of their father Jacob's special affection for Joseph, his brothers stripped him of the luxurious robe that Jacob had given him, threw him into a pit, and sold him into slavery, leading Jacob to believe that he had been killed (Genesis 37:1–35).

 at the hands of one person: For Jacob's conflict with his twin brother, Esau, see Genesis 25:19–34, 27:1–41.

2 *What Joseph would say:* After the events described in Ethopoeia 1, Joseph remains in prison, alongside Pharaoh's chief cupbearer. Joseph interprets a dream for the cupbearer, telling him that he will shortly be restored to his office, and his prediction comes true. When Pharaoh later has a dream that he cannot interpret, the cupbearer recommends that he ask for Joseph's help. When Joseph successfully interprets this dream too, Pharaoh makes him his second-in-command (Genesis 40:1–45).

2.1 *a woman's scheme took me prisoner:* For these events, see Ethopoeia 1.

2.5 *The fat cattle:* Predicted by dreams that Joseph interpreted. For this dream imagery and its interpretation, see Genesis 41:46–57.

2.6 *what the sheaves portended; . . . the sun bowing and the stars bending down:* For these two dreams, see Genesis 37:3–11.

 my very brothers: During the famine, Joseph's brothers came to Egypt to buy grain, unaware that Joseph was alive (Genesis 42:1–45:28).

for God also promised him: For God's promise to Abraham, see Genesis 22:17.

3   *What Samson would say:* The Philistines pay Samson's beloved Delilah to discover the secret of his great strength. After he tricks her three times, she pesters him until he finally reveals that, as a Nazirite (one consecrated to God), his head must never be shaved. Waiting until he is asleep, Delilah has his head shaved; the Philistines then blind him, shackle him, and put him to work turning a millstone. When his hair begins to grow back, they summon Samson to entertain them. Samson asks his attendant to place his hands on the support pillars of the house. Then he prays to God and destroys the house, killing many Philistines along with himself (Judges 16:4–30).

3.1   *the jawbone of an ass:* Samson used the jawbone of an ass to kill one thousand Philistines (Judges 15:15–17).

    a woman's captive: That is, of Delilah.

3.2   *a lion was defeated:* Samson killed a young lion in the vineyards of Timnah (Judges 14:5–6).

    I abided by the command: Before Samson's birth, an angel proclaimed to Samson's mother that his hair should not be cut (Judges 13:2–14).

    it put a stop to my thirst: After Samson used the ass's jawbone to kill the Philistines, God supplied him with water from a hollow place in the jawbone (Judges 15:18–19).

3.4   *the Midianites:* The Israelites destroyed Midian in a holy war (Numbers 31), and the Babylonians conquered their fortified cities (Deuteronomy 28:48–57).

3.10   *For you must go on living:* In the biblical account, Samson does not warn the boy (Judges 16:28–30).

4   *What David would say:* A scenario loosely inspired by 1 Kings 21:10–15; see also 1 Kings 27:1–28:2. In the biblical account, David fears that King Saul intends to kill him, so he flees from Jerusalem to Achish, king of Gath; when Achish's men recognize him, David fears for his life and feigns madness. However, in the biblical account, David is not held prisoner or explicitly threatened with death.

4.1   *The famous Goliath:* Young David killed the Philistine champion
       Goliath with his slingshot and then beheaded him with the gi-
       ant's own sword; see 1 Kings 17:1–54.

       scorning the army of the living God: See 1 Kings 17:36. This is the
       army of the Israelites.

       the uncircumcised: That is, the Philistines.

4.3   *joined to your family:* David married Saul's daughter, Melchol (1
       Kings 18:20–27).

       The plucking of the lyre: When Saul was tormented by an evil
       spirit, David's lyre playing often soothed him (1 Kings 16:14–
       23).

       armed your insane right hand against my music: While David was
       playing the lyre, Saul tried to kill him with a spear (1 Kings
       19:9–10).

5   *What David would say:* Basilakes combines elements from two
       similar stories, both related in 1 Kings. In one story, when
       the jealous king Saul is pursuing David in the wilderness in or-
       der to kill him, he stops to relieve himself (or to sleep) in a
       cave in which David and his men are hiding. David has the op-
       portunity to kill Saul but does not take it; he only cuts off the
       skirt of Saul's robe. When David reveals himself and shows
       Saul the skirt, Saul realizes that David has been merciful in
       sparing his life, and the two are reconciled (1 Kings 24:1–23).
       In the other story, when Saul is pursuing David in the wilder-
       ness, David goes to his camp at night. David has the oppor-
       tunity to kill the sleeping Saul but does not take it; he only
       takes Saul's spear and a jar of water. He then rebukes the army's
       commander from a distant hilltop for failing to protect the
       king, showing him the spear and jar. Saul overhears them.
       When Saul realizes that David has shown him mercy, the two
       are reconciled (1 Kings 26:1–25). In Basilakes's composite ver-
       sion, the setting is a cave, Saul and his men are sleeping, and
       David intends to rebuke Saul's bodyguards for failing to pro-
       tect their king, showing them part of Saul's garment and part
       of his spear.

5.1   *you have fallen into the ditch that you dug:* See Psalms 7:15.

6   *What David would say:* When David's son Absalom revolts, David is forced to flee from Jerusalem (2 Kings 15:1–17:29).

6.1   *I was a fugitive:* David was a fugitive from Saul. For the conflict between David and Saul, his father-in-law and king, see 1 Kings 16–31, and Ethopoeiae 4 and 5 in this collection.

6.3   *I stole a marriage bed:* David arranged the death of Uriah the Hittite in order to marry his widow, Bathsheba, with whom he had conceived a child (2 Kings 11:1–27).

6.5   *to do battle:* For the battle, see 2 Kings 18:1–8.

        to take Absalom alive: Despite David's order not to harm Absalom (2 Kings 18:5, 12), his general Joab killed him (2 Kings 18:14–15).

        when I caught him asleep: For this story, see Ethopoeia 5 in this collection.

7   *What Zacharias, the father of the Forerunner, would say:* When the angel Gabriel visits the priest Zacharias to announce that his barren wife Elizabeth will give birth to John the Baptist ("the Forerunner" of Jesus), Zacharias doubts the prophecy and is punished by losing his ability to speak. He regains his speech after the baby is born, and he follows the angel's command to name him John. For the story, see Luke 1:5–80.

7.1   *"he will not drink . . . he will be filled with the Holy Spirit":* See Luke 1:15.

        I was condemned to silence: See Luke 1:18–20.

7.2   *a descendant of Sarah:* Like Zacharias's wife, Abraham's elderly and barren wife, Sarah, was told by a visitor that she would have a child, and she did not believe him (Genesis 17:15–18:15).

7.3   *Samson:* As a Nazirite (from a Hebrew word meaning "consecrated"), the Israelite hero and judge Samson could not cut his hair or drink alcohol (Judges 13:2–14); he also struggled against the temptations of sex (Judges 16:4–30). Like John, he was born to a woman who was previously barren. See Ethopoeia 3 in this collection.

        Samuel: A prophet and judge of Israel (1 Kings 1–12). Like John, he was born to a woman who was previously barren.

        you too will be called prophet of the most high: Luke 1:76.

	inspired to say something even greater: For Zacharias's prophecy, see Luke 1:67–79.
7.4	*the Voice:* The prophet Isaiah's reference to "a voice of one crying in the wilderness" (Isaiah 40:3–5; Luke 3:4–6) has traditionally been interpreted as a prophecy about John the Baptist.
8	*What the Theotokos would say:* Jesus performs his first miracle, turning water into wine, at the wedding at Cana, which he attends with his mother, Mary, who in the Greek tradition is called the Theotokos ("mother of God"). For the story, see John 2:1–11.
8.2	*as a bridal escort:* See Luke 1:26–38.
	That star heralded your birth: See Matthew 2:1–12.
8.5	*Our forefathers drank water that came from a rock:* Moses struck a rock in the wilderness to produce water for the thirsty, complaining Israelites, whom he rebuked for asking God to prove himself (Exodus 17:1–7).
9	*What the man blind from birth would say:* Jesus heals a man who was born blind by combining clay with his own spittle and applying it to the man's eyes. For the story, see John 9:1–41. Both here and in Ethopoeia 12.15 in this collection, Basilakes portrays the miracle as an act of creation; that is, Jesus fashioned new eyes for a man who was born without them. The same interpretation expressed in similar imagery appears in some ancient Christian authors, such as Ephrem the Syrian, Irenaeus, Ammonius, and Caesarius of Arles; for these sources, see *John 1–10*, ed. Joel C. Elowsky (Downers Grove, Ill. 2006), 318–27.
9.2	*I have often been discouraged:* In John 9:8, people ask if the healed man is the same one who used to sit and beg. Basilakes plausibly explains that he chose to sit so that he would not harm himself by stumbling around.
9.3	*I marveled at the great Moses:* The formerly blind speaker marvels at Moses (the ostensible author of the Pentateuch) for his vivid description of God's first act of creation, in Genesis 1:1–5.
9.4	*He blended earth with water:* See John 9:6–7.
	a whole man from clay: God created Adam from clay (Genesis 2:7).
	not whole: Literally, "partially nonexistent."

9.5   *as your sin:* Before Jesus healed the man, the disciples asked him whether the man's blindness was due to his sin or that of his parents. Jesus rejected both alternatives, saying that his disability represented an opportunity to show God's miraculous power (John 9:2–3).

9.6   *into the synagogue:* The healed man was twice taken before the Pharisees to explain how he had been healed (John 9:13–34).

10   *What Hades would say:* Four days after the death of his friend Lazarus, brother of Mary and Martha, Jesus goes to his tomb and resurrects him by calling out, "Lazarus, come forth." Basilakes imagines the reaction in the underworld. For the story, see John 11:1–44. One of the two manuscripts ascribes this exercise to Psellos, possibly the eleventh-century Byzantine polymath Michael Psellos.

10.2   *the prophet Elisha:* Elisha raised a boy from the dead (4 Kings 4:8–37).

            a dead man: When a dead man was put into Elisha's grave, contact with Elisha's bones raised him from the dead (4 Kings 13:20–21).

            his teacher: Elijah ascended to heaven in a whirlwind (4 Kings 2:11).

10.4   *one lying on a bed:* See Matthew 9:1–8; Mark 2:1–12; Luke 5:17–26.

            a madman: See Matthew 8:28–34; Mark 5:1–20; Luke 8:26–39.

            restored a dead man to life: Jesus brought two others back from the dead: the daughter of Jairus (Matthew 9:18–26; Luke 8:41–55) and a widow's only son (Luke 7:11–15).

10.5   *His body had already begun to smell:* See John 11:39.

            the command: That is, Jesus's command that Hades release Lazarus.

10.6   *he wept:* John 11:35.

            Lazarus . . . put on his body: See John 11:38–44.

11   *What the slave of the high priest would say:* When the traitor Judas leads Jewish leaders to the garden of Gethsemane to arrest Jesus, one of his disciples attacks the slave of the high priest and cuts off his ear; Jesus orders everyone to stop fighting and heals the man. All four gospels recount the wounding of the slave (Matthew 26:36–56; Mark 14:32–52; Luke 22:39–53; and John

18:1–11), but only Luke 22:49–51 includes his healing, and only John 18:10 identifies Peter (Basilakes's "rash old man") as the disciple who strikes him.

11.3   *that rash old man*: The apostle Peter (as in John 18:10).

your fellow disciple: Judas.

11.4   *gold-loving disciple:* Judas.

my master and all the rest who are acquainted with scripture: The high priest and the chief priests, temple officers, and elders who had come to arrest Jesus (Luke 22:52).

expectation of nations: See Genesis 49:10.

the star: A star directed Magi from the East to the place of Jesus's birth (Matthew 2:1–12).

the voice from heaven: When Jesus was baptized in the Jordan, a voice from heaven declared him the Son of God (Matthew 3:13–17; Mark 1:9–11; Luke 3:21–22).

by no means answerable to us: After examining Jesus, Pilate declared him innocent of any charges that would merit death (Luke 23:13–16).

12   *What the Theotokos would say:* Basilakes draws upon the Bible, the *Protevangelium of James* (an apocryphal gospel), liturgical texts, and iconography to imagine Mary's lamentation over her son, Jesus, as she prepares him for burial after the crucifixion.

12.1   *the men who came from Persia:* See Matthew 2:11.

as Symeon foretold: See Luke 2:35.

the fire . . . to cast upon the earth: See Luke 12:49.

the Lord with me: See Luke 1:28.

12.2   *your virtue covered the heavens:* See Habakkuk 3:3.

more beautiful than the sons of men: Psalms 44(45):2.

glory the heavens describe: Psalms 18(19):1.

A hewn tomb: See Luke 23:53, where Jesus's tomb is called "cut into a rock."

a stone cut from an unhewn mountain: See Daniel 2:45. The stone cut from an unhewn mountain was thought to foretell the birth of Jesus from a virgin.

in the bush: See Exodus 3:2.

in Joseph: Joseph's brothers plotted against him and sold him into slavery (Genesis 37:1–35).

in Isaac: God tested Abraham by commanding him to sacrifice his son Isaac (Genesis 22:1–19).

in Jonah: The prophet Jonah was swallowed by a giant fish and released after spending three days and nights in its belly (Jonah 1–2; Matthew 12:40).

could raise up children for Abraham from the stones: See Matthew 3:9.

when stones had been broken: Stones were broken (that is, there was an earthquake) at the moment Jesus died; when the centurion and other soldiers witnessed this, they believed that Jesus was the Son of God; see Matthew 27:51–54.

12.3   *You did not have a place to lay your head . . . foxes:* See Matthew 8:20; Luke 9:58.

a right-believing thief: One of the thieves who were crucified along with Jesus (Luke 23:40–43).

"The sun has looked upon me": Song of Songs 1:6.

one who sings her song of rejoicing: A reference to the female lover who is one of the singers in the Song of Songs.

"The sun set while it was still midday": Jeremiah 15:9.

sun of righteousness: See Malachi 4:2.

stones were broken: Stones were broken in an earthquake at the moment of Jesus's death (Matthew 27:51).

12.4   *curdled like cheese:* Similarly, Job describes God's act of creating him as pouring him out like milk and curdling him like cheese (Job 10:10).

the ancient debt: This is the ancient debt of Eve, whose disobedience to God's command is often characterized as having been reversed by Mary's obedience to God's will.

you made the heavens bow: See Psalms 17(18):9.

you descended like rain on a fleece: See Psalms 71(72):6.

would raise up the bodies of saints laid to rest: See Matthew 27:52–53.

the immaterial fire of divinity did not burn up my inner organs: That is, Mary remained unharmed at the moment of conception (Luke 1:34–35).

pledges of joy from an angel: See Luke 1:26–38 for the story of the Annunciation of Christ's birth to Mary.

wiped away every tear from the face: See Isaiah 25:8. That is, by giving birth to Jesus.

You descend into Hades: According to tradition, between his crucifixion and resurrection, Jesus descended to the underworld to rescue Adam and Eve and other famous figures from the Old Testament.

12.5   *bound with thorns:* Jesus was forced to wear a crown of thorns on the cross (Matthew 27:29; Mark 15:17; John 19:2, 5).

you did not have a place where you could lie: See Matthew 8:20; Luke 9:58.

you sleep . . . like a lion: See Genesis 49:9.

beaten by a reed: Jesus's head was beaten with a reed just before the crucifixion (Mark 15:19).

broken: Basilakes is alluding to the verse, "A bruised reed he will not break" (Isaiah 42:3, quoted in Matthew 12:20).

12.6   *bitter gall and . . . sour vinegar:* These were drinks given to Jesus on the cross to increase his torment (Matthew 27:34, 48; Mark 15:23, 36; Luke 23:36–37; John 19:28–30).

raised a man dead for four days: For the story of Lazarus, see John 11:38–44; see also Ethopoeia 10 in this collection.

a treacherous kiss: Judas betrayed Jesus with a kiss (Matthew 26:47–50; Mark 14:43–45; Luke 22:47–48).

grasped the hand . . . from his fall: Jesus descended to the underworld to rescue Adam, who had disobeyed God by eating fruit from the tree of knowledge of good and evil (Genesis 3:7).

side pierced with a spear: A spear was driven into Jesus's side on the cross (John 19:34).

the first mother: Eve, who was created from Adam's rib (Genesis 2:21–22).

feet that walked on water: Jesus miraculously walked on water (Matthew 14:22–33; Mark 6:45–52; John 6:16–21).

12.7   *manna:* Manna was the food provided to the Israelites by God on their journey through the wilderness (Exodus 16:33–34; Hebrews 9:4); Mary was like the jar that holds manna because Jesus is the bread of life (John 6:35).

the unconsumed bush: Mary was like the burning bush (Exodus

3:1–6) because she burned with the fire of God at the time of her conception of Jesus but was not consumed.

the golden lampstand: Mary was like the golden lampstand that God commanded Moses to make (Exodus 25:31–40; Zechariah 4:2–3) because she bore the light of the world and remained unharmed by it.

you have placed your light under the bushel: See Matthew 5:15; Mark 4:21. Jesus tells the crowd that they are the light of the world and that they should not hide their light under a bushel basket but put it on a lampstand for all to see. Here, Mary laments that Jesus's death has hidden his light from her and from the world.

12.8   *To you alone . . . to promise me to you:* Mary's mother, Anna, wife of Joachim, was barren until God heard their prayers. As a child, Mary was dedicated to the Temple and raised there. For the story, see *The Infancy Gospel of James*, chs. 1–8, pp. 32–47, in *The Infancy Gospel of James and Thomas*, ed. Ronald F. Hock (Santa Rosa, Calif., 1995).

A human ate the bread of angels: Psalms 77(78):25.

12.9   *an old, dry staff:* an allusion to the budding of Aaron's staff in Numbers 17:1–11. Just as the old, dry staff became fruitful, so also did the older, childless Anna.

when Zacharias saw him: See Luke 1:5–25.

The baby inside his wife's womb exulted: The angel Gabriel announced to Mary that she would give birth to Jesus (Luke 1:26–38). When Mary went to visit her pregnant cousin Elizabeth, wife of Zacharias, Elizabeth's baby (John the Baptist) leaped in her womb (Luke 1:39–45).

"a mother rejoicing in a child": See Psalms 112(113):9.

the ancestor of God: In the Byzantine tradition, the Psalms were traditionally ascribed to David, Mary's ancestor.

surpassing all daughters: See Proverbs 31:29. Some of the Proverbs were traditionally ascribed to Solomon.

Kings came to me: For the description of the kings' journey to Bethlehem, see Matthew 2:1–12.

wider than the heavens: In the Liturgy of Saint Basil, Mary is called "wider than the heavens" because she was able to con-

tain Christ in her womb. This epithet, *platytera*, sometimes appears in her iconography.

most blessed among all generations: See Luke 1:48.

12.10   *a cloud of light:* The pillar of cloud that led the Israelites by day during their forty years of wandering in the wilderness is mentioned in biblical books traditionally ascribed to the prophet Moses (Exodus 13:21–22; Numbers 14:14; Deuteronomy 1:33).

"The daughter of Zion will . . . a vineyard": Isaiah 1:8.

wine that cheers the hearts: See Psalms 103(104):15.

12.11   *A new star shining by day at your birth:* A star guided Magi from the East to the place of Jesus's birth (Matthew 2:1–12).

you hid the visible sun: The daytime sky was dark for about three hours just before Jesus died (Matthew 27:45; Mark 15:33; Luke 23:44–45).

has removed far away: In the gospels of Matthew (26:56) and Mark (14:50), the disciples deserted Christ as he was being crucified.

a division of your garments and mockery and a crown of insults: Jesus was mocked (Matthew 27:27–44; Mark 15:16–37; Luke 23:33–39; John 19:19–22), and forced to wear a crown of thorns (Matthew 27:29; Mark 15:17; John 19:2, 5), while soldiers gambled to divide his clothes (Luke 23:34; John 19:23–24).

12.12   *were seeking a sign from heaven:* Luke 11:16.

Jews tear their garments: See 4 Kings 18:37.

this temple rips its curtain: The curtain in the temple was ripped at the moment of Jesus's death (Matthew 27:51; Mark 15:38).

The earth too quakes: There was an earthquake at the moment of Jesus's death (Matthew 27:51).

12.13   *the crowd of five thousand men:* Jesus fed a large crowd with a small number of fish and loaves of bread (Matthew 14:14–21).

Pilate and asked for your body: See Mark 15:43. See also Matthew 27:57–61; Luke 23:50–56; John 19:38–42.

the crowds of the sick . . . and raised from Hades: In addition to many other healings, Jesus brought back from the dead the daughter of Jairus (Matthew 9:18–26; Luke 8:41–55), a widow's only son (Luke 7:11–15), and Lazarus (John 11:1–44).

       Nicodemus alone: In John 19:38–42, Nicodemus assists Joseph of Arimathea with Jesus's burial.

12.14   *an infant in swaddling clothes:* See Luke 2:6–7.

       your grave clothes: Jesus was dressed in grave clothes by Joseph of Arimathea (Matthew 27:59; Mark 15:46; Luke 23:53) or by Joseph and Nicodemus (John 19:39–40).

       Symeon: See Luke 2:25–35.

12.15   *to be spat upon:* See Matthew 26:67, 27:30; Mark 10:34, 14:65, 15:19; Luke 18:32.

       with your spittle created new eyes: Jesus used clay and his spittle to heal a man blind from birth (John 9:1–41). See Ethopoeia 9, above, for this interpretation of the miracle.

       you endured the lashings: Jesus endured lashings at his interrogation (Matthew 27:26; Mark 15:15; Luke 23:16; John 19:1).

       drove them outside the temple walls: Jesus drove the moneychangers out of the temple (Matthew 21:12–27; Mark 11:15–33; Luke 19:45–20:8; John 2:13–16).

       pierced in your hands and feet: An allusion to Psalms 21(22):16, as well as a description of the crucifixion.

       stabbed in the side: Jesus was stabbed in the side with a spear while on the cross, and water mixed with blood flowed from the wound (John 19:34).

12.16   *band of your disciples:* The disciples had fled after the crucifixion (Matthew 26:56; Mark 14:50).

       You, their shepherd, were struck: See Matthew 26:31 and Mark 14:27, alluding to Zechariah 13:7.

       bowed your head . . . gave up your spirit: See John 19:30.

       your legs have not been broken: The legs of crucifixion victims were broken to hasten their death. See John 19:31–37, quoting Exodus 12:46 or Numbers 9:12.

       the washing of my rebirth: See Titus 3:5.

       the right-believing thief: One of the thieves who were crucified along with Jesus (Luke 23:40–43). There is no mention in the New Testament of Jesus's blood and water sprinkling the thief in a quasi-baptism, but this interpretation is found in the ancient Christian author Ephrem the Syrian, *Commentary on the Diatessaron* 20.26.

12.17   *that bitter taste of the tree:* Adam and Eve ate the forbidden fruit
         and were punished with mortality (Genesis 3:7–20).

         you sit with your Father: See, for example, Matthew 26:64; Mark
         14:62, 16:19; Luke 22:69.

         adulterous generation: Matthew 12:39, 16:4.

         the pearl before the swine . . . the dogs: See Matthew 7:6.

         wood is being put into the . . . bread: See Jeremiah 11:19.

         madness of avarice: The disciple Judas betrayed Jesus to the au-
         thorities for thirty pieces of silver (Matthew 26:14–16, 47–50;
         Mark 14:10–11, 42–46; Luke 22:3–6, 47–48; John 18:1–5).

         blessed the poor: See Luke 6:20; Matthew 5:3.

12.18   *the temple . . . three days:* See Matthew 26:61.

         I magnify your works, because you do them all with wisdom: See
         Psalms 103(104):24.

13   *What Saint Peter would say:* Simon Magus boldly told a crowd in
         Rome that he would command angels to raise him up to his Fa-
         ther in heaven and punish the people for refusing to follow
         him. As Simon begins to fly with the aid of demons, Peter prays
         to Jesus to stop him. The demons vanish, and Simon falls to the
         ground, dying in great pain the next day. The crowd turns to
         God. Later, in revenge for Peter's conversion of his two favor-
         ite concubines, the emperor Nero sentences Christians to
         death and orders Peter to be crucified upside down. For the
         story, see Symeon Metaphrastes's *Acts of Peter and Paul* (*BHG*
         1493): *AASS*, Jun. VII, 3rd ed. (Paris, 1867), pp. 374–86, esp.
         pp. 379–80.

13.2   *I traveled . . . hands of barbarians:* Peter was twice brought before
         the Jewish high court called the Sanhedrin (Acts 4–5); he trav-
         eled as a missionary to Lydda, Joppa, and Caesarea (Acts 9–10);
         he was imprisoned by King Herod in Jerusalem and freed by an
         angel (Acts 12). Peter can also be placed in Antioch (Galatians
         2:11) and Corinth (1 Corinthians 1:12). Noncanonical writings
         expand his travels further, including Rome.

         another man, his bodyguard, a tyrant: This is the emperor Nero
         (r. 54–68 CE).

13.3   *bragged that he could ascend to the very heavens and sit with the Fa-
         ther:* Satan does not make this boast in the biblical accounts of

Jesus's temptation: see Matthew 4:1–11; Mark 1:12–13; Luke 4:1–13.

those magicians in Egypt: See Exodus 7:8–13.

Aaron: Moses's brother and partner; see esp. Exodus 6:13, 6:26–7:7.

13.4   *dye my body:* Instead of merely being awarded a crimson toga, which victorious Roman generals wore at a triumph, Peter says he will dye his body crimson through his violent death.

I must invert the ending: As a mortal who came from the earth, he will die being pulled toward the earth (that is, crucified upside down).

14   *What Atalanta would say:* Atalanta is left in the woods to die soon after birth because her father wants a son. Raised by a she-bear, Atalanta grows up to be athletic and to love the outdoor life, and like her patron deity Artemis, goddess of the hunt, she protects her virginity. Unwilling to marry, she challenges all potential suitors to a footrace. If the suitor wins, he can marry Atalanta, but in some versions of the myth, if she wins, she will kill him. She remains undefeated, and so unmarried, until Hippomenes (in some versions, Melanion) takes up the challenge. Aphrodite helps Hippomenes by giving him golden apples, which he throws onto the course during the race to distract Atalanta and slow her down. He defeats Atalanta using this trick and so marries her. For the myth, see Apollodorus, *Library* 3.9.2; Ovid, *Metamorphoses* 10.560–707. See also the Refutation and Confirmation in this collection.

14.1   *my feet have been held fast*: As Aphrodite rushed to save her lover Adonis from a boar sent by Ares, she wounded her foot on a rose thorn and did not reach Adonis in time. Her blood gave the rose its red color.

Danaë: For the story of Danaë, see Ethopoeia 17 and Narration 5 in this collection.

14.3   *from his mother:* Love's mother, Aphrodite, received the golden apple from Alexander (also called Paris) as a prize for beauty. For this story, see the note on Confirmation 1.23, above.

shade and letters: Atalanta apparently means that she has no need to interpret obscure messages. For the expression, see, for example, *Sur Zacharie par Didyme l'Aveugle*, ed. and trans. Louis Doutreleau (Paris, 1962), 4.280 (= vol. 3, p. 948), in which he contrasts the letter with the spirit, and shade with the truth.

15 *What Heracles would say:* While Heracles is attempting to cross the river Evenus with his wife, Deianira, he allows the centaur Nessus to carry Deianira across. The centaur assaults her while in the river, and so Heracles shoots him with his bow. While dying, Nessus gives Deianira a vial of his blood, telling her that it is a love potion, when in reality it is poisonous. Later, when Deianira is jealous of Heracles's affection for a younger woman, she applies Nessus's blood to a garment and gives it to Heracles to wear. Putting on this garment brings about Heracles's death, thus fulfilling the prophecy that a dead man would kill him. Sophocles's play *Women of Trachis* elaborates the story of Heracles's death. See also Apollodorus, *Library* 2.7.6–7.

15.1 *Loxias:* An epithet of Apollo, but also reminiscent of the Greek adjective *loxos* ("slanting, crosswise"), which when applied to oracles means they are ambiguous.

15.2 *oracle and prophetic oak:* The oracle of Zeus at Dodona.

15.3 *I have fought against Giants:* The Giants were children of Gaea (Earth) who challenged the Olympian gods after the defeat of the Titans. Heracles assisted his father, Zeus, in defeating them.

I have killed a lion: Heracles killed at least two lions: in his youth he killed the lion of Mount Cithaeron, which was threatening his hometown of Thebes, and the first of his Twelve Labors was to kill the lion of Nemea.

15.4 *my descent to Hades:* Heracles's twelfth labor was to descend to the underworld and abduct Cerberus, Hades's watchdog.

the serpents in my crib: Zeus was Heracles's father, which made Hera jealous. When Heracles was still an infant, she sent two serpents into his crib to kill him, but he killed them instead.

after that Hydra: Heracles's second labor was to kill the Hydra of Lerna; see Narration 2 in this collection.

after the Centaurs: On his way to accomplish his third labor, the killing of the Erymanthian boar, Heracles had dinner with the centaur Pholus. He became drunk and killed several of the centaurs who lived nearby.

15.5 *stolen Cerberus:* See the first note to 15.4, above.

Ares came to realize: After Heracles killed Ares's son, Cycnus, Ares attempted to avenge his son's death. Athena kept Heracles from harm, while Heracles wounded Ares in the thigh.

Even Hera has tasted my arrows: According to Homer (*Iliad* 5.392–94), Heracles shot a three-barbed arrow and wounded Hera in the right breast.

you too, father, have tested my hands: Probably a reference to Heracles's support of his father, Zeus, in the battle against the Giants.

the three-night son of Zeus: When Zeus in the guise of Amphitryon seduced Alcmene, he tripled the duration of the night and fathered Heracles. Thus Heracles sometimes receives the epithet "of the three nights."

16 *What Ajax would say:* After Achilles dies while fighting at Troy, the Greek army holds a contest to see who deserves to wear his armor. Achilles was the best Greek warrior, and Ajax and Odysseus are considered best qualified after him. After letting each man make his case, the Greek commanders, Agamemnon and Menelaus, award the armor to Odysseus. Believing that he is the better fighter and convinced that Odysseus tricked the judges through his clever speech, Ajax kills himself out of shame. After the war, Odysseus is making his way home to Ithaca, when he is forced to visit the underworld. There he speaks with Agamemnon and Achilles, but Ajax still holds a grudge and refuses to speak with him. Sophocles's *Ajax* elaborates the events surrounding Ajax's suicide, and Homer (*Odyssey* 11.541–67) tells the story of Odysseus meeting Ajax in the underworld. See also Apollodorus, *Epitome* 5.5–7; Ovid, *Metamorphoses* 13.1–398.

16.1   *I lost my mind:* In Sophocles's play, Athena drives Ajax be-
       fore he commits suicide.

       Cerberus: The guard dog of Hades.

       Hermes: The patron deity of thieves and the father of Autolycus,
       Odysseus's maternal grandfather. He guided souls to the un-
       derworld.

16.2   *Aeacus:* An ancestor of Ajax who after death became a judge in
       Hades.

       the sons of Atreus: Agamemnon and Menelaus, who awarded
       Achilles's armor to Odysseus rather than to Ajax.

16.4   *Palamedes:* For the story of Palamedes, see Narration 15 in this
       collection.

       Minos and Rhadamanthys: Judges in the underworld.

       Tantalus: He was sentenced to sit under an enormous stone that
       appeared about to fall on his head because, in addition to his
       other crimes, he revealed the gods' secrets to humans.

       carry off Cerberus: As Heracles did; see Ethopoeia 15.5 in this col-
       lection.

       Sisyphus: Known as a trickster, he offended Zeus by witnessing
       the god's abduction of a girl, Aegina, and then informing the
       girl's father. In his anger, Zeus killed Sisyphus and condemned
       him eternally to roll a rock up a hill in the underworld. Each
       time Sisyphus reached the top of the hill, the rock would roll
       back down the slope.

16.5   *a son of Sisyphus:* In one version of Odysseus's myth, Sisyphus is
       his father.

       wronged by both father and son: In one version of his myth, Sisy-
       phus asked his wife not to perform his funeral in order to trick
       Hades into rejecting him for not being properly buried. In an-
       other version, when Death came to bring him to the under-
       world, Sisyphus put Death into chains, thus avoiding his own
       demise and keeping Death away from all mortals, until Zeus
       intervened.

16.6   *Lethe:* The river of oblivion in Hades.

16.7   *Tartarus:* Said to be located as far below Hades as earth is below

heaven, Tartarus was a place of punishment for the most infamous sinners and a prison for the Titans.

17   *What Danaë would say:* Danaë's father, Acrisius, receives an oracle that his grandson will grow up to kill him. Seeking to avoid his fate, Acrisius locks Danaë in a chamber to keep her from marrying and bearing a child. Zeus, however, sees the girl and is attracted to her. Entering the chamber by transforming himself into a shower of gold, he fathers a son with Danaë. The son, Perseus, grows up to be a hero in his own right, but eventually, while participating in some games, he throws a discus that accidentally strikes and kills Acrisius, thus fulfilling the oracle. For the myth, see Apollodorus, *Library* 2.4.1. See also Narration 5 in this collection.

17.1   *Mycenae, rich in gold:* In Homer (*Iliad* 11.46) and Sophocles (*Electra* 9), Mycenae is called rich in gold.

   Pactolus with its golden eddies: A river in Asia Minor (modern Turkey), famous for carrying gold dust from Mount Tmolus. In Greek mythology, King Midas was said to have washed himself in this river to rid himself of his golden touch.

   the whole city of Rhodes: When Athena was born, the people of Rhodes gave her unburned sacrifices, and her father, Zeus, rewarded them by raining down gold on their city.

17.2   *the gods' floor is golden:* An allusion to the floor of Zeus's abode on Mount Olympus; see Homer, *Iliad* 4.2.

   murex shell: Murex, a type of mollusk, was the source of the best purple dye from antiquity to well into the Byzantine period. Because of its expense, the dye was a luxury item, and the color purple itself was closely associated with the emperor and imperial power.

   The bronze was not indestructible: "Indestructible" is a common Homeric epithet of bronze; see, for example, *Iliad* 5.292, 7.247, 14.25.

   put even the Titans to rest with an unbearable fire: Zeus led the Olympian gods in defeating the Titans, the previous generation of gods. In Hesiod, *Theogony* 687–712, the earth is consumed in fire during the war.

17.3 *winged like a bird . . . bellow like a bull:* In the form of a swan, Zeus
seduced Leda and fathered Helen. In the form of a bull, he seduced Europa, conveyed her to Crete on his back, and fathered
Minos and other children.

18 *What Zeus would say:* Io is a young girl and priestess of Hera who
lives in Argos. Zeus falls in love with her and starts an affair,
which causes his wife, Hera, to become jealous. To protect Io
from Hera, Zeus turns the girl into a white heifer. Hera remains jealous, since Zeus has been known to visit Io (and other
girls) in the form of a bull, and so she sends Argus, who has one
hundred eyes, to guard the girl. Zeus sends Hermes to kill Argus, and in return Hera sends a horsefly to sting Io. The sting-
ing causes Io to run and to wander across the Greek world, visiting the Ionian Sea (to which she gives her name), crossing
into Asia at the Bosporus (which means "cow crossing"), and
eventually arriving in Egypt, where Zeus restores her human
form. For the myth, see Apollodorus, *Library* 2.1.3; Ovid, *Metamorphoses* 1.583–750.

18.2 *sing the song of the swan . . . bellowed once like a bull:* For Zeus taking
the forms of a swan and a bull, see Ethopoeia 17.3 (with note) in
this collection.

18.3 *flocks of birds:* Sophocles, *Ajax* 168; Euripides, *Ion* 106.

18.4 *the double fire*: The fire of intoxication combined with the fire of
love.

Ariadne's cheeks: Ariadne was one of the daughters of Minos and
Pasiphaë. After helping Theseus to slay the Minotaur and escape Crete, she was abandoned by him on the island of Naxos,
where Dionysus, also known as Bacchus, fell in love with her.

18.6 *a mortal girl rode on the back of Zeus:* For Zeus and Europa, see
Ethopoeia 17.3 (with note) in this collection.

Erotes: Personifications of desire, the equivalent of Cupids in
Latin.

the Graces will carry the baskets: A reference to the *kanephoros*
(basket-carrier), an honorary title for the young women selected to carry baskets at sacrifices in ancient Greece.

18.7 *I will appoint a cowherd:* This refers to Alexander, also called

Paris, who will judge the beauty of Hera, Aphrodite, and Athena and will award first prize to Aphrodite.

after my cow has passed away: The cow will metaphorically pass away when Io is restored to human form in Egypt. Zeus's statement about the hive alludes to the common belief that honeybees are generated in the bodies of dead oxen.

19   *What Heracles would say:* After Heracles kills Iphitus in a fit of madness, the oracle at Delphi reveals that he must be sold into slavery in order to compensate Eurytus, Iphitus's father, for the murder of his son. Heracles is sold to Omphale, queen of Lydia in Asia Minor, and serves as her slave for three years. For the myth, see Apollodorus, *Library* 2.6.1–3.

19.1   *I killed serpents:* Hera was jealous because her husband, Zeus, had fathered Heracles with Alcmene, a mortal. To kill the infant child, Hera sent serpents into his crib, but Heracles managed to kill them instead.

I became swifter than a deer: Heracles's fourth labor was to kill the deer that lived on Mount Ceryneia. This deer was sacred to Artemis and known for its swiftness.

braver than even a lion: Heracles killed at least two lions: in his youth he killed the lion of Mount Cithaeron, which was threatening his hometown of Thebes, and the first of his Twelve Labors was to kill the lion of Nemea.

When Hera was jealous: Fearing Hera's jealousy, Alcmene left the infant Heracles exposed in the countryside to die, but Athena returned him to his mother and urged her to raise him. Later, after Heracles married Megara and was living in Thebes, Hera made him temporarily insane, and in this state he killed his children. To expiate his sin, he became a servant to Eurystheus, who ordered him to perform the famous Twelve Labors. Athena is said to have assisted Heracles in several of them.

19.2   *bellowed*: Zeus transformed himself into a bull in order to seduce Europa.

the broad-chested one: A regular epithet of Poseidon.

Hades's helmet: This helmet made the wearer invisible; see Ho-

mer, *Iliad* 5.845. Perseus famously wore the helmet when he set
off to kill the Gorgon Medusa.

the all-seeing one: Probably a reference to the Sun, who in Greek
myth witnessed everything that happened on earth.

Lynceus: One of the Argonauts, who was known for his sharp vision and could even see under the earth; see Apollodorus, *Library* 3.10.3.

19.3   *Bacchus:* Another name for Dionysus, god of wine and, like Heracles, a son of Zeus.

one woman's girdle: One of Heracles's labors was to retrieve the
girdle of Hippolyta, queen of the Amazons. Theseus is one of
the mythical kings of Athens.

I contended with the Hydra: Another of Heracles's labors was to
kill the Hydra of Lerna, a beast with multiple heads. Whenever
Heracles cut off one of the heads, it would immediately grow
back. After struggling without success, he had his nephew, Iolaus, apply fire to the open wound left by each severed head,
thus preventing regrowth and allowing him at last to kill the
Hydra. See Narration 2 in this collection.

as though they were other heads spurting up: As with the heads of
the Hydra.

20   *What a sailor would say:* Daedalus is an artist and inventor. While
living in Crete, he becomes intertwined in the affairs of King
Minos and his wife, Pasiphaë, who had fallen in love with a
bull. Daedalus creates a hollow cow out of bronze, into which
Pasiphaë climbs and allows the bull to mount her. Their union
produces the Minotaur (literally, "the bull of Minos"), which
Minos hides away in an elaborate maze, called the Labyrinth,
which Daedalus also builds. In order to escape Minos's anger
for helping his wife mate with the bull, Daedalus invents wings
so that he and his son, Icarus, can escape from Crete. Icarus
ignores his father's warning not to fly too high, and so the sun
melts the wax that holds his wings together, causing him to fall
to his death in the sea. For Pasiphaë's passion for the bull and
Daedalus's invention of the artificial cow, see Apollodorus,

NOTES TO THE TRANSLATION

Library 3.1.3–4, 3.15.8; Ovid, Metamorphoses 8.131–37, 155–56. For the invention of flight and Icarus's death, see Apollodorus, Epitome 1.12; Ovid, Metamorphoses 8.183–235. See also Narrations 11–13 in this collection.

20.2   *his curved sword:* That is, the scimitar he used to behead the Gorgon Medusa.

    a flying horse: A reference to Pegasus, which Bellerophon rode when he killed the Chimera.

    pulled by dragons: After murdering her children, Medea escaped from Corinth in a chariot pulled by dragons.

20.3   *higher than the squids:* Basilakes seems to be referring to the flying squid, whose flight is described in Oppian's poem on fishing (*Halieutica* 1.427–37) and Pliny the Elder's encyclopedia (*Natural History* 9.84). Oppian says that they can fly high and far like birds.

    Phineus and . . . the sons of Boreas: Phineus, a blind seer, was plagued by Harpies, flying creatures that would swoop down and either snatch away his food or defecate on his table. Boreas is the North Wind. His sons, Calais and Zetes, could fly and so chased the Harpies away from Phineus.

    Prometheus: He is best known for restoring fire to humans after Zeus had taken it away, but one version of his story relates that he was responsible for the creation of humans.

20.4   *the Aloadae:* These "sons of Aloeus" were giant men who stacked up mountains in order to climb up and attack the gods in the sky. See Narration 7 in this collection.

20.6   *the Sun, who looks down on everything:* Homer, *Iliad* 3.277.

    He saw his daughter hidden in the bronze: Pasiphaë is the daughter of the Sun.

21   *What Xerxes's pilot would say:* In his history of the Persian wars (8.118–19), Herodotus records an anecdote about the return of Xerxes, the Persian king, from Greece to Asia. Having left his army in northern Greece to make its way home by land, Xerxes and his entourage board a ship and set out to sea. When the ship encounters wind and rough seas, the pilot advises Xerxes

that there are too many men on board for the ship to weather the storm. Xerxes then asks his entourage to jump overboard, to ensure his own safety. Upon reaching land, Xerxes rewards the pilot with a crown for his good advice, and then orders him to be executed for causing the loss of so many Persian lives. Herodotus disbelieves the story.

21.1   *a tiara:* A special headdress worn by Persians, especially on solemn occasions.

Telchis: Telchines (sing. Telchis or Telchin) were legendary inhabitants of Crete, known as spiteful and backbiting people.

the Erinyes: Spirits who avenged crimes. The Romans identified them with the Furies.

21.2   *a strange pancratium:* The *pancratium* was an ancient athletic contest, a combination of boxing and wrestling.

turned sea into land and turned land into sea: In order to bring his army into Greece, Xerxes bridged the Hellespont, turning sea into land, and dug a canal through the peninsula of Athos, turning land into sea (Herodotus, *Histories* 7.22–24, 33–37).

Nereids: Female deities who live in the sea.

a bitter and salty river: Herodotus, *Histories* 7.35.

21.3   *Acheron:* A river in the underworld.

21.5   *Mardonius:* When he returned to Asia, Xerxes left Mardonius in Greece to conclude the war (Herodotus, *Histories*, 8.107).

sons of Asclepius: A name for medical doctors in antiquity.

22   *What Love would say:* Myrrha (or Smyrna) falls in love with her father, Theias (or Cinyras), and tricks him into sleeping with her. He becomes furious when he learns that he has committed incest with his daughter. To escape his wrath, Myrrha prays to the gods for help and is subsequently transformed into a myrrh tree. The child of their union, Adonis, is born from the tree nine months later. On the same topic, see Narration 16. For the myth, see Apollodorus, *Library* 3.14.3–4; Ovid, *Metamorphoses* 10.298–502.

22.1   *a tree of Pan:* Pan was a god of shepherds and flocks whose cult originated in the Greek region of Arcadia. Pausanias, who trav-

eled widely and wrote a description of Greece in the second century CE, mentions a sanctuary of Pan in Arcadia, next to which stood an oak tree, also sacred to the god (8.54.4).

an ash . . . furnished, in turn, with a point: In Homer, spears are made of ash; see, for example, *Iliad* 19.390.

mask of a tree: In Greek tragedy, actors wore masks that represented the characters.

Hyacinthus . . . Narcissus . . . Daphne: All humans who were transformed into plants.

22.2   *an apple tree with its beautiful fruit:* Homer, *Odyssey* 7.115, 11.589.

who am both young and old: In Greek myth, Love is sometimes one of the first gods to come into being, and sometimes he is the very young son of Aphrodite.

22.3   *forefather of Zeus himself, more ancient than Cronus, more primal than Uranus:* This list represents three generations of gods: Uranus was the father of Cronus, who in turn was the father of Zeus.

22.4   *Bacchus:* Another name for Dionysus, god of wine and drunkenness.

22.5   *Adonis:* As a young man, Adonis became the lover of Aphrodite. In one version of the story, the god Ares, another of Aphrodite's lovers, killed him out of jealousy.

23   *What Adrastus would say:* After Oedipus is forced into exile, his sons, Eteocles and Polynices, share the throne in Thebes, with each serving as king in alternating years. Eteocles, however, refuses to yield the throne when his year is completed, and so Polynices seeks the aid of Adrastus, king of Argos, who has also taken in Tydeus, another man forced into exile from Thebes. Adrastus marries the men to two of his daughters and promises to restore both of them to their respective homes. He decides to march first against Thebes and gathers an army led by seven heroes, one for each gate of Thebes. The campaign ends in the utter defeat of Adrastus's army and the deaths of the brothers, Eteocles and Polynices, who slay each other on the battlefield. Contrary to Greek custom, the Thebans refuse to allow the Argives to bury their dead, and so

Adrastus appeals to Theseus, king of Athens, who leads an army to Thebes, defeats the city, and returns the fallen Argives to their kinsmen for burial. Ten years after the Argive defeat, the sons of the dead heroes lead a second, successful campaign against Thebes, thus avenging their fathers. For the myth, see Apollodorus, *Library* 3.6–7.4.

23.1   *outsiders from Phoenicia:* Cadmus, the founder of the city that eventually became Thebes, was from Phoenicia.

     Capaneus: One of the seven heroes who led Adrastus's army. He was struck dead by a thunderbolt from Zeus as he scaled the wall at Thebes.

23.2   *born from a serpent:* Cadmus slew a serpent on the site where he founded his city. Then he sowed the serpent's teeth, from which grew armed men.

     you tricked him with Semele: Hera convinced Semele, Cadmus's daughter and Zeus's lover, to ask Zeus to appear to her in his true form instead of disguising himself, as he usually did. Upon seeing Zeus as he really was, Semele was immediately consumed by fire.

     the Erinyes: Spirits who avenged crimes. The Romans identified them with the Furies.

23.3   *O prophetic Pythia:* The priestess of Apollo at Delphi, through whom the god revealed oracles, was called the Pythia.

     the tripod of Themis: The Pythia would sit on a tripod in the temple of Apollo to receive cryptic messages from the god, which she then relayed to inquirers. Themis, the goddess of law, was said to have controlled Delphi before Apollo and to have taught the younger god the art of prophecy.

     a father-in-law to beasts: Adrastus had received a prophecy that he would marry his daughters to a boar and a lion. Polynices and Tydeus had emblems of animals on their shields, one a boar, the other a lion.

     despised and contested trophy . . . by his own defeat: Both Polynices and Eteocles win (by killing the other) and lose (by being killed) at the same time. Because the brothers are vying for vic-

tory in the battle for Thebes, Polynices metaphorically gets to erect a victory trophy (because he kills Eteocles) but then must also tear it down (because he is killed himself).

23.4   *in retribution for Semele:* See note on Semele above, at 23.2.

Typhoeus: The personification of a typhoon, Typhoeus challenged Zeus after Zeus had defeated the Titans; see Hesiod, *Theogony* 820–85.

Ares was wielding the spear: Homer, *Iliad* 5.594.

the killing of the serpent: The serpent that Cadmus killed was sacred to Ares.

Amymone: A daughter of Danaus, she was a lover of Poseidon from Argos. Poseidon saved Amymone when a satyr was attacking her, striking a rock with his trident and causing a stream with three springs to appear.

a parched city: "Parched" is an epithet applied to Argos in Homer, *Iliad* 4.171.

a wise prophet: A reference to Amphiaraus, a seer and brother-in-law of Adrastus; typically, he is said to have been buried alive by Zeus, not Poseidon. He foretold that the attack on Thebes would fail but was forced to participate anyway.

23.5   *a mother to rage against her son:* Driven into a Bacchic frenzy by Dionysus, Dionysus's aunt Agave killed her son, Pentheus.

attacking his children with his own hands: Driven temporarily insane by Hera, Heracles killed his own children while living in Thebes. To expiate his sin, he became a servant to Eurystheus, who ordered him to perform the famous Twelve Labors.

One Argive: It is not clear which of the seven heroes Basilakes is referring to.

23.6   *they who are autochthonous:* According to legend, the Athenians grew from the earth around their city.

the Sown Ones: The first Thebans grew from the serpent's teeth sown by Cadmus. They are often known as the Spartoi, from the Greek word for "sown."

24   *What Ismenias the* aulos *player would say:* Alexander the Great became king of Macedon in 336 BCE, inheriting his father's hegemony over the cities of Greece. In 335, the Thebans attempted

to expel the Macedonian garrison from their city and reassert their independence, to which Alexander responded by besieging Thebes and demanding its capitulation. When the Thebans refused, he sacked the city and killed or sold into slavery nearly all of its inhabitants. Basilakes's exercise is based on a story not found in historical accounts but which appears in the Greek version of the Romance of Alexander (Richard Stoneman, ed., Tristano Garguilo, trans., *Il romanzo di Alessandro*, [Milan, 2007], 1:1.46a, pp. 104–19), a fictionalized narrative of Alexander's career, and in the later (thirteenth- or fourteenth-century) *Byzantine Alexander Poem* (Willem J. Aerts, ed., *The Byzantine Alexander Poem* [Boston, 2014], 1.46a, ll. 2260–399), a version of the *Romance* rendered into verse. In this story, a certain Ismenias (the name derives from the river Ismenus, which flows near Thebes) beseeches Alexander to be a merciful conqueror; Alexander responds by forcing Ismenias to play music as his men destroy the city. The instrument that Ismenias plays is the *aulos* (plural *auloi*), a wind instrument employing a single or, more often, a double reed, similar to the modern oboe.

24.1   *Cadmus:* The legendary founder of Thebes.

Bacchus: Another name for Dionysus, god of wine and revelry and the son of Zeus and Semele, Cadmus's daughter.

24.3   *Panhellenion:* The term Panhellenion usually refers to the united body of all Greeks or to the temple of Zeus founded in the second century CE by the emperor Hadrian on Aegina as their meeting place. There was a festival associated with this temple. Basilakes might be referring to this festival anachronistically, or he might be referring to earlier Panhellenic festivals at Olympia, Delphi, Nemea, and Isthmia.

the eye of Greece: The eye is considered the most precious part of the human body, and so Basilakes means to say that Thebes is "the most precious part" or "the pride" of Greece.

Pella: The capital of the kingdom of Macedonia.

palinode: A song in which the author retracts a view expressed in an earlier song.

the Argives who fell in Cadmus's field: This army was led by the leg-

endary Adrastus, king of Argos, who marched against Thebes on behalf of Polynices in an attempt to restore him to the throne. See Ethopoeia 23 in this collection.

the noble Spartans who were repudiated by the Thebans: The Thebans defeated the Spartans at Leuctra in 371 BCE. This was the first time the Spartans were defeated in a major battle, and in consequence they lost prestige and their hegemony over Greece.

24.4   *the Erinyes:* Spirits who avenge crimes. The Romans identified them with the Furies.

leaving the auloi *on the ground:* Athena is sometimes credited with inventing the *aulos*, but then discarding it after she noticed that playing it distorted her face in an ugly way.

Harmony: Daughter of Aphrodite and Ares, she was married to Cadmus.

those sprung from the earth: Cadmus slew a serpent sacred to Ares on the site where he founded Thebes. Then he sowed the serpent's teeth, from which grew armed men, called the Sown Ones.

as his father Zeus did: Zeus mourned his mortal son Sarpedon when he was killed by Patroclus on the battlefield at Troy (Homer, *Iliad* 16.419–61).

24.5   *the strings of Amphion:* Amphion played the lyre, which has seven strings. He ruled at Thebes with his brother Zethus, and when the two built the city's walls, Amphion moved the stones into place with his music.

transformed the city into a field: Turning "the city into a field" is a proverbial expression about how criminals treat their city; see Diogenianus 2.47 (*CPG* 1:202.13–15).

the flowing waters of the Ismenus: A river that flows near Thebes.

its responsive song might echo the songs of its founders: As it was also aided by music while Amphion was building its walls.

24.6   *Heracles in his madness:* When driven mad by Hera in Thebes, Heracles killed his own children.

you have leveled the walls: Literally, "shorn the wall of its hair."

You granted a house to the singer and to the Muses: When destroying

Thebes, Alexander spared the house of the poet Pindar and
pardoned his descendants; see Stoneman, *Il romanzo di Alessandro*, 1:1.27, pp. 176–77, 306–7.

*my mother, Thebe of the golden shield, I will put your interests above
my occupation:* See Pindar, *Isthmian* 1.1–3.

25   *What Pasiphaë would say:* For the story, see the introduction to
Ethopoeia 20 in this collection.

25.1   *entirely lovely, like Plutus, someone might say*: "Lovely" *(eperastos)* is
an epithet applied to Plutus, the god of wealth, in Lucian, *A
Professor of Public Speaking* 6; idem, *On Salaried Posts in Great
Houses* 42.

when Prometheus created humans: Prometheus is often credited
with the creation of human beings, in addition to providing
them fire. In fables, Zeus is sometimes said to have created
both humans and animals (see, for example, Perry 1952, 311), or
to have commanded Prometheus to create them (Perry 1952,
240).

when he abducted Europa: Zeus transformed himself into a bull to
seduce Europa. He carried her on his back to Crete and, in
some versions of the story, fathered her son Minos, Pasiphaë's
husband.

25.2   *the cattle of the Sun:* Odysseus's men famously killed the Sun's
cattle (*Odyssey* 12.352–70).

that constellation in the sky: That is, the constellation Taurus.

the curvature of Selene: A reference to the crescent moon. Selene
is the personification of the moon, who drives through the sky
on a chariot.

Endymion, the darling of Selene: Selene is said to have fallen in love
with the mortal Endymion, to whom Zeus granted eternal
sleep so that he would never age or die. Basilakes suggests that
Selene's love for Endymion disrupted the passage of the moon
through the sky.

25.3   *You hold a beehive in your mouth:* That is, your mouth is sweet.

it will give rise to a swarm of bees: An allusion to the belief that
honeybees are generated in the bodies of dead oxen.

25.4   *Europa loved a bull, and another woman in turn loved a horse:* Zeus

transformed himself into a bull to seduce Europa. Demeter attempted to evade Poseidon's amorous advances by disguising herself as a mare, but to no avail. Poseidon transformed himself into a horse, and their union produced another horse, Arion.

beguile . . . with a bull: Basilakes appears to play with a verb here (*boukoleo*) that can mean both to beguile and to herd cattle.

25.5   *golden Aphrodite:* "Golden" is a regular epithet of Aphrodite; see, for example, Homer, *Iliad* 3.64, 5.427, 9.389.

sea-dyed robe: Purple dye derived from the mollusk called murex was a luxury item.

25.6   *Io, the daughter of Inachus:* In most versions of the story, Zeus transformed his lover Io into a cow to protect her from Hera's anger. In Aeschylus, *Suppliant Women* 299, Hera is said to have changed Io. See Ethopoeia 18 in this collection.

Daedalus has hammered bronze: Daedalus was working as a sculptor for Minos and would have made statues out of bronze.

the yoke and the overseer of weddings among cattle, as well: A "yoke-mate" is a Greek term for a wife, and Hera is patron of weddings.

26   *What a gardener would say:* This exercise is unique in this collection for not taking an episode from scripture or classical literature as its theme.

26.1   *Alcinous:* King of the Phaeacians, mythical descendants of Poseidon who live on an island paradise. Homer describes Alcinous's garden in *Odyssey* 7.112–32: the fruit on the trees is abundant year round, grapes grow continuously and are pressed into wine, other sorts of plants are always in bloom, and two springs irrigate the garden and provide water for the palace.

"shining-fruited": At *Odyssey* 7.115, Homer applies this adjective to Alcinous's apple trees.

Erotes: Personifications of desire, the equivalent of Cupids in Latin.

Paris as judge: The son of Priam of Troy, Paris was asked to judge the beauty of the goddesses Aphrodite, Athena, and Hera after the goddess Eris (Discord) presented them with a golden apple

inscribed ambiguously, "To the most beautiful." Paris chose Aphrodite after she offered him Helen, the most beautiful human woman, as a bribe.

26.2   *the Persian apple:* The peach.

    a Pactolus: The Pactolus is a river in Asia Minor (modern Turkey), famous for carrying gold dust from Mount Tmolus. In Greek mythology, King Midas washed himself in this river to rid himself of his golden touch.

26.4   *Zephyr:* The west wind.

26.5   *my treasures to be ashes:* In the collection of Zenobius (2.1), the proverb reads, "The treasure was revealed to be ashes" (*CPG* 1:32.1–5).

    since I did not pour a libation to Prometheus, I am now intimately joined with Epimetheus: Prometheus ("Forethought") warned his brother Epimetheus ("Afterthought") not to accept a gift from the gods, but Epimetheus, living up to his name, ignored the advice and received Pandora, who appeared beautiful but brought along with her hardship and disease.

26.6   *just like the rather simpleminded fishermen:* Basilakes is referring to a proverb (Zenobius 2.14), which reads, "A fisherman will come to his senses after being struck" (*CPG* 1:35.1–6).

    "I would not buy at any price a man who is inspired by empty hopes": Sophocles, *Ajax* 477–78.

27   *What the girl from Edessa would say:* From the story of Euphemia and the Goth, which survives in both Greek and Syriac versions. Basilakes's composition is based on the redaction of Symeon Metaphrastes in his *Menologion* (November 15th = *BHG* 738). A widow, Sophia, is living with her unmarried daughter, Euphemia, in Edessa, a Mesopotamian city in ancient Syria, now Urfa in modern Turkey. While the city is under attack, the Roman army arrives and one of its soldiers, an unnamed Goth, is billeted in Sophia's home. He falls in love with Euphemia and, wishing to seduce her, attempts to convince Sophia that he desires a lawful marriage. She resists, but the Goth swears to God and on the tomb of the three martyrs of Edessa (Gourias, Samonas, and Abibos) that he is not already married and that he intends to settle down with Euphemia in

Edessa so that she (Sophia) will not be left alone. Sophia relents and the couple is married, and in time Euphemia becomes pregnant. When the war is over and the Roman army is withdrawing, the Goth reneges on his oath by leaving with the army and taking Euphemia with him. Once out of the city, he reveals that he is in fact already married, and he forces Euphemia to dress as a servant and pretend to be his slave. When they arrive at the Goth's home, his wife suspects the trick and in her jealousy abuses Euphemia. After Euphemia gives birth to a baby boy who looks just like his father, the Goth's wife poisons the child. Then Euphemia poisons the wife, and in turn the Goth's family shuts Euphemia in a tomb. There she prays to God and to the three martyrs for help. The martyrs perform a miracle by transporting her back to Edessa, where she is reunited with her mother. The story ends when the Goth returns to Edessa, is confronted by Sophia and her family, and is executed by the authorities. Basilakes's exercise refers to events up to the point where Euphemia is preparing to poison the Goth's wife, but it also acknowledges the eventual intercession of the martyrs. See further, Charis Messis and Stratis Papaioannou, "Histoires 'gothiques' à Byzance: Le saint, le soldat et le Miracle d'Euphémie et du Goth (*BHG* 739)," *DOP* 67 (2013): 15–47. A translation of the text on which Basilakes draws will appear in a forthcoming Dumbarton Oaks Medieval Library volume, *Christian Novels from the Menologion of Symeon Metaphrastes*, translated by Stratis Papaioannou.

27.2   *those very martyrs:* That is, Gourias, Samonas, and Abibos, who were known as the "martyrs and confessors" of Edessa.

27.6   *the precinct of the martyrs:* When the martyrs miraculously transported Euphemia back to Edessa, they hid her in their tomb, which had become a shrine and is where the Goth swore his false oaths to Sophia.

I enlist as my helper a child: Euphemia obtained the poison she used to kill the Goth's wife by soaking it from her son's lips with cotton.

The blows . . . children's darts: See Psalms 63(64):7.

Concordance of Exercise Numbers

	DOML Exercise	Pignani Number
FABLES	1	1
	2	2
	3	3
	4	4
	5	5
	6	6
	7	7
NARRATIONS	1	8
	2	9
	3	10
	4	11
	5	12
	6	13
	7	14
	8	15
	9	16
	10	17
	11	18
	12	19

CONCORDANCE OF EXERCISE NUMBERS

	DOML Exercise	Pignani Number
	13	20
	14	21
	15	22
	16	23
Maxims	1	24
	2	25
	3	26
Refutation	1	27
Confirmation	1	28
Encomium	1	29
Ethopoeiae	1	30
	2	31
	3	32
	4	33
	5	34
	6	35
	7	36
	8	37
	9	38
	10	39
	11	40
	12	41
	13	42

DOML Exercise	Pignani Number
14	43
15	44
16	45
17	46
18	47
19	48
20	49
21	50
22	51
23	52
24	53
25	54
26	55
27	56

Bibliography

EDITIONS

Hörandner, Wolfram. *Der Prosarhythmus in der rhetorischen Literatur der Byzantiner,* 98–104. Vienna, 1981.

Pignani, Adriana, ed. and trans. *Niceforo Basilace, Progimnasmi e monodie. Testo critico, introduzione, traduzione.* Naples, 1983.

Walz, Christian, ed. *Rhetores Graeci.* Vol. 1, 421–525. Stuttgart, 1832.

SECONDARY SOURCES

Clark, Donald L. *Rhetoric in Greco-Roman Education.* New York, 1957.

Failler, Albert. "Adriana Pignani, *Niceforo Basilace. Progimnasmi e monodie. Testo critico, introduzione, traduzione* (Byzantina et Neo-Hellenica Neapolitana 10) Bibliopolis, Naples 1983." *Revue des études byzantines* 43 (1985): 274–75.

Garzya, Antonius, ed. *Nicephori Basilacae orationes et epistolae.* Leipzig, 1984.

Hock, Ronald F., and Edward N. O'Neil. *The Chreia and Ancient Rhetoric: Classroom Exercises.* Atlanta, 2002.

Hörandner, Wolfram. "Zu den Progymnasmata des Nikephoros Basilakes. Bemerkungen zur kritischen Neuedition." *Jahrbuch der Österreichischen Byzantinistik* 36 (1986): 73–88.

Kennedy, George A. *Greek Rhetoric under Christian Emperors.* Princeton, N.J., 1983.

Magdalino, Paul. *The Empire of Manuel I Komnenos, 1143–1180.* Cambridge, 1993.

———. "The *Bagoas* of Nikephoros Basilakes: A Normal Reaction?" In *Of*

Strangers and Foreigners (Late Antiquity — Middle Ages), edited by Laurent Mayali and Maria M. Mart, 47–63. Berkeley, 1993.

Papaioannou, Stratis. "Byzantine Mirrors: Self-Reflection in Medieval Greek Writing." *DOP* 63 (2010): 81–101.

———. "On the Stage of *Eros:* Two Rhetorical Exercises by Nikephoros Basilakes." In *Theatron: Rhetorical Culture in Late Antiquity and the Middle Ages,* edited by Michael Grünbart, 355–74. Berlin, 2007.

Penella, Robert J. "The *Progymnasmata* in Imperial Greek Education." *Classical World* 105 (2011): 77–90.

Reinsch, Diether R. "*Nicephori Basilacae orationes et epistolae,* recensuit A. Garzya. [Bibliotheca Scriptorum Graecorum et Romanorum Teubneriana.] Leipzig, B. G. Teubner Verlag. 1984. *Niceforo Basilace, Progimnasmi e monodie.* Testo critico, introduzione, traduzione a cura di Adriana Pignani. [Byzantina et Neo-Hellenica Neapolitana. Collana di Studi e Testi, 10.] Neapel, Bibliopolis 1983." *Byzantinische Zeitschrift* 80 (1987): 84–91.

Robins, Robert H. *The Byzantine Grammarians: Their Place in History.* Berlin, 1993.

Webb, Ruth. "The *Progymnasmata* as Practice." In *Education in Greek and Roman Antiquity,* edited by Yun Lee Too, 289–316. Leiden, 2001.

Index

Asia, Narr. 8.1
Assyrians, Ethop. 10.2, 22.2
Atalanta, Ref. 1; Conf. 1; Ethop. 14
Athena, Conf. 1.7; Ethop. 15.6,
    16.1, 17.1, 19.1–3, 23.1, 23.4, 23.6,
    24.4
Athens/Athenians, Maxim 2.4, 2.8,
    2.15, 3.15; Ethop. 23.6
Athos, Ethop. 21.2
Atreus, Ethop. 16.2
Attica, Maxim 2.15

Bacchants, Ethop. 24.1
Bacchus, Ethop. 18.4, 19.3, 22.4,
    24.1. See also Dionysus
Bellerophon, Ethop. 20.2
Bethlehem, Ethop. 12.1
Boreas, Ethop. 20.3. See also North
    Wind

Cadmus, Ethop. 23.2, 24.1, 24.3,
    24.5
Capaneus, Ethop. 23.1, 23.4
Centaurs, Ethop. 15.4, 20.1
Cerberus, Ethop. 15.5, 16.1–2,
    16.4–5
Chastity, Ethop. 2.2
Chersonese, Narr. 14.2
Christ, Maxim 1.7; Ethop. 8, 11, 12,
    13.1–4, 27.2, 27.6. See also Jesus;
    Lord; Messiah; Savior
Cilicians, Enc. 1.2
Cithaeron, Ethop. 23.2, 24.5
Clytemnestra, Maxim 3.2, 3.4, 3.6
Coroebus, Enc. 1.9
Creator, Maxim 1.4; Ethop. 8.5,

9.4–5, 12.17. See also Christ; Fa-
    ther; God
Crete, Narr. 11.1; Ethop. 20.4
Cronus, Ethop. 22.3

Daedalus, Narr. 11, 12.2, 13.1–2;
    Ethop. 20, 25.6
Danaë, Narr. 5; Ethop. 14.1, 17
Daniel, Ethop. 12.2
Daphne, Ethop. 22.1
David, Maxim 1.10; Ethop. 4, 5, 6,
    12.8–9
Deianira, Conf. 1.17
Delilah, Ethop. 3
Demeter, Ethop. 19.2
Diomedes, Maxim 2.16
Dionysus, Narr. 16.2; Enc. 1.1;
    Ethop. 18.3–4, 19.3, 23.5, 24.5. See
    also Bacchus

Edessa (in Syria), Ethop. 27
Egypt/Egyptians, Maxim 2.15;
    Ethop. 1, 2, 13.3, 25.2
Electra, Maxim 2.2–3
Elijah, Ethop. 10.2
Elisha, Ethop. 10.2
Endymion, Ethop. 25.2
Ephialtes, Narr. 7.1
Epimetheus, Ethop. 26.5
Eridanus, Narr. 3.2
Erinyes, Ethop. 21.1, 23.2, 24.4–5
Erotes, Ethop. 18.6, 26.1
Ethiopians, Ref. 1.7
Euripides, Maxim 3.17
Europa, Ethop. 20.2, 25.1, 25.4
Europe, Narr. 8.1